EFFECTIVE TEACHING STRATEGIES IN SECONDARY PHYSICAL EDUCATION

THIRD EDITION

GREYSON DAUGHTREY

Adjunct Professor of Physical Education
Old Dominion University
Norfolk, Virginia

Former Director, Health, Physical Education
  and Intramurals
Norfolk Public Schools
Norfolk, Virginia

CLIFFORD GRAY LEWIS

Professor of Physical Education
University of Georgia
Athens, Georgia

Former Head, Department of Physical Education
  for Women
University of Georgia

W. B. SAUNDERS COMPANY   Philadelphia London Toronto   1979

W. B. Saunders Company: West Washington Square
Philadelphia, PA   19105

1 St. Anne's Road
Eastbourne, East Sussex BN21 3UN, England

1 Goldthorne Avenue
Toronto, Ontario M8Z 5T9, Canada

Effective Teaching Strategies in Secondary Physical Education   ISBN   0-7216-2887-7

Last digit is the print number: 9   8   7   6   5   4   3   2   1

To
Anne Scott Daughtrey
and
Mary Ella Lunday Soule

PREFACE

The survival of education in this country depends upon effective instruction. This premise is more evident today because the public is demanding account- ability and educators are advancing competency-based instruction as their reaction to the challenge. Public demand for a return to basic educational requirements is a genuine signal that something is wrong with the present curriculum. Students are performing below average in reading, writing, mathematics, and physical fitness.

Physical education must concern itself with learning and teaching strategies if it is to remain in the school program. The purpose of this text is to teach the foundations of physical education so that the objectives of the program will not only be achieved but will be recognized by students, parents, and the community.

Instruction in physical education involves more than teaching the skills of the activities included in the curriculum. Using the best teaching methods possible is essential, and for this, teachers must educate themselves about new and effective instructional techniques. Planning instruction, formulating curricula, organizing classes, coping with disruptive behavior, developing a philosophy, grouping by ability, and interpreting the program are a few of the strategies that must be developed before actual teaching begins. The text provides information relative to these responsibilities that will assist teachers in organizing and conducting sound programs.

Modern physical education is undergoing perpetual revision. Some changes have resulted from attempts to follow experiments in general education in areas such as performance objectives, flexible scheduling, competency-based instruction, and alternative education. Other changes are caused by evolutionary developments of physical education that are designed to alleviate some of the deteriorating trends in our culture. Greater emphasis is being placed on teaching the skills of lifetime activities, expanding the concepts of health and fitness, emphasizing individualized instruction, and providing for the exceptional child. This text documents the effects that these trends are having on physical education and assists students and teachers in implementing those revisions that are desirable.

The second edition of this text has been revised to include current information on performance objectives, mainstreaming, ability grouping, Title IX legislation, and similar areas. In addition, the text provides teachers and other secondary school personnel with detailed lesson plans for competency-based instruction in 12 different group and individual activities. Each plan includes performance objectives, detailed information on organizing for instruction, and information for grouping by ability.

The *Resource Manual and Student Guide,* which supplements the text, is a chapter-by-chapter analysis of the text based on five components: (1) performance objectives, (2) supplementary material, (3) media sources, (4) annotated bibliography, and (5) student assessments that include self-evaluative tests on the information in both the text and the *Resource Manual*.

An *Instructor's Guide* accompanies the text. This guide is a valuable asset to the teacher because it provides, for each chapter, (1) test questions and answers, (2) relevant insights into text content, (3) suggested performance objectives, and (4) recommended tasks or projects.

G.D.
C.G.L.

ACKNOWLEDGMENTS

We have never regretted being both teachers and administrators of physical education. The profession means a great deal to us; our institutions, the Norfolk Public School System and The University of Georgia, have given us more than we deserve, our colleagues have given us lasting friendships, and our students have made it all worthwhile.

We are indebted to Jennie Johnson and Vivian Johnson for typing the manuscript and to Juanita Tipton and Pauline Wiley for editing it. Eleanor King served as a skillful critic. Credit should be given to Meldine Maloney for the art work in chapter 9. For the endless hours of work and the faithful efforts of these individuals, the authors are extremely grateful. Students at the University of Georgia, both undergraduate and graduate, gave support and encouragement throughout the entire project. We also express appreciation to the many thousands of former students and teachers and the city directors who directly or indirectly assisted in the development of the concepts presented in this book.

The good will and cooperation of the other writers have made this undertaking a challenging and satisfactory one. Barb Landers is responsible for the *Instructor's Guide* and Charles Jackson is responsible for the *Resource Manual*. Their competence is evidenced in the quality and design of these guidebooks.

G.D.
C.G.L.

CONTENTS

Chapter **1**

      AFFLUENCE AND PHYSICAL EDUCATION 2

Chapter **2**

      THE EFFECTIVE TEACHER 16

Chapter **3**

      MEANING AND PHILOSOPHY IN PHYSICAL EDUCATION 38

Chapter **4**

      CURRICULUM DESIGN AND DEVELOPMENT 60

Chapter **5**

      MANAGEMENT AND METHODS IN TEACHING 80

Chapter **6**

      THE LEARNING PROCESS 100

Chapter **7**

      TEACHING AIDS AND STRATEGIES 118

Chapter **8**

      ESSENTIALS IN CLASS ORGANIZATION 140

Chapter **9**

      TEACHING STRATEGIES FOR SELECTED ACTIVITIES 178

Chapter **10**

      MAINSTREAMING IN PHYSICAL EDUCATION 270

Chapter **11**

      INTRAMURAL PROGRAMS 290

Chapter **12**

      SCHOOL-COMMUNITY RELATIONS 318

Chapter **13**

      ASSESSMENT AND EVALUATION 336

      INDEX 364

EFFECTIVE TEACHING STRATEGIES IN SECONDARY PHYSICAL EDUCATION

Chapter 1_____

THE AFFLUENT SOCIETY
EDUCATION AND SURVIVAL
CRISES IN AMERICAN CULTURE
    EDUCATIONAL PROBLEMS
        SCHOOL ATTENDANCE
        ACADEMIC ACHIEVEMENT
        DISRUPTIVE BEHAVIOR
    HEALTH PROBLEMS
        EMOTIONAL INSTABILITY

    GROWTH AND EXERCISE
    EXERCISE AND HEART FUNCTION
    TENSION
    PHYSICAL FITNESS
    HEALTH AND LONGEVITY
WHAT EDUCATORS MUST DO
QUESTIONS FOR DISCUSSION
REFERENCES
SELECTED READINGS

Chapter 1

AFFLUENCE AND PHYSICAL EDUCATION

THE AFFLUENT SOCIETY

As America approaches the twenty-first century, evidence of progress and affluence is clearly discernible. Unlike many civilizations that perished after having reached pinnacles of ease and prosperity, America is maintaining a strong and vibrant culture.

However, the same disintegrating influences that have always plagued prosperous nations are beginning to appear. In just 300 years, American society has reached a plateau of affluence that other civilizations attained over thousands of years. Superseded by today's highly industrialized way of life, the physical labors that brought this country its success have been forgotten. People no longer depend on their muscles to provide a livelihood. Moreover, 80 per cent of our population is concentrated around the industrial life of big cities. We have become victims of the atomic age, with its emphasis on speed of travel, the convenience of home and office appliances, television, and other facets of sedentary living that involve little muscular activity. It is amazing to realize how much of our daily routine requires no physical exertion. Hours are spent eating, viewing television, working at a desk, and riding, rather than walking, running, or performing physical labor in which muscles are used in the ways necessary for normal healthy living.

Other nations have failed to develop, or have been restricted in their development, because of inadequate education, political strife, war, and disease. This country, under its democratic system of free enterprise, has channeled scientific and technological advances toward more leisure time and higher living standards based on a peaceful society. Although these accomplishments are desirable, we are becoming victims of our own scientific ingenuity. It is indeed a paradox that as scientific progress brings more ease, comfort, and pleasure to our lives, the deteriorating influences increase. Delinquency, crime, crises in public education, lack of physical activity, and high incidence of drug usage and venereal disease all affect the health and physical fitness of the nation.

Our achievements have not gone unnoticed by others; this nation's actions and attitudes affect and are affected by other societies. We are generally aware that modern America is fighting for economic and political survival in a world seeking self-expression and individual betterment. In this struggle there are two forces that immediately threaten our people: aggression from without and deterioration from within. No other institution can offer a greater deterrent to these menacing forces than education.

EDUCATION AND SURVIVAL

Education in the United States has a twofold responsibility in preparing students for able citizenship. Students must be equipped to meet the threat of aggression — which will always be with us — and at the same time be able to function in a peaceful world and respond to the demands of a highly competitive society. The urgency of the world crisis should not be minimized; however, it must be realized that the efforts of this country center around life in a peaceful culture. Whether living at peace or preparing for conflict, the nation's citizens must be physically, emotionally, and mentally fit.

Educators must be concerned with upgrading all phases of the curriculum. To place major emphasis on mental growth and development without recognizing that students need guidance in their physical development is a serious mistake. It is disturbing to note that while educational administrators have been planning and improving the academic curriculum, they have left physical growth to chance. Approximately 60 per cent of the nation's schoolchildren do not participate in a daily program of vigorous activity. To substantiate the charge that physical education is treated lackadaisically, a very simple survey may be used. Answers to the following questions reveal the status of

physical education in American schools: Does the program have the same daily requirements as the academic curriculum? Is the teaching load comparable to that in other areas of the curriculum? Does the program have a separate budget, divorced from athletics? Does the program have teaching stations comparable to those allotted to other subjects? Are teachers chosen for teaching ability, or are they selected for coaching performance? Are adequate supplies and equipment available? Are physical education teachers supervised? Are both inside and outside facilities adequate? Are physical education teachers evaluated on quality instruction rather than on coaching success? Is Title IX implemented to give girls equal attention? Are students with handicaps given adequate instruction?

If the above questions can be answered affirmatively, then the plan is probably adequate. However, very few schools in the country can boast of programs that meet these criteria. Can boys and girls attain and maintain the strength, skill, and endurance necessary for normal growth and development if they do not have the opportunity to participate in a well-planned program of physical education? How will they be able to meet the challenge of the twenty-first century without the health and fitness essential for survival?

This imbalance in guiding the mental and physical growth of schoolchildren has created many problems that are contributing to the disintegration of the health and fitness of our youth. In addition, failure to understand and meet the needs of young people in the planning of curriculum content has made the educational system a contributor to the revolt of youth rather than an aid to learning and developing acceptable social behavior. Educators must accept the challenge that confronts them and make the necessary curriculum adjustments to assist our youth, not only mentally but physically and emotionally, in their preparation for a changing world. Some of the more serious areas of concern for American culture are discussed in this chapter.

CRISES IN AMERICAN CULTURE

All societies have problems. In advanced countries, many of the societal ills are materialistic outgrowths of invention and progress. Other problems, the disintegrating by-products of a progressive and permissive culture, are related to the mental, physical, and emotional factors involved in the growth and development of children. Generally, the concerns surfacing in the United States are educational and health problems. There are others, but those mentioned may be basically identified as the results of inadequate physical activity, which may be remedied through widespread participation in a well-organized physical education program. The seriousness of such problems, which pose a tremendous challenge to American educators, and their relationship to physical education are discussed in the following pages.

Educational Problems

As educators assume more responsibility for the development of American youth, a wide range of problems emerges. Difficulties vary, but no area is completely free of them. The inner cities, where the school population contains large numbers of disadvantaged children, suffer most from problems of attendance, academic achievement, and disruptive behavior.

School Attendance. Educators are deeply concerned by the apparent indifference to scholastic achievement felt by many students in school today. The number of dropouts, particularly in the secondary schools, has become so alarming that attempts to correct the situation are being made both locally and nationally. Approximately one fourth of the students who enter the ninth grade do not graduate. Many factors contribute to poor daily attendance and the dropout problem, but the basic causes are socioeconomic and cultural differences that lead to lack of motivation and failure in the various components of scholastic life.

When students lose interest in school, the curriculum should be examined and re-evaluated. Traditional curriculum, which does not provide opportunities for the development of individual potential, discourages some students and causes them to leave school. A curriculum must be interesting, flexible, and realistic if the needs of today's youth are to be satisfied. Many leaders in education, sociology, and psychology are strongly urging changes in program content. The need for curriculum change is described by the National Association of Secondary School Principals:

The basic responsibility of the secondary schools within this total context is to instruct students. Even as new understandings develop to the broader needs of youth, the secondary schools must make an honest appraisal of their own limitations to serve all needs of all youth.[1]

Partly because of television and other media of communication outside the school, today's students are more knowledgeable and sophisticated than students of the past. Experiences within the school must relate to and offer solutions for the many problems and needs confronting them. Attention in recent years has been focused on disadvantaged, culturally deprived, and physically, mentally, and emotionally handicapped children. Now, with the many federally designed programs for innovative curriculum procedures, concentrated efforts are being made. Standardized curricula do not incorporate the requirements of disadvantaged or handicapped children. Because of the lack of adequate individualized programs for these students, Title I of the Elementary and Secondary Education Act of 1965 focuses on assisting them. Programs funded by the Act are designed to improve learning and work skills, attitudes, and cultural environment, and to solve personal problems.[2]

In the past, traditional academic curriculum has been geared to the intelligence quotient (I.Q.). Until recently, many educators believed that there was a correlation between low mental ability and dropping out of school, but current studies show that this is not true.[3]

Moreover, it is known today that the I.Q. is not the only measure of ability. For example, educators are beginning to believe that the typical I.Q. test does not measure creative giftedness, except perhaps indirectly in some areas of cognition and memory. All children, the disadvantaged in particular, may discover a joyous new world when allowed to develop their creative potential. Creativity can be identified and encouraged. Albert Ayars, Superintendent of Schools, Norfolk, Virginia, said to physical education teachers:

> You have it within your power to help young people to fulfillment of the total purpose of education — to become equipped with resources that will endure as long as life endures. You can help them to make their lives more dignified, satisfying and useful. You can further the maximum development of each child's capacity. We hear a lot about accountability these days. You're responsible for an important segment of what the public holds us, collectively, responsible for.[4]

A review of curriculum offerings and teaching methods based on the individual needs of students should lead to teaching programs that stimulate students to learn the skills necessary for living in today's complex social structure. Implementation of an effective physical education program can relieve indifference toward scholastics because it is natural for children to be active. A program that is properly designed to meet these adolescent needs will inevitably stir student interest. The holding power of physical education is evident in the popularity of intramural sports, which are an extension of the physical education program. Organized intramural activities also encourage self-motivation in secondary school students; one only has to watch the thousands of skill-thirsty youths in the playgrounds after school, practicing the fundamentals of basketball and other sports, to substantiate this claim. Physical education class is the only place that provides the competent instruction necessary for satisfactory participation in these after-school programs.

At this point, the interschool athletic program as it relates to the school dropout needs to be examined. Competitive athletic contests offer dramatic appeal to the daring nature of many students. If outlets for these aggressive drives cannot be found, students will leave school to seek satisfaction in other activities. It was shown earlier that the traditional curricular philosophy that permeates American secondary education forces many students out of school.

Since relatively few students are able to participate in interschool athletics, its principles may be applied more extensively to the instructional and intramural phases of physical education programs. This is desirable because interschool athletics are designed for gifted individuals; physical education, when planned properly, meets the needs of all students.

Leaders in education have long realized the need for making the school a natural environment for pleasant experiences. Physical educators are indebted to John Dewey for his role in making physical education an important segment of the curriculum. Early in this century, he realized how to retain students in school. He stated that "experience has shown that when children have a chance to participate in physical activities which bring their natural impulses into play, going to school is a joy; management is less of a burden; and learning is easier."[5]

Academic Achievement. Even if the dropout problem were to be solved overnight, educators would still be faced with the problems posed by the great variation in the learning ability of those who remain in school. Reading deficiency, failure to retain acquired knowledge, and lack of creative effort are some areas that teachers and administrators are studying. Many innovations, such as programmed teaching, machine teaching, and team teaching, are being used in an effort to upgrade the teaching process and to develop the student's potential for academic achievement. The success of these experiments is, however, questionable. Administrators and teachers need to become thoroughly acquainted with accepted learning process theories and must review the numerous studies showing the connection between academic achievement and physical growth and development. A brief analysis of this relationship may clarify this point of view.

Lack of physical activity sometimes impedes mental development. The tendency to emphasize the development of the mind without concurrent physical growth and development is one of the major reasons students are inattentive in class, receive poor grades, and lose interest in school. Moreover, research reveals a high correlation between mental and motor performance.[6] As the mind develops, so does the body. Much has been written about the development of the mind as the basic objective of education. If this premise is accepted, the manner in which the brain cells are involved in the process should be understood. In studying the structure of the mind and the body and the relationship between them, one discovers that all knowledge is attained through the physical senses. For example, we acquire mathematical and scientific concepts through our ears, our eyes, and our kinesthetic sense. Therefore, every effort should be made to learn more about maintaining the health and efficiency of our avenues of learning. This theory is supported by Gallahue et al. in their observation that "the integration of physical education with academic concepts increases the possibilities of successful achievement in school."[7]

The development of the mind can be studied in another way. After accumulating knowledge about science, mathematics, or other subjects, the individual expresses or makes use of this knowledge. Furthermore, as the relationship of mind and body is studied, it is found that all thoughts and mental impulses must be manifested through the body. All knowledge, all flashes of genius, and in fact, all communication, must be expressed by speaking, by writing, or by some physical behavior. This necessitates efforts to develop the body's ability to express the mental manifestations of the glorious heritage of civilization. The Greeks and Romans, thousands of years ago, knew the answer — a sound mind in a sound body.

The mind and body function together and consequently are inseparable. Many great thinkers have pointed out the importance of physical education and its relationship to mental development. Studies have been made showing the relationship between normal physical development and mental acceleration. Gallahue reviews opinions concerning the effects of exercise on intellectual progress and concludes that the effects are positive.[8] Further evidence of the close relationship between mental and physical development is discussed by Paul Dudley White. He refers to the importance of leg exercise in furnishing adequate blood supply to the brain, stating:

Here are located both our mental activities and our very souls and personalities, and we must keep it healthy and free from the disadvantages of poor physiological and psychological functions, and from defects of blood supply due to obstructions in the arteries.[9]

There is considerable documentation of the relevance of organized physical education to mental development. Joseph Gruber, in an address to the American Association for the Advancement of Science, discussing seventy-one studies, stated that youngsters who exercise and are fit perform well scholastically. His research shows that exercises involving coordinated movements of the arms and legs are the key to promoting academic achievement. The report indicates that synchronized exercises that require a child to think through the performance patterns before execution tap the same learning mechanisms that are utilized when learning to read and write. Coordinated movements requiring reflective thinking exercise the mind, thus opening up wider avenues for mental development. All schoolchildren should receive daily instruction in appropriate physical activities carefully selected to increase their physical fitness; to deny such a program may in fact place limitations on their potential.

Gruber, in his summary, pointed out

that the following results of the study have far-reaching implications for physical education teachers:

1. Motor aptitude test items correlate positively and significantly with intellectual performance.
2. Items measuring coordination of the arms and legs contribute more to the mind-body relationship than do items measuring growth, strength, speed, and power.
3. It is possible to predict a child's level of academic achievement from a motor aptitude test battery utilizing multiple regression techniques.
4. Several experimental programs have demonstrated a significant improvement in the academic performance of children exposed to a physical education program.
5. Items measuring certain aspects of motor performance, intellectual achievement, and certain personality components appear to be interrelated.
6. There appears to be a significant positive relationship between physical fitness and grade point average.
7. There is a significant positive relationship between mental and motor performance in the mentally retarded.[10]

A more recent report by Clark, based on 33 studies, shows the relationship between physical status and mental achievement. It includes research projects taken from educational, psycholog-

ical, and medical journals. Clark's conclusion, drawn from an analysis of these studies, maintains: "As a consequence of the evidence presented . . . it may be contended that a person's general learning potential for a given level of intelligence is increased or decreased in accordance with his degree of physical fitness.[11] The report produces evidence that relates the individual's general learning potential to fitness and documents the need for maintaining physical fitness as an objective of education.

Physical education programs in our schools are the principal channels for providing adequate physical activity for the nation's children, since the majority of children are required to attend school and some form of physical education is found in most schools. Through a sequential program in physical education, proper instruction designed to meet the needs of youth may be initiated.

Disruptive Behavior. Since the turn of the century, educators have expressed strong convictions concerning the importance of the play life of chil-

Classification of Comments from Supervisors	Number of Times Reason was Checked as Characteristic of Superior Teacher		Number of Times Reason was Checked as Characteristic of Inadequate Teacher	
	POSITIVE	NEGATIVE	POSITIVE	NEGATIVE
Discipline, control of class, etc.	49	0	0	58
Rapport of parents, staff, students	82	0	0	34
Flexible	46	0	0	36
Personality	61	0	0	58
Attitude, enthusiasm, etc.	41	0	2	12
Ability to communicate	13	0	0	13
Subject matter good	52	0	19	10
Willingness to take advice, responsibility	38	0	2	45
Interest in child	24	0	1	7
Professional	39	0	2	14
Conscientious	38	0	7	9
Cultured (dress, community, etc.)	38	0	6	2
Takes suggestions	11	0	7	12
Organization	21	0	0	28
Lack of confidence	0	0	1	32
Health	12	0	2	3
Motivation	17	0	0	8
Community affairs	12	0	1	4
General impression	17	0	0	3

Figure 1–1. Reasons given by supervisors for success or failure of first-year teachers. (From Vittetoe, Jack O.: "Why First-Year Teachers Fail," *Phi Delta Kappan*, January, 1977, p. 429.)

dren. Dewey explained the need for activity:

If education does not afford opportunity for wholesome recreation and train capacity for seeking and finding it, the suppressed instincts find all sorts of illicit outlets, sometimes overt, sometimes confined to the indulgence of the imagination.[12]

Phi Delta Kappan recently published a survey to discover why teachers were ineffective in the classrooms. The responses of supervisors, who were polled over a ten-year period, revealed that the lack of class control was one overriding failure of educators. Figure 1–1 lists some specific results of the survey.[13]

Children are pressured toward activity by innate drives and thus will engage in some form of activity whether it is desirable or not. Their play life may be clean, socially acceptable, and healthful, or it may be outside tolerable social standards. It is the responsibility of parents and teachers to provide opportunity for and to guide children into the kind of play and activity that is socially admissible. Proper class control and instruction during activities, achieved through a well-planned physical education program, play an important role in combating delinquency.

It is logical to assume that if clubs, schools, recreational centers, the home, and community organizations were to plan purposeful activities for youth, delinquency would be curtailed. However, the schools are in a better position than any other medium to provide preventive programs, because (1) a school exists in every community; (2) schools work with children from all backgrounds; (3) schools receive children at an early age and have daily contact with them for 10 or 12 years; (4) teachers are trained to work with children; (5) schools have a more natural relationship with parents than the police; and (6) schools are in a position to detect children's emotional problems early enough to prevent them from leading to delinquency.

Physical education classes provide the greatest socializing medium in the school. The various games, sports, dances, and activities that constitute the curriculum are those in which students can find natural outlets for tension, suppressed desires, and aggressive urges. Through wise counsel and direction, the teacher may direct these urges into socially acceptable channels. Experiments have been made to determine the effects of recreational programs on delinquent behavior. One conducted in Dallas, Texas, in 1977, revealed that a planned program to raise the physical fitness level of delinquents through physical activity can prevent them from becoming more deeply involved in antisocial behavior.[14]

The assertion that physical education involves the teaching of skills that in turn are expressed in intramural and recreational programs should be properly expanded. Merely demonstrating skills and organizing games is not a guarantee for preventing delinquency. Solving the problem is not that simple. However, the guidance of individuals through their play life, emphasizing the values of fairness, the need for fitness, and the personal satisfaction in physical performance, may very well offer attractive substitutes for antisocial behavior.

Considerable support is given to physical education as a deterrent to deviant behavior and school dropouts by Paul Briggs, Superintendent of Schools in Cleveland, Ohio. He states:

I have seen young men headed for trouble — academic trouble, personal trouble, legal trouble — until they had a real experience in physical education or athletics, and suddenly begin to find themselves.[15]

Health Problems

Of the many issues troubling American culture, health problems are among the more serious. Current literature reveals factors such as emotional instability, growth and exercise, heart disease, tension, physical fitness, and exercise for the aged deserve considerably more attention than they have been given in the past.

Emotional Instability. Fifty per cent of all hospital beds in this country are occupied by emotionally disturbed people. Authorities state that one person in every ten (a total of 20,000,000 in the United States) has some form of mental or emotional illness that requires psychiatric treatment. Many of the causes of these illnesses are known. The economic and social reversals resulting from the two World Wars, the American involvement in the Korean and Vietnam conflicts, and the tension created by the continuing cold war have contributed to mental unrest. A terrific strain is created by the nuclear age in which we live; we simply have not had time to develop our emotional stamina sufficiently to bear the stress of the uncertainty we have created. The fast pace at which Americans live, the emphasis on individual achievement, the lack of proper recreation and exercise, and the unproductive use of leisure time are deteriorating influences that take their toll on the emotional well-being of the American people.

Numerous studies have shown the relationship between physical education and psychological improvement in children. One report indicates that:

One might well speculate that physical education programs that improve the physical fitness and motor abilities of boys and girls will have salutary effects in improving their psychological characteristics, in increasing their acceptance by and popularity among their peers, and in enhancing their concept of self.[16]

Emma Layman, in a review of several studies, states that most of them conclude that exercise and sports can contribute positively to the attainment of sound mental health. The studies also reveal that participation in sports leads to the acquisition of behavior patterns that assist in making social adjustments. She deduces, however, that if programs and sports are to make positive contributions to emotional health, several conditions have to be met:

1. The activities should be such as to encourage the development of organic health.
2. The activities should be available to all and not to a small, select group of "super athletes."
3. Activities should be geared to individual differences in ability and interests.
4. Physical education teachers and coaches

should avoid professional isolation and should work with parents and representatives from other disciplines.[17]

Growth and Exercise. Studies in physiology and medicine reveal that sequentially planned programs in physical education influence growth patterns in children. These studies emphasize not only the importance of vigorous exercise programs but also the need for teaching the skills of activities that can be used beyond school years and throughout life.[18]

Exercise and Heart Function. Although many factors are involved in degenerative circulatory diseases, recent research indicates the value of regular exercise in the prevention of such disorders. It is generally recognized that poor diet, heredity, lack of rest, smoking, stress, and obesity are linked to circulatory diseases. Lack of exercise is also a very important factor. Authoritative study and opinion support the premise that regular physical activity may prevent or postpone degenerative cardiovascular changes.[19]

Further evidence exists showing the beneficial results of exercise on the heart and blood vessels. It is widely accepted that coronary disease does not threaten people whose daily routines require physical activity, and that the hearts of active individuals have larger networks of arteries than those of sedentary individuals. The more active person stands a better chance of avoiding a heart attack, which is not an organic condition but is the result of blockage of a coronary artery caused by arteriosclerosis. Proper diet and physical activity seem to lower the incidence of arteriosclerosis. Don B. Chapman, a physician in Houston, Texas, believes that exercise is important in preventing heart attacks. He states: "The incidence of cardiovascular disease is greatly reduced in those who keep themselves physically and mentally fit."[20]

Tension. It is generally believed that moderate exercise aids in relieving tension. The use of drugs as a treatment is universally practiced, but drugs produce undesirable side effects. The *Physical Fitness Research Digest* reports several studies in which exercises had a greater effect in reducing tension without side effects than did the tranquilizers.[21] Activities such as walking, swimming, bowling, golf, tennis, and dancing are recommended. The fundamental skills involved in these activities should be taught in the secondary schools.

Physical Fitness. As a result of the tests done by Kraus and Weber, attention has been focused on the need for more concentrated physical fitness programs. Although there is disagreement among physical education leaders concerning the validity of the tests, they did serve as a catalyst in arousing the nation to the need for more physical activity. Alarmed by the Kraus-Weber findings, President Eisenhower created the President's Council on Youth Fitness. The original conferees, who met at Annapolis, suggested that the President of the United States create federal committees to promote the fitness of American youth.

In 1961, the Council, in its bulletin *Youth Physical Fitness,* set forth guidelines for an effective physical fitness program. Among them was the recommendation that physical fitness programs provide vigorous activities that will develop the physique, increase the efficiency of the cardiovascular system, and contribute to the development of physical skills. A school's physical education program should include a core of developmental and conditioning activities appropriate to each grade level, which should be carefully identified and stressed in progressive order.

The Council has provided the impetus necessary for action in regard to the need for fitness. It recognizes the existence of many excellent programs in the country, and has assisted those communities whose programs are inadequate. Probably the most significant contribution the Council has made is that it aroused the nation to the need for sound physical education programs in the schools. In May, 1973, operating under the new name of President's Council on Physical Fitness and Sports, with C. Carson Conrad as executive director and astronaut James A. Lovell

as chairman, the Council adopted a statement of basic beliefs. The first of these statements was devoted to school programs for grades kindergarten through 12. It is reproduced in Figure 1–2.

Health and Longevity. Too often, physical education leaders devise programs for elementary and secondary school students without taking into consideration the need for exercise in later years. The life span of people in this country is increasing each year, and the physiological and psychological effects of exercise benefit all age groups. Since the skills learned during adolescence are usually those practiced later in life, it is necessary to plan instruction in those activities that may be enjoyed in maturity. Rarely are new skills learned efficiently after age 60.

An increasing amount of evidence supporting the importance of exercise for good health and longevity appears in current publications. An example is a recent study by Nedra Belloc, of the California State Department of Public Health, and Lester Breslow, Dean of the University of California School of Public Health at Los Angeles. These researchers surveyed the living habits of 6928 people over a period of five and one-half years, and they found a significant relationship between seven health practices and good health. Exercising regularly was listed among the seven practices, as were: (1) sleeping between seven and eight hours each night, (2) eating breakfast, (3) not eating between meals, (4) staying within 10 per cent of proper weight, (5) not drinking to excess, and (6) not smoking cigarettes. The study reached several conclusions, including the following:

1. The two single most important health practices are getting sufficient exercise and refraining from smoking cigarettes.
2. A 45-year-old man who follows six or seven of the rules has a life expectancy of 11 more years than one who follows fewer than four.
3. A 70-year-old man who follows all seven rules is probably just as healthy as a 40-year-old man who follows just one or two.
4. The greater the number of practices followed, the less likely an individual is to be sick.
5. Access to medical science and yearly

Basic Beliefs

The President's Council on Physical Fitness and Sports is fully aware that education is a State and local responsibility. Through the cooperative efforts of school board members, school administrators, teachers and organized citizenry, our Nation has developed an increasingly effective school system and has improved specific areas of education. Continuation of such cooperation is heartily encouraged.

We believe that the following recommendations, which were developed after extensive consultation, offer a sound approach to improvement of the physical fitness of children and youth.

- All school children in grades K-12 should be required to participate in daily programs of physical education emphasizing the development of physical fitness and sports skills.

  Medical authorities recommend unequivocally regular vigorous exercise during school years, as such is essential to healthy development of individuals.

  In order to enjoy a sport, master the necessary skills and participate safely, a person must be physically fit. The popular slogan, **Get Fit by Playing,** should be **Get Fit to Play Safely.**

  Within the educational context of physical education programs, students should develop knowledge of the effects of activities for conditioning as well as the relation of activities to various aspects of health throughout life. Students need to understand the basic elements of physiology of exercise and the value of participating in regular vigorous activities. The need to continue activities in adulthood should be stressed at an early age and throughout the school physical education experience. Knowledge, understanding and participation should result in the development of desirable attitudes concerning the values of participation in regular vigorous physical activity.

  Special programs of physical education should be provided those pupils with orthopedic problems, obesity, perceptual motor problems, and other health-related problems. Such students must first be identified, along with those who may suffer from physical underdevelopment, malnutrition or inadequate coordination.

  Physical education programs should be planned to include physiological fitness goals along with other educational aims needed to meet the developmental needs of children; thus, activities must be adapted to individual needs and capacities and be vigorous enough to increase energy utilization and heart rate significantly.

  The school physical education program should include a core of developmental and conditioning activities appropriate for each grade level. Activities should be identified and stressed in progressive order. Demonstration standards for survival activities, particularly including swimming, should be established and competence maintained by periodic testing and training.

- Every pupil should have continuing supervision by his family physician and dentist, including periodic examinations and correction of remediable defects.

Through these resources, supplemented wherever necessary and feasible by school and community services, the health appraisal procedures should include:

Identification of pupils with correctable orthopedic defects and other health problems and subsequent referral to medical authorities.

A posture check, including foot examination; pupils with acute problems should be referred to medical authorities.

Height and weight measurements, interpreted in terms of individual needs; pupils who are obviously obese, underweight or malnourished should be identified and referred to medical authorities.

- The Community-School Concept should be encouraged wherever possible as a vehicle to enhance physical activity programs.

- Public school sports facilities belong to the people and should be available for community use when not being used for school activities.

School sports facilities—gymnasiums, swimming pools, tennis courts, etc.—should be available for public use when not being used for school programs and functions.

Figure 1–2.

checkups, although valuable, may have less to do with health than the care one takes of his health.[22]

Americans work hard to insure ease and comfort in later life. The tragedy is that when they reach this goal, they often become mentally and physically inactive — a state not conducive to longevity. Unless infectious disease is a factor, health and fitness result when efforts to exercise regularly are sustained throughout life. A major impediment to this concept is that most adults simply do not know how to exercise properly. Many would play golf and tennis and would bowl and swim if they had learned the rudiments of such sports during their school years. Thus fitness for older adults in this country is becoming a problem, and more than ever we are confronted with the need to provide recreational programs for them. A basic solution to this challenge in the future is to gear secondary students toward activities and sports that

are pleasurable, regardless of age. Attitudes concerning exercise and other good health practices must be formed and reinforced early in life.

It is particularly difficult to maintain sound health in a modern society. Evidence that we are victims of our own ingenuity is the sedentary life into which the products of our technology have placed us. American people are slipping into a state of inertia, weakness, and poor health. The advent of television and the popularity of spectator entertainment have contributed greatly to this unwholesome situation. Lack of exercise is evident everywhere; physicians must "prescribe" exercise, and "health studios" and reducing salons have become a million-dollar industry because simple exercise is missing from our daily lives.

There is a need in our culture for greater *participation*. We are rapidly becoming a nation of spectators — thousands of viewers will watch a football game in which only 22 players participate. Emphasis placed on interscholastic and intercollegiate sports is acceptable only if equal emphasis is placed on activities for everyone.

WHAT EDUCATORS MUST DO

Administrators must establish and maintain an equal balance in the curriculum between mental and physical education. Educators, authors, and other leaders have advocated the development of the whole child mentally, physically, emotionally, and socially. Yet in such vital matters as curriculum, monetary expenditures, and provisions for facilities and staff, the emphasis is too often placed on the offerings intended to educate only the mind. Health and fitness can be generated solely by systematic use of the body's muscles and by continual instruction in good health habits and practices. Unless the physical education program is given a proper place in the curriculum, our population will continue to be physically and emotionally unfit.

Physical development and mental growth are simultaneously occurring natural functions. We do not leave mental growth to chance and therefore cannot afford to leave physical growth and development to chance. Guidance in physical development through required physical education classes scheduled during the school day is as essential as guidance in mental development through such scheduled courses as English, science, or mathematics.

George Leonard, in his book *The Ultimate Athlete,* reveals how the desire and need for physical education is manifested in a new movement which promotes exercise. This movement can popularize healthful activities and impel the public to become involved in sports, physical education, and body improvement. The trend is exemplified by the growth in jogging, hiking, and cycling. Leonard also points out the sudden shift toward the pleasures of recreational pursuits on courts, lakes, streams, and fields. Increasing the emphasis on lifetime sports rather than on team sports in the secondary schools is another answer to the need for participation.[23] Educators should actively join the new exercise movement themselves. In addition, they should use their authority to provide students with a physical education program which is conducive to learning and practicing health and fitness.

QUESTIONS FOR DISCUSSION

1. Discuss the effect that scientific advancements have had on the health and physical fitness of the United States as a nation.
2. Explain what is meant by *deteriorating influences in society*, and indicate some of the educational problems that have resulted.
3. What guidelines can be used to insure the development of an adequate physical education program?
4. Explain how traditional education programs may contribute to the educational problems in American society.
5. How can physical education programs help alleviate school attendance problems?
6. Discuss the relationship between physical development and mental abilities.
7. Explain the significance of the statement, "Play gone wrong may produce delinquency."
8. How can physical education contribute to the emotional development of an individual?
9. What is the relevance of physical education to health programs evidenced in later life?
10. What innovations or changes can be made to make physical education more meaningful to today's student?

REFERENCES

1. "This We Believe," *National Association of Secondary School Principals* (Reston, Virginia, 1975), p. 17.
2. William M. Alexander, J. Galen Saylor, and Emmett L. Williams, *The High School, Today and Tomorrow* (New York: Holt, Rinehart and Winston, Inc., 1971), p. 269.
3. Chris DeYoung and Richard Wynn, *American Education,* 7th ed. (New York: McGraw-Hill Book Company, 1972), p. 35.
4. "A Superintendent Speaks Out for Physical Education," *Directions* (Washington, D. C., January, 1976).
5. John Dewey, *Democracy in Education, An Introduction to the Philosophy of Education* (New York: The Macmillan Company, 1916), p. 194.
6. David L. Gallahue, Peter H. Werner, and George C. Luedke, *A Conceptual Approach to Moving and Learning* (New York: John Wiley and Sons, Inc., 1975), p. 242.
7. *Ibid.,* p. 243.
8. *Ibid.,* p. 238.
9. H. Harrison Clark, ed., *Physical Fitness Research Digest* (President's Council on Physical Fitness and Sports, October, 1971).
10. Joseph J. Gruber, "Exercise and Mental Achievement" (From an address before the American Association for the Advancement of Science, Dallas, December, 1968).
11. Clark, *op. cit.*
12. Dewey, *op. cit.,* p. 241.
13. Jack O. Vittetoe, "Why First-Year Teachers Fail," *Phi Delta Kappan* (January, 1977), p. 429.
14. T. R. Collingwood and Mike Engelsgjerd, "Physical Fitness, Physical Activity and Juvenile Delinquency," *JOPER* (June, 1977), p. 23.
15. "An Inner City Superintendent Supports Physical Education," *Physical Education Newsletter* (June, 1971).
16. H. Harrison Clark, ed., *Physical Fitness Research Digest* (President's Council on Physical Fitness and Sports, January, 1972), p. 12.
17. Emma McCloy Layman, "Contributions of Exercises and Sports to Mental Health and Social Adjustment" (From Warren R. Johnson and E. R. Buskirk, eds., *Science and Medicine of Exercise and Sports*, New York: Harper and Row, Publishers, 1974), p. 419.
18. G. Lawrence Rarick, "Exercise and Growth," 2nd ed. (From Warren R. Johnson and E. R. Buskirk, eds., *Science and Medicine of Exercise and Sports,* New York: Harper and Row, Publishers, 1974), pp. 317–319.
19. H. Harrison Clark, ed., *Physical Fitness Research Digest* (President's Council on Physical Fitness and Sports, April, 1972), p. 9.
20. "Physicians Speak Out for Daily Physical Education," *The Physical Education Newsletter* (Physical Education Publications, Old Saybrook, Conn., March 15, 1974).
21. Clark, *op cit.*, April, 1977, p. 4.
22. "Ways You Can Save Your Life," *Virginian Pilot* (Norfolk, Va., October 11, 1977).
23. George Leonard, "Physical Education for Life," *Today's Education* (September–October, 1975).

SELECTED READINGS

Bucher, Charles A., *Foundations of Physical Education,* 4th ed. (Saint Louis: The C. V. Mosby Company, 1975).
Clark, H. Harrison, "Physical Activity and Coronary Heart Disease," *Physical Fitness Research Digest* (Washington, D.C., April, 1972).
Johnson, Warren and E. R. Buskirk, *Science and Medicine of Exercise and Sports* (New York: Harper and Row, Publishers, 1974).
Rarick, G. Lawrence, ed., *Physical Activity, Human Growth and Development* (New York: Academic Press, 1973).
Strom, Robert D. and Torrance, Paul, *Education for Effective Achievement* (New York: Rand McNally and Company, 1973).

Chapter 2

Courtesy Cedar Shoals High School, Athens, Georgia.

WHAT IS TEACHING?
    TEACHER EFFECTIVENESS
        LOVE–INFLUENCE–HUMOR–ETHICS
    GOALS AND OBJECTIVES
        TEACHERS MUST BECOME PERSONALLY
        INVOLVED
CHARACTERISTICS OF GOOD TEACHERS
    DEDICATION
    KNOWLEDGE
    PERSONALITY
    EMOTIONAL STABILITY
    INDIVIDUAL DIFFERENCES
    PROFESSIONAL INTEREST AND DIGNITY
    LEADERSHIP
    PERSONAL QUALIFICATIONS
        HEALTH
        APPEARANCE
        VOICE
        CHARACTER
        CREATIVITY
        GREGARIOUSNESS
        ENTHUSIASM
        HUMOR
        PROFESSIONAL RELATIONSHIP
TASK–CENTERED PERFORMANCES
    THE TEACHER IN THE SCHOOL
        GENERAL DUTIES
        SPECIFIC DUTIES
    THE TEACHER AND THE COMMUNITY
HUMAN-CENTERED PERFORMANCES
    INTERACTION COMPETENCIES
    COMMUNICATIONS
        LISTENING
        UNDERSTANDING
        CONCERN
SEEKING A POSITION
    APPLYING FOR A POSITION
        LETTER OF APPLICATION

THE INTERVIEW
    BE FAMILIAR WITH THE PHILOSOPHY OF
        THE SYSTEM
    BE ABLE TO ANSWER QUESTIONS
        ABOUT PHYSICAL EDUCATION
    BE PERSONABLE
    BECOME FAMILIAR WITH THE SCHOOL
        SYSTEM
    KEEPING A JOB
ACCOUNTABILITY
    TYPES OF ACCOUNTABILITY
        STATEWIDE ASSESSMENTS
        THE VOUCHER SYSTEM
        PERFORMANCE CONTRACTING
        PROGRAM PLANNING BUDGETING
            SYSTEM (PPBS)
        OTHER PLANS
    THE TEACHER IN CHANGING TIMES
    THE CHANGING STUDENT
    THE CHANGING CURRICULUM
    THE PRICE OF PRODUCTIVITY
        PROS AND CONS
    THE PROMISE OF COMPETENCE-BASED
        TEACHER EDUCATION
PREPARING PHYSICAL EDUCATORS FOR THE
FUTURE
    CAREERS IN TEACHING
    CAREER ALTERNATIVES
        PRIVATE TEACHING
        SPECIALIST IN THE HANDICAPPED
        WORK WITH THE AGED
BEING A PROFESSIONAL
    THE TEACHER AND THE SUPERVISOR
    THE TEACHER AND THE STUDENT
QUESTIONS FOR DISCUSSION
REFERENCES
SELECTED READINGS

THE EFFECTIVE TEACHER

accountability

Modern secondary school teachers face responsibilities and challenges far different from those of a decade ago. Educators of today's youth must be held accountable for the teaching-learning process. To be successful in the classroom, in the laboratory, in the gymnasium, on the playground, and in the community, a teacher must be able to elicit certain desired changes in behavior and must maintain a constant open attitude toward learning. The beginning teacher of one year, as well as the experienced teacher of 10 or more years, must continue to learn, to grow, and to change.

If young teachers are competent learners, physical education will be lively and meaningful. One seldom sees an effective physical education teacher past the age of forty or forty-five in the secondary school program, because most fail to maintain an ongoing teaching-learning process. In the past, teachers could rely on traditional teaching methods, which made the tasks involved in the educational expe-

rience seem somewhat simple. But innovations in modern education benefit today's teachers and students by stimulating new outlooks on the art and science of effective teaching.

WHAT IS TEACHING?

Teaching has been defined as "an art based in science." Educators have made great progress in evaluating that portion of teaching which is scientific, but only recently have they devoted time to exploring the artistic aspect of teaching. Teaching has been broken into component parts, dissected into alternative strategies, classified into behavior outcomes, assessed into taxonomies and hierarchies, and described as process and product. However, the goal of teaching remains constant: to bring about desired changes in behavior through experiences in education.

The aim of scientific inquiry has been to describe, predict, and control the cognitive aspects of teaching,

17

whereas the interpretation of the affective aspects are more reflective, and perhaps more difficult, to predict. If teaching is a total experience for the individual — as it should be — it has mental, emotional, physical, and social meaning. The terminology, with words borrowed from the fields of science and technology, does not completely describe the concepts and capacities that give teaching and learning a real sense of vibrancy. Interaction is essential. Spontaneity gives climax. Emergency needs reaction. Human senses are involved. Values and feelings are indescribable. Teaching is quite individualized. Teaching is personalized. Above all, teaching must be free, real, and total.

To achieve effectiveness, the teacher must be critical not only of the scientific evaluations that extend the mechanical or technological efficiency of educational endeavors but also of the artistic evaluations that extend the affective or humanistic capabilities of the teacher. Research has pointed out that intuition and feelings have an impact on learning. Knowledge of the teacher, educational technique, equipment, technology, and the buildings are all vital ingredients if children are to learn.[1]

A conscientious teacher is the core of effectual education. If student behavior imitates teacher behavior, and most research indicates that it does, then to become a more aware individual with an integrated self, a positive self-concept, and a warm personality, should be the goal of the teacher. An atmosphere of trust, warmth, freedom, and enthusiasm is essential for the meaningful experience in the teaching-learning atmosphere in secondary school physical education.[2]

Teacher Effectiveness

A secondary school physical education teacher should change as his or her curriculum changes. Physical education will continue to be an integral part of the secondary school program, but, as the curriculum broadens, the specialist is likely to be more in demand. It is improbable that a teacher will be expected to teach everything; the health instructor, the dance instructor, or even the specialist in gymnastics, aquatics, adapted physical education, intramural sports, or coaching will be employed as needed. Any teacher who assumes the role of facilitating the learning process for students has a difficult and complex task. Knowledge and skill are not sufficient attributes for the future teacher. Success and effectiveness will be reflections of individual beliefs, values, and personal characteristics.

What is the answer? How does one attain an inner harmony that can be translated into an outward harmony? There is no simple answer, there are only clues: simplicity of living to retain a true awareness of life; balance of the physical, intellectual, and spiritual being; work without undue pressure; space to appreciate things of significance and beauty; time for solitude and sharing; closeness to foster understanding; and faith in the strength of the spirit. The effective teacher assimilates these guidelines into wholesome living, and recognizes that love, influence, humor, and ethics are important ingredients of a satisfying professional life.

Love–Influence–Humor–Ethics. Love of teaching and service is essential for those who wish to enter the profession. Happy people are usually loving people, and to be content in teaching, one must be in harmony with self, with others, and with the outside world. One can best benefit students only when one realizes that each is a unique individual. A teacher's influence will then be reflected in emulation, respect, and concern on the part of the students. Teaching affects value concepts and depth of knowledge. Ultimately, what will last will not be what you have done for students, but what they have done because of you and your influence on their lives.

A teacher should learn to enjoy the profession. Humor can be serious, it can be playful, and it can even be senseless. If a teacher becomes bored with students, it is likely the students have long been bored with the class.

Generally, a meaningful career needs four things: (1) work with a clear purpose; (2) continued growth in a field; (3) a creative aspect; and (4) humor about the things you ought to do as well as the things you want to do. Ethics involves putting this theory into practice. There will be crises, issues, problems, strikes, or disagreements; but if the teacher is honest, loyal, sincere, mature, reasonable, reliable, and a person of integrity, then ethics will be in harmony with beliefs and values. The consistent application of a moral code is the crux of a professional career.

Goals and Objectives

Many students enter the teaching profession without a realistic idea of what teaching entails. Motivation for such prospective teachers is possibly the influence of a former teacher, a genuine liking for children, parental pressure, a favorable experience in teaching small children, or a personal love for sports and games. Learning is a two-way process involving self-reflection, which the teacher presents to students, and the teaching methods used in the learning experience. One must identify himself with self-honesty and interest in the values of the learning process. Behavior of both students and teachers should be modified if the educational experience is to be profitable.

Teachers Must Become Personally Involved. Physical education leaders feel that teachers must become more concerned with how they teach children than with which activities they teach. Each teacher should ask the following questions:

1. How do I develop an atmosphere of learning that is encouraging and supportive?
2. What activity sequence is most effective in helping the student develop a positive self-image?
3. What are the best methods for helping each student make a unique contribution to the group?
4. How can I gradually help to develop a feeling of confidence in those children who tend to be timid and reluctant to participate?
5. What do I really stand for —demonstrated by the example I set by my own behavior and the kinds of organizational procedures and teaching methods I employ?

CHARACTERISTICS OF GOOD TEACHERS

The physical education staff of any secondary school today is composed of all types of teachers. Some are there because they are dedicated and have a genuine interest in working with young people. On the other hand, many are unqualified and regard teaching physical education as an interim position before going on to assume other responsibilities. Regardless of why they are there, constant emphasis must be placed upon improving the quality of teachers.

The survival of physical education in America depends largely on quality programs in schools throughout the nation. Top rank programs will exist only where good teachers are continually doing commendable jobs. The urgent need for physical education teachers to meet the quest for excellence in instruction is obvious. Throughout America, particularly in large cities, the public is refusing to support education. Budgets are being cut, and in some instances, entire school systems are closing because of insufficient funds to support the educational effort and to pay teachers' salaries.

Unfortunately, when budgets are cut, the physical education program is often the first to suffer. Among the reasons for this is the poor quality of instruction practiced in some physical education classes. The teacher who uses the physical education class for extra practice for the varsity, who resorts to the play program instead of teaching, and who leaves the class to function without him, is the teacher who is contributing to the demise of physical education.

What is a good teacher? This question has been answered by many experts in the fields of education and psy-

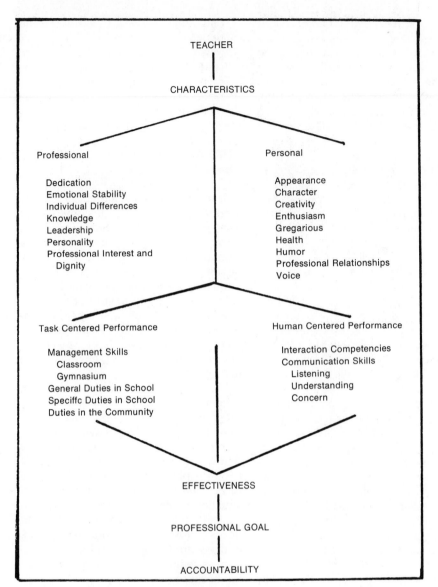

Figure 2-1. Characteristics and performances of an effective teacher.

chology. Not all agree exactly on what the characteristics are. A student feels, when he is in a class, that "this is a good teacher," but grasping or pinpointing the intangibles is a difficult task. What quality does this teacher possess to elicit response from students? How does a teacher motivate students to apply themselves to achieve, and, in some instances, overachieve? How does one teach students to appreciate the role of physical education and its value in their lives?

These are the characteristics that one sees and feels, but cannot always translate.

Fortunately, there are teachers who believe in the importance of quality instruction and who continually attempt to improve their abilities as teachers. These people are likely to have many of the characteristics that are discussed in this chapter. Although many factors interact between students and teacher, certain easily observed characteristics are present in a successful teaching-learning situation. Describing these traits is in no way an attempt to present a stereotype of the physical education teacher.

Dedication

Unless teachers are dedicated, it is difficult for them to maintain the enthusiasm and aggressiveness necessary for teaching. Students do not respond to a teacher who neglects the many little details involved in class management and teaching. A poorly managed class offers inadequate instruction and prompts students to turn their interests in directions unrelated to instruction. Classes conducted by unenthusiastic teachers provide little instructional value for the students, and they create a climate that is conducive to antisocial behavior and disciplinary problems. Devotion is vital for effective teaching.

Knowledge

Teachers of physical education must be familiar with all the skills and techniques that are necessary for satisfactory instruction. Students enrolled in physical education are eager to learn correct techniques in skill performance and have little respect for teachers who cannot adequately provide this knowledge. It is possible for teachers to teach an activity without actually demonstrating it, but the ability to show students the correct form stimulates learning and gains the admiration and respect of students.

Personality

Successful teachers are friendly, extroverted, and able to relate to students. No longer can embittered or unfriendly teachers produce the types of programs necessary for quality education. The ability to establish harmonious relationships and rapport with differing individuals — student, co-worker, administrator, and parent — is a highly desirable

characteristic for a physical education instructor.

Emotional Stability

One of the most important attributes of a good teacher is emotional stability. A nervous, irritable teacher will create disciplinary problems and will compound the seriousness of an otherwise trivial class incident. A study published in Today's Health revealed that many educators are unqualified and unfit to be in the classroom. It found that 9 per cent of today's teachers are maladjusted, create serious problems in their classes, and should be removed.[3] Teachers who are well-adjusted, happy, enthusiastic, and understanding usually develop the buoyant and relaxed atmosphere essential for effective teaching.

Individual Differences

Although it is generally understood that the students in a physical education class vary physically, mentally, and emotionally, teachers rarely consider this fact in planning their daily programs. Effective teaching cannot exist without considering individual differences in the process. Students progress at different rates in the acquisition of skills, and procedures must be developed that provide opportunity for each student to learn at his or her own rate. Physical education offers something unique to each student. Teachers must respect the students and allow for individual differences.

Professional Interest and Dignity

Teachers who constantly seek to improve themselves through research, study, and participation in professional efforts are usually superior educators. By keeping abreast of the latest developments in learning theories and the best methods for teaching skills, instructors are better equipped to achieve the level of performance expected of a superior teacher. Awareness of the advanced base of knowledge in sport psychology, sport sociology, exercise physiology, kinesiology, and perceptual motor skill should bring about a new emphasis in professional interest and dignity.

The degree of respectability that physical education enjoys in a given school is determined by the teacher. Successful physical education leaders are articulate, have a command of the English language, and leave a good impression with their fellow teachers. The teacher who calls the program "fizzed" or "gym," refers to teaching wrestling as "rassling," or who "throwed" the ball, should not be surprised to find that in the eyes of colleagues the program has very little prestige.

Leadership

Good leadership is vital to any physical education program. The teacher who is well prepared and creative is vastly more effective than the well-equipped gymnasium or the most expensive equipment. Genuine leaders are not satisfied with mediocrity. They are generally energetic individuals with socially valuable objectives who assume a sense of responsibility to create an excellent teaching-learning experience.

Personal Qualifications

Health. The teacher of physical education must be in shape, not only to set an example, but also because the nature of the work necessitates excellent health at all times. Physical education is the most emotionally and physically demanding subject in the curriculum. Instructors who fail to establish standards of healthful living cannot meet the challenge of teaching physical education for very long.

Appearance. Sometimes physical education teachers, in their efforts to relate to their students, disregard good taste in their dress and mannerisms.

This is undesirable, since teachers should distinguish themselves from students. Their job is to set an example, not to gain popularity by adopting student whims and fads. A student, for example, may wear a certain type of clothing that is acceptable to peers; but if the teacher were to adopt it also, both dignity and respect would be lost.

Voice. The tone in which a teacher addresses students is of extreme importance. A successful teacher is able to talk to a large class in a normal, well-modulated tone; he or she should never attempt to talk over the noise of a class. Nothing irritates students more than a screaming teacher who is trying to reach students by pitching his or her voice higher and higher as the noise of the class increases. A rapport should be established early, in which students remain quiet and attentive during instruction.

Character. Successful teachers of physical education set examples of how to live a good life. Physical education is the one area in the curriculum that should personify the character traits and the moral fiber essential for health, fitness, and happiness. The teacher must be a role model for these standards of conduct. Related to this are the elements of fair play, integrity, and honesty in all teacher-student relationships.

Creativity. Creative teachers are innovative. They may be dissatisfied with the traditional approach to teaching, and they may feel that there is a better way than that described in the text or the *Resource Manual*. In such situations, imaginative instructors will experiment, seeking a superior method of motivating students to learn and, at the same time, experience a greater thrill in the process.

Gregariousness. Effective teachers are usually fond of children and people in general, and thus enjoy associating with them. If teachers dislike children and the people with whom they work, it is extremely difficult to develop the rapport necessary for teaching. Daily problems that occur in teaching become unbearable if instructors are unable to relate to students. Although knowledge of skills is extremely important, teachers must be able to break through the barrier that may exist between them and their students. This is best accomplished by a friendly and gregarious attitude toward the students.

Enthusiasm. Lack of enthusiasm is a problem for many teachers. Teachers become efficient but bored in handling such routine duties as assigning lockers and taking attendance. Quality teachers in physical education maintain enthusiasm by being goal experimenters and by providing more challenging course material. Creating enthusiasm within oneself is a characteristic in teacher behavior that keeps a teacher alive and productive as the years progress.

Humor. Humor is not only effective in working with students but is also helpful in learning about oneself. Styles of humor are as varied as individual personalities. Humor can minimize friction in a faculty meeting; it can relieve tension in the classroom. Humor is indicative of good personality adjustment. In public education today there is a need for the appreciation of the humor of life.

Professional Relationship. Many qualities are equally important for the physical educator to possess. Maturity, good judgment, and a professional manner enhance the ability to function properly as a teacher in relationships with students, faculty, and the community at large. The physical educator is respected for more than just coaching ability or teaching skills.

TASK-CENTERED PERFORMANCES

Management is a time-consuming aspect of teaching physical education. Research indicates that more than 30 per cent of the teacher's time during the school day is spent in handling details. There is also observational evidence that far less that 50 per cent of any given instructional period is spent in the actual teaching-learning processes. The average physical education teacher spends too much time on de-

tails and too little on actual instruction. The structure of these tasks needs re-evaluation. Certain task-centered performances are always necessary, such as planning, organizing, conducting, and evaluating a concept for a completed project. Locker assignments, repairing equipment, and interruptions from the main office for announcements need more efficient organization.

The Teacher in the School

The physical education teacher assumes a responsible role in the functions of the total school program. Generally, teachers are expected to assume other duties of school life such as sponsoring a student activity, holding a homeroom, or coaching a team.

General Duties. These assignments not only enable teachers to see students in a different perspective but also provide a broader insight into the administration of the school. A number of administrators are selected from the physical education faculty, and assignments that furnish organizational and administrative experience enhance the teacher's chances of actually becoming an administrator. It was shown earlier in the chapter that one of the outstanding qualities of a successful teacher is the willingness to assist in the total operation of the school.

Principals and supervisors who work with and evaluate teachers are aware of the qualities that successful teachers must possess. Questionnaires sent to city and county directors often ask for indications of what they expect of a new teacher. The results reveal similar criteria. They expect a new teacher to:
1. Have a strong personality that reflects integrity, character, and emotional stability.
2. Be professionally prepared to teach physical education.
3. Have a broad cultural background.
4. Have a knowledge of child growth and development as a foundation upon which to plan learning experiences.
5. Possess the ability to establish effec-

tive professional growth and strive continuously to improve professionally.

6. Understand the *Why* of physical education and be able to interpret it to others.

7. Demonstrate a desire to work with all students, not just with talented athletes.

8. Have the ability to demonstrate basic skills and movements in a wide variety of physical education activities.

Specific Duties.   In addition to general expectations, teachers are expected to assume certain specific responsibilities. These are related to daily instruction and may be used as an integral part of teacher evaluation. Regardless of how they are used, effective instruction cannot exist without them. Specific duties depend on the philosophy of the school and the department. One guidebook expects teachers to comply with the following:

1. Attend faculty and departmental meetings.

2. Be responsible for all supplies for classes.

3. Check to see that student has a proper uniform.

4. Evaluate students with the plan outlined.

5. Enter grade and intramural records on permanent record cards.

6. Have students carefully fill out individual record cards.

7. See that leaders in each class are appointed or elected and have meetings with them at designated times.

8. Cooperate to the fullest extent with other teachers in the department.

9. Supervise dressing room while being used by class.

10. Be responsible for safety of students and proper facilities.

11. Acquaint students with their responsibilities.

12. Stay with their classes at all times.

13. Cooperate with department head in his or her efforts to improve instruction.[4]

The Teacher and the Community

Although a large portion of the instructor's time is spent in the school, the community plays an important part in the teacher's life. One of the biggest problems both single and married teachers have in a new community is the development of an interesting social life. It may be difficult for strangers in a city to meet people and make new friends. In some instances, teachers have resigned and left their jobs because of the lack of friends and a normal social life. Teachers accepting po-

Figure 2–2.   The teacher is the key to developing a sound school-community relations program.

sitions in unfamiliar cities need assistance in finding living accommodations, the church of their choice, shopping areas, and amusement centers, and with acquainting themselves with other facets of the community. Some school systems provide this information during orientation programs held prior to the opening of school.

Involvement of new teachers in the community not only facilitates the teacher's own adjustments but also brings the physical education program and the community together for a more effective relationship. Successful teachers accept this challenge. Because they are an integral part of community life, they learn about the needs of the students and the attitudes of parents toward education in general and physical education in particular. Inquisitive teachers learn about the local environment and use this information to provide a more meaningful teaching program. The community can serve as a laboratory and a resource for enriching instruction with those essentials that provide quality education. Students exposed to superior instruction acquaint parents with the purposeful program that exists in the physical education class. Community contacts and associations further develop a positive attitude toward physical education. The teacher's personality, the spirit in which the individual relates to community activities, and his willingness to work in community organizations go a long way toward creating a positive image of physical education and providing a more effective instructional program.

HUMAN-CENTERED PERFORMANCES

The teacher should be equally concerned with the affective and cognitive aspects of teaching. Although the task-centered performances are generally those for which the teacher is directly accountable, the human-centered performances are of crucial value to the effective teacher. If he or she generates a humanistic atmosphere in the classroom or gymnasium, he or she is acting responsibly for the personalized instruction and understanding of the individual students. Patterson suggests:

> The good teacher is not an instructor, who simply provides information, facts, and knowledge, but a facilitator of learning for the student. Good teachers are not those who are simply experts in subject matter, or experts in teaching methods, or curriculum experts, or who utilize the most resources, such as audio-visual aids. The best teacher is one who, through establishing a personal relationship, frees the student to learn. Learning can only take place in the student, and the teacher can only create conditions for learning. The atmosphere created by a good interpersonal relationship is the major condition for learning.[5]

Interaction Competencies

The degree to which teacher and student interact influences the value of the learning experience. No teacher will be successful in interpersonal relations with every student, because the human personality is such that values and interests vary greatly among individuals. Yet there are common interests that each teacher can develop, which will increase his or her ability to work with a student and to cope with a situation. The qualities of humanity and humility are essential to effective functioning in a school environment. Listening, understanding, and concern improve face-to-face relationships. There is little question that suspicion replaces trust, doubt replaces confidence, and competition replaces cooperation when a student struggles to seek recognition, understanding, and dignity.

Communications

Teachers must possess good communication skills if dialogue is to flow freely. Dialogue always involves interaction.

Listening. Teachers must learn to attend not only to verbal but also to nonverbal communication. Research on behavior through verbal communication is extensive, and has shown that teachers need to listen more sincerely to students. Nonverbal behavior also reveals the attitudes and feelings of students. These expressions can lead to more meaningful experiences if the teacher is attuned to various positive and negative responses.

Understanding. Each teacher is a complex of interests, needs, talents, motivations, and goals. To be effective, the teacher needs to understand the self before he or she can understand others. Self-awareness and self-concept further one's understanding of the student. From a deeper understanding comes acceptance of the individual and recognition of his worth.

Concern. Purposeful human relations are based on a concern for the individual and the group. Involvement of individualism has become significant in modern planning. The balance between personal and group goals is delicate, and some teachers forget the individual for the sake of the group or forget the group for the benefit of the individual. Cooperative concern is viewed as an integral part of the teaching-learning process, because it leads to better teacher-student relations.[6]

SEEKING A POSITION

The prospective teacher seeks the type of position that is compatible with personality, professional goals, and lifestyle.

Applying for a Position

It is advisable for the senior college student to write a letter early in the year, to the superintendent of the district in which he or she wishes to teach. (Sometimes students tend to postpone applying for a position and, as a result, will find that the best ones have been filled.) Upon receipt of the letter, the school administration will send an application blank to the student. The application should be carefully completed, with special attention given to spelling and neatness. A carelessly worded and hastily written application may have an adverse effect on

the candidate's chance of securing a position. If possible, the student should type the requested information.

Letter of Application. The prospective teacher should keep in mind that the letter serves as an introduction of the candidate to the employer. An application letter should be concise but informative. Pertinent details on educational background, previous experience, special competencies (e.g., aquatics), and names and addresses of references should be included. It is often desirable to include a telephone number and to declare one's availability for an interview. Employers are usually adamant about having their names spelled correctly and receiving typewritten, grammatically correct letters.

The Interview

The interview is a very important step in the future teacher's career. The manner in which the candidate approaches the superintendent, principal, or supervisor is extremely important. Even a dedicated person who is highly endowed with the capabilities of a superior teacher may not be offered a position because of the impression made at the interview. The following suggestions are valuable for the teacher in the interview situation.

Be Familiar With the Philosophy of the System. Before reporting for the interview, the applicant should, if possible, learn something about the philosophy of the program. Is emphasis placed on instruction? Does the administration believe in quality education? Does the school program include or sponsor innovative plans such as flexible scheduling, educational television, and team teaching? If these plans exist, are they successful? Knowledge about questions such as these will be of invaluable aid to the prospective teacher.

Be Able to Answer Questions About Physical Education. The applicant should be able to answer, in a straightforward manner, questions about physical education and professional philosophy. The interview gives the applicant a chance to express intelligently his or her capabilities as a teacher. Some questions that may be asked are:

1. Why did you decide to teach physical education?
2. What activities are you best able to teach?
3. What is your feeling about teaching as opposed to play?
4. Do you intend to make the teaching of physical education your life work?
5. What is your experience in physical education?
6. Why did you seek employment in this area rather than in some other place?

Be Personable. The prospective teacher can make a good impression by exhibiting good taste in dress and deportment. He should realize that the interviewer is observing and appraising his qualifications as an addition to the teaching staff in a particular school. In view of this, the applicant should be careful in answering questions and remain alert, poised, and relaxed. The employer is seeking a teacher who has the confidence, ability, and professional background to perform a satisfactory job and who will be an asset to the school.

Become Familiar With the School System. The interview is a two-way procedure. Although the basic purpose of the interview is the assessment of the applicant, the prospective teacher should use the interview to learn more about the position in question. The applicant has the right to know what the system has to offer. In a diplomatic way, the candidate should seek answers to the following questions:

1. Is the physical education program required?
2. Do the students receive credit for graduation? If so, how much credit?
3. Does the department have a supervisor?
4. Is there a guidebook available?
5. Does physical education have its own budget, or does it depend on gate receipts for survival?
6. What are the facilities for physical education? Does each teacher have a teaching station?
7. Is there sufficient equipment for conducting a quality program?
8. What are the retirement, insurance, sick leave, and personal leave plans?
9. Does the system provide an intramural program?
10. Are teachers evaluated? Annually? By what standards?

Keeping a Job

Educators need assessment criteria, evaluation studies, performance contracts, and other devices of accountability. Teachers will be held responsible for their positions through the courts by taxpayers, parents, and the school systems in which they are employed. No one wants to turn schools into mere production factories. If the teacher focuses on being a top quality teacher — if he or she works toward this goal each year — then the teacher will be able to remain on the job. Educators must keep abreast of changes in society that affect the subject field. Teachers should keep up with the latest research and conduct personal research. They should participate in professional organizations, experiment with new ideas, and employ creative teaching approaches. The teacher should welcome continuous evaluation and, whatever duty is undertaken, always keep *quality* in mind.

ACCOUNTABILITY

A factor teachers must face when they begin any teaching assignment is accountability to the public for the effectiveness of their instruction. Parents have been concerned with the quality of instruction for many years, but the pressure for measuring the actual results of teaching is now intense. Taxpayers insist on knowing how much education can be acquired for their investment.

Figure 2-3. Quality instruction in physical education is essential for accountability. (Courtesy Los Angeles Unified School District.)

Types of Accountability

As teachers enter the profession, they become aware of this public sentiment and should be apprised of the modes of accountability being employed. Girard Hottleman has identified some of these, which are described below.

Statewide Assessments. Statewide Assessment Plans all follow the same general design. A series of fairly broad minimum goals are set forth for the entire state, and the degree to which students conform to these goals is then measured. The state assessment programs assert that schools are successful according to the degree of conformity to state goals manifested by students. In some states, conformity to statewide objectives is used as a basis for distribution of state funds.

The Voucher System. The Voucher System provides assistance to parents who believe private schools offer a better education than public schools. The parent is given a voucher equal to the cost of educating a child in the public school and permitted to use it toward the cost of a private school.

Performance Contracting. The late 1960's witnessed the beginning of per-formance contracting, in which areas of instruction, such as reading, were placed in the hands of private, commercial firms. Education received a jolt; history may reveal this to be the greatest catalyst in improving instruction in the last 50 years. It grew out of the failure of many disadvantaged childred to learn reading and arithmetic and the failure of education to change in order to meet the needs of all children. Probably the most noticeable result in performance contracting is that it is producing educational reform.

Program Planning Budgeting System (PPBS). This venture into accountability is a type of systems planning that was introduced into General Motors and the Pentagon. The PPBS is applied to school operations tied to specific goals.

Other Plans. Performance Based Teacher Education (PBTE), Performance Based Teacher Certification (PBTC), Competency Based Teacher Education (CBTE), and Program Planning Teacher Education (PPTE) are all offshoots of the PPBS idea. The *Resource Manual* discusses other types of accountability. Both teacher education and teacher certification as they now exist are designed to guarantee at least a minimally acceptable skill level. Reformers suggest that certain measurable skills necessary for teaching can be isolated. Education degrees are being granted based on demonstrated proficiency in these skills.[7]

The movement to provide taxpayers with justification of monetary expenditures for education has initiated the development of performance objectives throughout the country. In the past, physical education has held back and waited to follow academic trends in education; therefore, it is somewhat late in showing the results of educational change. However, in the use of performance objectives, it should not wait for academicians to experiment before taking action. Physical education operates in the psychomotor domain and has been relying on performance measurements for many years. Teachers should use this means of evaluating motor performance in their teaching and in their school-community relations programs. Parents can understand the results of performance testing and, by relating these results to the need for physical education, teachers can easily justify expenditures for the student education program.

The Teacher in Changing Times

To summarize, the accountability movement was begun under the rubric of management by objectives (MBO). The MBO theory states that first you decide what you want to do, then you arrange your personnel and resources in the most effective patterns to achieve those objectives. The accountability movement was begun not as a way to improve learning opportunities for children but in response to problems rising out of the increased cost of education. Certain dangers may result from overemphasis on measurement, such as greater conformity, decrease in humanism, less individualism, more rigid controls, and more mechanization of teaching. What is needed is a flexible, quality teacher for the fluctuating times.

The Changing Student

Rapidly changing social conditions in the past few years have completely altered the climate of education in the nation's schools. For 50 years, teaching was more or less concerned with perpetuating the same curriculum, presented in the traditional manner. Although textbooks discussed the need to recognize individual differences, actual practice revealed very little application of this important facet of teaching. The major portion of the secondary school curriculum today is designed for students who plan to attend college. Little attention is given to students who are more concerned with developing the skills necessary to make a living.

Recent attempts to organize programs that will provide equal opportunity in education have revealed glaring inequities in the current system. Antiquated content and procedures must give way to innovations and approaches that will eventually reconstruct the entire complexion of the educational scheme. High on the list of teaching priorities is the development of management and methods, as shown in Chapter 5.

The Changing Curriculum

Just as teachers of academic subjects adapt their curricula to fit the times, so must physical education teachers be responsive to changing concepts and procedures. A leading educator has stated that:

The art of teaching is in about the same state as was the art of war in the 15th century, when the Roman legion had been supplemented by the English long bow, cross bow, and gunpowder. Educationally we now have other instruments—equivalent to the tank and the airplane—which we try out now and then. But we put our trust in the old weapons and an occasional cavalry charge.[8]

Constructive changes would involve more elective programs and fewer required subjects. Tomorrow's schools will place more emphasis on performance objectives, use of machines and audio-visual aids, specialization in teaching, individualized instruction, development of ungraded schools and classes, and lengthening of the school day, and will adopt the concept of the 12-month school. These are just a few of the revisions that are beginning to pervade our present educational system to form the nucleus of education in the twenty-first century.

All educational remodeling will be reflected in the physical education program. In fact, some of these changes have existed in physical education for years. Although they are probably unaware of it, physical education teachers have long been conducting programs involving behavioral objectives. Physical education basically is centered around the psychomotor field, and students have been evaluated on their performance in the skills which constitute the program.

All physical education teachers in changing times must have a flexible attitude toward teaching and must be able to contribute innovations to the curriculum reorganization.

The Price of Productivity

The accountability movement in educational institutions holds at least two positions that concern the performance of the school. Performance can mean *productivity*, or it can mean *responsiveness*. In most establishments, each level of authority sets goals for those below. Teachers set goals for students, administrators for teachers, and school boards for administrators. Even when goals are formulated at lower levels, the accountability data are reported from students to teachers, teachers to administrators, local agencies to state agencies, and so on.[9] In 1973, the National Education Association (NEA) developed Resolution 73–25 on Accountability, which states:

The National Education Association recognizes that the term "accountability" as applied to public education, is subject to varied interpretations. The Association maintains that educational excellence for each child is the objective of the education system. The

Association believes that educators can be accountable only to the degree that they have responsibility in educational decision-making and to the degree that other parties who share this responsibility — legislators, other government officials, school boards, parents, students, and taxpayers — are also held accountable.

The Association will seek the proper aim professionally, legally, and legislatively for educators to achieve optimum and appropriate accountability programs.[10]

Pros and Cons. There is little evidence to suggest that elaborate prespecification results in better learning. Recent research indicates that the more attention paid to planning objectives, the less paid to immediate student concerns. Accountability plans often have been mere attempts to save money. In actuality, the 1980's will determine the extent to which our social system and American education will accept or reject the accountability models. Tomorrow's students and teachers will have to bear the costs incurred by today's teachers, administrators, and school boards trying to meet the requirements of the accountability movement

The Promise of Competency-Based Teacher Education

The future of teacher education depends ultimately on the ability of professionals to demonstrate the relationship between teacher education curriculum and successful performance of students. The effort to document this correlation is based on the premise that an effective teacher will provide general knowledge and skills which will influence the achievements of students in the secondary schools. Materials are being field-tested to revise the training of preprofessionals. Because of the close association of teacher competence with certification requirements, many states have appointed state examiners to study the reliability of the standards used to determine the effectiveness of teacher behavior.

The competency-based teacher education movement shifts the criteria for certification away from completion of a

Teacher Self-Evaluation

Continuous attention to self-evaluation will result in self-improvement. Answer the following ''yes'' or ''no.''

_____Do I know the names of all my students?

_____Do I get my students to think instead of giving back ''rote'' memory of what I say?

_____Do I analyze my own classroom or gymnasium teaching?

_____Do I find myself available for student conferences?

_____Do I listen attentively to what students are saying?

_____Am I intuitive to the varying needs of students, such as the hypertense?

_____Do I know my subject matter well enough to be challenged by questions in class?

_____Do I really try to develop a positive teaching-learning climate in my classes?

_____Do I give individual attention to the excellent, the moderate, and the slow learner, and not concentrate just on the talented ones?

_____Do students talk to me freely inside and outside of class?

_____Are many students sleeping in class or getting restless?

_____Am I tolerant of students' mistakes as well as my own?

_____Do I keep up to date with my professional reading?

_____Do I grade fairly on learning objectives, rather than on likes and dislikes?

_____Do I really care about students and let them know it?

Give yourself 5 points for each ''yes'' answer. Score above 60 points and you are doing fine.

Figure 2–4. Teacher self-evaluation scale.

prescribed program at an accredited institution to presentation of evidence of particular expertise. The prospective teacher will be required to demonstrate, under actual classroom conditions, behavior that is either presumed, or has been established by research, to be associated with student performance. Permanent certification may become the licensing of the past. More states are moving toward continuing education to promote salary increases, release time, and professional pride. Conducting performance-based, field-centered teacher education programs will identify competencies that teachers need for successful careers in physical education.[11]

PREPARING PHYSICAL EDUCATORS FOR THE FUTURE

There is widespread belief that job opportunities for teachers of physical education will be limited to the quality programs that produce measurable and recognizable results. Physical education programs in schools of the future will have to show evidence of effectual teaching and learning experiences for the student in order to survive. Many agencies, including the National Education Association, have reported a decline in the number of teaching positions in schools and colleges. Economists believe that the academic labor market will be stable during the balance of the 1970's, but that a downward turn lies ahead in the 1980's. Several demographic factors have altered the picture of higher education in the last few years. The following data support this claim:

1. Decline in birth rate in late 1960's. Census figures list the size of the college–age group (18 to 21 year olds) today at about 15.5 million. Earlier projections were 21 to 23 million by the end of the century, but it now appears that in the year 2000 there will be approximately the same number as today.
2. The rate of students graduating from high school rose steadily for 15 years and peaked in the late 1960's. This rate has now dropped back 3 per cent.

3. The percentage of secondary school graduates entering college was 62 per cent in the late 1960's. In 1974 it was 58 per cent.
4. The rate of students graduating from college was 57 per cent in 1970 and 54 per cent in 1974.
5. The percentage of college graduates going to graduate and professional schools was 24 per cent in the late 1950's, 41 per cent in the late 1960's, and 30 per cent in 1973.[12]

This ample supply of qualified teachers provides an unprecedented opportunity for improvement in quality programs. The stronger the program, the less likely the curtailment of the physical education programs in times of economic stress.

Careers in Teaching

Prospective teachers must move toward more meaningfully centered approaches in the secondary school program. A major factor influencing these programs is the understanding of the differences between interscholastic athletic programs and quality instructional physical education programs. It is difficult to predict the future of athletic programs. Perhaps at the junior and senior high school levels, there will be a broadening of interscholastic activities offering greater variety to schoolchildren, including the handicapped, and with more students in each activity and less emphasis on only three or four sports. Maybe this trend will necessitate the establishment of more sports clubs and better intramural and recreational programs within the secondary school environment.

Teachers in future programs of physical educaton will become specialists as areas such as modern dance, adapted physical education, and motor therapy become popular. As stated previously in this chapter, types of certification will change. The undergraduate teacher education curriculum will become more flexible to meet the changing needs of teachers. There will be a "buyer's market" for teachers in the 1980's, and school officials will be more selective in the hiring process. The profession has reassessed the supply and demand for teachers. As a result, alternative career opportunities will need to be developed for the undergraduate, graduate, and professional student.

Career Alternatives

Career opportunities are increasing rapidly in work with the elderly, the exceptional, the very young, the fit, and the unfit.

Private Teaching. Evidence confirms the need for trained leaders to work in fitness programs, tennis camps, ski clubs, health centers, golf courses, industrial fitness programs, and various activities of personal choice in today's affluent society.

1. CLINICS AND CAMPS. Sports touch peoples' lives in many different ways. Various kinds, levels, and degrees of involvement are desired by the young, the old, the rich, the poor, the male, the female, the healthy, and the unhealthy. The average American watches sports, talks sports, reads sports, and plays sports. The physical education professional student needs to study the theory of sport, the management of sport, the safety of sport, and the business administration of sport. Opportunities exist not only to teach skills such as skiing, surfing, and swimming but also to serve as club managers, athletic trainers, facility supervisors, hotel managers, sports reporters, media technicians, hospital administrators, and specialized professional sports teachers.

2. HEALTH CENTERS. There are now approximately 1200 health clubs operating in the United States, and they will continue to be lucrative enterprises. The medical profession recognizes the need for quality exercise programs and adult fitness. Some health clubs have been criticized for a lack of medical clearance, untrained staff, and poorly designed exercise programs. Numerous states are currently contemplating laws requiring certification of health club personnel. Preparation is needed for future physical educators in this field.

3. BUSINESS AND INDUSTRY. Programs such as the Young Christian Associations (Y. M. C. A. and Y. W. C. A.), the Young Hebrew Associations (Y. M. H. A. and Y. W. H. A.), and the Catholic Youth Organization (C. Y. O.) have long been employing trained physical education teachers. Opportunities also exist in municipal recreation programs, summer camps, and other types of summer or part-time employment. Only recently have American businesses and industries given serious consideration to hiring full-time personnel for the development of fitness programs, recreational periods, and participative sports during the regular working day. General Motors (GM), International Business Machines (I. B. M.), and American Telephone and Telegraph (A. T. & T.) are expanding their recreational programs to include jogging, whirlpool therapy, exercise rooms, and game centers. For these programs, qualified physical educators and physical therapists are in great demand.

Specialist in the Handicapped. The Education for the Handicapped Act of 1974, enacted in 1975, upholds the right of all children and adults to equal educational opportunities. Attitudes toward the needs of handicapped individuals for physical education and recreational activities are changing. Significant modifications are being made to help teachers deal with mainstreaming the exceptional child in education. (These programs are discussed in detail in Chapter 10.) It becomes the responsibility of the physical educator to be equipped to handle these programs within the school environment as well as within the community. Teacher preparation has met the challenge so far through new courses, innovative programs, and interdisciplinary avenues. Schools, resource centers, hospitals, and rehabilitation centers need professionally prepared specialists. Career options are varied, depending upon the training and interest of the individual. Teachers are needed to work with perceptual motor learning for the child who is emotionally disturbed, mentally retarded, blind, deaf, neurologically handicapped, has cerebral palsy, or is afflicted with other learning disabilities. Institutions and industries welcome professional programs to alleviate the problems of adult alcoholism and drug addiction.

Work with the Aged. The population of men and women over 65 years of age is growing rapidly in this country. Nationwide interest is now centered on the exercise and activity needs of the elderly. More research is being devoted to low stress level exercises for the aging. A need exists for trained individuals to work in programs sponsored by private and public agencies in this field. Senior citizen centers, churches, nursing homes, retirement homes, and private resort clubs require qualified instructors. The current interest in fitness for the elderly appears to be growing, and opportunities are available for professionals to specialize in this area. Contributions to the general feeling of well-being, relaxation, and improved emotional attitudes among the elderly are opportune avenues for professional growth.

BEING A PROFESSIONAL

Teaching is the best way to learn. The teaching profession is a satisfying one that includes commitments to the student, to the public, and to the profession. It also includes a commitment to yourself for lifetime professional development. Many options are available for career enrichment. The degrees of success attained will be largely a matter of personal involvement. In-service education, graduate training, professional organizations, professional workshops and clinics, as well as personal research and reading, will enhance the development of the young professional. Responsibility is personal, and the commitment to continuing education and improvement is individually fulfilled.

The Teacher and the Supervisor

Dedicated teachers are quite frank both in stating that they need help and

in describing the type of help and guidance they want from their supervisors. Beginning teachers should expect assistance and should make their wishes known diplomatically. *Physical Education Newsletter* compiled a list of some of the areas in which teachers feel that supervisors can help them:

1. Teachers want more contact with their supervisors.
2. Teachers want their supervisors to help them become better teachers by supplying the leadership and inspiration.
3. Teachers want their supervisors to help them learn the proper lines of authority and supervision.
4. Teachers want their supervisors to help them find the compromise point between the ideal and the practical.
5. Teachers want their supervisors to keep them informed about new equipment, instructional materials, trends, and techniques.
6. Teachers want their supervisors to provide and coordinate the K–12 program.
7. Teachers want their supervisors to have the courage to lead, to make decisions, to try new ideas.
8. Teachers want their supervisors to give them some responsibility for developing the core program of activities based on a sequential progression.
9. Teachers want their supervisors to make better use of individual teachers' talents and specialities.
10. Teachers want their supervisors to give expert advice and guidance and to make constant, forceful (but not authoritarian) efforts to improve the teaching situation.
11. Teachers want their supervisors to provide more opportunity for physical education teachers to share ideas and teaching techniques with each other.
12. Teachers want their supervisors to keep the lines of communication between them and the staff open and functioning smoothly at all times.
13. Teachers want their teaching performance evaluated by a specialist in physical education.[13]

The Teacher and the Student

New teachers sometimes discover a gap between theory and practice that seems insurmountable. Teachers crave practical answers to the many problems that confront them. A background in theory is desirable, but success in teaching is measured by sound methods and procedures. The educator facing his or her class for the first time

On Becoming a Professional

You will be entering the teaching profession shortly and will be faced with many problems and situations that—as a professional—you will be expected to resolve in an expert manner. Here are some. What are your reactions?

1. The Department of Health, Education and Welfare in a Title IX proposal states that:

   A recipient school district may not require segregation of boys into one health, physical education, or other class, and segregation of girls into another such class.

   What is your reaction? Do you think boys and girls should participate in the same physical education activities?

2. You are employed in an area which has no supervision in physical education. You have the sole responsibility for planning and organizing your teaching activities. What activities would you teach? Why?

3. You have been asked to appear before the school board to justify physical education as a part of the school curriculum. What would you say?

4. As a future teacher, have you developed a philosophy of physical education? What is it? A big problem in physical education is impressing teachers with the importance of teaching.

5. In your opinion, what is meant by teaching physical education, as opposed to play?

6. You are required to teach perceptual-motor skills. What are they? At what grade level should they be taught?

7. There is considerable discussion about humanizing in education. What do you think this means? How is it applicable to physical education?

8. The State of Virginia requires that teachers of academic subjects write performance objectives for their classes. What are performance objectives? Are they applicable to physical education?

9. Ability grouping is extremely important in teaching physical education. Why?

10. Curriculum activities are roughly classified into two groups, team activities and individual activities. Which group dominates the curriculum? Why? Which group should receive the most emphasis? Why?

Figure 2–5. On becoming a professional. Courtesy VAHPER, Student Section, 1977.

needs to have basic knowledge of kinesiology, philosophy, history of physical education, and other subjects, but without equal knowledge of effective organization and teaching methods, the results will be unsatisfactory. Physical education is a movement program; when a class of 30 to 40 students begins to move into the techniques of skill acquisition, common sense and practical experience are essential for success.

The need for student teachers to acquire practical experience is so great that the importance of the student teaching program in college cannot be overemphasized. Future instructors should take advantage of every opportunity to practice teaching to learn about daily problems and ways to alleviate them. In situations in which the student teacher is closely supervised, he or she may receive valuable assistance. If practice teaching is done in a school where considerable freedom reigns and little supervision is given, students may profit by experimentation. Regardless of the manner in which the practice teaching program is handled, the student will find that experience is invaluable when real teaching begins.

QUESTIONS FOR DISCUSSION

1. What are the goals and objectives of effective teaching?
2. What are some of the characteristics of a successful teacher?
3. What are the major differences in task-centered performances and human-centered performances?
4. What is meant by accountability? What are the current models used in accountability?
5. How does the prospective physical educator prepare for career alternatives in changing times?

REFERENCES

1. Arthur L. Costa, "Affective Education: The State of the Art," *Educational Leadership* (January, 1977), pp. 260–263.
2. Marion E. Kneer, "How Human Are You." *JOPER* (June, 1974), pp. 32–34.
3. Myron Brenton, "Troubled Teachers Whose Behavior Disturbs Our Kids," *Today's Health* (November, 1971), p. 17.
4. "Building Healthier Youth," (Norfolk Public Schools, 1976), p. 6.
5. C. H. Patterson, *Humanistic Education* (Englewood Cliffs: Prentice-Hall, Inc., 1973), p. 98.
6. Helen M. Heitmann and Marion E. Kneer, *Physical Education Instructional Techniques: An Individualized Humanistic Approach* (Englewood Cliffs: Prentice-Hall, Inc., 1976), pp. 67–70.
7. Girard D. Hottleman, "The Accountability Movement," *Education Digest* (Vol. 39, April, 1974), pp. 17–20.
8. William C. Trowe, "New Educational Arsenal," *Innovator* (The University of Michigan School of Education, October 14, 1971).
9. Ernest R. House, "Feature on Accountability," *Today's Education* (Vol. 62, September–October, 1973), pp. 65–69.
10. Terry Herndon, NEA Executive Secretary (Speaking at an accountability conference, Denver, Colorado, May, 1973).
11. Benjamin Rosner, "The Promise of Competency-Based Teacher Education," *The Education Digest* (Vol. 39, September, 1973), pp. 25–28.
12. Allan M. Cartter, "Academic Jobs: Stability in the 1970's." The Chronicle of Higher Education (Vol. II, No. 12 December 9, 1974), p. 3.
13. "What Physical Education Teachers Want From Their Supervisors," *Physical Education Newsletter* (Croft Educational Services, Inc., September 15, 1964).

Calandra, Gerald N., "Job Hunting for Fun and Profit," *JOPER* (November–December, 1975), pp. 19–22.

Goldberger, Michael, "Studying Your Teaching Behavior," *JOPER* (March, 1974), pp. 33–36.

Heitmann, Helen, ed., Conference Report, "The Whole Thing," Special feature on report of the First National Conference on Secondary School Physical Education, *JOPER* (May, 1973), pp. 21–36.

McClusky, Mildred G., ed., *Teaching Strategies and Classroom Realities* (Englewood Cliffs: Prentice-Hall, Inc., 1971).

National Association for Physical Education of College Women and The National College Physical Education Association for Men, "Careers in Physical Education," *Briefings 3* (1975).

Ornstein, Allan C. and Harriet Talmage, "The Rhetoric and the Realistics," *Today's Education* (Vol. 62, No. 6, September–October, 1973), pp. 70–80.

Siedentop, Daryl, *Physical Education: Introductory Analysis* (Dubuque: William C. Brown Company, Publishers, 1972).

Sugarman, Stephen D., "Accountability Through the Courts," *School Review* (February, 1974), pp. 233–257.

Ulrich, Celeste, "The Physical Educator as Teacher," *Quest* VII (December, 1977), pp. 58–61.

Walker, June and Arthur G. Miller (consultant). Cowell and Schwehn's *Modern Methods in Secondary School Physical Education* (Boston: Allyn and Bacon, Inc., 1973).

Chapter 3

Courtesy Los Angeles Unified School District.

FACTORS INVOLVING A SEARCH FOR MEANING
   ACADEMIC DISCIPLINE
      CHARACTERISTICS OF A DISCIPLINE
WHAT IS PHILOSOPHY?
   WHY DOES A PHYSICAL EDUCATOR NEED A
   PHILOSOPHY?
   PERSONAL PHILOSOPHY
      SEARCH FOR MEANING
GENERAL OBJECTIVES OF EDUCATION
   OVERVIEW OF THE BASIC AIM OF PHYSICAL
   EDUCATION
   REDEFINITION AND REASSESSMENT
      INNOVATIONS IN THE SECONDARY
      SCHOOL
HISTORICAL SIGNIFICANCE OF OBJECTIVES IN
PHYSICAL EDUCATION
   DEVELOPMENTS IN
   1920–1930
   1930–1940
   1940–1950
   1950–1960
   1960–1970
   1970–1980
CONTEMPORARY DESIGNS IN PHYSICAL
EDUCATION
   THE PLAY PATTERN
   THE PHYSICAL FITNESS PATTERN

   FITNESS FOR WHAT?
   ANATOMICAL COMPONENT
   PSYCHOLOGICAL COMPONENT
   PHYSIOLOGICAL COMPONENT
   DEFINITION OF PHYSICAL FITNESS
THE CARRY-OVER LEISURE SPORTS
   PATTERN
THE HUMAN MOVEMENT PATTERN
PERFORMANCE APPRAISAL
   PERFORMANCE OBJECTIVES FOR TEACHERS
      PERFORMANCE CATEGORIES
   PERFORMANCE OBJECTIVES FOR STUDENTS
      THE COGNITIVE DOMAIN
      THE AFFECTIVE DOMAIN
      THE PSYCHOMOTOR DOMAIN
   BEHAVIORAL CATEGORIES
DESIRABLE OUTCOMES OF THE SECONDARY
SCHOOL PROGRAM
   SELF-REALIZATION
   SOCIALIZATION
   SPORTSMANSHIP
   POSITIVE HEALTH
   VALUE IDENTIFICATION
QUESTIONS FOR DISCUSSION
REFERENCES
SELECTED READINGS

MEANING AND PHILOSOPHY IN PHYSICAL EDUCATION

The profession took its most serious look at the purpose and meaning of physical education during the 1970's. Certain aspects of the post-industrial society, the maturing of the "baby-boom" population of World War II, the vast expansion of knowledge, the debate between the concepts of teaching as an academic discipline or a profession, the effect of the "athletic revolution," the influence of the female model in athletics, and the continuing search for meaning in teaching by physical educators in high school and college programs all have led the profession to its most searching quest for philosophic beliefs.

FACTORS INVOLVING A SEARCH FOR MEANING

History indicates that a profession advances as a result of an overriding urge to seek truth. Philosophers in physical education are examining the contributions that physical education makes to society in broad, cultural terms. The physical education program in the nineteenth century and in the first half of the twentieth century was concerned with pragmatic and sometimes short-term goals. Professional personnel have been considered "doers" rather than "thinkers." The average secondary teacher or administrator has not made a serious study of the meaning and significance of human movement to the culture as a whole. These studies become more vital as the profession approaches the realities of the twenty-first century.

Academic Discipline

Since the early 1960's, leaders in physical education have studied the scholarly directions of the art and science of human movement. Numerous conferences led to changes in the professional curriculum. Research flourished in sport sociology, anthropology, motor learning, sport history, sport psychology, sexism in sport, and the philosophy of physical education and sport. These studies were added to the already expanding knowledge in biomechanics, exercise physiology, adapted physical education, tests and measurements, and comparative physical education. Most of the major institutions training teachers of physical education introduced courses, re-evaluated curricula, and made significant changes in undergraduate and graduate offerings.

Some may say that "it is a whole new ball game," while others contend that the profession is simply "putting the old wine in new bottles." But the study of philosophy is important because it develops within the individual teacher or administrator an awareness of the importance of physical education in the schools. Goals and objectives must be based upon a sound philosophy that reflects scientific evidence and scholarly endeavors.

Characteristics of a Discipline. Franklin Henry defined academic discipline as "an organized body of knowledge collectively embraced in a formal course of learning."[1] He further stated that an area of subject matter should meet four criteria in order to be considered an academic discipline. Physical education leaders should determine (1) Does physical education have a definable body of knowledge? (2) Is there suitable subject matter for scholarly and scientific investigation? (3) Is there an orderly and logical sequence of increasing complexity? (4) Is there a technology for transmitting and applying knowledge? Thus, as physical educators defined the conceptual structures of human movement, theorists and scholars began to distinguish their beliefs from those of technical and professional educators.

WHAT IS PHILOSOPHY?

Aristotle once said, "What is, is. What is not, is not." There will be contrasting opinions and beliefs whenever concerned men reason. Philosophy asks questions in its attempts to understand life's problems. It is based on a science of facts in which rational theory, basic principles, and reflective thinking give rise to a "philosophic" way of viewing one's basic beliefs. Philosophy has long been a nebulous concept to students; the eclectic is universal. Yet the young professional student is beginning to study more seriously the relation of philosophic thought to the purpose of physical education in today's world.

What the individual does is a function of what he or she believes; actions reflect philosophy. For the professional student, the process is to establish a system of values. The original meaning of philosophy was a "love of truth" or "love of wisdom." Philosophy is concerned with questions of right and wrong, freedom, and discretion. There is a distinction between philosophy and science: philosophy evaluates the worth of things and synthesizes facts, science describes, discovers, and analyzes facts.

Why Does a Physical Educator Need a Philosophy?

Davis and Miller have identified five forces indicating the need for philosophy:

1. Philosophy uses a common language which ties together the diverse educational areas and invites communication with other subject content fields. The development of a theoretical and philosophical position will be helpful in interpreting physical education to the general public.
2. Philosophy enables the profession to expand if it undertakes the study of physical education beyond isolated concerns. The contributions to moral values, the culture, and the individual can be introduced through the interdisciplinary approaches to sociology, psychology, anthropology, history, and science.
3. Philosophy highlights a professional purpose. It states what the profession does in relation to what needs to be done. The individual in the profession obtains more satisfaction if he understands the basic purpose or purposes of the secondary school program.
4. Philosophy encourages examination of basic assumptions. Young professional

teachers are changing the course of phys-ical education as students question values and purposes. Reflective thought has to be given to the question of "why."
5. Philosophy stimulates self-examination and independent work. The teacher reads and talks with other individuals, but he needs to build his own philosophy.[2]

Personal Philosophy

What is the purpose of education? How do secondary education in general and physical education in particular make a contribution to society? Who should be educated? What is the purpose of physical education in the elementary school, the middle school, the secondary school? Where should the emphasis be in physical education? How do athletics contribute to the well-being of the individual? How does a teacher view the student in the teaching-learning process? How does the school evaluate learning? Who is held accountable to whom and for what? These questions and their answers are not merely abstractions. Answers have meaning and purpose as the teacher relates his or her own beliefs and personal philosophy to the profession. Mature thinkers search for meaning. Students should use philosophy as a process for analytical thinking.

Search for Meaning. A personal philosophy allows the individual to think, to discuss, and to write. It is a mental activity, a part of the process of self-examination and professional growth. A young teacher needs to express personal beliefs, to experiment with new ideas, to examine and reexamine current ideas, to be flexible in forming a philosophy, and to reach a balance in the real worth of his professional contribution. How a teacher *feels* about a problem or an issue is important. Past experience, valid knowledge, personal thoughts, and creative ideas portray an individual's own basic beliefs. The challenge is to *think*. One learns through the thinking process — mental wandering, intuitive thinking, creative thinking, problem solving, musing, comprehending, recalling, and rationalizing.

This chart is a simple explanation of how to build a personal philosophy:

Personal Philosophy
as one studied

Foundations
as one found

Beliefs
as one based

Opinions-Speculations
on

Facts-Judgments
as one structured

Hypotheses
as one generated

Theory
as one developed

Principles
as one discovered

Laws

A person's philosophy is reflected in his teaching. Since values vary, no teacher wants his performance evaluated by judges who are unaware of the teacher's own standards of excellence. Davis offers the following sample of various philosophies concerning the central focus of physical education:

Now the first teacher can be informed that he is to be judged for excellence in teaching. Teacher A, *an idealist*, replies, "Well, all right, but before you do so may I remind you that my central concern—first, last, and most importantly—in the entire teaching-learning procedure is that the students be helped to reach their highest potential, to work toward attaining perfection, each to become a complete personality and fulfill the best self-image. In fact, I do not believe that there can be excellence in teaching unless this is the major concern."

Teacher B, *a realist*, is next. His response runs something like this: "Don't judge my teaching for excellence unless you know that my central concern is to motivate, prod, push, pull, encourage, and help the student adjust to life and his Universe as the way toward happiness. Such a concern determines all that I do, say, think, and aspire to, as a teacher."

Next, Teacher C, *an aritomist*, responds

with these words: "You could not possibly judge the excellence of my teaching unless you knew that my central concern was improving the student's ability to reason, make better decisions, draw sounder conclusions, and perform sharper mental activities. These considerations control all of my part of the teaching-learning procedure."

Teacher D, *a pragmatist*, says, "You are unable to consider whether my teaching is excellent or not until you know what my central concern is. In brief, it consists of such provisions as offering chances for the student to learn by doing, to solve his own problems in his own way, to work cooperatively with others on common chores, to arrive at jointly-made solutions—all in terms of, and because of, the results obtained."

The fifth and last, Teacher E, is *an existentialist.* Here is his reaction to our suggestion: "Any and all teaching assumes the student has developed some degree of self-responsibility. The trouble is that almost all teachers take this for granted and do little or nothing to help the student gain his self-responsibility. You cannot judge the excellence of my teaching unless you know beforehand that the central concern in all my teaching is that the student develop more and more self-responsibility. This, in turn, means that a good deal of my work also is devoted to his self-discovery. He must learn to 'know thyself.' "[3]

GENERAL OBJECTIVES OF EDUCATION

Individuals and groups from time to time have endeavored to formulate the general purposes of education. One of the most outstanding clarifications was offered in 1918, when the Cardinal Principles of Secondary Education were designed. Education was then undergoing a transition from a more formal curriculum to one designed to meet the needs of a changing society. The cardinal principles are:

Health
Command of the Fundamental Processes
Worthy Home Membership
Vocation
Citizenship
Worthy Use of Leisure
Ethical Character.[4]

Just prior to and during World War II, the need for another look at the purposes of education became evident. In 1938, the Educational Policies Commission of the National Education Association condensed the aims of educa-

tion into four broad areas, which are still widely accepted:

1. The objectives of self-realization.
2. The objectives of human relations.
3. The objectives of economic efficiency.
4. The objectives of civic responsibility.[5]

Physical education, like all other disciplines, plays an important role in the attainment of all four goals; however, the first — the objective of self-realization — is the one to which physical education makes its greatest contribution.

In 1961, the Education Policies Commission again reviewed the aims and objectives of American education:

The purpose which runs through and strengthens all other education purposes — the common thread of education — is the development of the ability to think. This is the central purpose to which the school must be oriented if it is to accomplish either its traditional tasks or those newly accentuated by recent changes in the world.[6]

Overview of the Basic Aim of Physical Education

Before attempting to initiate any program of physical education, leaders must define a basic aim or purpose. The basic objective of any subject is the result of years of thought, application of principles, and a final analysis obtained through the practical application of all known phenomena around which the existing programs revolve. It is the statement of purpose that really sets the direction for what is to be accomplished and helps to determine whether the effort is approaching the desired goal.

The American Alliance for Health, Physical Education and Recreation lists five major purposes of physical education, which clearly show the transformation of the profession from the old program of *physical training* to a comprehensive and modern program of *physical education:*

1. *To help* children learn to move skillfully and effectively not only in exercises, games, sports, and dances but also in all active life situations.
2. *To develop* understanding of voluntary movement and the ways in which individu-

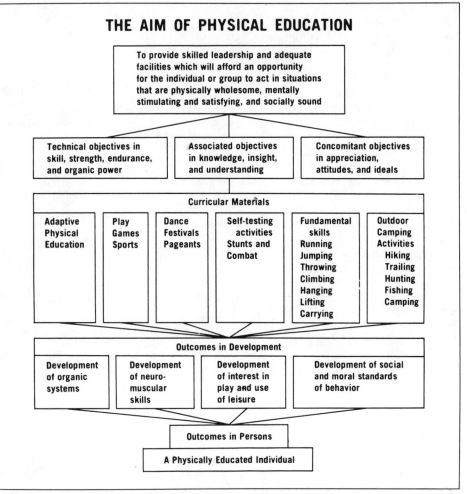

Figure 3–1. The aim of physical education. From Williams, Jesse F., *Principles of Physical Education* (Philadelphia: W. B. Saunders Company, 1964), p. 331.

als may organize their own movements to accomplish the significant purposes of their lives.

3. To *enrich* understanding of space, time, mass-energy relationships, and related concepts.

4. To *extend* understanding of socially approved patterns of personal behavior, with particular reference to the interpersonal interactions of games and sports.

5. To *condition* the heart, lungs, muscles, and other organic systems· to respond to increased demands by imposing progressively greater demands upon them.[7]

Redefinition and Reassessment

By the mid 1970's, the identification of a specific body of knowledge based on scientific facts caused the profession to redefine and reassess its purposes. A condensation of the aims listed above might result in one general objective that would link physical education more closely to the total health and well-being of the individual:

Physical education in a democratic culture should place before all students those phases of activity, guidance, and instruction which allow for manifestation and development of inherent human potentialities, contributing to the total health and well-being of the individual, and allowing him to become adjusted to the physiological and sociopsychological goals that lead to a self-actualizing individual.

Although few would suggest that physical fitness should shape the entire program at the expense of sociopsychological objectives, it may be appropriate as one goal of a comprehensive program. Justification for maintenance of physical education in the curriculum includes projected life expectancy of 120 to 150 years before the turn of the century, manipulation of the genetic code, development of plastic and metal organs and arteries, organ transplants, wonder drugs, and individually tailored diets.[8]

Innovations in the Secondary School. The old "p.e." or "gym" program had as its goal the exercise of young bodies so they would grow stronger and better. The purpose of secondary physical education in the latter part of the twentieth century goes far beyond that aim to include instruction in lifetime sports, relaxation for both stress and leisure, stronger self-concepts, higher levels of perceptual motor skills, good body movement skills, and an understanding of how to use these skills in individualized programs.

Whereas teachers should always have an ideal aim in mind, they must deal practically with stark reality. Scheduled to attend their classes are all kinds of students — short, slender, fat, strong, weak — and teachers have to provide a program to suit all of them. In order to do this, teachers must have guidelines to help them utilize to the best advantage the time allotted for instruction. These guidelines or steps leading toward the ultimate aim are the objectives of the program. These should always be brought to the attention of teachers, administrators, and the public when programs in physical education are planned and executed.

HISTORICAL SIGNIFICANCE OF OBJECTIVES IN PHYSICAL EDUCATION

The current and future objectives of physical education reflect philosophical study. A capsule view of these past developmental years is helpful in understanding where the profession has been and where it is going.

1920–1930

Clark Hetherington classified the goals of physical education into five groups:

1. The immediate objectives in the organization and leadership of child life as expressed in big muscle activities.
2. The remote objectives in adult social adjustment and efficiency.
3. The objectives in development.
4. The objectives in social standards as applied to the activities, the development, and the adjustment.
5. The objectives in the control of health conditions.[9]

1930–1940

Sharman outlined three general objectives of physical education:

1. To provide opportunities for controlled participation in physical activities that will result in educative experiences.
2. To develop the organic systems of the body, to the end that each individual may live at the highest possible level.
3. To develop skills in activities and favorable attitudes toward play that will carry over and function during leisure time.[10]

1940–1950

Four standards for assessing and judging the physical education program proposed by Williams revealed the thinking developed during the war years. These standards are as effective for judging outcomes today as they were many years ago:

1. Provide physiological results, scientifically determined, indicative of wholesome, functional activity or organic systems, and sufficient for the needs of the growing organism.
2. Have meaning and significance for the individual and provide a carry-over interest.
3. Provide opportunity for the individual to satisfy those socially desirable urges and impulses of nature through engagement in motor activities appropriate to age, sex, condition, and stage of development.
4. Offer opportunity to the individual under wise leadership to meet educative situations as one of a social group.[11]

World War II brought an increased emphasis on health and fitness. Stimulated by the high proportion of rejections from military service because of physical deficiencies, many educators lent their support to the physical education effort. After the war, leaders in the profession came forward with objectives that influenced the physical education program. Bucher reflected the thinking of those years in his list of four objectives: (1) the physical development objective, (2) the motor development objective, (3) the mental development objective, and (4) the human relations objective.[12]

1950–1960

During the 1950's, several leaders in physical education made contributions to the philosophical approach to physical education. Cowell advocated a balanced curriculum and grouped both general and specific objectives in the following categories:

1. Organic power or the ability to maintain adaptive effort—in which one attempts to strengthen muscles, develop resistance to fatigue, and increase cardiovascular efficiency.
2. Neuromuscular development—in which one attempts to develop skills, grace, a sense of rhythm, and an improved reaction time.
3. Personal-social emotional attitudes and adjustment—in which one attempts to place students in situations that encourage self-confidence, sociability, initiative and self-direction, and a feeling of belonging.
4. Interpretative and intellectual development—in which students are encouraged to approach whatever they do with active imagination and some originality, so that they contribute something that is their own.
5. Emotional responsiveness—in which students express joy and "fun" in games and sports, get a thrill out of cooperative success or teamwork, and develop an increased appreciation of aesthetic experiences in the dance, game, or water ballet.[13]

era but also influenced planning for the 1970's. Among the writers of that decade were Nixon and Jewett, who proposed five broad, general objectives which were designed for use in the creation of immediate or specific objectives. These objectives were designed to serve as forerunners in the design of performance objectives:

1. *To develop a basic understanding and appreciation of human movement.* This broad objective involves (a) the development of understanding and appreciation of the deeper, more significant human meanings and values acquired through idea-directed movement experience; (b) an appreciation of human movement as an essential nonverbal mode of human expression; (c) the development of a positive self-concept and body image through appropriate movement experience; and (d) the development of key concepts through volitional movements and closely related nonverbal learning activities.
2. *To develop and maintain optimal individual muscular strength, muscular endurance, and cardiovascular endurance.* It is customary to refer to this purpose as the "physical fitness" objective. Many authors expand it to include such factors as flexibility, balance, agility, power, and speed. It is essential to develop not only skills but also knowledge and understanding relevant to physical fitness.
3. *To develop individual movement potentialities to the optimal level for each individual.* Physical education instruction concentrates on the development of selected neuromuscular skills, and on the refinement of fundamental movement patterns basic to specific skills.
4. *To develop skills, knowledge, and attitudes essential to satisfying, enjoyable physical recreation experiences engaged in voluntarily throughout one's lifetime.* Normal mental and emotional health is enhanced by participation in voluntary physical recreation.
5. *To develop socially acceptable and personally rewarding behavior through participation in movement activities.* Physical education instruction seeks to develop desirable social habits, attitudes, and personal characteristics essential to citizens in a free, democratic society.[14]

1960–1970

The 1960's saw a revival in objectives that not only affected the thinking of physical education leaders for that

1970–1980

New directions for secondary school physical education emerged in the 1970's. In a conference on Curriculum

Improvements in Secondary School Physical Education, Jan Felshin gave a rationale for and delineated the purposes of physical education. She stated:

There is, however, another reason for widespread and continuous efforts to identify purposes for physical education programs in schools. All of the beliefs and values that provide the sources for purposes (1) are changing continually, as knowledge is developed and as value priorities are redefined and (2) are always available for interpretative refinement. Physical educators have not agreed upon the theoretical concerns of the field and that means that purposes for programs, which are the most commonly used expressions of attitudes towards theory, have been confused. This confusion has had several unfortunate but familiar manifestations:

1. Lack of ability to discriminate among purposes has resulted in purposes becoming additive; that is, new insights or formulations of intent have simply been added to existing ones with the resulting long lists of unordered purposes.
2. Confusion between intent and effect has led to alleged benefits of physical education being identified as purposes without reference to theoretical appropriateness.
3. Beginning with the Seven Cardinal Principles of Education in 1918, physical education has accepted all educational obligations and commitments as its purposes and the integrity of the field is frequently obscure in its statement of intent.
4. The conventional wisdom of familiar purposes means that they are often ignored altogether, and curriculum process is likely to be approached by assuming that purposes are obvious and need no attention.[15]

She further concluded:

Purposes, therefore, can provide an ordered expression of theoretical positions, and because of their viable and interactive relationship with program and experiences become crucial elements of the process of the continual evaluation and refinement that are cornerstones of curriculum development.

1. Purposes must be directly related to knowledge appropriate to the concerns of physical education.
    a. They may reflect the importance of knowledge about man as he pursues movement activities; the ways in which movement is related to human functioning; ideas about effective or efficient movement; the nature of sport, dance, or exercise as movement forms, or the experiencing of movement forms.
    b. They may reflect the importance of experience and/or development and functioning in relation to movement itself or to sport, dance, and exercise.
2. Purposes must be defined and understood as contributions to goals and commitments of education.
    a. Foundational assumptions about the role of education, social realities and/or commitments, and beliefs and knowledge about individuals and how they develop and learn must be identified and related to purposes.
    b. The implications of purposes must be clarified so that the presumed effects of the experiences they suggest are explicit.[16]

Siedentop contends that we are entering a period that may be characterized by a diversity of physical education programs. Several types of programs reflect a lack of unanimity of purpose. There are those that emphasize physical fitness or lifetime sports or team sports. Some stress the multiactivity approach; some specialize in fewer activities. Movement exploration may dominate one program; the cognitive development others. It is becoming increasingly important for physical educators to examine program aims and program content to determine the basic concepts which undergird the program.[17]

It is with the foregoing overview of the aims and objectives of education in general and physical education in particular that the authors present the contemporary concepts of physical education. These realistic ideas should be helpful in planning programs not only for the 1980's but also for the incoming twenty-first century.

CONTEMPORARY DESIGNS IN PHYSICAL EDUCATION

The four patterns of physical education that are discussed are play, physical fitness, leisure sports, and human movement.

The Play Pattern

Play is synonymous with movement and is one of the four basic drives of man. Play, exercise, activity, or movement—the name does not matter—is basic to all life. Whereas basic drives

Figure 3–2. Golf provides students with components of play, leisure sport, and human movement. (Courtesy Rosemont Junior High School, Norfolk, Virginia.)

have been broken down into rather extensive categories by some psychologists, they can generally be grouped into four basic urges: sex, ego, gregariousness, and play. The play urge is the first to manifest itself. A newborn baby takes its first and most important fitness test when it utters its first cry at birth. This manifestation of life is a muscular demonstration and initiates the child's career in fitness for survival. In quick order, this muscular movement is followed by rolling, sitting, crawling, pulling up, walking with support, standing alone, and walking alone. Hilgard states that the development in these movements is orderly, and 95 per cent of all individuals pass through these stages in 14 months.[18]

As children grow, fundamental movements such as walking, running, hanging, carrying, jumping, leaping, climbing, and other natural inherited movements develop organic vigor. The dynamic urge for activity is a natural biological impulse of all normal healthy individuals and is manifested by outward responses in play activities.

These provide a means of normal self-expression for the natural biological drives that are so dominant in children.

The fundamental movements of man, which are part of his inheritance and which have been basic to our culture for thousands of years, include activities that provide the movements necessary for normal growth and development. Fink points out the meaning of play:

> Play is a fundamental possibility of social life. To play is to play together, to play with others; it is a deep manifestation of human community. Play is not, as far as its structure is concerned, an individual and isolated action; it is open to our neighbor as partner. There is no point in underlining the fact that we often find solitary players playing alone at personal games, because the very meaning of play includes the possibility of other players. The solitary player is often playing with imaginary partners.[19]

Latchaw and Egstrom offer a comprehensive outline of the fundamental movements. They classify gross movement skills into three groups: (1) basic movements; (2) skills of locomotion;

and (3) skills for overcoming inertia of external objects. The classifications and movements involved are shown below:

Basic Movements	Skills of Locomotion	Skills for Overcoming Inertia
Bending	Walking	Pushing
Stretching	Running	Pulling
Twisting	Leaping	Throwing
	Jumping	Kicking
	Hopping	Striking
	Skipping	Batting
	Sliding	Catching
	Galloping	Blocking[20]

This concept of play shows that children do not need external, artificial programs imposed upon them by parents, teachers, or others. What they need is guidance. Opportunity must be provided for students to participate in activities that allow desirable manifestations of their natural play urge. These activities need to be scientifically selected so that children have opportunities for the fullest mental, physical, emotional, and social growth.

The writings of Luther Gulick, Clark Hetherington, Joseph Lee, and Jesse Feiring Williams have promoted the play pattern as a basic means of education. Currently, writers such as Harold Vanderwagg and Daryl Siedentop are extending the concept of play in theoretical terminology. As skill competencies increase, the motivation for play increases. Recent trends indicate that Americans enjoy the freedom, excitement, and enjoyment of "the play pattern."

A recent survey revealed 15 theories purporting to explain why children play.[21] These were classified into groups and evaluated. A description of the classical theories of play is shown in Figure 3–3. Examination of these theories may be helpful to teachers in relating play to the physical education program. Other descriptions appear in the *Resource Manual*.

The Physical Fitness Pattern

Physical fitness is a phase of total fitness and an integral part of the physi-

cal education program. The problem confronting many teachers and administrators is interpretation. Many individuals have their own definitions of physical fitness and the activities that should be used to achieve it. Those interpretations in many instances are without scientific foundation and represent an empirical approach to teaching.

Fitness for What? It should be understood that physical fitness is a relative state and varies from individual to individual and from program to program. In discussing program objectives, one must ask, "Fitness for what?" Anatomical, psychological, and physiological differences as well as varying lifestyles necessitate consideration of individual needs in terms of physical fitness.

Recent research in exercise physiology has made the general public increasingly aware that physical fitness can be defined in terms of circulatory-respiratory efficiency. This definition substantiates the current interest in running, jogging, and cycling. DeVries suggests that the concept of "physical working capacity" (PWC) should be an important part of the physical educator's attempt to measure physical fitness. He states:

The best approach to the measurement of PWC is to have a subject perform successive work bouts of from three to six minutes duration, and of increasing intensity, with adequate rest periods between successive bouts. During each work bout the O_2 consumption is measured, and, when the O_2 consumption fails to rise with increased load, this "maximum O_2 consumption" value is a measure of the subject's aerobic capacity, or PWC.[22]

There are three components of fitness — anatomical, psychological, and physiological. All three are vitally important in the approach to the physical fitness pattern.

Anatomical Component. The anatomical component has to do with an individual's heredity. Certain anatomical structures may hinder an individual in the performance of a given "fitness test." Those with physical handicaps, such as loss of an arm or leg or varying degrees of deformities, do not perform as well on certain standardized tests, yet they may be as fit physiologically as an Olympic athlete.

Psychological Component. This relates to the emotional factors involved in fitness performances. Competition may so deeply affect an individual that his emotions may hinder performance. It would not be scientifically sound to say that one who fails to start quickly because of some emotional deviation, and who thereby gives a poor performance in the 50-yard dash, is not physically fit. Yet psychology does play a role in physical development.

Physiological Component. The physiological component involves four factors: skill, speed, endurance and strength. These basic factors of physiological fitness will be considered separately. The curriculum should include activities that involve all these factors, because each is important in the quest for physiological fitness.

1. *Skill.* The attainment of skill in various activities may be called the epitome of physical fitness. Practice of skill activities develops other factors of fitness and is, at the same time, interesting to the participant. Morehouse and Miller summarize recent opinion on the importance of teaching skills:

The development of motor skills of various types, one of the major objectives of physical education, consists primarily of improvement in the speed and accuracy with which the nervous system coordinates activity.[23]

In addition to the need for skills instruction in physiological development, the importance of skills to intellectual achievement is well documented. The teaching of skills involves perceptual motor movements that are vitally important in learning to read and write.

2. *Speed.* In most life situations, muscular speed is necessary in varying degrees. For growing boys and girls, to be able to run fast, throw fast, and combine speed with strength, skill, and endurance are basic for normal growth and development.

Speed is based on quick muscular reaction, and practicing speed activities improves coordination and reaction time. Through participation in activities combining endurance and strength, the organs of the body are developed during the formative years, enabling individuals to perform the tasks of later life.

In many instances, speed combined with skill may offset a lack of strength. This is one way individual differences are provided for in physical education; the compensating factor causes greater interest in participation.

3. *Endurance.* To be able to compete, to participate, and to prolong certain efforts with a minimum of fatigue is important in the development of physical fitness. There are two kinds of endurance: muscular and circulatory-respiratory. The former is the ability of the muscles to perform work, as in pull-ups; the latter is the ability of muscle groups to contract for long periods of time, as in distance running. Exercises of endurance, therefore, are essential. They develop the heart, promote healthy metabolism, and provide an overall physiological development that is not attained through exercises of skill, speed, or strength.

4. *Strength.* Strength is basic to performance and is essential in the development of muscular efficiency. The ability to lift, carry, hold, squeeze, and push is important for the development of strength. It must be borne in mind that strength should be developed concurrently with speed, skill, and endurance. Overemphasizing strength while neglecting the other components is undesirable. The type of strength illustrated by bulging muscles is no longer considered an example of good development. Strength developed through vigorous participation in sports and games is much closer to the physiological ideal.

Definition of Physical Fitness. In summarizing the foregoing considerations of physical fitness, it may be stated that *physical fitness is a relative condition that varies from individual to individual and that depends on the ability of the individual to adjust to the tasks demanded with as little effort as possible and without undue fatigue.*

In striving for physiological fitness, physical education teachers must continually search for the scientific approach in the selection of activities that make the greatest contribution to strength, speed, skill, and endurance. They must realize that exercise is an

CLASSICAL THEORIES OF PLAY

Name	Play is caused:	This explanation assumes:	It can be criticized because:	Verdict
Surplus Energy I	by the existence of energy surplus to the needs of survival.	1. energy is stored. 2. storage is limited. 3. excess energy must be expended. 4. expenditure is made on play, by definition.	1. children play when fatigued or to the point of fatigue so a surplus is not necessary for play. 2. the process of evolution should have tailored the energy available to the energy required.	Inadequate
Surplus Energy II	by increased tendency to respond after a period of response deprivation.	1. response systems of the body all have a tendency to respond. 2. response threshold is lowered by a period of leisure.	after periods of disuse, eventually all available responses should reach a low enough threshold to be discharged. Some responses available to the person are never used.	Inadequate as written but has been incorporated in learning theory.
Instinct	by the inheritance of unlearned capacities to emit playful acts.	1. the determinants of our behavior are inherited in the same way that we inherit the genetic code that determines our structure. 2. that some of those determinants cause play.	1. it ignores the obvious capacity of the person to learn new responses that we classify as play. 2. the facile naming of an instinct for each class of observed behavior is to do no more than to say "Because there is play, there must be a cause which we will call an Instinct."	Inadequate

Theory				
Preparation	by the efforts of the player to prepare for later life.	1. play is emitted only by persons preparing for new ways of responding, and in general is the preserve of the young. 2. the player can predict what kinds of responses will be critical later. 3. instincts governing this are inherited imperfectly and are practiced during youth.	1. it requires that the player inherit the capacity to predict which responses will be critical. This requires the inheritance of information about the future. 2. play occurs most frequently in animals that live in rapidly changing circumstances. 3. when acceptably prepared the person should stop playing.	Inadequate. However play may have by-products that are advantageous later.
Recapitulation	by the player recapitulating the history of the development of the species during its development.	1. critical behaviors occurring during evolution of man are encoded for inheritance. 2. person emits some approximation to all these behaviors during his development. 3. since they are currently irrelevant they are play. 4. the stages in our evolution will be followed in the individual's development.	1. no linear progression in our play development that seems to mirror the development of a species. At one point, late boyhood and adolescence, there may be similarity between sports and games and the components of hunting, chasing, fighting, etc., but before and after there seems little relation. 2. does not explain play activities dependent on our advanced technology.	Inadequate
Relaxation	the need for an individual to emit responses other than those used in work to allow recuperation.	1. players work. 2. play involves the emission of responses different to those of work.	1. it does not explain the play of children—unless they are clearly working some part of their day. 2. does not explain the use in play of activities also used in work.	Inadequate

Figure 3–3. Classical Theories of Play. (From Ellis, M. J.: "Play and its theories re-examined." *Parks and Recreation,* National Recreation and Parks Association, August, 1971.)

important factor in weight control, relief of tension, and circulo-respiratory efficiency.

The Carry-over Leisure Sports Pattern

In the carry-over leisure sports pattern, the secondary school reaches beyond the school setting and attempts to prepare the students to meet the challenge of the increasing amount of leisure time. Through the years, a great number of leaders and groups have emphasized the importance of teaching the skills of individual sports that can be enjoyed in later life. Jay B. Nash was emphasizing leisure sports, carry-over activities, and lifetime recreational skills as far back as 1935. Elmer Mitchell promoted the concept of participation for a lifetime, and Obertueffer and Ulrich have shown why the carry-over activities are far superior to "blind alley" activities which lead nowhere

after the class period is over. Cobb and Lepley discuss new directions for secondary school physical education:

Secondary education represents the termination of formal education for a large segment of our population. For these people education must provide adequate training for life. They need not only the basic communicative and quantitative skills which are prerequisite to successful social and vocation endeavors, but these people also need recreational skills. It is the responsibility of the physical education program to ensure that as many as possible of these skills are developed.

The secondary school physical education program must be carefully and completely coordinated with the elementary school program so as to provide continuity and progression, increasing both the complexity and the scope of curricular offerings. We must continually strive to build upon that which the child already knows, to broaden his range of capabilities and at the same time allow him to develop high levels of performance in activities that are of particular interest to him.

Although these appear to be decisive influences, we would maintain that activities promoted in the physical education and ath-

Figure 3–4. Camping can provide a worthwhile carry-over leisure activity. (Courtesy Los Angeles Unified School District.)

letics programs can also play an important role in stimulating the development of new recreational interests in the community. This notion places the school's physical education program in a leadership position. It is often necessary and desirable to create new interests within a community. This can only be accomplished when the needs of the young people are being met—when they genuinely believe that these recreational pursuits are enhancing the quality of their lives.[24]

The Human Movement Pattern

Terms such as *movement exploration, movement education, developmental physical education,* and *human movement* have appeared in professional literature over the past 20 years. The most significant work in these areas is of Rudolf Laban. He began his mastery of movement in the English schools of the mid 1930's. Laban developed his theories through emphasis on dancers and dance teachers. American interest in movement increased through the writings of Eleanor Methany on the meaning of movement. Methany introduced the use of symbols for defining the concepts of human movement. Perhaps the widespread interest in movement education developed because the profession was beginning to question philosophically the theoretical bases of the art and science of human movement. For this reason, the elementary schools in particular accepted an approach to the teaching-learning process through the human movement theory. Kate Barrett states:

A physical education program of value that can develop progressively into more complex directions needs a meaningful framework or structure of the content. The content of such a program is *human movement.* Using Laban's theory of movement as a model, I view all movement as having four major components: the *body* or what the body can do, *space* or where the body can move, *effort* or how the body can move, and *relationships* or with what relationships the body can move. Upon careful examination of these four components, a framework or structure for studying movement results. It is from this structure that the content of physical education emerges and develops.

Besides giving a sense of order and wholeness to movement, two additional reasons support the use of such a model: it can be applied to all forms of movement no matter the purpose, and it allows for the constant creation of new learning opportunities. All people who use the same model do not necessarily have similar programs. It is the *way* each of us uses such a model, in relation to his beliefs about both education and physical education, that gives individual programs their own directions and unique characteristics.[25]

The secondary school should expand upon the skills and concepts that the student already knows. Content and method are not the same in the more advanced movement approach. Problem-solving techniques afford differing degrees of opportunity for the secondary school student. The mechanical principles that govern efficient movement are emphasized.

Basically, the program should make a significant contribution to body development through the achievement of movement competence. Perhaps the stimulation that the student gets from "learning to move as he moves to learn" heightens his ability to reason. The learning environment must allow the student to experiment, explore, create, and choose for himself the movement pattern he or she deems most effective. A student thus acquires body awareness in learning what his body can do and how it moves.

Siedentop captures the relationship between physical education and human movement as succinctly as possible in his four approach summations. They may be discerned as prescriptions for school programs of physical education:

1. The approach which views human movement as the central core of meaning for what has heretofore been called physical education.
2. The approach which views physical education as an applied field of the broad discipline of human movement.
3. The approach which views human movement as a part of physical education.
4. The approach which views human movement as the catalyst for bringing about an entirely new program of physical education.[26]

Siedentop further states:

At least two predictions are possible. First, I suggested earlier that approaches one and two were far apart in terms of program implementation and could conceivably join together if some differences on the theoretical level could be worked out. This is a distinct possibility; the two together may in the future provide one distinct movement within the profession. It is also possible to foresee a wedding of approaches three and four. The movement education approach was seen to be almost exclusively the interest of elementary school physical educators. On the other hand, approach four was seen to be most applicable to high school and college programs of physical education. Such a union would provide a total human movement curriculum that would be radically different from anything we have known in physical education.[27]

PERFORMANCE APPRAISAL

Teachers themselves are complex personalities. They have, in the past, contributed constructively to the teaching-learning process, but never before in history have their efforts been subjected to such scrutiny and appraisal. The philosophy of the physical educator, the goals of education, the aims and purposes of programs in the secondary school, the historical objectives of the profession, the contemporary concepts of the approaches to physical education — all affect the performance of the teacher. The reader should, at this point, review the chapter in relation to his goals, aims, purposes, objectives, and concepts. The significance of his role in the future will be determined by his performance appraisal. A creative performance appraisal involving goals, judgment, development, and growth will indicate how well the teacher is doing his or her job.

As yet, the authors are not convinced that organizational management is the most effective means of improving the performance of the teacher. Human needs vary. Work qualities are difficult to determine, and therefore results may not be evaluated objectively. Any administrator realizes that there are different types of individuals within the school system. These include the "procrastinator," who thinks about getting the job done; the "grouper," who wants to call a committee meeting to decide everything; the "buck passer," who sloughs off unpleasant tasks to the inexperienced teacher; the "no-hitter," who possesses great style and charisma but achieves no results; the "echo," who says what the boss wants to hear; and the "doer," who has his goals in mind at all times and the knowledge and ability to accomplish the task.[28]

Performance Objectives for Teachers

Result-oriented appraisal is gaining respect in the educational arena. An effective performance appraisal system provides the school administrators with awareness of individual performance and provides teachers with feedback and the opportunity to improve. Evaluations can reveal potential for advancement or promotion. They also are used to make decisions pertaining to salary, promotions, transfers, and dismissals. A performance appraisal system must be constructive, objective, operational, and, above all, understood and accepted.

The system must be designed to measure the right things. Systems have often failed because the evaluations have not been planned carefully. Some of these programs demand too much time, standards and ratings are often unfairly reported, and frequently personal bias becomes involved. The lack of communication between the evaluator and the teacher causes concern. Sometimes this places the administrator or supervisor in the role of judge rather than that of helper.

Performance Categories. There are many variations of performance appraisal, but four basic techniques are generally used: essay appraisal, checklist appraisal, interview appraisal, and assessment center appraisal. Lahiti has summarized these four categories as follows:

In the *Essay Appraisal Technique*, the manager writes a paragraph or more covering individual strengths, weaknesses, and potential. The biggest drawback of this technique is its inconsistency. There can be great variation in assessment depending on a manager's individual values and sensitivities.

The *Checklist Appraisal Technique* has three common variations: a forced choice technique, a field review technique, or a graphic rating scale. In each of these cases, there generally exists a form which has been standardized and agreed to by top management, with the manager told to check off a level of performance for particular traits or value characteristics felt to be critical to the job. There are many drawbacks to this technique. The process sometimes becomes too mechanical and does not demand the manager to think and review performance; since the checklist need not be filled out in the presence of the subordinate, the subordinate may never be appraised of his performance; and though the technique may yield reliability, its validity is often doubted.

The *Interview Appraisal Technique* is frequently conducted in three variations: the work standards approach, the management by objectives approach, and the "critical incident" approach. The work standards and MBO approach have an advantage in that both subordinate and manager know in advance and agree to an expected performance. However, both techniques rely heavily on trained managers and mature personalities. The critical incident technique looks good on the surface because it provides managers with actual facts of incidents accumulated in a "little black book." However, the negative factor is that instead of arguing over traits, the managers end up discussing behavior. It also requires managers to jot down incidents on a daily or weekly basis, thus causing delay in feedback to an employee. Nor does it allow the standards used for judging to be discussed in advance.

In the *Assessment Center Appraisal Technique*, which is gaining popularity in large industrial organizations, an attempt is made to assess future performance or potential. In most other performance appraisals, one generally talks about assessing past performance. In any employment decision or promotion decision, some prediction of future performance is necessary.

In the assessment center appraisal technique, individuals from different departments are brought together to spend two or three days working on individual or group assignments similar to the ones they would be handling if they were promoted or employed. The pooled judgment of observers leads to a merit selection of each participant by comparison or alternate ranking. There is some evidence that managers chosen by assessment center methods work out better than those not chosen by these methods. The advantages of this system are the individualizing of opportunity, improvement of morale, and the enlargement of the organization's manpower resource of promotable personnel.[29]

Teachers are often evaluated by the assessment appraisal system, which includes a look at total teacher behavior.

Performance is measured against agreed-upon goals. Objectives of the teacher should be well planned, well stated, and well reviewed. The process of assessment will allow the individual teacher to better understand his own contribution to the entire school system.

Performance Objectives for Students

Having established an overview, the teacher is ready to focus attention on devising performance objectives for the instructional program. These objectives are not only necessary for providing direction and meaning for each class period, but they are also desirable for evaluating student performance and teacher efficiency.

Evaluation can be approached successfully through behavioral objectives. Behavioral objectives have been classified into three main groups or domains: cognitive, affective, and psychomotor. In the mid-1950's, a committee of college and university leaders published the "Taxonomy of Educational Objectives," which explored the cognitive domain.[30] During the early 1960's, objectives for the affective domain were published,[31] but very little material about the psychomotor domain has been published. The three fields are briefly discussed below. The reader should refer to the *Resource Manual* for a complete description of the major categories in the cognitive and affective domains. Examples of general instructional objectives for the psychomotor domain also appear in the *Resource Manual*.

The Cognitive Domain. The cognitive domain consists of behavior involving the intellectual process symbolized by knowledge, comprehension, application, analysis, synthesis, and evaluation.

In physical education, the cognitive domain includes learning and solving problems related to objectives, materials, methods, procedures, rules, guidelines, and other related areas that involve students. Evaluation in these areas should be made in behavioral terms.

The Affective Domain. The affective domain consists of behavior involving attitudes, emotions, and values and is reflected in the learner's interests, appreciations, and adjustments. It is symbolized by response, organization, and characterization.

In physical education, the affective domain pertains to attitudes that may be expressed in interests, apprecations, and values affecting physical education. In evaluation, written behavioral objectives should be used to measure such areas as leadership, self-discipline, responsibility, sportsmanship, self-concept, and respect for rules of the game.

The Psychomotor Domain. The psychomotor domain places emphasis on neuromuscular skills and is symbolized by frequency, energy, and duration. Physical education is built around the development of neuromuscular skills and has always been evaluated by performance in these skills. Although instructional objectives in the psychomotor domain include some cognitive and affective elements, the performance in motor skills is the basic outcome of the learner's experience.

Behavioral Categories

Many books and articles have been written describing the domains and the categories that may be included in behavioral objectives. Teachers and students may find it difficult to formulate a working procedure to assist them in defining these objectives. They should be written and graded from the most simple to the most complex. For example, the cognitive domain starts with the knowledge category and proceeds through the increasingly more complex categories — comprehension, application, analysis, synthesis, and evaluation.

Outlining behavioral objectives for the physical education program may have some advantages, particularly in the psychomotor domain. On the other hand, the considerable body of opinion concerning the disadvantages of using behavioral objectives should be weighed carefully before definite decisions as to their development are made. Elliot Eisner discusses the disadvantages of curriculum construction and teaching based on behavioral objectives. He argues that the theory has four limitations:

1. The dynamic and complex process of instruction yields outcomes far too numerous to be specified in behavioral and content terms in advance.
2. A limitation of theory concerning educational objectives is its failure to recognize the constraints various subject matters place upon objectives. In some subject areas, such as mathematics, languages, and the sciences, it is possible to specify with great precision the particular operation or behavior the student is to perform after instruction. In other subject areas, especially the arts, such specification is frequently not possible and when possible may not be desirable.
3. The assumption that objectives can be used as standards by which to measure achievement fails, I think, to distinguish adequately between the application of a standard and the making of a judgment. Not all — perhaps not even most — outcomes of curriculum and instruction are amenable to measurement.... The judgment by which a critic determines the value of a poem, novel, or play is not achieved merely by applying standards already known to the particular product being judged; it requires that the critic or teacher view the product with respect to the unique properties it displays and then, in relation to his experience and sensibilities, judge its value in terms which are incapable of being reduced to quantity or rule.
4. Educational objectives need not precede the selection and organization of content. The means through which imaginative curriculum can be built is as openended as the means through which scientific and artistic inventions occur. Curriculum theory needs to allow for a variety of processes to be employed in the construction of curriculums.[32]

The task of writing behavioral objectives could become insurmountable if the objectives had to be stated in specific detail. There are many people who feel that a few general objectives satisfactorily serve the cause of education and that explicit objectives are not necessary.

DESIRABLE OUTCOMES OF THE SECONDARY SCHOOL PROGRAM

As the program begins to function, certain outcomes should be observed which may be classified according to evaluative criteria. At this point, the reader should review the basic aims and purposes of physical education discussed in this chapter. Note the important role these desirable outcomes play in the meaning and philosophy of physical education. Although there are several beneficial results of physical education, the more outstanding ones are self-realization, socialization, sportsmanship, positive health, and value identification.

Self-Realization

Recognizing and accepting one's own potentials, achievements, expressions, and satisfactions are worthwhile outcomes of an effective program. Individual students should understand and accept their own abilities as well as the abilities of others. Students should realize also that it is an individual responsibility to pursue one's own understanding of physical activity and human movement. Coming to a self-realization or reasoned judgment of one's own competencies and skills is essential for sound self-development and self-appraisal.

Socialization

Participation in physical education activities provides one of the truly natural channels for social adjustment and behavior. Through the ages, sports, dancing, and other play activities have been used as outlets for social drives. The physical education program, when organized carefully and taught properly, can make an outstanding contribution to the socialization process in the school curriculum.

Sportsmanship

The practice of good sportsmanship has been an aspect of physical education for many years. The teacher should use proper methods of guidance to assist students in developing sportsmanlike attitudes.

Positive Health

Good health is the basic aim of physical education. It is largely because of physical education's tremendous contribution to health that physical education leaders can continue to demand time in the curriculum. Improvement in health habits and attitudes is a natural outcome of a well-planned, scientific program of physical education.

Value Identification

A carefully organized program of physical education incorporates qualities that assist the student in developing a well-integrated personality, which is the major aspect of his total self-concept. It is likely that positive character traits will be an outgrowth of such a program. Mere participation in physical education activities, however, does not insure character development. In fact, the exact opposite may take place. The very nature of participation and competition may lead to negative character manifestations. It is at this point that guidance by the teacher is necessary if positive character traits are to be formed. Participants must be educated along the criteria of socially acceptable behavior.

Using physical education to develop positive values is only one method offered by the total environment. The home, church, peer group, community, and cultural setting have various influences on individual value identification. The aims and purposes of the school and the objectives of committed physical educators should lead to sound individualized and group values.

As teachers and students examine their value systems, they gain insight into their own individual moral codes. Accepting new value systems is not easy. Leaders in the secondary school should strive to abide by certain standards in their own professional and personal lives. Perhaps one of the most desirable outcomes of secondary school physical education is the identification of positive values in the development of the total human personality.

QUESTIONS FOR DISCUSSION

1. What is meant by "academic discipline?" How are theorists and scholars distinguished from technical and professional educators?
2. Why does a secondary school physical educator need a basic philosophy?
3. What have been the major objectives in physical education during the past 40 years?
4. Discuss the four contemporary designs of physical education.
5. What are performance objectives for teachers? For students? How can you appraise these performances? What are the advantages? Disadvantages?
6. What are five desirable outcomes of the secondary school program? Distinguish between objectives and outcomes.

REFERENCES

1. Franklin Henry, "Physical Education: An Academic Discipline," *JOHPER* (Vol. 37, September, 1964), pp. 32–33.
2. William A. Harper, Donna Mae Miller, Roberta J. Park, and Elwood C. Davis, *The Philosophic Process in Physical Education,* 3rd ed. (Philadelphia: Lea and Febiger, 1977), pp. 274–279.
3. E. C. Davis, *Philosophies Fashion* (Dubuque, Iowa: William C. Brown Company, Publishers, 1963), pp. 126–127.
4. Commission on the Reorganization of Secondary Education, *Cardinal Principles of Secondary Education* (Bulletin No. 35, Washington, D.C., Bureau of Education, 1918), p. 9.
5. Educational Policies Commission, *The Purposes of Education in American Democracy* (Washington, D.C., National Education Association, 1938), p. 2.
6. Educational Policies Commission, *The Central Purpose of American Education* (National Education Association, 1961), p. 12.
7. American Association for Health, Physical Education and Recreation, *This Is Physical Education* (Washington, D.C., 1965).
8. Dorothy L. Fornia, "Signposts for the Seventies," *JOHPER* (October, 1972), p. 34.
9. Clark W. Hetherington, *School Program in Physical Education,* (New York: World Book Company, 1922), p. 34.
10. Jackson Sharman, *Introduction to Physical Education,* (New York: A. S. Barnes and Company, 1934), pp. 66–68.
11. Jesse Feiring Williams, *Principles of Physical Education,* 8th ed., (Philadelphia: W. B. Saunders Company, 1964), p. 325.
12. Charles A. Bucher, *Foundations of Physical Education.* (St. Louis: C. V. Mosby Company, 1952), pp. 144–150.
13. Charles C. Cowell, *Scientific Foundations of Physical Education.* (New York: Harper and Row, Publishers, 1953), p. 173.
14. John E. Nixon and Ann E. Jewett, *An Introduction to Physical Education,* 8th ed. (Philadelphia: W. B. Saunders Company, 1974), p. 97.
15. Jan Felshin, "Rationale and Purposes for Physical Education," *Curriculum Improvement in Secondary School Physical Education.* (Washington, D.C.: AAHPER Publications, 1973), pp. 61–62.
16. Ibid., pp. 64–65.
17. Daryl Siedentop, *Physical Education: Introductory Analysis,* 2nd ed. (Dubuque, Iowa: William C. Brown Company, Publishers, 1976), pp. 83–84.
18. Ernest R. Hilgard, Richard C. Atkinson, and Rita Atkinson, *Introduction to Psychology,* 5th ed. (New York: Harcourt Brace Jovanovich, Inc., 1971), p. 71.

19. Eugene Fink, "The Ontology of Play," *Philosophy Today* (Vol. 4, Spring, 1960), p. 102.
20. Marjorie Latchaw and Glenn Egstrom, *Human Movement,* (Englewood Cliffs, New Jersey: Prentice-Hall, Inc., 1969), pp. 29–39.
21. M. J. Ellis, "Play and Its Theories Re-examined," *Parks and Recreation* (National Recreation and Park Association, August, 1971), p. 51.
22. Herbert de Vries, *Physiology of Exercise,* 2nd ed. (Dubuque, Iowa: William C. Brown Company, Publishers, 1974), p. 230.
23. Lawrence E. Morehouse and Augustus T. Miller, *Physiology of Exercise,* 7th ed. (St. Louis: C. V. Mosby Company, 1976), p. 287.
24. Robert A. Cobb and Paul M. Lepley, eds., *Contemporary Philosophies of Physical Education and Athletics,* (Columbus, Ohio: Charles E. Merrill Publishing Company, 1973), pp. 88–89.
25. Kate R. Barrett, "I Wish I Could Fly — A Philosophy in Motion," from *Contemporary Philosophies of Physical Education and Athletics* (Columbus, Ohio: Charles E. Merrill Publishing Company, 1973), p. 7.
26. Daryl Siedentop, *Physical Education: Introductory Analysis,* 2nd ed. (Dubuque, Iowa: William C. Brown Company, Publishers, 1976), pp. 144, 146, 148, 150.
27. Ibid., p. 153.
28. Robert E. Lahiti, "Improving Performance Appraisals," *Community and Junior College Journal* (Vol. 45, No. 6, March, 1975), p. 8.
29. Ibid., p. 9.
30. Benjamin Bloom, ed., "Taxonomy of Educational Objectives, Handbook 1, Cognitive Domain," (New York: David McKay Company, Inc., 1956).
31. David R. Kralhwohl, ed., "Taxonomy of Educational Objectives, Handbook 2, Affective Domain" (New York: David McKay Company, Inc., 1964).
32. Elliot W. Eisner, "Educational Objective Help or Hindrance?" *The School Review* (Vol. 75, No. 3, Autumn, 1967), pp. 254–259.

SELECTED READINGS

American Alliance for Health, Physical Education and Recreation, Frost, Reuben B. and Edward J. Sims eds., *Development of Human Values Through Sports* (Washington, D.C., 1974).

Bloom, Benjamin S. et al., *Handbook on Formative and Summative Evaluation of Student Learning* (New York: McGraw-Hill Book Company, Inc., 1971).

Freeman, William H., *Physical Education in a Changing Society* (Boston: Houghton Mifflin Company, 1977).

Gerhard, Muriel, *Effective Teaching Strategies with the Behavioral Outcomes Approach* (West Nyack, New York: Parker Publishing Company, Inc., 1971).

Gronlund, Norman E., *Stating Behavioral Objectives for Classroom Instruction* (Toronto: The Macmillan Company, 1970).

Lansley, Keith L. and Maxwell Howell, "Play Classification and Physical Education," *Journal of Health, Physical Education and Recreation* (September, 1970).

Lewis, Clifford G., *He Who Thinks, Better* (Athens: University of Georgia Printing Department, 1974).

Plowman, Paul D., *Behavioral Objectives* (Chicago: Science Research Associates, 1971).

Vanderzwagg, Harold J., *Toward a Philosophy of Sport* (Reading, Mass.: Addison-Wesley Publishing Company, 1972).

Zeigler, Earle F., *Physical Education and Sport Philosophy* (Englewoods Cliffs, New Jersey: Prentice-Hall, Inc., 1977).

Chapter 4

Courtesy Rosemont Junior High School, Norfolk, Virginia

THE DECADE OF INNOVATION
   GOALS OF SECONDARY EDUCATION
      CONTENT GOALS
      PROCESS GOALS
PRINCIPLES IN CURRICULUM CONSTRUCTION
   PLANNING THE CURRICULUM
      DEFINING CURRICULUM
      DESIGNS AND STRATEGIES
      COMMITTEES IN CURRICULUM
         PLANNING
           POLICIES AND PROCEDURES
   LEGISLATION AND CHANGE
      CURRICULUM REVISION
CURRICULUM PROGRAM MODELS
   THE TRADITIONAL MODEL
   THE PERFORMANCE-BASED
      INSTRUCTIONAL MODEL
   THE PURPOSE-PROCESS CONCEPTUAL
      FRAMEWORK MODEL
   OTHER ALTERNATIVE MODELS
      COEDUCATIONAL LOTTERY SYSTEM
      BUSH SCHOOL PROCESS MODEL
      POWAY HIGH SCHOOL MODULAR PLAN
DEVELOPING CURRICULUM COMPONENTS
   THE CURRICULUM GUIDE
      DEFINITION
      CHARACTERISTICS OF THE
         CURRICULUM GUIDE
      CURRICULUM GUIDE COMMITTEE

PLACEMENT OF CONTENT
   THE CYCLE PLAN
   GRADE PLACEMENT
   SEASONAL PLACEMENT
YEARLY CALENDAR
SCOPE AND SEQUENCE
UNIT TEACHING
   GUIDELINES FOR DEVELOPING THE
      UNIT
THE DAILY LESSON PLAN
   DEFINITION
   EVALUATION OF THE LESSON PLAN
THE SCIENTIFIC APPROACH IN SELECTING
   ACTIVITIES
   CRITERIA THROUGH THE YEARS
   CRITERIA FOR THE FUTURE
   CRITERIA OF RELATIVE VALUE
PROCEDURES FOR SELECTING ACTIVITIES
   FOR THE PROGRAM
   FORMATION OF A COMMITTEE
CHALLENGES IN CURRICULUM DESIGN FOR
THE FUTURE
   ROLE OF THE STUDENT IN PLANNING
   DEVELOPMENT OF HUMAN VALUES
      THROUGH SPORTS
QUESTIONS FOR DISCUSSION
REFERENCES
SELECTED READINGS

CURRICULUM DESIGN AND DEVELOPMENT

Curriculum content in secondary school physical education is limited by what is taught in elementary and middle schools and in higher education. Questions such as "What is curriculum?" "What is a good curriculum?" "How can we decide what to teach?" are basic to the design and development of a practical curriculum in secondary school physical education.

Developing the curriculum in physical education is a very tedious and challenging task. Social pressures, lack of facilities, overcrowded programs, and austere budgets are a few of the elements that complicate the planning. Other factors, such as local philosophy, purposes of physical education, divisions of the physical education program, and time allotment also influence curriculum construction.

In designing a physical education curriculum, problems arise concerning procedures, construction, and leadership. These problems and others emphasize the importance of careful planning. Although many colleges and universities offer courses in curriculum, it is extremely difficult to separate curriculum from method.

THE DECADE OF INNOVATION

The decade between 1962 and 1972 was one of experimentation and innovation in the schools, an era during which a major effort was made to create strategies for change. The most common approach was modeled on the work of the Department of Agriculture in the 1930's and 1950's, when improvements in farming technology were introduced through "agricultural agents," whose farms were more productive than those of less enlightened neighbors. Education, too, would have its "change agents." The following plans attracted the most funding from foundations and the United States Office of Education during the decade of innovation:

1. Team teaching
2. Modular scheduling

3. Non-graded schools
4. Programmed learning
5. Individualized instruction
6. Computer-assisted instruction
7. Independent study
8. Learning centers
9. Open plan schools
10. Language laboratories
11. Behavioral objectives
12. Differentiated staffing.[1]

However, the 1973 Report of the National Commission on the Reform of Secondary Education concluded that the decade of change and innovation in the schools had little or no lasting effect on the content of school programs or the quality of teaching and learning.

Goals of Secondary Education

The recommendations in the report of the National Commission on the Reform of Secondary Education dealt with the following thirty-two items:

1. Defining secondary school expectations
2. Community participation in determining secondary school expectations
3. The basis for curriculum revision
4. Teacher training
5. Bias in textbooks
6. Bias in counseling
7. Affirmative action
8. Expanding career opportunities
9. Career education
10. Job placement
11. Global education
12. Alternative paths in high school completion
13. Local board responsibilities for funding alternatives
14. Credit for experience
15. Secondary level examination program
16. Broadcast television
17. Classroom use of broadcast materials
18. Cable television
19. Flexibility of alternative programs
20. Rank in class
21. Planning for school security
22. Records of violence
23. Code of student rights and obligations
24. School newspapers
25. Right of privacy
26. Corporal punishment
27. Student activities
28. Compulsory attendance
29. Free K−12 public education
30. Youth organizations
31. Sexism
32. Females in competitive team sports[2]

The goals suggested by this Commission Report were learner-centered. Responsibility for achieving these goals was placed with teachers, administrators, school board members, parents, and students. The objectives of secondary education fell into two groups: content goals and process goals.

Content Goals. There were seven content goals:

1. Achievement of communication skills
2. Achievement of computation skills
3. Attainment of proficiency in critical and objective thinking
4. Acquisition of occupational competence
5. Clear perception of nature and environment
6. Development of economic understanding
7. Acceptance of responsibility for citizenship

Process Goals. There were six process goals:

1. Knowledge of self
2. Appreciation of others
3. Ability to adjust to change
4. Respect for law and authority
5. Clarification of values
6. Appreciation of the achievements of man[3]

Whatever goals or recommendations are used as guidelines, the planner should consider the following statement carefully before undertaking curriculum revision:

The high schools should no longer be required to perform purely custodial functions. Attempts to keep in school adolescents who do not wish to be there damage the environment for learning. The content of traditional high school curricula should be revised to eliminate busy-work components designed merely to occupy the time of adolescents who are in school only because the law requires it. Revitalization of the curriculum will require attention to the earlier maturation of adolescents. Intelligent evaluation of curricular revision must grow from valid measurements of the degree to which students are achieving the stated goals and objectives of their schools.[4]

PRINCIPLES IN CURRICULUM CONSTRUCTION

Physical education leaders today are willing to experiment with new ideas in curriculum development. Changing concepts are based on the need of students to cope with tomorrow's world.

Selection of activities, improvement of instructional methods, and organizational procedures are guided by a determined set of principles. Oberteuffer and Ulrich list nine principles of curriculum construction that continue to be valid:

1. The curriculum should be planned to allow for progression in learning, with a minimum of repetition of activities.
2. The curriculum should be arranged so that students have consecutive time to learn.
3. There should be cooperative planning on conceiving and executing the curriculum.
4. The curriculum should consist of activities in which values are inherent, which are intrinsically interesting, and with which the student can develop a compatibility.
5. The curriculum should be constructed in relation to community needs and facilities and with some consideration given to the interests which may be engendered by national backgrounds or ethnic characteristics.
6. The curriculum should provide activities which are susceptible to informal rather than formal teaching methods.
7. Curriculum materials should be selected in relation to age, sex, and physical condition of students.
8. The curriculum should make ample provision for those learnings associated with motor activity.
9. Integration as an education process and concept has a bearing on physical education, and its premise should be examined.[5]

Planning the Curriculum

One cannot overemphasize the importance of planning. Learning occurs as a result of planned or unplanned experiences; however, the outcomes of random experiences are often random and unpredictable. If the teacher has no particular learning goals in mind, no particular curriculum is needed. The likelihood of achieving particular goals without a plan is remote whether the teacher is committed or not. It seems to make sense that the teacher not only plan for learning but also determine what kind of plan is needed. The potential teacher needs to review the preceding chapter, *Meaning and Philosophy in Physical Education*, very carefully, for the characteristics of the curriculum plan will depend largely upon the teachers, administrators,

school board members, parents, and students who have stated the goals and objectives for their school. The type of curriculum will depend upon (a) what one thinks "desirable" learning is, and (b) what one believes about how, or by what process, such learning occurs.

Defining Curriculum. Curriculum is defined by authorities in many ways. Ehrenberg states:

Curriculum is a plan that describes the necessary and sufficient "means" for achieving particular learning "ends." Its purpose is to specify the amount and kinds of resources and "doing" experiences that must be provided to learners for them to have sufficient and appropriate opportunities to develop specified learnings to the desired quality and/or degree and with as many secondary gains and as few negative side effects as possible.[6]

Such a purpose suggests that curriculum should be structured to include these elements:

1. Learning objectives with rationale stated
2. "Means" for achieving learning objectives
   a. Content information
   b. Instructional materials
   c. Sequenced learning activities
   d. Instructional sequence of learning strategies.[7]

Designs and Strategies. Organization for instruction and scheduling is usually developed around four phases: large group instruction, small group instruction, independent study, and laboratory practice. These are handled by traditional, flexible, or individualized scheduling. Selection and adaptation of the design and strategy are dependent upon personal teaching philosophy and the nature of the material. Time allotments may vary according to the needs and capabilities of the individual student. Although curriculum, scheduling time, and organizational patterns are interrelated, this chapter deals with designs and strategies in terms of changes needed to improve the curriculum.

Some scheduling elements, however, are absolute. Teacher-student ratios are among these unvarying numerical relationships. In a traditional schedule (150 students in five classes of about 30 each), a high school teacher has about two minutes per student per day. If the teacher spends an additional hour or two beyond class meetings working with individuals, the teacher gets as much as three minutes per student per day. If the teacher uses a percentage of the time in flexible scheduling or individualized guidance, the time for individual attention may be increased. The teacher still has two or three minutes per student per day to distribute, but the advantages of using various categories and strategies allow for various kinds of instruction. Chapter 8, *Essentials in Class Organization,* deals fully with organizational patterns.

Committees in Curriculum Planning. In the past, experts were usually given the responsibility for curriculum construction. Now, however, this responsibility is divided among several groups. Administrators, physical education teachers, and other interested persons are assigned to various committees, each of which has a specific curriculum component to examine. Figure 4–1 suggests an arrangement of committees for designing a curriculum in physical education.

POLICIES AND PROCEDURES.   The committees are responsible for the overall planning of the curriculum in physical education. They study the needs of the community, evaluate the existing program, and determine present weaknesses. Other responsibilities of the committees include arranging schedules, coordinating the efforts of any other committees, procuring materials for committee work, and editing the final materials compiled by other committees.

Legislation and Change

Recent legislation in Title IX of the Education Amendments of 1972 is designed to end sex discrimination in American education. The deadline for secondary school compliance was July 21, 1978, and school systems have adjusted policies, procedures, programs, and facilities to reorganize the instructional programs in physical education. Many school systems have surveyed

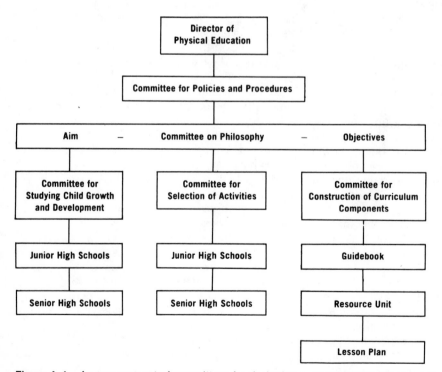

Figure 4–1. An arrangement of committees for designing a curriculum in physical education.

student interests, faculty reactions, and administrator concerns in an attempt to implement popular curriculum change. The *Resource Manual* reviews several of the effects of the Title IX legislation on curriculum revisions.

Curriculum Revision. Coeducational physical education lends itself to a variety of teaching methods. Refer to Chapter 5, *Management and Methods in Teaching,* for suggestions in methods that lead to effective learning. Excellent ideas on coeducational activities are contained in the AAHPER publication, *Ideas for Secondary School Physical Education.*

Several states have prepared materials through their departments of public instruction to assist physical educators in formulating changes. The state of Maryland has a publication entitled *Guidelines to Implement Title IX of the Education Amendments of 1972 and to Implement State Board Resolution, 1974–75.* It contains state and federal guidelines for three areas: guidance, physical education (including athletics), and vocational education. The physical education section contains the Title IX regulations and a set of guidelines, along with a useful checklist for identifying bias in physical education and athletics.

A State of Delaware publication entitled *A Suggested Policy Guide for School Districts Prohibiting Sex Discrimination in Education* contains a variety of information including policies, guidance, admissions, recruitment, and special data on physical education, health education, interscholastic athletics, extracurricular activities, and grievance procedures. Included in the physical education section are several practical implementation suggestions, such as methods of grouping, types of supervision, and techniques for effective staff utilization.

The New Hampshire Department of Education also provides a packet of information useful in planning and implementation. Special emphasis is given to program description, facilities and equipment, administration and supervision, activity offerings, program requirements and options, and plans for evaluation.[8]

CURRICULUM PROGRAM MODELS

Widespread experimentation and adoption of new models of teaching physical education have taken place during the past decade. The strengths of the traditional model have been redirected as meanings and philosophies have been given changing emphases. The success of alternate teaching styles depends upon the compatibility of the style with existing conditions in a local school district. The reader should examine the variety of alternatives. Only a few of the existing models are discussed here.

The Traditional Model

The traditional model has incorporated explanation, demonstration, drills, practice, lead-up activities, basic skills correction, and game or sport participation and competition. The unit system of instruction is used, with progression in methodology, ranging from the simple to the complex. Subject matter is based upon a wide selection of activities. Team sports, individual sports, aquatics, rhythms, and self-testing activities are selected according to age, growth, and development. Much of the content is dependent upon what is taught in the elementary and middle schools. The traditional model is generally teacher-focused, with organization, order, and control being characteristic of this plan. The teacher observes and analyzes movement skills, then gives individual or small group attention by both positive and negative reinforcement. Many physical educators in the secondary school environment continue to embrace the traditional model, as it has proved effective in helping students to learn. Individual teacher personality often blends easily with the model.

The Performance-Based Instructional Model

Competency-based education is a design in which both teachers and students are held accountable for knowledge, behavior, and skill levels in specialized areas of physical education. (This model is discussed in detail in Chapter 5, *Management and Methods in Teaching,* and in Chapter 13, *Assessment and Evaluation.*) The demand for it came at a time when accountability legislation was being enacted in states and school districts. Competency-based teacher education programs provide theoretical methods to assist the secondary school teacher in designing more effective programs in the teaching of sport skills.

Performance is the core of this model. Teacher behavior rather than teacher knowledge is the measure used in determining the competence of the teacher in "delivering the message" to the learner. Elements such as specified criterion-referenced measures, behavioral objectives, realistic teacher roles, and individualized instruction are used in this model. Thus the emphasis is on the way learners learn.

The recent work of A. M. Gentile provides a very useful model for skill acquisition. Translated briefly, Gentile's model divides learning into two stages: (1) getting the ideas of the movement and (2) fixation/diversification. The first stage consists of seven steps:

The Learner
1. Perceives what is to be learned and desires to try.
2. Identifies the relevant stimuli in the environment.
3. Formulates a motor plan.
4. Emits a response.
5. Attends to the results.
6. Revises the motor plan.
7. Emits another response (and repeats steps 5, 6, and 7).

Steps 1 through 3 can be categorized as "preparation" and steps 4 through 7 as "action." Perceiving what is to be learned, identifying the relevant stimuli, and formulating a motor plan prepare the learner to perform, after which movement can be initiated. Emitting a response, attending to the results, revising the motor plan, and emitting another response indicate movement or action and suggest a continuous recycling process. While the distinction between the preparation and action phases may not be extremely important to motor skill acquisition per se, it does help to conceptualize the model.[9]

The objectives of the model are clear-cut, with the final outcome measuring the degree of competency. Physical education classes have always been performance-based. The model develops sound evaluative criteria for the student in the school program.

The Purpose-Process Conceptual Framework Model

Ann E. Jewett and associates contend that "teachers need to be guided by some conceptual framework in making key curricular decisions. If the curriculum is developed in terms of a purpose-process framework, clarification of purpose concepts will help to define the scope of the subject content, and classification of movement processes will guide the ordering of learning sequences."[10]

In this model, the key purposes of movement delineate the important curricular content of physical education. Man moves: (1) to fulfill personal development potential, (2) to develop movement skills utilized in adapting to and controlling the physical environment, and (3) to assist himself in relating to other persons. Each of these key purposes has subpurposes. Furthermore, each subpurpose embraces several essential elements.

Figure 4–2 may guide the prospective teacher in the development of a secondary curriculum following the conceptual framework.[11] This model focuses on the responsibility of physical educators to develop some degree of physical fitness, recreational competence, and skillful movement. The experiences selected for inclusion in the secondary curriculum center on human movement goals.

Other Alternative Models

A theoretical framework for curriculum planning has been presented in the preceding three models. There are other models to be considered, such as the core program or interdisciplinary

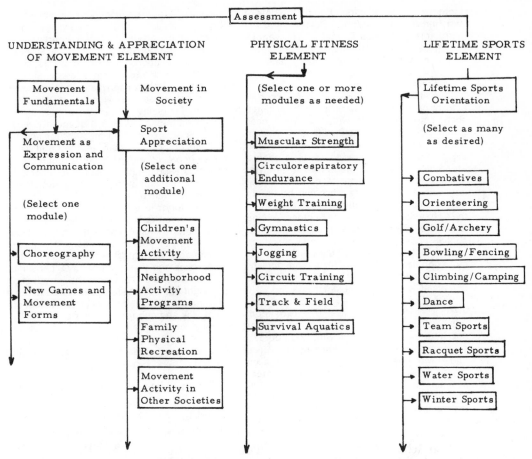

Figure 4–2. Development of the secondary curriculum. (Courtesy Ann E. Jewett, AAHPER Publications, *Curriculum Improvement in Secondary School Physical Education*, 1973, p. 36.)

curriculum, the conceptual structure of human movement, and the process-product designs. Three examples of alternative program models are those being used by Highland Park Senior High School in St. Paul, Minnesota; Bush Secondary School in Seattle, Washington; and Poway High School in Poway, California.

Highland Park. The Physical Education Department at Highland Park developed a new program because the faculty (three men and two women) had become discouraged with the traditional program of teaching. In the first year of the new program, Highland Park was on the traditional six-period, 55-minute class day. At the present time, they operate on a six-day rotating cycle with two-hour block classes, and see each class for two hours every other day.

At the beginning of the year, the school administration, by computer, programs the boys into the men's department and the girls into the women's department. (In all they handle 600 sophomores and 150 juniors and seniors.) Each department divides the number of students equally and alphabetically for each section. Each instructor is responsible for those students in a section of the alphabet—called the "home base" group. The instructor is also responsible for grading those students for any problems that may arise.

After the year begins and home base groups have been assigned, each instructor gives a group a two-week orientation program. During this time, they issue locks and uniforms and familiarize students with the program and facilities. Each unit is seven sessions (14 hours of instruction) in length, and there are three units per quarter. At the beginning of each unit, the faculty decides what each instructor might like to teach—depending on the time of year, the teaching station available, and the instructors' individual strengths. The various activities are given enrollment limits according to the type of activity, the facility, and the number of home base students taking physical education in that section.

Each student is required to sign up for an activity on the first day of a new unit. First, each instructor meets with the home base group and a lottery is held, with each student drawing a number from a receptacle containing as many numbers as there are students. All home base groups then meet in the gymnasium, where each instructor sets up a station with a sign stating what will be taught for the unit. Then the numbers are called out, the students with lower numbers being assured of being able to sign up for their first choice activity. Higher numbers are more limited in their choice of activity, since the more popular activities are filled more quickly, but there is always a next time. The program is completely coeducational.

What about the advanced or junior and senior classes? Some are assigned two hours every other day; others are programmed for one hour every day. Those with two hours of class sign up for two different activities. Those with one hour every day may sign up for the same class every day or two different activities on an every-other-day basis. Advanced classes are on an elective basis, and the numbers involved are smaller than in the required sophomore classes. [12]

Bush School Process Model. Bush's physical education program rests on the following assumptions: (1) The program should help students integrate new skills and knowledge with their previous experiences; (2) The student's abilities to rationally employ skills and knowledge to real life problems should be refined; (3) In addition to learning how to solve problems themselves, students should learn how and where to acquire additional resources outside the school; (4) The student's learning should be personalized, self-paced, and often voluntary; (5) Sports and games provide superb mechanisms for the experiential learning of intellectual concepts.

The intent of the structure is to provide active, enjoyable learning experiences for students by using experience in sports and games as a jumping-off point for the knowledge and understanding depicted in the goals of the program. Additionally, planning has included efforts to have instruction in physical education coincide with related units in other subjects. For example, while heart rates are studied in conjunction with a soccer unit,

science classes are studying the cardiorespiratory system as a part of physiology; while cooperation and teamwork are stressed in soccer, peer group relations are being stressed in human relations course. Teachers in all subject matter areas can thereby aid the student in integrating material from what might otherwise be viewed as separate, unrelated subjects.

Skill instruction in this procedure is used more as an experiential medium for accomplishing other goals than as an end in itself. An example of the program structure in a soccer-speedball unit is related to other subjects: cardiorespiratory system (physiology); graphs (mathematics); sport in England (European history); leverage (physics); situational ethics (human relations).

Content in conjunction with activity: evolution of these sports; specificity of training principle; physiological reactions to exercise, pulse rates and their relation to O_2 consumption and caloric expenditure, and introduction to weight control; levers of the body and force production; ethical factors in participation; team play and cooperative efforts.

Basic skills: goalie play, kicking-passing, trapping, dribbling, heading, shooting, tackling, dodging, strategy and rules, throwing patterns. [13]

Poway High School Modular Plan. This physical education program is based on the premise that students with a high degree of skill will enjoy their activities and feel a sense of personal achievement.

The current program has four phases: *first*, students are enrolled in a small group class in a skill area of their choosing. This class meets twice each week for a total of 2 or 2-1/2 hours, and the emphasis is entirely instructional. Fifty-seven separate skill sections have been scheduled with class sizes ranging from 9 to 36 students, depending upon the activity. The average number of students to each instructor in the skill section is 29. It is believed that with this ratio, skills can be taught and just not presented to the student with the hope that he learns.

In the *second* phase, each student is scheduled for a physical fitness laboratory, where he is regularly tested and records are kept on his progress. The class is 15 minutes in length, twice a week, and is attached to the skill section.

The *third* phase of the program involves regularly scheduled competitive laboratories. On Fridays, each student is given the opportunity to compete with other students of a similar skill level in a team or individual activity which interests him. Four blocks of time (60 minutes each) are set aside for this program, and all physical education teachers participate.

The competition lab is intentionally large for two purposes. First, one instructor can schedule, supervise, and administer the lab (teachers help as supervisors) in a large group of 200 to 300 students. Second, making the lab ratios 70 to 1 allows the teacher time to meet with small classes in the instructional phase of the program and leaves the instructor with more than the usual unscheduled time. The unscheduled time is used to meet with students in open labs for further skill development. Third, the lab must be large to offer enough choice to the student and enough competition within each activity. The competition lab gives a choice of novice or open competition in the following areas: tennis, badminton, volleyball, handball, touch football, and basketball.

The open laboratory period is the *fourth* phase of the physical education program. Since teachers are scheduled to meet regular classes approximately 15 hours a week, they have considerable time to meet with individual students in open laboratory sessions where skills are developed and refined. To guide the student in the open labs, and to provide a basis for evaluation, Poway's staff has developed a performance curriculum for each activity.[14]

DEVELOPING CURRICULUM COMPONENTS

As discussed earlier in this chapter, the responsibility for developing the curriculum in physical education usually is vested in the school administration. However, recent trends give the teacher a more vital role in assisting with the development of the curriculum. In many schools, the physical education teacher is given entire responsibility for the program. Whether the teacher is partially or fully responsible for this planning, instructors everywhere should be familiar with the procedures for the construction of (1) the curriculum guide, (2) the resource unit, and (3) the daily lesson plan.

This chapter presents a brief outline to assist the teacher. Considerable additional material on the various aspects of planning is available, and selected references are provided at the end of the chapter for students who wish to read more about curriculum development.

The Curriculum Guide

The first part of this chapter demonstrates the necessity of sound principles in curriculum construction and of careful planning in program development. The next logical step is to place the content sequentially in a guide so that teachers can use it effectively.

Each school should have a guidebook outlining the areas to be covered in the physical education program. It should be written by teachers, administrators, and students who have a background in physical education and should include those subjects recom-

FIGURE 4–3. Modern dance is an excellent activity in the secondary school curriculum. (Courtesy Edmund Burke Academy, Waynesboro, Georgia.)

mended by various national education organizations, successful school systems, and current authors; in addition, it must be designed to meet local needs. Procedures for studying these areas should be determined by the committees organizing the guidebook.

The construction of a physical education guide serves many purposes. It not only results in a necessary instruction plan, but also provides teachers with valuable experience in the democratic processes involved in educational procedures. The research and interaction develops individual leadership, increases in-depth knowledge, and assures more effective use of the guide.

Definition. The curriculum guide may be defined as a written outline of the essential content to be covered in a specific discipline or of a course within that discipline. The guide serves as an aid to teaching and usually contains units of instruction relating to a central theme. It may also contain methods for presenting the sport activities, student activities, supplementary resources, and independent study projects.

Although some writers differentiate between such terms as *curriculum guide, teacher's guide, guidebook,* or *course of study,* all essentially serve the function we have defined.

Characteristics of the Curriculum Guide. The curriculum guide should reflect the local preference in teaching procedure. If the school system encourages the subject matter approach, this approach will dominate the development of the guidebook. On the other hand, if the experience curriculum is dominant, the guidebook will reflect the more informal experience approach. Regardless of the type of curriculum, a number of elements are common to effective guidebooks:

1. Definition of curriculum
2. Statement of the philosophy of physical education, including aims and objectives
3. Selection of areas of instruction
4. Scope, sequence, and time allotment
5. Organization of program content
6. Suggested teaching procedures

7. Reference materials
8. Evaluation procedures
9. Anticipation of future needs

It is generally agreed that no curriculum guide is absolute. Education itself is a dynamic function, and physical education is continually changing its emphasis and direction. Curriculum planners should anticipate future changes and make recommendations that will be easily adaptable to them.

Curriculum Guide Committee. The selection of this committee is very important to the construction of the guidebook. It is obviously more expedient to select teachers who are interested in the project. Although the general development of the guidebook should be undertaken by a large group, it is advisable to delegate the actual writing to a small group or perhaps to one member who is qualified to perform this function.

The general committee is divided into subcommittees that study the various areas of instruction to be included in the curriculum guide. A uniform pattern of reporting is agreed upon by the general committee. Results are reported by subcommittees to an editing committee, which prepares the final product for printing. It is helpful for teachers to study guides from other cities as they proceed with their planning. Figure 4–4 gives an outline of a guidebook from Arkansas State Department of Education.

The curriculum guide should be developed in a manner that will help teachers provide more meaningful instruction for students. It should be evaluated regularly to determine whether it is serving its purposes. The following criteria, reflective of current thinking, suggest that a guide should be:

1. Constructed by committees composed of teachers and administrators with a background in physical education.
2. Broad in scope, containing the necessary resource units that will be helpful to all teachers.
3. A reservoir of suggestions, references, teaching aids, and physical education procedures that teachers may refer to when the need arises.

ECTION I—EVALUATIVE CRITERIA FOR
PHYSICAL EDUCATION

Part I.   Organization
          Background Information
          Recommended Standards and Procedures
          Evaluative Criteria
          Evaluations

Part II. Nature of Offerings
          Background Information
          Evaluative Criteria
          Evaluations

Part III. Physical Facilities
          Background Information
          Evaluative Criteria
          Evaluations

Part IV. Direction of Learning
            Instructional Staff
              Background Information
              Evaluative Criteria
              Evaluations
            Instructional Activities
              Evaluative Criteria
              Evaluations
            Instructional Materials and Equipment
              Evaluative Criteria
              Evaluations
            Methods of Evaluation
              Evaluative Criteria
              Evaluations

SECTION II—THE PHYSICAL EDUCATION
CURRICULUM

          Types of Activities and Time Allotments
          Suggested Yearly Program by Grades
          Suggested Plan for Class Period
          Modified Program

SECTION III—PHYSICAL EDUCATION ACTIVITIES

Part I.   Team Sports
Part II. Individual or Dual Activities
Part III. Dance
Part IV. Gymnastics and Tumbling
Part V.   Developmental Activities
Part VI. Outdoor Education
Part VII. Extra-Class Activities

Figure 4–4. A guidebook outline. (Courtesy Arkansas State Department of Education.)

4. So constructed that sequential treatment of content will be provided.
5. Flexible, allowing for teacher creativity, yet maintaining consistency of purpose throughout.

The curriculum guide in which content is broken down into various topics provides the framework within which the teacher presents the units of instruction.

Placement of Content

The three types of plans for including activities in the curriculum are the cycle plan, grade placement, and seasonal placement.

The Cycle Plan. In the cycle plan, the program is arranged to offer certain activities in yearly rotations. For example, in a school requiring physical education in grades 7 through 12, swimming may be offered during the 7th, 9th, and 11th grades; bowling may be taught in the 8th, 10th and 12th grades.

The major criticism of this plan is the long interval of time which exists between cycles. To teach an activity and then wait a semester or even a year before it is offered again is not a sound instructional procedure.

Grade Placement. In this plan, activities are assigned to specific grade levels. However, systems that use this plan usually resort to repetition in several grades by breaking certain activities into elementary and advanced fundamentals.

Placement of activities according to class level is often unsatisfactory to students, since they may not continue to participate in a sport that they like once they have completed the school year. This situation can be avoided by using the seasonal placement of content.

Seasonal Placement. This plan calls

for introduction of the same activities each year on a seasonal schedule. Although the activities are the same each year, the approach, lead-up, and other instructional techniques vary from grade to grade. Content is sequentially developed. Students are guided toward improvement each time the activity is offered; progressively higher goals would therefore minimize repetition.

For instance, assume that basketball is a basic activity. The curriculum content in an 8th grade class might consist of foul shots, various shots from the floor, dribbling, basic passes, and so forth. If, after taking an inventory of performance in the class, it is found that dribbling was adequately covered in the previous grade, it should not be necessary to continue dribbling instruction except for an occasional review. Briefly, in the seasonal approach, the method of instruction and the skills content develop progressively upward.

The seasonal plan is the most practical and the most satisfactory for the following reasons:
1. Many schools do not have more than one or two grades of physical education; this rules out the use of the grade placement plan in various activities.
2. Some activities are popular at certain times every year. To progressively teach skills of the activity at these times would greatly stimulate the interest and participation in the activities as an after-school effort.
3. A great deal of time is needed for teaching the skills of sports and for learning them properly. If they are taught progressively each year, the results will be more satisfying.

Yearly Calendar

For an effective balance of the various activities included in the curriculum, each activity or group of activities should receive a predetermined amount of time. Some activities require considerably more time for instruction than others. Local and national emphasis on certain activities can affect the amount of time necessary for adequate instruction. Activities that receive great national attention, such as football and basketball, may not require as much instruction as a leisure-time activity that has previously received little attention.

If teachers are to instruct efficiently, they must develop yearly calendars that include the sequential placement of content and time allotment for each activity or group of activities. Without such a calendar, orderly arrangement of material and equal-time emphasis on activities are impossible.

Teachers may find it interesting to use the material outlined above to evaluate the activities included in the yearly calendars. A combination of the three plans is often the most feasible approach.

Scope and Sequence

A successful curriculum depends largely on the scope and sequence of the instructional content. *Scope* means the materials and body of knowledge that will be included in the total curriculum. *Sequence* refers to the order in which the body of knowledge is taught in the various grades.

Unit Teaching

The unit approach to physical education instruction is practical, functional, and motivational. Teachers of physical education therefore should become skilled in construction of resource units. The many advantages of unit teaching are well documented in educational literature. Unit teaching, when planned properly, provides a thorough, sequential approach to instruction. The method takes students' different interests and abilities into account and motivates them to learn. Teachers enjoy their work more because they are better able to stimulate the interest and enthusiasm of the students; in addition, both they and the students are able to see progress more readily.

The philosophy of the school, the purposes of the course, and the available resources influence the selection of the central concerns around which the resource units are to be developed. The needs of students always should be foremost in the planning. Physical education is so close to everyday living and so vital for health and happiness that material for developing a unit is always available. The resourceful teacher need not look far to tap the vast reservoir of materials. A few of them are:

Textbooks. Current textbooks from reputable publishers serve as authoritative sources for facts and information. There are many excellent education texts that may be used to aid the teacher in construction of the unit.

Needs of students. Many student needs are obvious. Students who are physically weak, poorly coordinated, and emotionally unstable are noticed by the observant teacher. The need for coeducational activities should guide the teacher in the selection of instructional units.

Courses of study. Teachers may secure curriculum guides from other sections of the country to assist them in the development of local resource units. Many guides are composed of resource units that can be adapted to the local teaching situation.

Community. The community is a rich source of materials for developing resource units. Many community groups, such as local health organizations, sports clubs, medical associations, and departments of public health, are most cooperative in supplying materials and data.

Records. Many schools keep records of student progress through the years. Medical records, guidance studies, and other demographic data provide a fertile reservoir of materials for the guidebook.

Guidelines for Developing the Unit. Several elements are common to all good resource units. These provide guidelines that will assist the teacher in developing a unit to serve local purposes. Some of the important points to consider in planning the unit are outlined below:

1. Needs of students should always be the basic consideration. They should be encouraged to participate in developing the unit.
2. Desirable results and objectives should be established; all materials and activities should contribute to the realization of these goals.
3. Content should be current, factual, and appropriate.
4. Content should include a wide variety of materials, activities, and resources that will meet individual needs, interests, and abilities.
5. Material should be extensive and detailed enough to insure ease in using the unit.
6. Content should motivate the students to carry their interests and efforts in the activity beyond the class period.
7. Evaluation should include a variety of techniques involving the students, the teacher, and the parents. Emphasis should be on student growth in health awareness and health habits.

The Daily Lesson Plan

The unit is a collection of materials, activities, and resources that covers a block of time within the school term. Obviously, the unit must be broken down into smaller sections for daily presentation. The true test of effective teaching is the manner in which the teacher introduces the body of knowledge from the unit into the daily class routine. The value of daily planning, therefore, cannot be overestimated.

Criteria. The daily lesson plan is the teacher's best guide to effective teaching. The plan must be concise and developed to utilize every moment of class time. Nothing is more conducive to poor instruction than the teacher who faces the class without specific preparation. Students can readily tell when a teacher is floundering, wasting time, or waiting for the bell to ring. It is better that the teacher reach the end of the period with considerable information uncovered than to finish the lesson halfway through the period and then assign aimless work to fill in remaining time. Both these situations, however, can be avoided with proper planning.

Evaluation of the Lesson Plan. Assessment is a part of all phases of teaching; the lesson plan is no exception. The following criteria may be used to evaluate daily lesson plans:

The lesson plan must have meaning for the learner. The teacher should construct the lesson on the basis of the student's needs, interests, and abilities. This means that student participation should be stimulated by the presentation of the material.

The plan should be brief. The teacher already has the guidebook, which serves as a source of material, and the teaching unit, which specifies the material to be learned. The daily lesson plan should be taken from the unit and should be a simple guide for the day's lesson.

The lesson plan must be interesting. The lesson should be organized so that all of the appropriate tools of learning can be brought into the presentation. The type of plan that provides for the teacher to lecture for the entire period will fail because it does not utilize the methods necessary for effective teaching. Modern teaching principles dictate that interest is generated more readily when students actively participate in the instructional process.

The plan must stimulate extra-class activity. Motivation is the key to all learning. The lesson should be planned so that students will desire to continue learning beyond the class period.

The plan should be complete. Although brief, the lesson plan should be complete. Included in the plan should be the title of the lesson, objectives, equipment and supplies needed, value of the activity, time allowed for each phase, homework, and evaluation.

The Scientific Approach in Selecting Activities

It is the purpose of this section to show how activities may be selected scientifically. It should not be concluded that the plan shown is the only way to select activities. Nevertheless, the information should help the teacher realize the importance of the scientific approach and emphasize the need to justify the curriculum.

Criteria Through the Years. It is important that definite criteria be used to evaluate each activity considered for inclusion in the curriculum. These criteria, to be fundamentally sound, must be based on the educational needs of boys and girls. Criteria are different from objectives. Objectives furnish the *guides* that assist in the step-by-step approach to the ultimate goal. Criteria are the *standards* used to select the material necessary to attain the objectives.

In the early 1940's, the results of one of the greatest efforts to select activities for the physical education curriculum were published. A committee consisting of national leaders worked for nine years, evaluated twenty activities, and ranked them according to the opinions of outstanding experts throughout the country. The following criteria served as a basis for evaluating activities by showing:

1. The contribution to the physical and organic growth and development of the child and the improvement of body function and body stability.
2. The contribution to the social traits and qualities that go to make up the good citizen and the development of sound moral ideals through intensive participation under proper leadership.
3. The contribution to the psychological development of the child including satisfaction resulting from stimulating experiences both physically and socially.
4. The contribution to the development of safety skills that increase the individual's capacity for protection in emergencies, both in handling himself and in assisting others.
5. The contribution to the development of recreational skills that have a distinct function as hobbies for leisure-time hours, both during school and in after-school life.[15]

Other writers have selected criteria for the evaluation and selection of activities. Brownell and Hagman used eleven criteria based on the thinking of leaders during the 1950's:

1. Does the activity contribute directly to the achievement of program objectives?
2. Does the activity have greater relative value than any other possible choice?
3. Does the activity have meaning for the current social life of the learner?

4. Does the activity have carry-over value for the out-of-school and adult life of the learner?
5. Is the activity of interest to the learner?
6. Is the activity within the range of ability of the learner?
7. Does the activity grow out of previous experience and will it lead to further developmental experiences?
8. Has the activity been adequately presented in a previous grade or within a previous experience of the learner?
9. Can the activity be learned better through an available non-school agency?
10. Does the activity contribute to a correlative function with other experiences in the curriculum?
11. Is the activity reasonably safe, or does it lend itself to reasonable safety precautions?[16]

During the 1960's, leaders began to develop criteria that would reflect the times and serve as indicators for the next two decades. Bookwalter and Vanderzwagg proposed eleven criteria that provide teachers and others who are designing curricula with a comprehensive set of selection principles. These criteria are reproduced in their entirety:

Validity. The activities selected must contribute to one or more of the objectives of physical education.
Totality. The total of the activities selected for each sex and any grade level must have the potential for making an optimum contribution to all valid objectives for each sex and for that grade level.
Relativity. Activities must be selected according to their relative contribution to the totality of the purposes for physical education and for the needs of the learner.
Acceptability. Activities must be meaningful and purposeful and thus acceptable to the learner even if they are not of greatest interest.
Continuity. Activities must lead on to continued use of more of the same and to related activities.
Desirability. Activities must be of interest to the child. Contribution to other desires enhances potential or latent interest.
Utility. Activities must have carry-over value today and in the future, out of school and in after-school years.
Capacity. Activities must be within the ability of the learner according to his age, sex, and physical capacity.
Intensity. Activities should be treated sufficiently intensively to assure that the learner acquires the proper degree (beginning, intermediate, or advanced) of competence set for the grade or course level.
Social Adaptability. Activities must offer leadership-followership opportunities in a social situation so as to promote social adaptability in life activities.
Feasibility. Activities must be feasible in a particular school in terms of time allotment, facilities, teacher competence, and geographical or community differences.[17]

Criteria for the Future. The purpose of preparing the extensive list of criteria used through the years is twofold: (1) to show the importance of criteria in the selection of activities and (2) to assist in the development of a set of criteria that will stand the test of the future. This double purpose is accomplished by choosing standards that have been most prevalent through the years. The following have been selected as a guide to planning activity programs of the future.

MAJOR CRITERIA. Several criteria outweigh all others in importance and accordingly should be given greater consideration in the selection of activities. These major criteria are:

1. Does the activity meet its basic objectives? No activity should be included in the curriculum that does not contribute to the attainment of the basic objectives and purposes of physical education. (See Chapter 3 for basic objectives.)
2. Is the activity reasonably safe? It is the responsibility of the teacher to assure parents and children that the environment for the physical education program is safe and that dangerous activities have been excluded. Teachers are responsible by law for the safety of their students and may be liable if negligence can be proved in the conduct of the program. *Teachers should consider seriously their legal responsibilities for the safety and welfare of their students.*
3. Are the activities teachable? An inventory of the various movements of which the human body is capable would show thousands of possibilities. Natural play activities alone involve hundreds of kinds of movements. When "frill activities" and all the movements using machines and gadgets are added, the selection of activities becomes increasingly complicated. *Teachers should be exceedingly careful in promoting activities that may be included in the curricu-*

lum. Activities that do not involve instruction should be scrutinized carefully before being used. This is important not only because of the growth and developmental needs of children but also for teacher security.

MINOR CRITERIA. If an activity satisfies the major criteria, it is evaluated by a set of minor criteria. Many activities seem to be acceptable until these secondary standards render them invalid.

1. Is the activity too expensive? The cost of any activity must, of course, be considered. If several activities measure up to all criteria but one is less costly, this should be the ground for selecting it in preference to the others. Lack of local facilities may be the determining factor for excluding an activity.

2. Is the activity generally interesting? Other things being equal, the interest of students should be considered, but interest fluctuates with age and experience. Instruction can also affect interest. An activity that is not accepted today may be interesting next week, depending on how well it has been presented and what degree of success students have had in it.

3. Does the community accept the ac-

tivity? The schools belong to the people. An activity may be safe and meet all basic objectives and still not be acceptable to the community. An illustration is dancing. There are other activities, more acceptable to the community, that make the same contribution to physical development.

4. Is the activity too time-consuming? There are many activities which would meet all the criteria, but because of large classes are not feasible time-wise. An illustration is the apparatus program that is included in some schools. The parallel bars, for instance, are seldom purchased in multiple sets; a school would be fortunate to have one set.

Criteria of Relative Value. Sometimes two or three activities meet all the established criteria. However, because the time element allows the inclusion of only one, the teacher must decide which has the greatest relative value. An illustration would be a choice among touch football, speedball, and soccer. All three of these activities meet the accepted standards. However, touch football might be selected because it is an American activity or because it would be more acceptable in a given locality; it also provides greater motivation for after-

Figure 4–5. Selection of coeducational activities is vital. (Courtesy Cedar Shoals High School, Athens, Georgia.)

school participation because of the national interest developed through television.

Procedures for Selecting Activities for the Program

Several steps should be followed to achieve a more scientific approach to the formation of curriculum content and to initiate a more cooperative effort by teachers in planning and teaching after the activities have been selected.

Formation of a Committee. A committee should consist of physical education teachers and administrators who are sincere, dedicated, unselfish, unbiased, and experienced. The committee should:

1. *List activities for study.* In selecting curriculum content, each member lists the activities that he or she feels should be studied.
2. *Eliminate certain activities.* All activities that are extremely hazardous should be ruled out immediately.
3. *Formulate criteria.* Evaluative criteria should be established to measure each activity.
4. *Assign weight values.* The committee should assign to each criterion a weight value in points. Certain criteria should have greater weight than others.
5. *Evaluate activities by major criteria.* The activities that have not been eliminated because of the safety factor should be evaluated by the major criteria that have been selected. Forms should be made up, listing the criteria and activities to be evaluated.
6. *Arrange activity by rank.* From the total points given to activities by the committee members, the activities should then be arranged by rank.
7. *Evaluate activities by minor criteria.* Each member of the committee, or each teacher in the system, or teachers in other systems may subject the group of activities to minor criteria for the selection of activities for the individual school or schools.

CHALLENGE IN CURRICULUM DESIGN FOR THE FUTURE

One authority on curriculum development, Ralph Tyler, states that he finds no reason to modify the fundamental questions he raised 25 years ago in his book, *Basic Principles of Curriculum and Instruction:*

- What should be the educational objectives of the curriculum?
- What learning experiences should be developed to enable students to achieve the objectives?
- How should the learning experiences be organized to increase their cumulative effect?
- How should the effectiveness of the curriculum be evaluated?

These issues are still at the core of physical education. Tyler believes, however, that some changes in emphasis are necessary. First, educators should give much more attention to the *active role of the student in the learning process* and to the implications of student involvement in curriculum development. Second, educators also should give greater emphasis to the need for a comprehensive examination of the *nonschool areas of student learning* as they relate to curriculum development.[18]

Role of the Student in Planning

Teachers must meet the challenge of seeking student opinion. There are many ways to involve students. It has been helpful to use "Student Interest Surveys" to suggest points of departure for curriculum revision in course offerings, intramurals, elective programs, independent study, and mini-courses.

An evaluation of the nonschool areas of learning is necessary because other agencies of society are placing greater emphasis on physical education. Experiences in social clubs, religious institutions, home, and community, have extended the individual's basic interests, values, attitudes, and skills. Television viewing, specialized summer camps, and private lessons in sport activities have supplemented and complemented the opportunities that were once provided only by the school. Work experiences for adolescents are changing, and students' interest in learning what the school teaches fluctuates. Physical educators in secondary schools need to improve the curriculum by maximizing the school's resources and strengthening the out-of-school environment.

Development of Human Values Through Sports

Perhaps one of the greatest forces of the 1980's will be the influence of sport on the development of human values. Never before have youth been so pressured to identify a personal value system. Most of us believe that the behavior which emphasizes the dignity and worth of the individual in a democratic society can be fostered through sports participation. This profession has preached good sportsmanship, tolerance of others, brotherhood of man, self-realization, and acceptance and understanding of others; yet, we as a professional group continue to condone exploitation of the athlete, violence in sports, commercialism, and varying degrees of cheating and dishonesty. If the high school physical education class and the intramural sports program are to develop a positive learning experience that encourages human values, teachers, students, and administrators must be willing to change.

The scientific selection of curriculum content in physical education is an intricate procedure and requires considerable research. Teachers should responsibly accept the challenge and devise other methods of curriculum construction with emphasis on the scientific approach.

As educators face revision of the traditional curriculum construction, serious consideration should be given to experimental learning theories about skill acquisition. This chapter has presented only a few of these innovations. Grouping by ability in a coeducational setting with an emphasis on individualized instruction may lead to more effective instruction. Successful performance of the high-school student that results in lifetime participation in physical activities and self-realization of human movement should be the goal of a good secondary school physical education curriculum.

QUESTIONS FOR DISCUSSION

1. What are the differences between content goals and process goals? List several areas of consideration for change discussed by the National Commission on the Reform of Secondary Education.

2. What steps should be taken in planning the curriculum?

3. What are the major curriculum revisions as a result of the Title IX legislation?

4. Describe three program models and list the advantages and disadvantages of each.

5. What are the characteristics of a good curriculum guide? Outline a sample guide.

6. Why should activities in the physical education program be selected scientifically?

REFERENCES

1. The National Commission on the Reform of Secondary Education, B. Frank Brown, Chairman, *The Reform of Secondary Education, A Report to the Public and the Profession* (New York: McGraw-Hill Book Company, 1973), p. 7.
2. *Ibid.*, pp. 13–22.
3. *Ibid.*, pp. 32–34.
4. *Ibid.*, p. 39.
5. Delbert Oberteuffer and Celeste Ulrich with Charles Mand, *Physical Education*, 4th ed. (New York: Harper and Row Publishers, Inc., 1970), pp. 289–302.

6. Sydelle D. Ehrenberg, "The Case for Structure," *Educational Leadership* (ASCD, Vol. 34, No. 1, October, 1976), p. 48.
7. *Ibid.,* p. 48.
8. Barbara J. Kelly, "Implementing Title IX," *JOPER* (Vol. 48, February, 1977), p. 28.
9. The National Association for Physical Education of College Women and The National College Physical Education Association for Men, *Competency-Based Teacher Education, Briefings 2* (1976), pp. 42–43.
10. AAHPER Publications, American Association for Health, Physical Education and Recreation, *Curriculum Improvement in Secondary School Physical Education* (Washington, D.C., 1973), p. 48.
11. *Ibid.,* pp. 42–43, p. 55.
12. Larry Overskei, "A Coeducational Lottery System," *JOHPER* (Vol. 44, September, 1973), pp. 27–28.
13. Hal Lawson, "An Alternative Program Model for Secondary School Physical Education," *JOPER* (Vol. 48, February, 1977), pp. 38–39.
14. AAHPER Publications, American Association for Health, Physical Education and Recreation, *Organizational Patterns for Instruction in Physical Education* (Washington, D. C., 1971), pp. 70–71.
15. William R. LaPorte, with revisions by John M. Cooper, *The Physical Education Curriculum,* 7th ed. (Los Angeles: The University of Southern California Press, 1968), p. 9.
16. Clifford L. Brownell and E. Patricia Hagman, *Physical Education* (New York: McGraw-Hill Book Company, 1951), p. 193.
17. Karl W. Bookwalter and Harold J. Vanderzwagg, *Foundations and Principles of Physical Education* (Philadelphia: W. B. Saunders Company, 1969), pp. 217–218.
18. Ralph W. Tyler, "Two New Emphases in Curriculum Development," *The Education Digest* (Vol. 42, February, 1977), p. 11.

SELECTED READINGS

AAHPER Publications, *Curriculum Improvement in Secondary School Physical Education* (Washington, D.C.), 1973.

AAHPER Publications, *Ideas for Secondary School Physical Education* (Washington, D. C., AAHPER, 1975).

Heathers, Glen, "A Working Definition of Individualized Instruction," *Educational Leadership* (ASCD, Vol. 34, No. 5, February, 1977), pp. 342–345.

Hulac, Georgia M., et al., "Developing Competency Waivers in the Three Educational Domains," *JOPER* (Vol. 46, June, 1975), pp. 20–21.

Jewett, Ann E., ed., *Curriculum Design: Purposes and Processes of Physical Education Teaching-Learning* (Washington, D. C., AAHPER Publications, 1974).

·Lomen, L. D., "Upgrading the Physical Education Curriculum," *JOPER* (Vol. 46, June, 1975), p. 29.

Mackenzie, M. M., *Toward a New Curriculum in Physical Education* (New York: McGraw-Hill Publishing Company, 1969).

National Association for Physical Education of College Women and National College Physical Education Association for Men, *Quest: Educational Change in the Teaching of Physical Education* (Vol. XV, January, 1971).

Siegel, Judith E., "Task No. 1: Writing 'Practical' Curriculums," *Educational Leadership* (ASCD, Vol. 34, No. 7, April, 1977), pp. 540–544.

The Physical Education Framework Committee, *Physical Education Framework for California Public Schools, Kindergarten through Grade Twelve* (California State Department of Education, Sacramento, California, 1973).

Vaughn, Jacqueline B., "The Expanding Role of Teachers in Negotiating Curriculum," *Educational Leadership* (ASCD, Vol. 34, No. 1, October, 1976), pp. 21–23.

Chapter 5

Courtesy Los Angeles Unified School District.

IMPORTANCE OF METHODS AND MATERIALS
  MEANING OF METHODOLOGY
  CRITICAL AREAS OF CONCERN
    CLASSROOM AND GYMNASIUM
      DISCIPLINE
    CULTURALLY DISADVANTAGED
      STUDENTS
    SELECTION OF MATERIALS
METHODS IN TEACHING PHYSICAL EDUCATION
  MANAGEMENT DEVICES
    INSTRUCTIONAL OBJECTIVES
    SYSTEM INSTRUCTION
    CONTRACT TEACHING
    OTHER MANAGEMENT DEVICES
  METHODOLOGY IN KNOWLEDGE, SKILL,
    OR ATTITUDE
    TEXTBOOKS
    QUESTIONS AND ANSWERS
    LECTURES
    GROUP DISCUSSIONS
    DEMONSTRATIONS
    PROJECTS
    EXPERIMENTS
    CONSULTANTS AND OUTSIDE
      SPECIALISTS
  SKILL ACQUISITION
    CLOSED-OPEN CONTINUUM
    MULTI-SENSORY APPEAL
    PROGRAMMED INSTRUCTION
    BEHAVIOR MODIFICATION
    WHOLE METHOD AND PART METHOD
  APPROACHES TO TEACHING PHYSICAL
    EDUCATION

    FORMAL APPROACH
    INFORMAL APPROACH
    COMPROMISE APPROACH
  KINDS OF LEARNING
    PRIMARY LEARNING
    ASSOCIATED LEARNING
    CONCOMITANT LEARNING
TOOLS FOR EFFECTIVE TEACHING IN
PHYSICAL EDUCATION
  AUDIO-VISUAL AIDS
    FILMS
    FILMSTRIPS AND SLIDES
    VIDEOTAPES AND CASSETTES
    TELEVISION
    GUIDELINES FOR USE OF
      AUDIO-VISUAL AIDS
  VISUAL AIDS
    BULLETIN BOARDS
    WALL BOARDS
    MAGNETIC BOARDS
    FLANNEL BOARDS
    CHALK BOARDS
ENRICHING INSTRUCTION THROUGH FREE
MATERIALS
  CRITERIA FOR SELECTING
    SUPPLEMENTARY MATERIALS
CLASSIFICATION AND TIME ALLOTMENTS FOR
PHYSICAL EDUCATION ACTIVITIES
  INDIVIDUAL ACTIVITIES
  GROUP ACTIVITIES
QUESTIONS FOR DISCUSSION
REFERENCES
SELECTED READINGS

MANAGEMENT AND METHODS IN TEACHING

Arguments about systems, management, and methods, pro and con, vary greatly. There are those who believe that if teachers have adequately prepared subject matter, they will develop appropriate methods. Others contend that content can be acquired if teachers have mastered the skills of teaching. Educators may be at one end of the continuum or the other, and between these two extremes are many differing points of view.

In teaching, method refers to the structuring of the educational material to achieve an effective teaching-learning process. It should be noted that there is no one best method of teaching physical education. Attempts have been made to apply teaching theories to all physical education activities; the results sometimes have been confusing. Traditional methods employed by general educators are not always applicable to physical educa-

tion. A method must be compatible with the personality of the teacher, as well as the subject matter, in order to foster a positive relationship and interaction with students. One method may be more appropriate to use in a tutorial program, another is more effective in team teaching.

To understand the significance of management and methods, the reader should keep in mind that a teaching *system* will incorporate several methods. A teaching *method* is a manner of prescribing the appropriate means to students. The term *teaching technique* refers to the tools used for effective results in the teaching-learning process.

IMPORTANCE OF METHODS AND MATERIALS

Chapter 6, *The Learning Process*, points out the kinds of feedback, reinforcement, and rewards that affect the choice of systems, methods, or techniques used by the teacher. It is obvious today that instructors in professional schools who teach sports, such as skiing, tennis, bowling, and other commercial-type activities, focus on methods of teaching. These teachers provide the kind of help and instruction that the learner desires. The success of these private learning programs points out that the secondary school teacher needs and wants help in management devices and methodology. It is apparent that although they vary, methods are important and apparently make a difference in the educational experience.

Meaning of Methodology

The traditional method of teaching physical education in the secondary school involves the cognitive, affective, and psychomotor domains. The emphasis has been on teaching skills and facts, with very little meaning given to the method used in the affective domain. The traditional method is used in most levels of education — elementary, middle, junior high, and senior high schools — and is supported by methods courses taught in the undergraduate and graduate professional preparation programs in physical education. The application of teaching theory has resulted in the characteristic sequence of explaining a skill, demonstrating a skill, practicing a skill, analyzing and correcting a skill, and evaluating the results of the skill performance. Teachers tend to prefer a traditional teacher-directed method wherein the teacher is the focus of the class. Several authorities in psychology call this method the *command style* of teaching. Some find other means of teaching more likely to motivate the student to learn. Chapter 4 discusses alternative curriculum construction and program models.

An analysis of current literature indicates that almost all innovations in the past 10 years have been either organizational (management) or methodological (methods). Innovations such as the nongraded classroom, team teaching, specialized staffing, learning centers, modular scheduling, the middle school, contingency management, and computer-assisted instruction reflect, basically, a change in management (or ganization). This may or may not include new methods. Other recent changes concentrate primarily upon methodology. These increasingly popular trends in the school program include individualized, prescribed instruction, role playing, programmed learning, diagnostic teaching, problem solving, independent study, and teaching for specific behavioral objectives, to name only a few.[1]

Educators today have developed instruments and techniques for evaluating the effectiveness of teachers. It is significant that many of these relate to the methodology used by the teacher. In reviewing students' opinions of teachers, one finds that they often judge "good" or "poor" teachers by their characteristic methods of teaching. Research in the late 1970's indicates that methods are extremely important. No one approach is best for all situations; no one method is successful for all teachers. The pre-service and in-service teacher education programs should familiarize the beginning teacher with a variety of methods. The prospective teacher can then choose those that can be implemented to obtain the most desirable results with the student.

Secondary schools exist for students. Baughman has reported that youth want their schools to provide: (1) a quality education, (2) teachers who know how to teach, (3) opportunities for self-identity, (4) demanding and understanding teachers, (5) guidance and direction, and (6) success and peak experiences.[2] Teachers testify that it is becoming more and more difficult to teach students in the secondary school. The needs and problems that they face often concern management and methodology. In fact, the proper selection of a teaching method and an efficient management device are critical to the development of an effective teacher.

Critical Areas of Concern

The implications of any teaching method are determined by several factors. Methods are dependent upon age level, ability, classification, type of activity, purpose of activity, special problems of discipline, goals of the teacher, and the extent of federal legislation concerning race, sex, and accommodating the handicapped. What the teacher expects to teach and what the students expect to learn necessitate not only a variety of teaching methods but also a basic understanding of classroom and gymnasium discipline, a genuine appreciation of the culturally disadvantaged, and a sound foundation in the guiding principles of the learning process.

Classroom and Gymnasium Discipline. Discipline is an essential part of education. Both the general public and educators are concerned about the problems of discipline in the secondary school. Two complications occur at this age level. First, our laws of universal schooling force into school some students who have no desire to be there. Until teachers discover the needs and motivations of such students and devise ways of meeting the resultant challenges, there will be a continual source of aberrant behavior in the school. The second complication arises from the complexity of our technological society. The more complex the society, the more demands it places on its members. To the extent that high school students face increasing demands, the school can anticipate an increase in deviant behavior.[3]

Discipline problems are basically of two orders: real and perceived. A real discipline problem arises from a student's infringing on the freedoms of the teacher or other members of the class. A perceived discipline problem is caused by the teacher's imagining a problem when there is none. Far too many so-called discipline problems are wrongly interpreted as such by the teacher. A perceived discipline problem, however, is no less real to the teacher than the actual ones. The teacher may err in either direction: by failing to perceive real discipline problems, or by perceiving problems that do not exist.[4]

Secondary school educators should establish a positive learning environment. Preventive discipline not only affords students as much freedom of behavior as they can handle without infringing on the rights of others but also minimizes conflicts between teachers and students. If threat is minimized and levels of tolerance are maximized, discipline problems will be greatly reduced. Misbehavior frequently occurs because lesson content is not relevant, the student is not involved in the learning process, or the mode of presentation is uninteresting. Preventive discipline enhances the learning environment, examines the relevance of the curriculum, and challenges traditional methodologies.[5] Teachers must learn to deal with discipline problems. These suggestions may be helpful:

1. Establish a threshold level of tolerance.
2. Establish an environment that is free but not chaotic.
3. Re-establish rapport after dealing firmly with a student.
4. Understand adolescents' desire for attention, recognition, and status.
5. Understand adolescents' frustrations and tensions in striving for adult independence.
6. Be friendly, yet firm; act confidently.
7. Be prompt, consistent, and reasonable in actions.
8. Avoid spending too much time enforcing discipline.
9. Avoid rejection of a student because of misbehavior.
10. Avoid assuming the role of "pal."
11. Remember, the more rules and limitations, the more potential discipline problems.
12. Remember to do anticipatory planning.
13. Remember to help students over difficult hurdles in behavior.
14. Remember to encourage constructive behavior by defining the limits.
15. Remember the teacher's role is to be sensitive and understanding.

Culturally Disadvantaged Students. The child who has never been exposed to a varied environment or to parental encouragement of education may face a difficult adjustment when placed in a predominately middle-class public school. The 1960's and 1970's have not solved the problems created by the inner city school, busing for cross-cultural student population, or the multiplicity of federal regulations.

However, from all the studies and experiments conducted, a new image of the disadvantaged child, as well as more suitable teaching methods, has emerged. The disadvantaged child suffers psychologically from any or all of the factors listed below:

1. *Poor motivation.* The ghetto child does not have the same desire to learn and become educated as does the middle-class child. He learns to hate school and to compensate by resorting to antisocial behavior.
2. *Lower expectations on part of teachers.* Teachers are prone to expect less of the ghetto child, and the treatment that follows this expectation causes the child to develop a negative attitude toward learning.
3. *Poor self-perception on part of students.* Children from the ghetto, because of the affluence portrayed on television which is in sharp contrast to the environment in which they live, develop a poor self-concept. They must be provided with the opportunity to live in more acceptable situations and have a chance to develop their innate potentialities. Some of the most outstanding accomplishments in sports have been made by schoolchildren from the ghetto when given the opportunity.
4. *Antagonism toward school and teachers.* Disadvantaged children develop a negative attitude toward school and antagonism toward their teachers. This is easily understood when individual study reveals that their parents were dropouts and cared little for school and education. In addition, the middle-class child, by the time he enters junior high, is already thinking about college. This is not true of the ghetto child. He does not have parents who are prodding him to further his education; nor are the members of his peer group college-bound.[6]

Physical education teachers have a tremendous opportunity to encourage the education of the disadvantaged child. The self-image of the ghetto child in sports is generally superior. There are few high school, college, and professional teams in the country that do not have among their members many players from the ghetto. Physical performance is an area in which these children can excel and develop a positive self-concept. The physical education programs throughout the country have done a tremendous job in providing opportunity for the disadvantaged child to develop his or her potential. In view of the unique situation, there are certain implications for teaching disadvantaged children. Biehler lists them:

1. Do everything possible to satisfy the deficiency needs — physiological, safety, belongingness, esteem.
   a. Allow for the physical condition of your students.
   b. Make your room physically and psychologically safe.
   c. Show your students that you take an interest in them and that they "belong" in your classroom.
   d. Arrange learning experiences so that all students can gain at least a degree of esteem.
2. Strive to enhance the attractions and minimize the dangers of growth choices.
3. Direct learning experiences toward feelings of success in an effort to encourage a realistic level of aspiration, an orientation toward achievement, and a positive self-concept.
4. Be alert to the damaging impact of excessive competition.
5. For students who need it, encourage the development of a desire to achieve.
6. Take advantage of natural interests and try to create new ones, and encourage learning for its own sake.
7. Provide encouragement incentives for learning that is essential but not intrinsically appealing.[7]

Selection of Materials. Teachers must seek their own methods and techniques for best working toward productive results. It is critical, however, that the teacher base these decisions on sound principles of learning. (Detailed emphasis is placed on the learning process in Chapter 6). Guiding principles for the learning process have been summarized most effectively by Oberteuffer and Ulrich. These 20 points should be kept in mind when selecting the methods for teaching physical education in the secondary school:

1. The heart of the physical education program is in the development of skills and behaviors in a variety of activities chosen for and by the individual in relation to his interests, needs, and capacities.
2. The orderly format which governs the

universe and man seems to suggest that learning also is an orderly process and can be understood.

3. Teaching methods may vary from teacher-directed to student-solved approaches. The good teacher will use the correct teaching methods for each learner and will seek shared goals with his students.

4. Teachers must expect spurts, plateaus, and drop-offs in the curve of learning.

5. Skill classes should be classified for the beginner and the advanced.

6. Learning must be understood if it is to be meaningful to the learner.

7. Learning is affected by interest span; the span is shorter in children and novices than it is in adults and experts.

8. Practice should be distributed throughout the learning period, with frequent, short practice sessions rather than infrequent, long sessions.

9. "Mental practice" can be of benefit, especially to the advanced performer.

10. There is no substitute for learning by doing.

11. Errors should be corrected early in the learning procedure.

12. An adverse environment is a detriment to learning.

13. The attention of the learner should be directed to as large a part as he is able to comprehend.

14. Extraneous elements that act as distractions for beginners and inhibit learning may be of little consequence to advanced students.

15. Learning satisfactions are related to individual needs and desires, and such satisfactions are essential to learning.

16. Visual aids may abet learning if they are used intelligently by the teacher and if they are related to the task being learned.

17. Learning will produce behavioral change in the learner, but that change will be specific to the learner unless inferences are drawn for similar behavioral circumstances.

18. Transfer of learning may take place if the new situation presented is similar to that in which the skill was first learned, and if the performer recognizes the similarity.

19. Learning fosters economy of effort.

20. Overlearning abets retention of learning, while interference with retention is brought about by subsequent ideas which alter and erase the initial learnings.[8]

METHODS IN TEACHING PHYSICAL EDUCATION

Teachers view motivation, or the lack of it, as the key to student success or failure in physical education. In some school districts, chief administrators have adoped innovative methods in instruction that affect the total school system. Educators continue to search for more effective systems, teaching methods, and techniques to improve the quality of the school program. Methods include a variety of educational experiences such as lectures, demonstrations, or independent study that motivate, produce results, and modify behavior. The following devices are grouped under management and methodology in knowledge, skills, or attitudes.

Management Devices

A management plan can be established to help the teacher attain the goals of the lesson or the unit. A teacher finalizes the purposes and objectives, continues the plan, develops the material in a logical manner, brings the results to an educational climax, and then evaluates in terms of the objectives sought. There are several devices currently in use as management or organizational tools.

Instructional Objectives. Goals and objectives are often general in nature. One of the difficulties in this age of accountability is to prove that the learner has satisfied the objectives of the educational system. In order to make them more specifically measurable, instructional objectives are stated in terms of student behavior. Learning can be inferred when a relatively permanent change in behavior is observed. Goals are set for the cognitive, psychomotor, and affective domains. Instructional objectives are measured by the criterion of acceptable performance. A teacher can use this device to measure the results of the teaching-learning process.

To evaluate objectives is essential to the process. The teacher should be prepared to write instructional objectives clearly and accurately. In this type of careful planning, the teacher can focus on what needs to be learned; what skills, knowledge, and attitudes the secondary school student should develop and retain. Many schools across the United States are using the outcomes of the instructional objectives as a key to evaluating the performance of the student, the success of the instructional unit, and the effectiveness of the secondary physical education program. A concentrated effort is being made in many states to define more clearly, on a state-wide basis, the goals of physical education in the junior and senior high schools. The *Resource Manual* includes helpful examples of general instructional objectives.

Systems Instruction. Systems instruction is not new in American education. By 1968, the United States Office of Education had contracted with the Systems Development Corporation to study ongoing public school programs in Alabama, Florida, Michigan, and Utah. Many colleges and universities have included systems instruction in research and development projects. Examples of these projects are the Individualized Prescribed Instruction (IPI), Plan for Learning According to Needs (PLAN), Project READ of Behavioral Research Laboratory (BRL), Teaching Learning Units (TLU), and Learning Activity Packages (LAP). Most of the systems have these factors in common: (1) concept focus, (2) behavior-stated objectives, (3) multiple activities and methodologies, (4) diversified learning resources, and (5) evaluation instrumentation. Differing terminology is used, but the components are essentially the same: desired competencies are predetermined, behavior is identified, and task analysis is completed.[9]

The teaching profession is undergoing critical changes. California, Florida, Georgia, and Texas are using systematic approaches in teacher evaluations, in-service education, and pre-service education. These developments provide management devices to use as tools and techniques in the learning process.

Contract Teaching. One of the management devices used in the 1970's to motivate students to learn is contract teaching. It is cited here as an example of the numerous approaches of individualized instruction used to in-

volve the student more actively in the responsibility of learning. Contract teaching probably arose because students lacked the motivation to learn. It allows the student to select the learning activities and to determine the level of academic marks he or she wishes to achieve. In physical education, the student may be presented with a list of tasks and allowed to choose a standard of performance. The student and teacher may wish to develop a contract or establish a contract point system together. Patterns in contracts include progression from simple to complex skill development, adaptation of facilities and community resources, use of audio-visual materials, and the provision of resources, teachers, and internships. The contract device provides clearly defined objectives, permits self-direction, and establishes objective criteria for evaluation. Educational philosophies differ, however, and some school systems may not permit this type of flexibility.

Other Management Devices. Computers are being used increasingly in school systems to schedule classes, catalog books, accomplish non-instructional services, and program instruction. The computer also is used for drills, tests, dialogues, and diagnosis. In the 1980's, the ability of the teacher to identify the specific needs to management and methods that can be handled by the computer will be in demand.

Problem solving, role playing, microteaching, and modeling are other devices by which the teacher can encourage changes in behavior. These techniques may accompany the traditional method or be used as primary or supplementary designs in the learning process.

Team Teaching. Team teaching generally means that two or more teachers, because of their individual expertise, are assigned to handle a certain class or specific material within a unit of instruction. Having more than one teacher bear instructional responsibility for a class is a management device that requires careful planning. The increase in coeducational activities in the secondary school program has developed this concept even further. Besides utilizing individual teaching talents, the instructors often use a paraprofessional to assist with many of the non-instructional duties in the classroom or gymnasium.

Methodology in Knowledge or Attitude

Many successful methods in the teaching of academic subjects may be applied to teaching physical education theory. Several of these may be used for the activity program also. Some of the more commonly used methods are discussed below.

Textbooks. Textbooks are used widely in physical education. Although texts are very important, they sometimes become mere sources of information that is digested and fed back to the teacher without the necessary reinforcement for retainment of the acquired knowledge. Teachers may use the text as a crutch without exploring other methods of teaching. A text is a helpful source of information but should always be used in conjunction with a guidebook and supplementary materials.

The teacher of activities in physical education whose use of texts has been limited to pamphlets and brochures of game rules may encounter some difficulty in selecting a text for the physical education class. Teachers must have some means of evaluating texts in terms of the philosophy and objectives of the program as well as their appeal for the students. A great deal of improvement has been made in textbooks in recent years; publishers and authors alike are to be commended for their efforts in updating textual materials to reflect as closely as possible both authoritative research findings and prevailing educational philosophies. The task of the teacher is to determine which text will be most effective in a particular situation for developing the proper physical education knowledge and attitudes for the students.

Selection of the text may be made by a state or city agency, or by a school committee; in a small school, one teacher may have to make the decision. In any case, some guidelines are needed to aid in the selection. Textbook evaluation in the past frequently involved the use of a chart that assigned numerical values to important factors; this method is used rarely today because of the many variables that arise in each locality. Nevertheless, certain aspects of these charts still must be considered in selecting a text. The following questions reflect the most important criteria:

1. Is the content current, factual, and objective?
2. Is the content developed in a logical progression or in independent units? Is the spiral of learning principle evident in unit development?
3. Does the content conform to the pattern of physical education instruction adopted by the school? For example, a text based on the grade placement pattern should be selected in a school that follows this plan of instruction.
4. Is the textbook appropriate in vocabulary, examples, and level of difficulty?
5. Are there appropriate end-of-chapter activities? Are these of the nature and scope to provide for the various levels of ability among the students?
6. Is the book sufficiently illustrated to clarify the material presented?
7. Is the book authoritative? Is there evidence that the authors are qualified both in the specific field and in sound educational principles?
8. Is the book attractive in format and design? Is the type easy to read? Is the size appropriate? Are the cover and binding durable?
9. Is the cost reasonable?
10. Are supplementary materials available, such as a teacher's manual, workbook, transparencies, or standardized texts?

Questions and Answers. The question and answer method is an effective way to hold attention and keep pertinent topics foremost in the student's mind. Although this method should not be used too frequently, it has several distinct advantages: it arouses student interest, it gets to the heart of certain problems, it serves as a quiz to ascertain extent of knowledge, and it promotes discussion. The question and answer method is teacher-oriented and offers very little opportunity for student exploration, but it can be valuable in conjunction with other methods.

Effective use of the question and answer method requires considerable skill on the part of the teacher. Not every person has the ability to develop a point or lead to a generalization through questioning. In the question and answer technique, the classic Socratic method, teachers ask questions to elicit desired responses from stu-

dents. In the hands of the unskilled examiner, however, this practice frequently degenerates into a form of non-thinking textbook recitation.

Lectures. The lecture, except in rare instances, is the poorest method of teaching, as secondary students quickly become bored and lose interest. Sometimes, however, when a special topic needs to be presented with authority, the lecture method should be used.

It has been said that the person who learns most from a lecture is the lecturer himself. Students should have experience in exploring and finding out for themselves the answers to physical education problems. Students are the ones who should be doing research and ferreting out information; it is assumed that teachers already have a

Figure 5-1. Fencing demonstration can be an effective method of instruction. (Courtesy Los Angeles Unified School District.)

good background of knowledge pertaining to the problem. Special effort should be made to guide students toward seeking answers themselves. In this way students will retain much longer what they have learned.

Both the question and answer session and the lecture are carry-over methods from the formalized, traditional educational scene of the past. Although both have value for specific instructional situations, their use has been curtailed in secondary schools in favor of more effective, student-oriented methods of instruction.

Group Discussions. Teachers using the discussion method may stimulate the interest of their students and therefore attain a high level of retention. Because it challenges and develops students' intelligence and reasoning process, the discussion method is one of the most satisfactory means of teaching on the secondary level. Discussion may be an activity for the entire class, or students may be placed in small groups to examine assigned topics. In the latter case, reports are made by leaders from each group. Teachers should be alert to see that unrelated topics are not brought into the discussion, that discussions are summarized, and that conclusions are reached.

The teacher should encourage the timid student to participate and not allow the talkative, extroverted student to dominate the discussion. Moreover, teachers should limit their own participation to what is needed to stimulate the students, to clarify a point in question, to correct the misinformed, and to summarize what has been discussed. They should be careful not to inhibit students *during* the discussion by criticizing an expression or correcting grammar; constructive criticism is necessary but should be given at a more appropriate time.

A variation of the group discussion technique is to have a panel of students discuss a topic in front of the class and to organize a follow-up discussion in which the whole class participates. The panel's presentation may either be pre-pared or extemporaneous. A summary by a student leader or the teacher may reveal the need for further study and research by the class on the topic discussed, particularly when the technique has been used as an introduction to a unit.

Demonstrations. Physical education instruction can be more meaningful when portrayed through actual demonstration. This technique may be used by the student or the teacher. Demonstrations must be well planned, and the necessary equipment and materials must be ready at the designated demonstration site. The demonstration must be scheduled to coincide with relevant class instruction, as poor timing may result in an anticlimax, thus preventing the attainment of maximal benefits. Demonstrations also provide a type of visual incentive that may enhance retention.

Projects. Assigning projects to be prepared by students and placed on display is an effective technique when implemented by an enthusiastic teacher. The physical education curriculum is a fertile field for the development of projects. Safety surveys can be assigned and reported, booklets can be written and collated on a competitive basis, and models can be constructed to illustrate a topic. These are only a few of the numerous projects that are suitable for the physical education curriculum.

However, a word of caution should be given to the inexperienced teacher about the use of projects as a teaching device. It is imperative that the project be a meaningful learning experience for the student. Too frequently, projects are mere busy-work assignments that consume more time and energy than they are worth. If a project is assigned, it should be within the ability range of the student and at the same time offer a sufficient challenge; it should allow for individual interest relating to the topic; and it should provide the student with an opportunity to explore the topic outside the classroom.

Experiments. Many topics in physical education invite a direct classroom or home experiment. This is an excellent way to supplement classroom instruction and aid in the retention of knowledge. For example, an experiment might be conducted using psychophysical tests to show the relationship of depth perception, peripheral vision, and reaction time to good performance in physical education.

Care should be taken to see that experiments do not endanger human health. No student should be allowed to participate in a crash diet program, for example, to see how much weight he or she might lose in a week. On the contrary, the dangers of such practices should be emphasized by the instructor.

Consultants and Outside Specialists. Social agencies and private groups will usually agree to furnish speakers and lecturers to assist teachers in providing instruction in specialized areas. The use of guest speakers can provide a valuable instructional medium if certain precautions are taken. The guest should represent a reputable agency, be a recognized authority in the field, and be able to present ideas clearly to the class. Many associations and firms have a speakers' bureau composed of representatives who have demonstrated their ability to discuss their topics effectively and who can speak at the level of their audience. Before inviting a particular speaker, the teacher should explain to the agency the ages and general backgrounds of the class, the topic being studied, and the kind of information that will be helpful in developing the unit. Usually the speaker will be willing to answer questions from the students after the presentation.

The speaker should be met at the school and escorted to the place where he or she will meet the class. A letter of thanks from the class following the presentation is suggested also. School policy should be followed regarding outside speakers at the school, and the principal should be kept informed of the progress of the event.

Skill Acquisition

Experiments have been conducted on the teaching of motor skills. Several methods derived from these test studies are generally used. Teachers should understand these methods before beginning the teaching process.

Closed-Open Continuum. To analyze and classify physical education skills, the concept of a "closed-open" continuum has been introduced in the professional literature. The term "closed" is used for the motor skills requiring a stationary, stable, or unchanging condition or environment. Situations in which conditions change will vary depending upon the number and nature of the changes. Hence, "open" continuum describes moving changes. In physical education, the performer himself may be moving; the object or implement used in the skill may be moving; other performers may be moving; or any combination of these conditions may occur. The variables include the performer's body, the instrument used to execute the skill, the location of the object, the opponent in space, the timing, and the physical environment. In teaching skill development in the closed-open continuum, the methods the teachers will use to demonstrate a golf swing will be quite different from those required to show dribbling a basketball in a game situation. The skill level of the performer may also be a determining factor in the secondary school program. The open and closed skills are dependent on spatial relationships, coordination, and kinesthetic abilities of the individual learner.[10]

Multi-Sensory Appeal. Research has shown that learning takes place through the senses, especially the visual, auditory, and kinesthetic senses. It also has been proved that the more these three senses are brought into the learning situation, the more lasting the retention of knowledge will be. The teacher who effectively combines visual and auditory aids with demonstrations involving movement will have far better results than the teacher who appeals to only one sense.

After considerable research, Bryant Cratty found that visual cues are very important in teaching skills. He states:

> Thus, it would seem that whenever possible, visual cues in the form of films, demonstrations, or the like are superior to movement cues when learning skills. Attempts to teach a skill by first blindfolding the learner have not seemed as effective as permitting the individual simultaneously to attend to visual cues which may be present.[11]

Programmed Instruction. Behavioral objectives are developed to guide the student in accomplishing the desired performance level. Generally, in programmed instruction, the goal is defined. The student initiates the behavior to perform the task. Steps along the way are completed in sequence, with constant feedback or reinforcement given to the learner. As each step is successfully mastered by the student, he progresses on the criterion scale to the next sequence. The performance objective is met by the student at his own rate of learning. If he is to learn the serve in tennis, a series of performance objectives, say five to six, is developed. Each objective becomes more difficult until the final goals of accuracy, speed, and height are reached.

Behavior Modification. Behavior modification can be applied in the knowledge (cognitive), feeling (affective), or skill (motor) domains. If a student has an efficient throw in softball, the skill can be analyzed and changed. Body mechanics may be modified to motivate the student to respond differently to the stimuli. Behavior modification involves the application of the principles of behavioral psychology. The learner must be aware of his degree of inefficiency for the particular skill, and methods are used to increase or decrease certain behavior. The learner must desire to change, recognize the difficulty in the movement pattern, have the strength to attempt to modify the behavior, and be reinforced frequently by the teacher, in order to achieve success.

Whole Method and Part Method. The premise of the "whole" method of teaching is that demonstrating the entire movement from beginning to end is superior to teaching only a part of the movement at a time. Proponents of this method feel that the student must visualize the activity in its entirety and that the components should be thought of as means to an end not as ends in themselves. This method is the actual utilization of the cognitive theory of learning.

"Part" method teaching is based on the premise that the part is more important than the whole and should, therefore, receive the most emphasis. The stimulus response theory of learning is employed in the part method procedure.

Neither method can be superior for all activities. In teaching swimming, it would be absurd to use the whole method at first. A beginning swimmer cannot be thrown in the water without having had some orientation. Not only would fear prevent effective learning, but the individual might drown. On the other hand, in teaching the Fosbury Flop in high jumping, the whole method must predominate.

The teacher should study each skill in regard to safety, class size, facilities, equipment, and past experiences of the students to select the method that gives the best results. Teachers may find that both methods may be used successfully. Some activities are best taught by the part method followed by the whole method. Other activities should be introduced by the whole method, followed by the part method; finally, by putting the parts together and teaching the whole method again, the skill can be refined.

Approaches to Teaching Physical Education

There have been several approaches to teaching physical education activities. Three approaches that have been used most widely are described below.

Formal Approach. This approach is just what the name signifies. Everything in the class is done according to teacher command. Exercises are given and activities are taught by dictates, resulting in a formal, regimented program that rules out individualism and limits activity to the pattern set by the teacher. This type of instruction dominated physical education in this country until the early 1920's.

Informal Approach. The informal approach provides opportunity for the individual to progress at his own rate as he acquires various skills. The teacher presents the subject in an informal manner, taking into consideration individual differences within each class. The informal approach may have an advantage over the formal approach in the teaching of skills. One criticism of the informal approach is the faulty manner in which many teachers interpret and apply it. The informal approach does not imply free play or the "throwing out the ball" type of physical education.

Compromise Approach. This is a combination of the two mentioned above; the formal approach is used for some activities while the informal is used for the others. For example, when conditioning exercises are given to a group, they should be formally and precisely presented in order to save time and to attain the desired results. The informal approach is more effective in teaching basketball, although certain aspects of teaching basketball skills may be formal. The compromise approach employs those aspects of the formal and informal approaches that are appropriate to the specific learning situation.

The compromise approach also provides the inquiry and discovery factors so important to effective teaching. After demonstrating the skill, the teacher allows the students to practice in the various ability groups. As they learn by trial and error, with occasional assistance from the teacher, they are able to experience the satisfaction of accomplishment in each particular skill.

Kinds of Learning

Educational leaders generally agree that three kinds of learning are involved in any learning situation — *primary, associated,* and *concomitant.*

Primary Learning. Primary learning in physical education constitutes the body of fundamental technical skills of each activity in the program. The basic movements in a skill or activity, such as punting a football, serving a tennis ball, or learning the crouch start or the forward roll, are all examples.

Associated Learning. Associated learning is acquired after the student has mastered the primary movements. Having learned the skills of golf, for example, the student needs to learn the rules of the game, the selection of clubs, and the playing procedures and courtesies essential for participation. Students also should have an in-depth knowledge of the history and values of golf.

Concomitant Learning. Concomitant learning is acquired concurrently with primary learning. Concomitant learning may reflect the desirable outcomes of the program beyond proficiency in skills. In physical education, the cognizant teacher will take the whole individual into consideration and will realize that concomitant learning is a function of the innate qualities in all individuals. Attitudes of character and sportsmanship, evaluation of the teacher, and appraisal of the fellow student or competitors are all outgrowths of the primary learning process.

TOOLS FOR EFFECTIVE TEACHING IN PHYSICAL EDUCATION

Teachers often employ auxiliary materials to enrich the educational experience. (Chapter 7 describes effective teaching aids fully.) Audio-visual in-

Figure 5–2. Audio-visual aids are useful teaching devices. (Courtesy Cedar Shoals High School, Athens, Georgia.)

structional materials extend the teacher's ability to meet this challenge.

Audio-visual Aids

Sources for audio-visual aids related to the various areas of physical education are almost unlimited. Teachers should plan instructional units that will incorporate these aids, since many students learn more readily through such media than through the verbal approach. In combination, verbal and audio-visual aids greatly enhance the learning situation.

Films. Films on almost every aspect of physical education are available. Some are full length; many are loaned free of charge for extended periods. Films are very effective in introducing a new area of instruction, but should not be considered a substitute for the teacher or an opportunity for the teacher to take a break. Their main value is to stimulate interest.

Filmstrips and Slides. Filmstrips and slides, which are readily available, are powerful teaching devices. They are more valuable than films for specific instruction. Slides can be flashed on the screen for as long as needed, allowing ample time for discussion, and can easily be returned for review. They serve well for introducing, developing, and reviewing a unit.

Videotapes and Cassettes. Videotapes and cassettes are gaining popularity as supplements in teaching activity skills. Video cameras and videotapes allow immediate playback of individual or group performance. These aids are available commercially for most activities that are taught in the physical education program.

Television. Instructional television has taken several directions. It can present a quiz program on cancer, a viewing of the World Series in baseball or a replay of Olympic events. There are city, state, and nationwide programs such as "Shape Up" and "Ready Set Go." Television can be used in a telelecture system, allowing a speaker

Figure 5–3. Instant replay units provide powerful tools for effective teaching. (Courtesy SONY Corporation of America.)

in one section of the country to deliver a lecture in another section; with the help of a telephone hook-up, a question and answer session can follow. Closed circuit filming and instant playback of events or skills can make valuable contributions to teaching physical education.

Guidelines for Use of Audio-visual Aids. Although audio-visual aids are very helpful teaching devices, certain guidelines must be observed if they are to be effective. Some of these are:

1. The audio-visual aids should be carefully selected and timed in relation to the subject matter and interests of the students.
2. Films and filmstrips should motivate and supplement instruction. They should never replace the planned sequential procedures but should extend the instruction.
3. Planning well in advance for the showing of films or filmstrips is very important. Such routine procedures as examining the screen and projector, locating outlets, providing extension cords, and insuring proper lighting should be checked prior to the meeting of the class. The film or strip should be threaded and ready for projection before the class assembles.
4. The audio-visual aids should be previewed to acquaint the teachers with the content and allow them to formulate plans to raise questions, comment, and anticipate questions from students. This is essential to relate the content to the unit of instruction.
5. Class discussion should follow immediately after showing the film. Discussion may also take place during the filmstrip.
6. The film or strip may be shown

again, if necessary, to clarify details and to re-emphasize various points.

7. The film or strip should be evaluated by the teacher and the students to determine the extent of its contribution to the unit of instruction.

8. After the projection and discussion of the film or strip, the planned class procedures should be continued, relating the contents of the film or strip to the remainder of the instructional unit.

Visual Aids

Bulletin Boards. The teacher may appoint committees to keep the bulletin board filled with information pertaining to the subject being taught. Items should be changed frequently to keep the information current. Portable boards may be used to illustrate talks before civic clubs, parent-teacher associations, and other groups. An informative bulletin board is a solid teaching device.

Wall Charts. Wall charts are almost indispensable in presenting facts about physical education. They are invaluable when used to illustrate various aspects of physiology, for example. There is usually an abundant supply of these from many sources, for instance, school safety charts from the American Automobile Association.

Magnetic Boards. There are several aspects of physical education in which magnetic boards may be used to assist in the instruction. These boards may be purchased or constructed locally.

Flannel Board. The flannel board, with careful preparation and planning, is an excellent tool for presenting physical education material. Diagrams may be used to illustrate a topic, or multicolored charts may be arranged to provide vivid emphasis on a particular problem.

Chalk Boards. Although the chalk board has lost its popularity as a teaching device because of new, improved aids, it remains unsurpassed as a means for instant emphasis. The teacher can always rely on the effectiveness of the chalk board to reinforce or clarify a statement. Many occasions arise in the class when instant visual illustrations are necessary. For this purpose the chalk board is the best tool.

ENRICHING INSTRUCTION THROUGH FREE MATERIALS

There are many schools that would improve their physical education instruction if the cost of supportive materials were not prohibitive. Although standard textbooks are desirable, they are not mandatory; when they are used, it is considered a good teaching practice to use supplementary materials as well. Some systems use texts in certain areas and free materials in others. Subjects and topics are outlined in the guidebook of instruction, but teaching units are developed around free materials and textbooks.

Many agencies will furnish free literature in quantities large enough to provide a copy for each student. Not only does the introduction of these materials enrich the instructional offering, but it also provides both student and teacher with the results of the latest research in many areas.

In addition to the educational and public relations values derived from the use of free materials, economic aspects are important as well. The use of these free supplies, if planned wisely, may save the school thousands of dollars annually. Some materials and items of equipment are quite costly, and their purchase would put a considerable burden on the school budget.

Criteria for Selecting Supplementary Materials

Because there is an abundance of supplements available for physical education, the teacher should have some standards by which to judge those that are most effective for instructional purposes. In the professional literature of general education, the teacher will find various criteria for determining the value of auxiliaries for classroom use, such as:

1. *The material must be factual.* It is particularly important that physical education materials be reliable. Because the physical education area is vulnerable to quackery in medical and pharmaceutical claims, special care must be taken to select only the very best materials. The teacher may need to establish or consult a medical-dental advisory board to help him with this task.

2. *The material must be current.* Medical research results in frequent and important changes in physical education knowledge. Supplementary materials should reflect current thinking.

3. *The material must be relevant.* Common sense dictates that the materials be related to the unit being studied.

4. *The materials must aid in developing understanding, ability, and attitude.* One should select only those materials that serve as an extension of the text or the teacher's instruction to help the student understand the unit, broaden his knowledge, and improve his attitude toward physical education.

5. *The material must be appropriate for classroom use.* Materials that go beyond the scope of the unit objectives should be excluded. This is obviously true in such areas of instruction as isometrics.

6. *The material must be appropriate to the level of difficulty.* The teacher should review the materials with the abilities of the students in mind. Generally speaking, lower-ability students need more graphically illustrated material than students with high verbal ability; this is also generally true for students in lower grades. Vocabulary as well as illustrations should be evaluated to determine the level of difficulty of the materials. It is through this evaluation that the teacher plans for individual differences, selecting materials over a range of difficulty comparable to the ability range of the class.

7. *The material must be wihin the financial means of the school.* There is an abundance of free materials in physical education from which the teacher can make selections. Commercially prepared materials, on the other hand, may be desirable but too expensive for the school's budget. It is usually not difficult to find free or inexpensive substitutes to be used with the unit until more desirable materials are within the means of the school.

8. *Other factors of less critical importance should also be considered in selecting supplementary materials.* For example, the materials should be attractively prepared with good format and readability. They should also be of a size and type that make handling and storing relatively easy.

CLASSIFICATION AND TIME ALLOTMENTS FOR PHYSICAL EDUCATION ACTIVITIES

The physical education program draws from thousands of activities that may be included in the curriculum. Teachers should be familiar with the classification of activities in order to evaluate the merits of the program, to assure a balance of activities, and to facilitate research.

Activities have been classified by many authors and professional groups in the professional literature through the years. One such categorization is the following:

1. *Games, sports,* and *athletics:* individual activities such as archery or golf; dual activities such as tennis or badminton; team activities such as football or field hockey.

2. *Rhythmic activities:* such as square, folk, or modern creative dance.

3. *Aquatics:* such as swimming, sailing, or boating.

4. *Self-testing activities:* such as tumbling or running in track and field.

5. *Camping and outdoor activities:* such as canoeing, hiking, or skiing.
6. *Social-recreational activities:* such as skating parties, social dance activities, or cook-outs.
7. *Body-building, corrective, and preventive activities:* such as special conditioning or jogging.

Individual Activities

Individual activities are those in which performance is based entirely on the individual's prowess. The student may be a part of a team of individual performers who represent a school, but individual accomplishment is not dependent upon another person. Bowling is an illustration. Although the participant may be a member of a team, scores are not dependent upon the activity of others.

The need for individual sports is quite apparent. Too often the curriculum consists of a program in team sports, with very little attention given to those activities that will carry over beyond school years. There is overwhelming evidence — from doctors, school administrators, teachers, psychologists, and actual participants —to support the inclusion of individual sports instruction in the physical education curriculum.

One of the reasons that individual sports have received little attention is the difficulty of teaching them. New building blueprints invariably include facilities for basketball and football; there are probably very few high schools in the United States today that do not have gymnasia planned for the basketball team. Only recently, however, have provisions been made for tennis, bowling, golf, wrestling, and other individual activities.

The instructor who wishes to teach tennis skills will find it difficult to arrange a program when only a basketball court and a football field (frequently restricted to football use) are available. It is not difficult to teach volleyball or basketball skills to a class of 40 students in an average gymnasium.

However, to give lessons in tennis skills effectively in this situation requires a great deal of organizational ability.

Group Activities

Group activities are those in which the successful performance of the individual depends upon close teamwork with others. An end in football cannot receive a pass unless the passer performs properly. Individuals cannot play football without teammates. Although individual sports are of great importance for their lifetime value, they do not, as a rule, provide the rugged physiological development that comes from team sports. For growing boys and girls, team sports are essential. The strength, speed, skill, and endurance developed through hockey, touch football, soccer, or basketball are not acquired in many of the individual activities.

The importance of team activities, when kept in perspective, cannot be questioned. For immediate carry-over and physiological development, they are unsurpassed in value. They are of inestimable importance for normal growth and development. Moreover, team competition develops qualities of cooperation, leadership, and teamwork, and provides emotional release and social acceptance — qualities essential to health and personality development.

It is impossible to measure the extent of the deterrent effect that a well-planned intramural program of team activities may have on delinquency. The importance to healthy personality development of associating with other students and receiving intelligent adult supervision cannot be overemphasized. It is natural and normal for children of all ages to form groups and play together. The gregarious drive and the play urge are inherent in human nature. A combination of these two urges brings children together on the playground, in the gymnasium, and in areas near the home. It is the responsibility of physical education teachers to organize and guide the activities of these groups along socially accepted channels.

QUESTIONS FOR DISCUSSION

1. In what ways are a teaching system, a teaching method, and a teaching technique different?

2. Why is it important to understand management devices and methodology?

3. Discuss three critical areas of concern in the secondary school today.

4. What are the advantages in using management devices? Disadvantages? Select one device and apply it to the teaching of a unit in volleyball.

5. What are the most effective methods in teaching skills? In teaching knowledge? in teaching attitudes? Which would you use? Why?

6. List some tools in teaching physical education. Which do you feel are the most important?

7. Why is it important to classify and to allot time for physical education activities?

REFERENCES

1. Maurice R. Ahrens, "Methods Can Make A Difference," *Educational Leadership* (May, 1973), p. 701.

2. Dale Baughman, "What Youth Wants from School," *Phi Delta Kappa Fastbacks* (No. 12, 1972), pp. 27–32.

3. George H. Thompson, "Discipline and the High School Teacher," *The Education Digest* (October, 1976), p. 23.

4. *Ibid.*, p. 20.

5. *Ibid.*, p. 23.

6. Robert F. Biehler, *Phychology Applied to Teaching,* 1st ed. (Boston: Houghton Mifflin Company, 1971) p. 352.

7. Robert F. Biehler, *Psychology Applied to Teaching,* 2nd ed. (Boston: Houghton Mifflin Company, 1974), p. 480.

8. Delbert Oberteuffer and Celeste Ulrich with Charles Mand, *Physical Education,* 4th ed. (Harper and Row Publishers, Inc., 1970), pp. 213–214.

9. Marjorie Prentice, "Systematic Instruction," *Educational Leadership* (Vol. 30, May, 1973), p. 707.

10. Joan E. Farrell, "The Classification of Physical Education Skills," *Quest* (Monograph XXIV, Summer, 1975), pp. 63–67.

11. Bryant, J. Cratty, *Movement Behavior and Motor Learning,* 3rd ed. (Philadelphia: Lea and Febiger, 1973), p. 121.

SELECTED READINGS

Barnes, Ron, "Learning Systems for the Future," *Phi Delta Kappa Fastbacks* (No. 9, 1972).

Davis, Robert, "Writing Behavioral Objectives," *JOHPER* (April, 1973), pp. 47–49.

Ezersky, Eugene M., "Mini-Gyms and Fitness Corners," *JOHPER* (January, 1972), pp. 38–39.

Freischlag, Jerry, "Competency Based Instruction," *JOHPER* (January, 1974), pp. 29–30.

Gentile, John, "Cleveland South High School Lifetime Sports Program," (Cleveland Public Schools, Mimeograph Materials, March, 1977).

Goldberg, Robert A., Schwarts, Steven, and Manard, Stewart, "Individual Differences in Cognitive Processes," *Journal of Educational Psychology* (Vol. 69, No. 1, 1977), pp. 9–14.

Medsger, Betty, "The 'Free' Propaganda that Floods the Schools," *The Progressive* (December, 1976), pp. 42–46.

Pease, Dean A., "Competency-Based Teacher Education," *JOPER* (May, 1975), pp. 20–22.

Shockley, Joe M., Jr., "Needed: Behavioral Objectives in Physical Education," *JOHPER* (April, 1973), pp. 44–46.

Soares, P. L. and E. M. Heimerer, "Use of Formative Evaluation Procedures to Individualize Instruction in Tennis," *Motor Theory into Practice* (Vol. 1, No. 1, Fall, 1976), pp. 5–11.

Stoops, Emery and Joyce King-Stoops, "Discipline or Disaster," *Phi Delta Kappa Fastbacks* (No. 8, 1972).

Wilde, Sim O., "Is Compulsory Attendance Necessary?," *The Education Digest* (March, 1977), pp. 2–5.

Chapter 6

Courtesy Los Angeles Public Schools

QUALITY INSTRUCTION
TRADITIONAL THEORIES OF LEARNING
   THE STIMULUS-RESPONSE (ASSOCIATIVE)
     THEORY
      LAW OF EXERCISE
      LAW OF EFFECT
      LAW OF READINESS
   THE COGNITIVE-FIELD THEORY OF
     LEARNING
   READINESS IN LEARNING
     THE NATURAL APPROACH
     THE CRITICAL PERIOD APPROACH
   TRANSFER OF LEARNING
MODERN LEARNING CONCEPTS
LEARNING IN PHYSICAL EDUCATION
   BASIC AND REFINED SKILLS
   STEPS IN TEACHING SKILLS
GROWTH AND DEVELOPMENT
   THE JUNIOR HIGH SCHOOL STUDENT
     PHYSICAL CHARACTERISTICS
     SOCIAL CHARACTERISTICS
     EMOTIONAL CHARACTERISTICS
     MENTAL CHARACTERISTICS
   THE SENIOR HIGH SCHOOL STUDENT
     PHYSICAL CHARACTERISTICS

     SOCIAL CHARACTERISTICS
     EMOTIONAL CHARACTERISTICS
     MENTAL CHARACTERISTICS
STRATEGIES FOR DEVELOPING MOTIVATION
   MAKE TEACHING INTERESTING
     FEELING OF ACCOMPLISHMENT
     NEEDS OF STUDENTS
     EFFECTIVE TEACHING PROCEDURES
     CHALLENGING SITUATIONS
     COMPETITION IN SKILLS
     TEACHING LIFETIME ACTIVITIES
     RECOGNITION OF ACHIEVEMENT
      INTRINSIC REWARDS
      EXTRINSIC REWARDS
   CULMINATING ACTIVITIES
     COMPETING AGAINST ONESELF
     PARTICIPATING AGAINST OTHER
      INDIVIDUALS
   AVOIDING OVERMOTIVATION
   AVOIDING FAILURE
   TEACHER CHECKLIST
QUESTIONS FOR DISCUSSION
REFERENCES
SELECTED READINGS

THE LEARNING PROCESS

Educators are finding it increasingly difficult to make learning more meaningful to students. Various innovative techniques such as flexible scheduling, team teaching, and educational television have been tried but have not produced the desired results.

Lack of motivation is the most important factor in the poor performance of students. Motivation is the foundation of all learning; without it very little knowledge is absorbed. Psychologists tell us that learning is reflected in behavioral changes, and that this occurs only when the student is stimulated to acquire knowledge. Therefore, the purpose of education essentially is to arouse students' desire to learn.

Developing the play urge is crucial in physical education. This urge, which may be dormant, is one of the basic drives of man and is expressed through natural movements such as running, climbing, and jumping. The medical profession and other authorities have established a minimum amount of activity as necessary for normal growth and development, but the time allotted to physical education during the school day is not adequate to meet this need. Therefore, physical educators must use selected activities and effective instruction to create a desire within the students to participate in certain physical activities during after-school hours.

It is obviously impossible to cover the total volume of knowledge in any subject — mathematics, science, or physical education — within the regular class period. Students must be motivated to learn, to explore, to rehearse, and to apply after school what they have learned in the classroom. Because the physical fitness of youth depends on adequate activity, the school cannot abdicate its responsibility to encourage students in this direction.

Physical education programs in our schools are ideal for guiding youth into activity patterns that will contribute to their health and fitness. First, with a few exceptions, children are required by law to attend school, and thus nearly all children can be reached. Second, schools are designed to bring the appropriate physical facilities and professionally trained personnel together in an environment conducive to learning. Even with these conditions, motivation remains the greatest challenge to the teacher, who must stimulate interest not only within the class period but for lifetime activity as well.

The modern urban environment, where the majority of our youth live, often inhibits or prevents the basic play urge from finding its natural expression. This situation usually intensifies when the child enters school. If readers of this volume were to consider the changes in their own activity, for example, from early childhood until the present, chances are they would find their activity has decreased progressively each year. This is the usual pattern.

Children from birth to their sixth year usually have the opportunity to attain the minimum three to five hours of vigorous activity required daily for normal growth and development. They romp, fall down, climb, run, dodge, chase, and rest as nature demands. Most children satisfy this need in the home or the immediate neighborhood. At the age of six, most children enter school — a predominantly inactive environment. No longer can children spontaneously run, climb, romp, dodge, and engage in the fundamental movements of life freely, as they did before entering school.

In later years, the majority of students become even more inactive. Riding buses and autos, viewing television and motion pictures, preparing homework, and other sedentary activities occupy the hours between the close of the school day and retiring. America probably has the greatest interscholastic sports programs in the world. These programs are important, providing the same opportunity for the physically gifted that advanced study programs provide for the academically gifted. Yet the grass-roots program of sports activities for the masses of boys and girls has not improved much over the years. The urge for activity continues to be stifled. Schools must counteract this situation by motivating youth through carefully planned, effectively taught physical education programs.

QUALITY INSTRUCTION

A major concern of physical education today is the need to improve instruction. It should be emphasized that both motivation of the play urge and encouragement to carry it into afterschool participation depend upon excellent classroom teaching. Through quality skill instruction for sports that may be played after school, students can be stimulated to carry their activity program into the community environment and establish good exercise habits for life.

Every teacher should have a basic understanding of what is known about the way students learn. Considerable psychological research has been conducted through the years, and most teacher-preparation programs require a course in this area. It is not our purpose here to duplicate instruction received elsewhere; instead we review the content of such a course and clarify some of the basic concepts about the learning process. Additional informational sources are provided in the *Resource Manual* that supplements this text.

TRADITIONAL THEORIES OF LEARNING

It is important for teachers to understand that most experiments in learning theories have been planned around academic subjects. Teaching physical education activities, which consists largely of instruction in motor skills, requires different approaches and strategies from those used in teaching academic subjects. However, physical education instructors should have an overall knowledge of how students learn and should understand to what extent theories of learning can be adapted to teaching in physical education. Although we are not sure how learning actually takes place, two concepts now dominate the education field: the *stimulus-response theory* and the *cognitive-field theory*. (The *Resource Manual* gives a composite overview of these learning theories.)

The Stimulus-Response (Associative) Theory

Proponents of the stimulus-response (S-R) theory feel that learning means associating and conditioning. They also believe that the whole is the sum of the parts and that the best way to teach is step by step. The student is asked to perform an act, and if the act is accompanied by pleasure or satisfaction, it will be remembered and repeated. Thorndike is credited with fostering this concept; through his efforts it has played a dominant role in learning theory for many years.

Although the S-R theory has been described in different ways, it has certain intrinsic characteristics. Readers will notice that according to this theory, learning involves correcting and remembering and is basically passive, with emphasis on drills. They will also be aware that teaching is designed to arrange situations that lead to satisfying bonds, and that manipulation is more important than construction.

Three laws of learning are involved in the S-R theory as developed by Thorndike: (1) the law of exercise; (2) the law of effect, and (3) the law of readiness. These have had a tremendous influence on the teaching process for many years.

Law of Exercise. The law of exercise states that the effort (response) made in a situation (stimulus) becomes linked to the situation; the more it is exercised, the more strongly it becomes linked to the situation.

The law of exercise is clearly applicable in the teaching of skills in physical education. Students should participate in activities that are interesting and that satisfy the basic play urge. Instructors teaching physical skills are responsible for providing the best possible demonstration of the skills. Teachers should constantly assist all students in improving their performance in order to maintain a satisfying learning situation. Students will learn skills quickly and effectively if they are shown the correct form and are taught the procedure clearly. Continual practice in the proper techniques will assure improvement, which in turn will bring about satisfaction. Figure 6–1 illustrates how the law of exercise may be applied to an activity.

Law of Effect. The law of effect, or operant learning, is based on the premise that the associations which connect

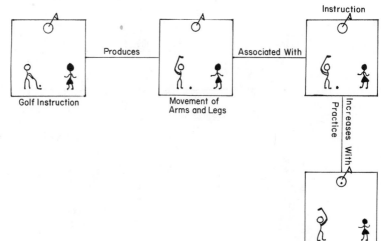

Figure 6–1. Law of exercise.

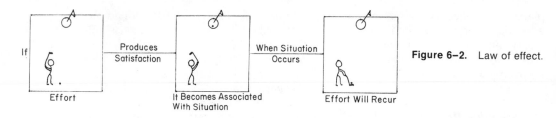

Figure 6–2. Law of effect.

the situation (stimulus) and the effort (response) are strengthened when the effort is satisfying, successful, and pleasant. On the other hand, if the effort is unsuccessful the association is weakened. Figures 6–2 and 6–3 illustrate how the law of effect may be applied to teaching golf and the handspring.

Physical education teachers often express concern about the lack of interest in their classes and about the numerous problems of discipline and inattention. They might profit from the advice of coaches, professional dance teachers, and dramatic club directors — all successful teachers who seem to have no difficulty in persuading participants to report on time, to dress quickly, and to take an active part in the same activity that was repulsive to them in the instructional class. The diagrams point out the importance of good teaching in the application of the law of effect to physical education.

Law of Readiness. The law of readiness postulates that students learn when they are ready to learn. This points to the need for adjusting instruction to the maturity level of the learner, setting the stage for learning by establishing a wholesome teaching climate, and applying the principles of growth and development.

Thorndike's theories have been strongly supported over the years by leaders in education and psychology such as Guthrie, Hall, and Skinner. In recent years, Skinner probably has been the strongest supporter of the view that learning consists of *associations* between stimulus and response. He is known for his extensive experiments with rats and pigeons, from which he developed the programmed instruction that is prevalent in many schools today. Skinner is also one of the most vocal critics of present-day education. He maintains that education is failing because (1) most efforts to im-

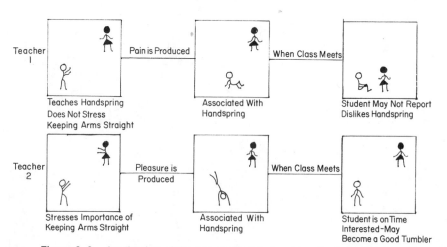

Figure 6–3. Application of the law of effect to teaching the handspring.

prove instruction place little emphasis on method; (2) teachers do not teach — they simply hold the student responsible for learning; and (3) they measure results but neglect teaching and plan examinations designed to show what the student does not know.[1] Skinner also feels that teachers fail because of aversive control, a form of discipline that is less severe but more insidious than corporal punishment. He sees the student as a captive attempting to escape from the threats of a series of minor aversive agents, such as the teacher's displeasure, criticism, or the ridicule of his peers. A serious consequence of aversive control is the student reaction of stubbornness and unresponsiveness.[2] The reader studying the S-R theory may draw the obvious conclusion that the teacher is in absolute control of the learning situation. The ultimate in the S-R theory of learning is the "teaching machine."

Although the S-R theory is the most widely practiced in America, it has been vigorously attacked. Some of the criticisms of the associative view are stated by Biehler: (1) Skinner experimented with lower animals such as rats and pigeons; (2) programmed teaching prevents creativity and borders on regimentation; (3) the programs are so designed that the student answers all responses correctly and will in turn forget quickly; (4) programmed learning is a glorified version of animal-training techniques that are centuries old and are obvious to everyone; and (5) machines may replace teachers.[3] (For a more detailed discussion of the S-R theory see the references in the *Resource Manual*.) Biehler offers suggestions for relating S-R conditioning to the instructional program:

1. Remain aware of the extent and disadvantages of aversive control.
2. Provide as much reinforcement as possible — in most cases, immediately after a student responds.
3. If students generalize erroneously, use selective reinforcement to teach them to discriminate.
4. If you are teaching a subject that has clearly specified terminal behavior, organize the work into units, or steps, and present them in sequence.
5. If you are attempting to shape behavior by leading your students through a progressive sequence of stages, vanish your prompts properly.
6. Keep in mind the impact of different reinforcement schedules on the rate of extinction.
7. Be sure to consider the potential value of programmed instruction when working with the disadvantaged, with slow learners, or with students who lack self-confidence.
8. When appropriate, apply operant conditioning principles in shaping desirable forms of behavior and establishing and maintaining classroom control.[4]

The Cognitive-Field Theory of Learning

The cognitive-field theory proposes that learning is not a response to a stimulus; it is a reaction to the learner's personal reconstruction of the stimulus in terms of the whole situation. The entire learning process is a sequence of intelligent behavior.

Various psychologists claim that learning is best accomplished when the total concept is understood. This approach to learning sometimes creates a chaotic situation because it is based on the simultaneous perception of the many parts of the whole. The teaching situation may seem hopeless until the student suddenly develops the insight to grasp the proper procedure and attain the desired objective.

The cognitive-field theory is characterized by certain principles, which stipulate that learning is (1) a form of intelligent behavior, (2) stimulation of inner forces, (3) based on insight and intuitive thinking, and (4) not repetitive. Finally, the cognitive-field theory involves the whole relationship; learning is not a response to the stimulus but a response to the learner's inner perception of it.

In the cognitive theory of learning, although the teacher still plays an important role in the learning process, *the major emphasis is on the discovery approach*. Instructors place students in situations that require insight to determine the solution to the problem. Advocates of the cognitive theory oppose the stimulus-response theory on the ground that too much time is wasted in the classroom on dull routines, boring drills, and formality, and that children are not allowed to think through a problem or situation, but are coerced into following authoritarian procedures.

There are many people, however, who look with disfavor upon the cognitive theory. Some of their criticisms are that (1) the discovery approach is designed to absolve the teacher from a sense of failure by making instruction unnecessary; (2) the teacher arranges the environment in which discovery takes place, and although he or she suggests lines of inquiry, he or she tells the student nothing; (3) it is impossible for students to discover for themselves any substantial part of the wisdom of their culture — great thinkers build upon the past; they do not waste time discovering it; (4) the position of the teacher who encourages discovery is ambiguous — students may feel that he or she does not know enough of the subject; and (5) a few students may make all the discoveries.[5] Some suggestions for introducing the cognitive-field theory into the instructional program are advanced by Biehler:

1. The first step is to establish a relaxed atmosphere.
2. Next, structure the discussion by presenting a provocative issue or question that will encourage the development of insight.
3. Once the discussion is under way, do your best to keep it on the track. Redirect digressions back to the original subject. Question and analyze points made.
4. Keep in mind the importance of structure in promoting comprehension of new relationships.
5. Consider the possibility that the discovery method is most appropriate for bright, confident, highly motivated students and for topics that lack clear terminal behavior.
6. Make use of the techniques of open education.
7. Consider the possibility that attitudes are more important than subject matter; that how you teach is more important than what you teach.[6]

As they study the theories of learning, teachers and students usually become confused, since it is difficult to apply theories to the actual classroom situation. Each of the two concepts discussed in the foregoing paragraphs has distinct value in planning teaching procedures. Although wide differences seem to exist between the two theories, in reality there are several similarities. Hilgard shows how they complement each other, neither being complete in itself, by suggesting that learning can be graded on a scale with the associative theory placed at one end of the continuum and the cognitive at the other. On the left, habits are learned automatically without awareness and with a minimum of understanding. Tasks that require reasoning and understanding fall to the right of the continuum. Most learning falls somewhere between the associative and the cognitive domains.[7]

A practical application of this premise can be illustrated in learning to serve a tennis ball correctly. Not only does the act involve hitting the ball (associative), but it also entails awareness of the opponent's position on the court, height of the net, position on the court after the serve, placement of the ball in the opponent's court, and anticipation of the opponent's type of return (cognitive).

Readiness in Learning

While it is generally agreed that a state of readiness for learning is essential to education, opinions differ as to just how instructional programs should be structured to create such an atmosphere.

In the course of teaching, moments occur in which the student is optimally ready to learn skills. The teacher should attempt to recognize these opportune moments and to take advantage of them in his or her efforts to make instruction more effective. This is a difficult task, since all students mature at different rates; but if such moods are not recognized and attempts are made to force learning at the wrong time, negative attitudes may result. The "teachable moment" depends on maturation, on which psychologists offer various views. Havighurst believes that children learn developmental tasks at various stages of growth. He relates these tasks to the teachable moment in the following statement:

When the body is ripe, and society requires, and the self is ready to achieve a certain task, the teachable moment has come. Efforts at teaching which would have been largely wasted if they had come earlier, give gratifying results when they come at the *teachable moment* when the task should be learned.[8]

A review of the prevalent theories in psychology regarding the approaches to readiness reveals two concepts as distinctly different as they are controversial. They are described by Biehler as (1) the natural approach and (2) the critical period approach.[9]

The Natural Approach. Some educators and psychologists support the premise that the development of the child depends on natural inner growth and maturation. They feel that children should not be subjected to formal teaching until they have reached that level of maturity at which they are ready to benefit from the instruction.

Hilgard reviews several experiments in human behavior and arrives at generalizations concerning the relationships of maturation to proficiency through training. These are studied in order to relate maturation to learning: (1) skills that build upon developing behavior patterns are most easily learned; (2) the rate of development remains uniform within wide ranges of stimulation; (3) the more mature the organism the less training is needed to reach a given level of proficiency; (4) training given before maturational readiness may bring either no improvement or only temporary improvement; and (5) premature training, if frustrating, may do more harm than good.[10] However, some theorists disagree with the natural or maturational view in structuring educational programs. They feel that the critical period approach is better.

The Critical Period Approach. Proponents of this approach to learning believe that growth and development consist of a series of critical stages through which children should be guided. They feel that the natural approach is too permissive and wasteful and that children learn more when they are guided through the various stages of instruction, with the teacher accelerating the learning process when advisable.

Transfer of Learning

Transfer of learning describes the improvement of a mental or motor function not by direct practice but as a result of practice at a related activity. Teachers of physical education are concerned with transfer from one sport to another, such as adapting learned tennis skills to badminton. Of course, there are sports between which there can be little or no transfer, for example tennis and basketball.

Although the effectiveness of the educational system is dependent on the degree to which the material learned in class transfers to actual life, the premise has definite limitations. Many former beliefs involving transfer have been found to be fallacious:

1. Memorizing facts strengthens the mind.
2. Studying "logical" subjects, such as Latin and geometry, improves one's powers of reasoning.
3. Educating students for "real life" by teaching them specialized, practical skills is unworkable mainly because it is impossible to anticipate the great variety of skills that will be required of different individuals in a rapidly changing civilization.[11]

Regardless of the difficulties that seem to exist in the transfer of skill capacity, there are several principles that may assist in transferring learning to life situations or from one activity to another.

1. *Relate the instructional activities to the actual situations existing beyond the classroom.* This premise places emphasis on the need for a broad intramural program. Instruction in skills is essential but the application should occur as soon as possible in an actual game situation. For example, an inventory may be conducted in the class to determine the performance level of students in basketball skills. It might disclose that some students perform poorly in the lay-up shot, some find difficulty in dribbling, and so on. A wise teacher will pro-

vide opportunity for instruction in these skills; after the instruction the students will transfer what they learn in class to the intramural program on the playground.

2. *When teachers emphasize transfer, maximum transfer can occur.* It should be pointed out to students how skills learned in class will make them better performers beyond the classroom.

3. Effective instruction should always be the goal. Transfer is more likely to occur when instruction is planned. Teachers should bear in mind that seeds for future participation are being planted.

MODERN LEARNING CONCEPTS

Recent views on the ways children learn question the theories advanced by Thorndike and other writers. Gagne summarizes the research of several psychologists that shows that in teaching subjects in school, repetition is not necessary; an item once learned is fully learned. The older concept of learning, which emphasizes strengthening connections, is too simple and does not take into account events that transpire both outside and inside the learner. Theorists sometimes call this concept *information-processing.* Gagne suggests that the most important factor in insuring learning is the awareness of prerequisite capabilities. In other words, the student can learn if he or she is prepared for it.

Conclusions drawn from research in new methods of learning have definite implications for instruction. Gagne offers these guides to the learning process:

1. It is generally recognized that each learner has different prerequisite skills as he attempts to learn a new activity. A complete diagnostic survey should be made of what the child can and cannot already do.
2. The teacher should have available the prerequisites the child has not already mastered.
3. Students do not need additional practice to insure retention but should be subjected to periodic and spaced reviews.[12]

If these modern theories of learning have a message for instructors, it is that teaching is not primarily communicating something to be retained. Teaching should stimulate the student's use of his or her capabilities and must encourage students to realize that they possess requisite abilities for present and future tasks.

LEARNING IN PHYSICAL EDUCATION

Life in the space age necessitates a search for means of better, faster learning. Consequently, new approaches to teaching and fresh theories on the way students learn are constantly emerging, making education in our present culture an ever-changing, dynamic function. The constant change is reflected not only in *what* we teach but also in the *way* we teach. Physical educators, therefore, must not only be familiar with the traditional theories of learning and their applications and their shortcomings but must also be alert to improved concepts and new applications in learning mechanisms.

Basic and Refined Skills

Basic movements, such as crawling, walking, running, and climbing, are assimilated in the course of normal growth. These movements are kinetic, and are part of the general kinesthetic pattern established early and instinctively, since movement is an essential part of life. More refined movements, such as serving a tennis ball, swinging a golf club, pole vaulting, high jumping, wrestling, tumbling, and hundreds of other skills included in the physical education curriculum require instruction and guidance, even though they are closely associated with kinesthetic sense. It is to the acquisition of these skills that learning theories must be applied. At the same time, learning of most skills includes the coordination of muscles, which involves both basic and refined movements.

Steps in Teaching Skills

It is essential that certain prescribed steps be followed in the demonstration and practice procedures of all teaching programs. Students need to be guided through the learning experience; without expert assistance, motivation may not develop. Biehler makes the following suggestions to teachers for making learning experiences proceed smoothly and effectively:

1. If possible and appropriate, analyze the skill to ascertain the specific psychomotor abilities necessary to perform it, arrange these component abilities in order, and help students to master them in this sequence.
2. Provide demonstrations, and as students practice, give verbal guidance to aid mastery of the skill.
   a. Demonstrate the entire procedure straight through, then describe the links of the chain in sequence, and finally demonstrate the skill again step by step.
   b. Allow ample time for students to practice immediately after the demonstrations. (Remember the importance of activity, repetition, and reinforcement.)
   c. As students practice, give guidance verbally or in a way which permits them to perform the skill themselves.
3. Be alert to generalization and interference.[13]

A program for applying learning theories to physical education instruction has been developed in the Omaha, Nebraska, public schools. The plan calls for a pretest of students to determine their level of performance in various activities. Students are then given an individual prescription based on their status. With the help of other students and self-directed learning processes, the students reach a level of performance which is then evaluated by the teacher. This evaluation includes challenge activities as well as psychomotor and cognitive tasks. If the students successfully complete these tasks, the information is placed in their folder and they are provided with a new learning pack based on need. Reinforcement occurs at intervals during the progression. If students fail to complete their tasks, they are given alternatives. At this point the teacher provides individualized instruction with emphasis on encouragement and stronger reinforcement.

The personalized learning program in Omaha includes student-centered learning and individualized instruction. The success of the program depends on certain basic principles:

1. Learning is enhanced by the use of a variety of learning strategies.
2. Learning is enhanced by the use of self-pacing methods.
3. Learning is enhanced through self-direction or self-learning.
4. Learning is enhanced by determining the individual needs of each student and then prescribing a program to meet these needs.
5. Learning is enhanced by stating objectives clearly and in behavioral or performance terms.
6. Psychomotor learning is enhanced by first acquiring understanding of relevant cognitive factors.
7. Learning is enhanced through successful experiences that are positively reinforced.[14]

GROWTH AND DEVELOPMENT

The main purpose of education is to assist young people in their mental, physical, and emotional development as they grow from childhood to adulthood. Effective teacher-preparation programs should therefore provide a thorough background in child growth and development. Physical education teachers are responsible for guiding students through the critical years of maturation. For the program to influence children properly, the content must be geared to their growth needs. You are probably aware of programs that impose adult-type activities upon young children. However, such practices violate all medical research and common sense and may adversely affect the health of children.

Most teacher-preparation programs include several hours in courses such as child growth and development and child and adolescent psychology. These provide insight into the growth needs of various age groups. The requisites for proper child development should always be carefully studied before teaching begins.

Developmental challenges are necessary throughout the growth period if boys and girls are to experience achievement. Havighurst lists eight of these encompassing the junior high school through the senior high school years:

1. Achieving new and more mature relations with age-mates of both sexes.
2. Achieving a masculine or feminine social role.
3. Accepting one's physique and using the body effectively.
4. Achieving emotional independence of parents and other adults.
5. Preparing for marriage and family life.
6. Preparing for an economic career.
7. Acquiring a set of values and an ethical system as a guide to behavior — developing an ideology.
8. Desiring and achieving socially responsible behavior.[15]

The third "developmental task" has challenging implications for physical education. Many problems in behavior and achievement may be alleviated if students are shown that although their particular developmental patterns may differ from those of the average person, they are still normal. Physical education has a responsibility to help students develop a positive self-image. Havighurst suggests the following guidelines:

1. Use criteria of skill and physical development in grouping students for physical education.
2. Teach about the physical changes of adolescence, stressing the normality of variability.
3. Apply criteria of physical development in grouping students at the junior high school level.
4. Use dancing to build up appreciation of the beauty of the human body.
5. Make it easy for a student to ask for information and assurance with respect to his own physical development.[16]

These concepts and developmental tasks are deeply involved in child growth and development throughout the school years. They also stress the range of problems a teacher may face in guiding the students assigned for instruction during these years. Since physical education is concerned with the health and fitness of children, learning about their mental, physical, social, and emotional characteristics facilitates the task of developing relevant and effective curriculum content. Teachers should use the information presented on the following pages to assist them in their planning.

The Junior High School Student

The junior high school student has certain characteristics that affect educational procedures. Teachers should understand these traits, since the anatomical and physiological changes that adolescents undergo have a definite bearing on their psychological attitudes toward school in particular and society in general.

Physical Characteristics. Most girls complete their growth spurt at the beginning of the junior high school period. Boys' growth spurt, however, usually is not completed before the eighth or ninth grade, and it may be quite sudden. Some boys add as much as 6 inches and 25 pounds in a single year.

By this age, almost all the students have reached puberty, and secondary sex characteristics are becoming increasingly apparent. These include the development of breasts and hips in females and the deepening of voice and development of shoulders in males. Adolescent concern about the physical and psychological changes associated with puberty is almost universal. Awkwardness — probably due as much to self-consciousness as to sudden growth — and a great deal of anguish about appearance are common. Both boys and girls take pains with their grooming, and what they may lack in finesse, they more than make up for in imagination and verve.

Although this age period is marked by relatively good health, the diet and sleeping habits of many junior high students are poor. In a television interview, one dietitian estimated that only 10 per cent of all students of junior high school age have an adequate diet.

Physical and mental endurance is limited at this time, probably as a result of several factors: the diet and sleeping habits just mentioned, the draining of energy by the process of growth, and the disproportionately small size of the heart. Although there is no clear-cut agreement on this last point, many authorities stress that the heart does not spurt in its development as the rest of the body does.

Social Characteristics. In junior high, the peer group becomes the source of behavioral codes. Conflicts frequently erupt between the peer code and the adult code, owing partly to the drastic cultural changes that have taken place within the last 20 years. Junior high school students feel a need to conform because they want to be part of the crowd, and they are greatly concerned about what others think of them. As a result, *cliques* are formed, and both friendships and quarrels become more intense. Best friends often replace parents as confidantes.

Girls are generally more advanced socially than boys of the same age. They therefore tend to date older boys, who are at about the same point of maturation. In reaction to this, many younger boys may try to compensate for their immaturity and lack of confidence by teasing and being obstreperously critical of girls.

Emotional Characteristics. At this age, a student is likely to be moody and unpredictable — partly as a result of the biological changes associated with sexual maturation and partly because of his own confusion about whether he is a child or an adult. The lack of self-confidence often manifests itself in boisterous conduct and outbursts of anger. Behavioral patterns at the junior high school level are commonly caused by a combination of psychological tension, biological imbalance, fatigue from overexertion, improper diet, and insufficient sleep.

Adolescents tend to be intolerant and opinionated, probably because it is reassuring for them to think that they possess some type of absolute knowledge. In junior high school, students begin to look at parents and teachers more objectively. Many become angry and disappointed, feeling that they have been deluded into attributing omniscience to mere mortals.

Mental Characteristics. Students at this age can comprehend abstract concepts to an increasing degree and therefore are better able to understand moral and ethical principles. And although the attention span of junior high school students can be quite lengthy, there is usually a tendency to daydream.

The Senior High School Student

Senior high school students must be studied separately from students in junior high school. Their needs are different, and problems that were minor in junior high school may be of major concern in the senior high school years. Conversely, problems that perplexed the junior high school student diminish or disappear as the student matures into senior high school age.

Physical Characteristics. Most students attain physical maturity and virtually all reach puberty during the high school years. Whereas almost all girls reach their ultimate height, boys may continue to grow even after graduation. Tremendous variation exists in height, weight, and rate of maturation. The physical changes associated with puberty cause the older adolescent to have the appearance of an adult. His realization that there will be no further physical changes due to growth may add to an already extreme self-consciousness.

Sexual maturity is linked to glandular changes and imbalance. General health is quite good — again, in spite of the eating and sleeping habits of most adolescents.

Social Characteristics. The peer group dominates the lives of most students and the conflict between the peer and the adult codes increases. Pressures to conform are extreme, the most obvious sign of this being fads in dress.

The most pervasive preoccupation of many students is the opposite sex. Dating, going steady, and marriage dominate the thoughts and conversation of adolescents during this period. Girls are still more mature socially than boys of the same age and continue to date older boys. They tend to have a small number of close girl friends, whereas boys usually maintain a wider circle of male friends on a more casual basis. But because of the competitive nature of both dating and schoolwork, neither boys nor girls may feel that they can completely trust these friends.

Emotional Characteristics. Adolescent revolt is a universal expression of the maturation from childhood to adulthood. Our society does not have any clearly prescribed forms of behavior for coping with this difficult transition. As a result, the adolescent takes matters into his or her own hands. Because of their increasing independence, many adolescents are in frequent conflict with their parents. They may turn to the teacher for sympathy and advice.

Students at this age are given to daydreaming, especially about their future. Many tend to overestimate their abilities and their chance of entering the professions or of holding other high-status jobs.

Mental Characteristics. People of high school age have close to maximum intellectual efficiency, but their lack of experience limits both their knowledge and their ability to use what they know. Students' realization that they need to develop their own "philosophy of life" in regard to ethical, political, and religious matters may be threatening and frightening, but it offers an excellent opportunity for guided discussion in the school.[17]

Various learning theories and teaching skills have been presented to assist teachers in improving instruction. *Motivation underlies all efforts to improve the quality of teaching. Motivation is the key to all learning, and teachers who are able to stimulate children successfully will find teaching more interesting and satisfying.*

Fortunately, physical education teachers do not have the same motivational problem that besets teachers of academic subjects. Earlier in this chapter it was pointed out that boys and girls are by nature self-motivated to move and play. This play urge continues throughout life in varying degrees unless it is inhibited by poor programs or other factors that interfere with its normal manifestation.

The remainder of the chapter is concerned with techniques for developing motivation and how these may be applied to physical education.

STRATEGIES FOR DEVELOPING MOTIVATION

As teachers plan programs of physical education, they should include strategies that motivate students to learn. Principles that teachers must remember are (1) motivation is the key to all learning, (2) motivation is a continuous process, and (3) different strategies should be used since each student reacts differently to learning situations.

Many strategies may be involved in motivating students to learn. The more common techniques include (1) capturing interest, (2) including a culminating activity, (3) avoiding overmotivation, and (4) avoiding failure.

Make Teaching Interesting

The teacher domination method of instruction that is prevalent in today's schools does not motivate students. However, it is possible for teachers to give instruction in what they feel is important without becoming boring. Interest may be developed by (1) allowing students to gain a feeling of accomplishment, (2) basing the activity on student needs, (3) using effective teaching procedures, (4) creating challenging situations, (5) providing competition in skills, (6) teaching life-time activities, and (7) recognizing achievement.

Feeling of Accomplishment. Teaching units should be planned to provide students with a feeling of accomplishment at the end of each class. This satisfaction should be great enough to motivate the student to continue the effort beyond the class period. Classes in which large numbers of students dress in their uniforms, come to class, behave themselves, and otherwise meet all the requirements for the class period, and never have the opportunity to hit a softball, shoot a basketball, or serve a volleyball because of faulty organizational procedures provide very little feeling of self-worth to the student.

An illustration of this regrettable situation is the manner in which softball is frequently introduced. Teachers will divide a class into two or four groups and tell the students to play softball. One group goes into the field and another remains at bat. Day after day the procedure continues, and many of the students never field a ball or bat even once. It is impossible to justify such a program. Not only is interest in a generally popular activity diminished by such procedures, but the development of fitness is nonexistent. An alternative to this procedure would be to divide the entire class into five groups with five balls and five bats. Each group would have a catcher, a pitcher, three batters, and three fielders. Emphasis would be on teaching skills in which all students field and bat several times during the class period.

Needs of Students. Largely because of certain anatomical limitations, as well as psychological and physiological deviations, boys and girls develop desires for certain activities and keen prejudices against others. After students have been subjected to a required program through the elementary school and usually in the junior high school, they are usually qualified to decide what activity they wish to pursue. A valuable teaching procedure is to allow students in the senior high school to participate in the activities appropriate to their capabilities. However, the choice should be made only after proper orientation to a wide variety of activities.

Effective Teaching Procedures. The importance of good teaching to motivation has been discussed earlier in this chapter. Effective procedures are essential to the total program, and teachers must experiment to discover which methods are best for each class. Poor teaching is probably the single most important reason why many students dislike the physical education class. For instance, the teacher who gives a skill test to a class of 40 students and allows the entire class to sit while each student takes the test is sure to elicit boredom and disgust instead of interest. Moreover, improper teaching procedures often create disciplinary problems; effective teaching procedures, on the other hand, usually elicit wholesome behavior from the students.

Challenging Situations. Students enjoy measuring their ability to perform a skill or proficiency test, and the instructional period should provide this challenge. An illustration is the procedure employed in giving group proficiency tests. Teachers periodically give fitness tests in the pull-up and standing broad jump. In order for these to be challenging and effective, they must be administered in a dignified atmosphere, the procedures must be well organized, and the student must understand the purpose of the tests. One way of accomplishing all this is to post the averages for each test, by grade, on the wall close to the testing location. As the student takes the test, he sees the average for his grade and is challenged to equal it or to exceed it. These standards are not used for classifying the student into a fitness category nor are they used for evaluation. Instead, they motivate the students to extend themselves — which in turn contributes to fitness — and to explore their own potential.

Competition in Skills. Each skill taught in the instructional period should be placed on a competitive basis. The teacher must be creative in finding ways to do this. One example might be teaching dribbling and passing a basketball to a class. After the students have learned the dribble and the pass, the two skills may be combined into a dribble and pass relay race. Note, however, that placing the skill on a competitive basis does not mean placing the entire *sport* on a competitive basis during the class period.

Teaching Lifetime Activities. In order for learning to be truly effective, it must be transferable to broader fields of activity. Studies have been made in academic subjects showing the lack of retention after the student completes the course.[18] Learning should not stop at the end of the period or term or at graduation. Students should be inspired to further their efforts through investigation and activity beyond the school day and school years if the learning is to be of any value.

Recognition of Achievement. It is basic in our culture to receive some type of award or recognition for practically everything one does. In school, grades are given for different levels of achievement, and monograms or certificates are presented to athletes in recognition of accomplishments. Community service is recognized by presenting the individual with a citation, certificate, or prize. Various organizations, educational and otherwise, have awards ranging from the Phi Beta Kappa key to automobiles. Of course, people receive salaries for services rendered.

In education, considerable attention has been focused on the types of rewards for accomplishment that follow the learning process. These rewards may be classified as intrinsic or extrinsic.

INTRINSIC REWARDS. Practical observation supports the claim that people receive many lasting rewards from educational effort that are more valuable than material awards, which are soon forgotten. These lasting rewards are intangible, or intrinsic. The intercollegiate football player, hero of the campus during college years, receives letters, makes speeches at banquets, and is the most sought-after individual of the school. The third-string tennis player is unknown and never receives a letter. Years later the letters and certificates given to the football player are forgotten and have no value. The intrinsic values acquired by the third-string tennis player carry over into later life and contribute to his health and happiness.

EXTRINSIC REWARDS. Extrinsic rewards are those of a tangible nature and may have monetary value. It has been common practice for many years to give rewards in all aspects of education. Grades, monograms, cups, and certificates are examples. Students are aware of awards and, traditionally, expect something for their efforts.

Many people feel that overemphasizing extrinsic awards may be undesirable. Extrinsic awards can become repetitious, which decreases their motivational value. Athletes strive to win the first letter award; succeeding awards become less important and provide very little motivation. However, the desire for competition furthers the participating effort. Extrinsic awards have little effect on accomplishment if the potential is insufficient. For example, if a student, because of anatomical limitations, performs poorly in the pull-ups, no amount of extrinsic awards will produce satisfactory results.

The fallibility of extrinsic recognition is illustrated by the use of marks and grades in our schools and colleges. Competition for credit has become so intense that the real values of education frequently are lost. Leaders in education should attempt to place values on dedication to a given field rather than on the credit involved. Intrinsic motivation should precede extrinsic motivation. The desire to excel should precede the award that may be given for excelling.

Culminating Activities

Teachers should arrange for some type of culminating activity at the end of the instructional cycle that provides the opportunity for students to test their ability. When students continually practice skills without testing their progress, the instructional program becomes stale and unstimulating. A football team that practices during the week and never participates against an opponent will eventually disintegrate because of lack of interest. There are two means by which individuals may test their progress: competition against themselves or an average score and competition against other individuals.

Competing Against Oneself. Psychologists speak of the advisability of limiting competition for young children to that in which they contend against themselves or a predetermined score. Bowling and proficiency tests such as pull-ups, sit-ups and the broad jump are activities in which the individual participates against himself or against a previous score. Many psychologists feel that there is already enough competition in the present educational system. Biehler states:

> To avoid these disadvantages, encourage students to compete against themselves, try to give each student some experiences of success by arranging situations in which everyone has a fairly equal chance in a variety of activities, and make use of group competition situations that stress fun rather than winning.[19]

Participating Against Other Individuals. The current American system is based on competition. People compete against each other for jobs, recreation, and social status. To end these contests would amount to tampering with the very roots of our culture. The idea is not to eliminate or inhibit competition but to use it wisely.

The majority of individuals benefit from competition with each other in activities that are suited to their normal growth and development and their age level. The qualities developed through competition on teams or with other individuals — such as perseverance, fortitude, and give and take — parallel the qualities needed for living in a democratic culture. Competition is a great motivator for beyond school participation. Successful teachers will study its effects and devise plans to make competition work most effectively in their instruction.

Avoiding Overmotivation

There are many natural channels for motivation in physical education. Unless the teacher is careful, it is comparatively easy to overemphasize an activity. This leads to overmotivation, which may retard learning and de-crease the child's desire for further participation.

Teachers, coaches, administrators, and parents make a grave error when they impose certain types of adult activities upon young children. The adverse effects of Little League baseball, midget football, and other types of activities not suitable for young children are well known. These activities vividly illustrate overmotivation and violate all laws of growth and development. If parents would leave children to themselves after the initial organization of a program, the results would be more satisfying.

It was pointed out early in this chapter that the natural play urge of boys and girls will progress on its own initiative, but that proper guidance is necessary. However, the play urge may be suppressed if there are too many awards, too much pressure, and too much criticism — all of which have adverse effects on the emotional stability of children.

Avoiding Failure

Children respond to failure in various ways. Some students react by exhibiting aggressive and antisocial tendencies, whereas others respond by withdrawal from the situation. Withdrawing from reality can lead to psychotic behavior.

Teachers of physical education should try to motivate students and provide opportunities for success and self-expression. Emphasis should be placed on individual differences, students' interests, and planning the curriculum to allow for individual improvement and expression. Activities in which a student may compete with himself or a given score should receive considerable attention in planning the program.

Teacher Checklist

A checklist for motivating strategies may be a valuable tool for the teacher. Such a checklist is shown in Figure 6–4.

	Yes	No
Do your students participate in planning programs?	( )	( )
Are students' suggestions incorporated in the program?	( )	( )
Are you fair and consistent with your students?	( )	( )
Do you determine students' abilities and capitalize on them?	( )	( )
Do you compliment students when they deserve it?	( )	( )
Do you give recognition for outstanding performances?	( )	( )
Do you show students that you enjoy your work?	( )	( )
Do you maintain an adequate level of fitness yourself?	( )	( )
Do you maintain an open-door policy for students?	( )	( )
Is your grading system including improvement in skills?	( )	( )
Do you know the interests of students?	( )	( )
Do you provide adequate time for individualized instruction?	( )	( )
Do you allow students to evaluate units of work?	( )	( )
Is your instruction clear, articulate, and adequately projected?	( )	( )
Do you explain the purpose of the program?	( )	( )
Is a variety of exercises provided in the program?	( )	( )
Are the values of exercises discussed?	( )	( )
Are rhythmic movements involving music involved?	( )	( )
Do you exercise with students occasionally?	( )	( )
Do your provide individualized help during the exercise period?	( )	( )
Do you incorporate basic skills as part of the exercise program?	( )	( )
Is the dressing area always clean and attractive?	( )	( )
Do you explain the importance of dressing properly?	( )	( )
Do you dress appropriately?	( )	( )
Are dressing requirements adequately explained?	( )	( )
Are procedures for being on time defined and implemented?	( )	( )
Are efficient plans for organizing the dressing area made?	( )	( )
Do you provide time for discussing the activity?	( )	( )
Do you maintain an adequate climate, free from distractions?		
Is equal time given to the unskilled?	( )	( )
Is your organization of the class practical and efficient?	( )	( )
Do you vary routine occasionally to prevent boredom?	( )	( )
Are participation and effort included in grading?	( )	( )
Are assignments for extra credit provided?	( )	( )
Is information available enabling absentees to keep up?	( )	( )
Are multi-media generously used for improving instruction?	( )	( )

Figure 6-4. Checklist of motivating techniques. (*Physical Education Newsletter.* Adapted from "Motivational Techniques to Use in Secondary Physical Education," Physical Education Publications. Old Saybrook, Conn., March 15, 1975.)

QUESTIONS FOR DISCUSSION

1. Explain what is meant by motivation and its importance in education.
2. What is the play urge, and how has it been affected by urban life?
3. What is learning?
4. Briefly differentiate between the two general learning theories.
5. Discuss the characteristics of Thorndike's theory as they relate to traditional physical education.
6. How would the implementation of the cognitive-field theory affect the instructional program?
7. Distinguish between the two concepts on readiness that affect the structure of an educational program.
8. How can learning theories be applied to physical education instruction to provide optimum learning experiences?
9. Discuss the learning strategies of developing motivation.
10. Using the concepts discussed in this chapter, explain the importance of developing a broad intramural program in schools.

REFERENCES

1. Robert F. Biehler, *Psychology Applied to Teaching,* 2nd ed. (Boston: Houghton Mifflin Company, 1974), p. 211.
2. *Ibid.*
3. *Ibid.,* p. 222.
4. *Ibid.,* p. 229.
5. *Ibid.,* p. 248.
6. *Ibid.,* p. 252.
7. Ernest R. Hilgard, et al., *Introduction to Psychology,* 6th ed. (New York: Harcourt Brace Jovanovich, 1975), p. 218.
8. Robert J. Havighurst, *Developmental Tasks and Education,* 3rd ed. (New York: David McKay Company, 1972), p. 7.
9. Biehler, *op. cit.,* p. 98.
10. Hilgard, *op. cit.,* p. 71.
11. Biehler, *op. cit.,* p. 357.
12. Robert M. Gagne, "Some New Views of Learning and Instruction," *Phi Delta Kappan* (Journal of Phi Delta Kappa, May, 1970), p. 468.
13. Biehler, *op. cit.,* p. 373.
14. *Physical Education Newsletter* (Old Saybrook, Conn.: Physical Education Publications, March 15, 1977).
15. Havighurst, *op. cit.,* p. 45.
16. *Ibid.,* p. 75.
17. Biehler, *op. cit.,* pp. 171–183.
18. "Little Improvement in Skills," *Education USA* (August 7, 1972).
19. Biehler, *op. cit.,* p. 435.

SELECTED READINGS

Bucher, Charles A., *Foundations of Physical Education,* 4th ed. (Saint Louis: The C. V. Mosby Company, 1975).
Clarke, H. Harrison, "Physical Activity and Coronary Heart Disease," *Physical Fitness Research Digest* (Washington, D.C., April, 1972).
Johnson, Warren and E. R. Buskirk, *Science and Medicine of Exercise and Sports* (New York: Harper and Row, Publishers, 1974).
Leonard, George, "Physical Education for Life," *Today's Education* (October, 1975), p. 75.
Rarick, G. Lawrence, ed. *Physical Activity, Human Growth and Development* (New York: Academic Press, 1973).
Stanley, Philip L., "Implementing Off-Campus Athletics," *JOPER* (June, 1974), p. 20.
Strom, Robert D. and Torrance, Paul E., *Education for Affective Achievement* (New York: Rand McNally and Company, 1973).

Chapter 7

Courtesy Belvedere Junior High School, Los Angeles City Schools.

PHYSICAL EDUCATION: A TEACHING PROGRAM
BEYOND SCHOOL ASSIGNMENTS
    ALTERNATIVE PROGRAMS
WHEN CLASSES ARE LARGE
    OVERFLOW PLAN
SELF-EVALUATION
SKILL COMPETITION
RECOMMENDED DAILY HOURS OF EXERCISE
    INTENSITY OF THE EXERCISE PROGRAM
    MENTAL EFFORT AND EXERCISE
INTERPRETATION THROUGH DISCUSSION
THE DRESSING AREA
HOW MANY ACTIVITIES SHOULD TEACHERS
SUPERVISE SIMULTANEOUSLY?
CLASSIFICATION FOR ASSIGNMENT TO
PHYSICAL EDUCATION
    GROUPING FOR INSTRUCTION
        ABILITY GROUPING
            TITLE IX AND ABILITY GROUPING
        HEIGHT AND WEIGHT
        AGE AND GRADE
THE WARM-UP
CREATIVITY

RHYTHMICAL MOVEMENT
    INNOVATIVE TEACHING STRATEGIES
THE TEACHER AND LEGAL LIABILITY
    CONSTANT SUPERVISION
    TEACHING SAFE ACTIVITIES
    CORRECT TEACHING PROCEDURES
    TEACHING GUIDE
    HEEDING EXCUSES
    ORGANIZING THE FACILITIES
    INSTRUCTION
STRENGTH AND PHYSICAL EDUCATION
    THE PRINCIPLE OF OVERLOAD
        NATURAL OVERLOAD
        SPECIAL OVERLOAD FOR SPORTS
        TRAINING
        NONFUNCTIONAL OVERLOAD
    PHYSICAL EDUCATION AND OVERLOAD
    LAW OF RECIPROCAL INNERVATION
THE HEALTH OBJECTIVE
UNDESIRABLE ACTIVITIES
QUESTIONS FOR DISCUSSION
REFERENCES
SELECTED READINGS

TEACHING AIDS AND STRATEGIES

PHYSICAL EDUCATION: A TEACHING PROGRAM

Education today is struggling through a transitional period so replete with cross-currents and uncertainties that the future of all areas of instruction is unclear. One likelihood, however, is that *accountability* will be a key factor in whatever form of education survives. Physical education leaders must establish and fulfill higher standards for education if they expect their programs to remain in the curriculum. As a rule, a physical education department can maintain a respected position within the school and the community when teaching of high caliber is practiced consistently. Departments that implement informal play-type programs, on the other hand, often discover that physical education is either completely excluded from the curriculum or relegated to an obscure position.

There is no justification for unstructured play in the instructional program. Early leaders in physical education pointed out the importance of using the time allotted in the school day for teaching those skills that would be used spontaneously in the after-school programs.[1] The same principle is just as valid today. Instruction should be the major objective of the physical education class and play should be restricted to after-school hours.

Many problems are involved in teaching physical education successfully, and students of the profession should be prepared to cope with them when they become teachers. In this chapter, teaching aids for new as well as experienced teachers are discussed.

BEYOND SCHOOL ASSIGNMENTS

Experience has shown that assigning tasks to students that extend beyond the school day is valuable not only for interpreting physical education but for improving of skill performance. Within the school program, students are screened by objective tests in skill. Those who do not achieve the suggested level of performance for their age are encouraged to practice outside of school and report the results to the class. This procedure carries the program into the home and assists students in attaining the desired results. Projecting physical education activity beyond the school day has been successfully developed by Dean Rippon at Rutland High School, Rutland, Vermont. He bases half of the physical education grade on outside activity.[2]

Alternative Programs

Closely related to the concept discussed above is the movement toward alternative programs. Many schools do not have adequate facilities for teaching the skills of lifetime sports such as bowling and swimming. Teachers with a little imagination are providing instruction in these activities by using community facilities. For example, bowling alley proprietors are interested in promoting this sport and frequently are eager to cooperate with schools in the use of their facilities.

Students and teacher may be bused to the alleys for instruction. When flexible scheduling exists, it is relatively simple to provide sufficient time in the school day for alternative programs.

WHEN CLASSES ARE LARGE

Teachers are often faced with the problem of teaching fundamental skills to large classes in small spaces. Sometimes the situation becomes so untenable that teachers abandon desirable activities and resort to informal play, with undesirable results. Leaders must constantly seek effective and interesting ways of teaching skills to motivate the students. They must also keep in mind certain principles of organization, which apply to all activities, whenever they are working with large classes:

1. Teach skills — this should be the objective. Play should take place after school.
2. Divide the class into as many small groups as possible.
3. Use all equipment or tools available. Get more if possible.

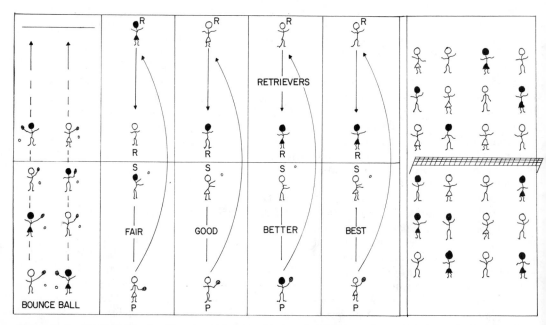

Figure 7–1. Teaching the backhand and forehand in tennis to a large class using the volleyball overflow. Players are designated as *P*, set-up students as *S*, and retrievers as *R*.

4. Classify groups according to ability. Place the more gifted students together.
5. Use small groups to simulate actual game situations.
6. Always emphasize the value of the activities to the students. Discuss the importance of learning skills for carry-over and better performance.
7. Use the overflow plan.

Overflow Plan

Many sports are difficult to teach because of the need for individualized instruction. While the teacher is working with a few students in the basic activity, the majority of the class may remain idle. This presents a disciplinary problem. In order to avoid wasted class time, the principle of overflow is used. The teacher gives instruction in the skills of a basic activity to one group and the remainder of the class participates in a team activity that accommodates large numbers safely without the need for intensive supervision. Volleyball is the best activity to use for the overflow. Figure 7–1 illustrates how this principle is employed in teaching tennis to a large class (48 students) and Figure 7–2 shows a golf class using the overflow principle. See Chapter 9 for the teaching procedures involved.

SELF-EVALUATION

From time to time teachers should evaluate their program to determine whether they are reaching their goals. In the daily routine of teaching, it is easy for teachers to deviate from the standards that distinguish a good program from a mediocre one. Good teaching, like charity, begins at home; thus any program evaluation must logically begin with the teachers themselves. Self-appraisal has been found helpful in guiding teachers and, when necessary, in redirecting their daily teaching efforts. The motivational chart found in Chapter 6 may be helpful to both beginning and experienced teachers in making an inventory of their attitudes and teaching procedures. Figure 7–3 itemizes specific details involved in self-evaluation.

SKILL COMPETITION

Students might enjoy practicing skills, but their objective is to be able to play the actual game effectively. To make students continually practice without actual participation is a sure way of destroying interest and motivation.

The bulk of participation will, of course, occur after school in intramural competition, recreation programs, and

Figure 7–2. The principle of overflow in teaching the skills of golf. Volleyball overflow is shown in the background. (Courtesy Rosemont Junior High School, Norfolk, Virginia.)

	Yes	No
Class Organization		
Do I organize my classes to provide maximum use of time?	( )	( )
Are all students participating at all times?	( )	( )
Do I use student leaders to assist with the program?	( )	( )
Instruction		
Do I group students by ability?	( )	( )
Do I use grouping by ability to provide individualized instruction?	( )	( )
Is the program based on the needs and interests of students?	( )	( )
Do I use all available facilities, supplies, and equipment?	( )	( )
Do I include lifetime activities in the program?	( )	( )
Do I provide ample time for students to master their chosen activities?	( )	( )
Do I allow students a periodical selection of activities?	( )	( )
Rapport		
Do the majority of students seem to respect me?	( )	( )
Do students cooperate with me?	( )	( )
Do I assist students with their individual problems?	( )	( )
Do other members of the department cooperate with me?	( )	( )
Interpreting the Program		
Do I interpret the program to parents?	( )	( )
Do I publicize the program throughout the community?	( )	( )
Do I organize demonstrations and invite the public?	( )	( )
Do I familiarize the principal with the program?	( )	( )
Do I explain the purposes of physical education to the faculty?	( )	( )
Safety		
Am I familiar with tort law, negligence, and liability?	( )	( )
Do I teach elements of safety for each activity to students?	( )	( )
Do I implement all safety rules within my activity?	( )	( )
Supervision		
Do I stay with my class at all times?	( )	( )
Do I supervise no more than one activity simultaneously?	( )	( )
Am I able to see all students at all times in all places?	( )	( )
Discipline		
Do I handle most of my discipline problems?	( )	( )
Am I able to maintain decorum in my classes?	( )	( )
Do I communicate with parents regarding discipline?	( )	( )
Do I employ current measures for discipline problems?	( )	( )
Care of Equipment		
Do I take care of equipment?	( )	( )
Do I teach students the proper care of equipment?	( )	( )
Do I keep a record of all equipment used each period?	( )	( )
Have I developed a sound plan for storing equipment?	( )	( )
Have I developed a sound plan for checking equipment each period?	( )	( )
Professional Preparation		
Do I hold membership in professional organizations?	( )	( )
Do I seek self-improvement through workshops, etc.?	( )	( )

SELF-EVALUATION

In view of the above I feel that I am a:
Superior teacher
Good teacher
Fair teacher

Figure 7–3. Self-evaluation of teaching efficiency. (Every teacher is not expected to have done all the things suggested above. However, this check list is intended to serve as (1) an aid to improving instruction, (2) a guide to self-evaluation, and (3) a means of determining programs planned toward the objectives of a quality program.)

informal play in backyards. Regardless of where the activity takes place, skill proficiency is basic to motivation. Lack of knowledge of the skill destroys interest, especially when students reach a performance plateau and are not led into higher levels of competency.

Basic skills should, however, be placed in highly competitive situations during the instructional period. For example, the basketball dribble-and-shoot relay may be used to provide competition in the class. All the students can be involved, thus eliminating the undesirable practice of allowing two teams to play a game with the remainder of the class on the sidelines.

RECOMMENDED DAILY HOURS OF EXERCISE

It is generally recognized that children need between two and three hours of vigorous exercise daily. However, it is difficult to prescribe the amount of daily exercise needed by all students. It would be better to provide the opportunity for activity participation and then allow the natural urge for movement to determine the amount of exercise necessary for each individual. The following guides to exercising have a great deal of merit:
1. Students should always warm up before performing vigorous movements. The warm-up is discussed later in this chapter.
2. Students should follow a definite pattern of exercise, ranging from an absolutely quiet formation at the beginning of the period, with a gradual increase in the vigor and intensity of movement, to the point where maximal effort is reached. After a period of sustained movement, the exercise program should diminish in intensity until the effort is inhibited as it was at the beginning of the period. From this intensity curve, the daily lesson guide is formed. This is shown in Chapter 9.
3. Exercises should be scientifically selected. Many exercises used today

are contraindicated and some may do more harm than good.

Intensity of the Exercise Program

Given the average daily activity requirement of two to three hours, the question arises of how strenuous the exercise should be during the physical education class. The needed intensity level of exercise varies with the individual and is related to the play urge. What is mandatory for the development of the interscholastic athlete is not necessary for most students. No one can say how much running is necessary or how many times an individual should chin the bar to promote normal growth and development. Who, then, should determine how intense the exercise should be? The answer is the students themselves. Each individual knows his or her physiological limits because nature has implanted in each person a built-in urge for activity that, if allowed to follow its natural pattern, will lead to enough exercise for normal growth and development. The physical education program should provide the motivation and the outlet for this natural urge.

Teachers tend to prescribe a certain amount of calisthenics or activity for an entire class. This cannot be justified scientifically because some students may not be able to attain the level demanded, whereas others could easily surpass it. Instead of telling an entire class to do 10 push-ups or 20 sit-ups, it is wiser to ask all students to do as many, correctly, as they are able to. This would allow for personal differences and would provide each individual with activity sufficient to his or her needs. Similar procedures should be followed in all physical education activities. It is the responsibility of the teacher to explore each activity and to find out how students can be motivated to perform within their physiological limits.

There are many advantages to allowing students to follow their own patterns of activity, some of which are:
1. The plan by which students exercise

at their own rate is scientifically sound. The exercise is defined at the students' level and is not a teacher-prescribed movement. Participants will proceed at their own paces, and the self-interest that grows out of this procedure will motivate them to practice and improve. Because the urge comes from within and not from teacher domination, the interest will be more lasting and the values accrued more meaningful.

2. When students practice and perform these movements on their own, the teacher has the opportunity to walk around the class and to assist individuals in their efforts.
3. Teachers are able to conserve their energy and strength, and at the end of the day they are not nearly so exhausted as they were when they dominated each class period.

Mental Effort and Exercise

Educators are concerned about the effects of strenuous activity on mental effort in the classroom. Opinion points to the need for short and moderate exercise during the instructional period, with the severe muscular work performed after school hours.[3] Many teachers propose strenuous exercise plans, subjecting students to an exhausting series of activities that does not follow a scientific intensity curve for training and that taxes participants beyond their physiological limits. This is educationally unsound, since our aim is to provide just enough exercise for the health needs of students.

Of all the activities that can be included in the curriculum, the formal, teacher-dominated types are the most exhausting. For exercise to assist normal growth and development, it should be carried on for many hours. To exhaust students in a short time is not conducive to physiological development and may have adverse effects on their health and fitness. Learning and practicing skills provides an adequate amount of activity for the school day. If motivated properly, the student will find the opportunity to participate more vigorously after school.

INTERPRETATION THROUGH DISCUSSION

Teachers should always explain the purpose of the activity being taught. It is worthless to walk into the classroom and begin teaching an activity without explaining why it should be learned. Skills and exercises become more interesting when students understand their importance. Sometimes they may question the value of certain conditioning exercises, particularly those involving the abdominal area. After the purpose of these exercises has been discussed, both interest and motivation increase, and students will often practice the exercises at home.

THE DRESSING AREA

The physical education class begins in the dressing room. Organizing dressing room procedures is essential to the overall success of physical education. Smooth traffic flow, locker assignments designed to prevent congestion, orderly use of showers and towels, and plans to save time and prevent confusion are some of the factors that should be considered when one is organizing each period of physical education.

HOW MANY ACTIVITIES SHOULD TEACHERS SUPERVISE SIMULTANEOUSLY?

Safety and effective instruction should always be uppermost in the mind of the teacher. These two requirements indicate that the teacher should be concerned with only one activity at a time. Each activity should receive an allotted amount of time, with the teachers concentrating all their efforts on improving skills in that activity. To teach the skills of basketball in one area and simultaneously to allow a group to practice tumbling in another will present safety problems; moreover, such situations are not conducive to good instruction and effective supervision. One exception to this principle is the overflow plan described earlier in this chapter.

CLASSIFICATION FOR ASSIGNMENT TO PHYSICAL EDUCATION

Teachers should never minimize the importance of classifying students *before assignment* to physical education. The need for this is emphasized by the Committee on Exercise and Physical Fitness of the American Medical Association. The committee maintains that unnecessary restriction of physical activity can interfere with the students' development and that when suitable programs exist, excuses from physical education are unnecessary. The Committee's objectives for classification of individual needs are:

1. To safeguard the health of participants. Adequate protective measures are necessary for safe and enjoyable participation.
2. To group students for effective learning. Some degree of homogeneity within a group is essential to optimum learning.
3. To equalize competitive conditions. Reasonable matching of players is a requisite for safe and equitable competition.
4. To facilitate progress and achievement. Similar levels of skill among students are helpful to satisfying performance.

The committee recommends four general categories for classifying all students in physical education. These groups are based on the findings of medical examinations:

1. Unrestricted activity — full participation in physical education and athletic activities.
2. Moderate restriction — participation in designated physical education and athletic activities.
3. Severe restriction — participation in only a limited number of events at a low level of activity.
4. Reconstructive or rehabilitative — participation in a prescribed program of corrective exercises or adapted sports.[4]

In conjunction with the classification of students, the committee strongly advises cooperation between the school and local physicians. Figure 7–4 shows a form that was developed jointly by physicians and schools for categorization and is highly recommended for general use.

Categories 2, 3, and 4 are applicable for handicapped students, students who are convalescing, and other students who need special attention. Students with these problems are discussed in Chapter 10. Grouping of students in the "unrestricted" category after they have been scheduled to physical education class is discussed in the following sections.

Grouping for Instruction

After having been assigned to physical education class, students may be grouped for instruction in several ways. Teachers should familiarize themselves with the methods and select the most practical for each situation. No program in physical education is complete or adequate if it does not include some sound form of grouping. When students are grouped by using one or several of the categories shown in this section, the competition will be more balanced; instruction will be more scientific; the program will have more continuity; and the health and safety needs of students will be met.

Ability Grouping. Classifying students by ability is an extremely effective teaching strategy. Such grouping may be carried out through the use of scores in motor ability tests, fitness tests, and skill tests.

Recently, much publicity has been given to ability grouping in education. Physical education teachers are in a better position to group and to teach by this procedure than instructors in any other subject in the curriculum, yet it has become a lost art in physical education. Alert teachers can easily observe students and classify them as good or poor, beginners, intermediates, and advanced. Each class has students with varying degrees of skill, and a

*REPORT TO SCHOOL ON SIGNIFICANT FINDINGS OF HEALTH EXAMINATION

This half to be sent to the school

Name of Pupil_____ School_____ Grade_____

Name of Parent_____ Address_____

Physical findings which are of significance to the school

Recommendations to the School:

Is pupil capable of carrying a full program of school work?   Yes_____No_____

Should there be restrictions on up and down stairs travel?   Yes_____No_____

Is special seating recommended?   Yes_____No_____

Would special exercises help to improve posture?   Yes_____No_____

Do you advise supplementary in-between meal feeding?   Yes_____No_____

Does pupil have any irremediable defects?   Yes_____No_____

Is there evidence of emotional upset?   Yes_____No_____
REMARKS:

Classification for Physical Education Activity.   Record Roman Numeral_____
  Code I.   Unlimited activity
  Code II. Slightly modified – under observation
  Code III. Definitely restricted – i.e., cardiac disease, post acute infectious diseases, potential
             chests, etc.
  Code IV. Individual physical education
  Code V.   Rest

Recommendations for the Home (to be used as basis for school-home contact):

Is the present food intake adequate?   Yes _____No_____

If not, what changes are advised?   _____

Is more rest needed?   Yes_____No_____

Do you recommend curtailment of extra-curricular activities?   Yes_____No_____

Should work at home be restricted?   Yes_____No_____

Should a work permit be issued for pupil, if requested?   Yes_____No_____
REMARKS: (please indicate also any specific need for dental, psychiatric, medical or surgical care).

Date_____Signature of Examining Physician_____

Report of Follow-up: (To be filled out by school personnel – please be specific).

_____
*School Health Examinations – A guide for physicians and school authorities.
School Health Committee of the State Medical Society of Wisconsin. August, 1954.

Sample form for reporting health examination data to schools.

Figure 7–4. Classification of students for physical education. (*JAMA*, January, 1967, p. 266.)

teacher can divide the students into as many groups as desired, depending on facilities, equipment, ability of the class, and safety factors.

Ideally, all classes are formed according to grade, but in many school systems grades are too small to permit this. Regardless of whether the grades are mixed or scheduled separately, ability grouping should be used. In junior high school, the performance of a seventh-grade student may be comparable to that of a ninth grader. It is advisable to place students in several ability groups because students who have attained a high level of proficiency become bored if they have to practice with beginners. Figure 7–5 illustrates ability grouping in a hypothetical class that is being taught the basketball lay-up shot. This example explains a simple ability-grouping procedure that might be applied throughout the program for teaching skills.

TITLE IX AND ABILITY GROUPING. Title IX mandates that classes be coeducational. Placing male and female students in the same classes might present instructional difficulties.

Ability grouping seems to be the answer to problems arising from the implementation of Title IX, since Title IX allows grouping of ability in physical education classes. Skill differentiation in coeducational classes may be resolved by placing students in groups as shown in Figure 7–5. As performance improves, students may progress, without embarrassment, to a group with a higher level of performance.

In Norfolk, Virginia, ability grouping has been practiced for 25 years. Title IX guidelines were easily implemented since the structure for grouping already existed. Mr. James Whaley, department chairman of Rosemont Junior High School, describes why grouping students by ability is so important:

Ability grouping is a necessity in a well-planned, well-structured physical education class as physical education classes often have both large enrollments and many different levels of ability. The advent of coeducational classes offers added advantages to this instructional method.

In order to give students the individualized instruction needed, they must be grouped by ability. Once students are thus grouped, the special skills needed by each level can be

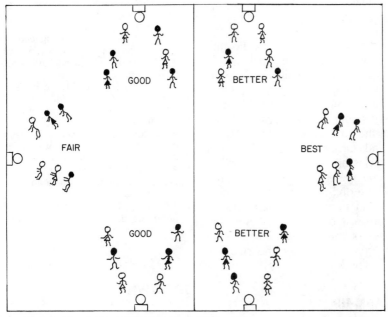

Figure 7–5. Grouping a class by ability for the lay-up shot in basketball.

determined, properly demonstrated, and practiced. This procedure provides for equal attention given to the less skilled as well as the gifted. Students in all levels benefit by grouping since skill competition is keener among equals no matter what level the performance. Competition among peers fosters better performance and mastery of skills. Instruction also benefits in that grouping makes for more efficient use of class time. Under the instructor's direction, more advanced students can be utilized to help less skilled students.

Grouping can be achieved by evaluating the performance of individual students in the basic skills employed in any activity. From this point, students, after mastering sets of skills, may advance to higher ability groups. Knowing that they can advance acts as an incentive to all students, motivating them to learn the techniques needed to participate more successfully in the desired activity.

A strong argument in favor of ability grouping is that when students are placed in such groups, there are fewer accidents and injuries. Court records list many cases in which students have been injured and teachers have been judged negligent because they classified students improperly. For example, in wrestling, if a more skillful student is matched with one who has had no instruction and the unskilled student is injured, the courts have found the teacher negligent. This fact alone should stimulate teachers to use ability groupings based on a sound inventory of performance.

Height and Weight. Classification by height is applicable to such activities as basketball and volleyball. Sports such as wrestling involve the students' weight; it is imperative that for such activities students be classified by weight if the competition is to be fair.

Age and Grade. Age is the most common classification because students of the same age are usually in the same grade. These divisions provide the most practical classification for administrative purposes and scheduling. Any disadvantages of this arrangement can be offset by regrouping after the students have assembled.

THE WARM-UP

Over the years there has been considerable argument both for and against the warm-up as a part of the instructional program. Some physical educators feel that the warm-up is a waste of time. They say that nature takes care of this physiological process and the sooner the basic activity is introduced the better, since time is of the essence in the physical education class. On the other hand, proponents say that related warmups prior to vigorous participation in the activity program are essential. They feel that the sudden demand for vigorous effort by a particular muscle group is physiologically unsound and may injure the muscles involved. A report to the American Heart Association indicated that sudden vigorous activity without warm-up may be hazardous to the heart. A group of firemen who participated in sudden running exercises registered abnormal electrocardiograms. When warm-up exercises were done, the symptoms did not occur.[5]

A comprehensive study of 22 research papers on the values of the warm-up reveals that 95 per cent of the studies indicated that performance improved when the warm-up was used. Six conclusions drawn from the study are of inestimable value to teachers in their overall planning:

1. Fourteen of 22 studies showed significant improvement in performance following warm-up.
2. Seven of the 22 studies showed improvement in performance following warm-up, but the improvement was not statistically significant.
3. One of the studies showed a decrease in muscular strength following passive warm-up, but muscular endurance was not affected.
4. A vigorous, long warm-up appears to contribute more to better performance than does a moderate, shorter warm-up.
5. A related type of warm-up seems to improve performance more than an unrelated warm-up.
6. Attitude appears to have an influence upon the degree of improvement in performance following warm-up.[6]

CREATIVITY

The opportunities for developing the creative potential of students in physical education are unlimited. The imaginative teacher not only will look for creativity in students but will develop a class environment conducive to creativity. The instructional period offers many opportunities to use original procedures to enhance the prestige of the program and in turn to increase motivation.

Rhythmical Movement

Movement is the basis of all physical education. Constructive movement is manifested in those activities that incorporate the basics such as running, jumping, dodging, and climbing.

Paralleling the natural movements are rhythmical movements that have been used through the years to express human conditions and emotions. These rhythmical patterns, with or without musical accompaniment, have been a part of every human culture and are still prevalent. Rhythmics provide not only a natural activity but also an opportunity for creativity on the part of both students and teacher.

The physical education teacher should guide rhythmic activities along educational channels. Folk, modern, and interpretive rhythms contribute to health and fitness and encourage creativity. Many innovations in modern dance have grown out of the efforts of individuals who wished to explore beyond the traditional boundaries of content and procedure.

One of the most popular and productive forms of rhythmical movement is jumping rope to music. Not only is jumping rope a skill, but it has tremendous circulatory-respiratory value. Many dance steps may be combined with rope jumping, creating an interesting and effective warm-up exercise.

Innovative Teaching Strategies

Developing innovative teaching strategies is a challenging phase of program planning. Teachers can enrich the educational experience by formulating and implementing unique instructional techniques. The old method of using one ball for basketball and volleyball or one shot-put and one hurdle for track will be replaced by more functional procedures; for example, many balls will be used for teaching basketball and volleyball skills, and several hurdles for track. In addition, the teacher should quickly see the advantages of such simple techniques as dividing the class into as many small groups as possible for instruction. Teaching will be more effective and disciplinary problems will diminish for the teacher who employs well-planned procedures. Chapter 5 discusses innovative teaching strategies.

THE TEACHER AND LEGAL LIABILITY

Teachers of physical education, more than teachers of other subjects, must be aware of their responsibility for the safety and welfare of their students. Little attention is paid to accidents that occur in the physical education class. They are viewed as anticipated accompaniments to the program and thus legal action is taken infrequently. Parents accept the situation passively because they are unaware of tort liability. As a result, the physical education class and the athletic field continue to be sites for the majority of accidents in the school. However, the situation is now changing, and teachers can no longer remain ignorant of their liability under the law. They must carefully appraise the class environment and the accident potential of each activity they teach.

The enormous increase in accidents in physical education is largely the result of expanded curricula, inadequate supervision, and substandard instruction. Most programs now include track, wrestling, football, gymnastics, golf, hockey, tumbling, and many other activities that can be dangerous if not taught and supervised properly. Accidents are most liable to occur when teachers leave their classes unattended, attempt to supervise groups that are too large, or allow too many activities to proceed simultaneously. The importance of *quality instruction as a deterrent to accidents* cannot be overemphasized.

Every American possesses the legal right to be free from physical injury caused by others, whether intentional or a result of carelessness. When accidents occur in the physical education class, the injured party can initiate legal action against the teacher, claiming negligence. Teachers are often sued in accident cases, and many court decisions have been handed down against them. These suits involve *torts,* which have been defined as "any private or civil wrong by act or omission for which a civil suit can be brought, but not including breach of contract."[7] However, for a teacher to be held liable under tort law, it must be proved that he or she was negligent in the supervision of the class at the time the injury was sustained. No court has held a teacher liable for negligence when sufficient evidence was available to show that he or she prudently and cautiously performed the teaching duties.

Teacher liability involves a rather complicated aspect of legal procedure. In some states, governmental agencies are immune from suit; thus the entire legal responsibility lies with the teacher. In other states, responsibility is shared by all parties concerned. Regardless of who is legally responsible, conducting a program that stresses accident prevention is always the teacher's obligation. There are several administrative and organizational principles that teachers can follow to insure the safety of students and to reduce the possibility of negligence: constant supervision, teaching safe activities, using correct teaching procedures, following a guidebook, heeding excuse notes, checking facilities for safety, and providing adequate instruction.

returned a verdict of $300,000 against a New Jersey physical education teacher for negligence because he was out of the room during a regular class period and an injury was sustained on the springboard.[8] Recently, courts have handed down decisions involving injuries resulting from assaults and other violent behavior that occurred in unsupervised classes. These rulings also apply to accidents caused by individuals who are not members of the particular class. The courts reason that because teachers are aware of the aggressive natures of certain students, it is their duty to provide constant and responsible supervision.

The use of unqualified personnel as substitute teachers is an ill-advised supervisory practice. This is illustrated in the case of the individual who volunteered to take over the wrestling class when the regular teacher resigned. The plaintiff in the case, who had had no previous wrestling experience, was matched with an opponent who was experienced and who had injured a boy the year before. The plaintiff was not given instruction in how to escape from a dangerous wrestling hold and as a result suffered a severe injury in which his spine was severed. Negligence was declared, and the jury awarded the plaintiff $385,000.[9]

Cases similar to these in which the court has ruled against teachers, administrators, and the district should be of concern to all school personnel. Action should be taken to insure that there is competent supervision by qualified personnel. When this is not possible, the activity should be discontinued until a qualified teacher is available. Sports such as tumbling, wrestling, golf, and certain track and field events should definitely not be supervised by untrained, inexperienced individuals.

Constant Supervision

Teachers sometimes leave their classes unattended, ignoring the hazards of doing so. If an accident occurs while they are away, it becomes a simple procedure to prove negligence. One case is recorded in which a jury

Teaching Safe Activities

Research has shown that certain activities and pieces of equipment are considerably more dangerous than others and that their instructional value is not great enough to warrant inclusion in the physical education program.

One such example is the trampoline. The objective of any activity is the development of the highest possible degree of performance efficiency. Yet, as Helen Zimmerman states in a study of the trampoline, "Based on the number of hours of participation, injuries occurred twice as frequently in colleges as they did in high schools. Therefore, the teaching of this sport is not only dangerous, but it loses all carry-over value for the student."[10] There are other activities, such as tumbling, that meet the objectives of physical education with a much lower accident potential. Further discussion of unsafe activities is found in the *Resource Manual*.

Boxing is another dangerous sport that is unnecessary in a school physical education program. In boxing, the objective is to score a knockout, which is achieved by a severe blow to the head area that causes a concussion of the brain, rendering a person unconscious. When a concussion occurs, there is permanent damage to the brain in the form of scar tissue. Any activity that is actually geared toward physical injury should be excluded from the curriculum. It is wiser to teach wrestling, which meets all the objectives of physical education and is a much safer sport than boxing. Other activities, such as judo, boxing, karate, and certain types of calisthenics are considered too dangerous for the physical education class. It would not be difficult to prove negligence in any accidents that occurred during instruction of these activities. Although these activities may be popular, it does not mean they are educationally sound or safe.

Teachers cannot afford to become lackadaisical in their planning, organization, and teaching. They are not only legally liable but morally obligated to plan and teach so well that students will continually progress toward the health objective without injury.

Correct Teaching Procedures

Violations of the standard procedures involved in teaching activities recognized as sound and safe can constitute negligence. In many recorded cases, teachers have been successfully sued as a result of tumbling accidents. In most instances, the focus of the complaint has been improper teaching methods. A case in point involved a girl who was assigned to a tumbling class under protest. She claimed that the teacher did not provide her with adequate instruction in the stunts required and that the teacher used students to demonstrate the stunts. Although the defendant school district denied negligence and claimed that the girl was guilty of contributory negligence, the court ruled in favor of the plaintiff and awarded her $5000.[11] In New York City a teacher was charged with negligence when a boy was injured while performing a somersault. The student claimed that he had received no instruction in tumbling, and that he was told to perform the stunt although he was incapable of doing it. Both the trial court and the appellate court ruled in favor of the plaintiff.[12]

On the other hand, courts will rule in favor of the teacher when proper procedures were followed. Evidence that the instructor used the recognized method of teaching, from the simple to the complex, is usually sufficient to disprove negligence. This is illustrated by the case of a 16-year-old boy who was practicing take-downs in wrestling. The 30 students in the class had been introduced gradually to the various holds, and the boy had practiced these activities with the others. The court ruled against the plaintiff and found that the instruction was competent, having conformed to recognized standards in teaching wrestling.[13] Another example of the courts' ruling in favor of the teacher occurred in New Jersey. A high-school student was injured while doing leap-frog jumps over a vaulting horse. The court held that the teacher was not negligent since he had demonstrated the jump, warned the students of the possible danger, and asked that they not participate if they were concerned about being able to perform the activity.[14]

Teaching Guide

Educators who do not follow a teaching guide and give instruction in activities not included in it may be found negligent. In New York a boy broke his leg when attempting a somersault, which was not in the Regents' guide. The court ruled in favor of the child because he had not received instruction in how to perform the stunt.[15] Teachers who deviate from the rules, regulations, and standards listed in the guidebook may be held responsible for their actions if injuries result.

Heeding Excuses

Too often teachers disregard notes sent by parents informing administrators of the physical condition of their children. It is advisable to have a written policy concerning excuses that will provide some flexibility in dealing with such cases. Teachers will find it difficult to argue against a charge of negligence when notes from parents that have specified physical limitations of their children have been ignored.

Organizing the Facilities

Equipment and facilities should always be tested for safety before organizing physical education classes. A study of court records reveals many decisions confirming teacher negligence for allowing the use of dangerous equipment and facilities. In California a girl was injured when a locker fell on her while she was seated on a bench in the dressing room. She sued the school district for negligence for failure to provide safe equipment, and the court ruled in her favor.[16]

An excellent illustration of the need for careful organization in physical education is a case in which a boy was injured while playing three-man basketball. A class of 48 boys was participating in various activities in an area of 80 feet by 43 feet, causing overlapping in eight areas. The plaintiff was injured when he attempted to shoot the ball and his opponent blocked him. Evidence showed that the injury occurred because the gymnasium was overcrowded. The court ruled in favor of the plaintiff and severely criticized the school board. The organization of this gymnasium, with a large number of students participating simultaneously in a number of strenuous games that required a great deal of movement over a wide area, created a condition of danger that the defendant should have anticipated.[17]

The environment in physical education includes the gymnasium, the swimming pool, and the playground. A list of all the conditions and situations in which accidents might occur would be too extensive for this text. Placement and types of equipment used, classroom planning, and location are a few factors involved in creating a safe setting for physical education.

Adequate Instruction

In reviewing cases in which teachers have been found guilty of negligence, the authors found that there was usually little or no instruction in the class. This further stresses the importance of using the physical education class for an *instructional* program rather than as a period for play. Instruction should consist of *teaching the skills* of the various activities that are included in the physical education program; injuries rarely occur when these skills are taught properly. A teaching program, as opposed to a play period, not only enhances the atmosphere for learning but reduces the possibility of accidents. Other precautionary measures that teachers should take in their classes are:

1. Inspect all equipment and facilities periodically. Report any deficiencies in writing to your building principal, supervisor, and the central office. Things to look for in-

clude defective playground equipment, holes and defects in the playground surface, worn-out athletic equipment and materials of all kinds; apparatus and mats that are in unsafe condition; lockers that are loose and not attached to the floor.

2. Be sure that all physical education students have had recent medical examinations.
3. Remove overly fatigued students from practice, games, or class activities. Research shows that injuries are more likely to occur when students are overly tired. Concentrate on developing endurance and provide extra work in this aspect of fitness for students who need it.
4. Do not permit students to attempt stunts or any other physical education activity until they have been properly taught to execute the maneuver.
5. Follow a definite progression in each activity. Don't permit students to move ahead until they have mastered the previously taught stunt or technique. Make sure your students have mastered particular skills before you require them to use these skills or techniques in class or in a game.
6. Don't overcrowd your individual play areas. Too many students running, jumping, and exercising in any one area can be dangerous and lead to accidents and injuries.
7. Avoid mismatches in class activities and intramurals. Try to group students equally, considering such factors as skill, height, weight, fitness, and experience in specific sports, games and activities.
8. Never leave a class alone, no matter what the reason. This is doubly important when potentially dangerous equipment is being used.[18]

STRENGTH AND PHYSICAL EDUCATION

In Chapter 3, the anatomical, psychological, and physiological components of physical education were briefly discussed, and the four aspects of the physiological component were described. It is now important to examine the strength factor, since too often attention has been focused on it to the exclusion of other important factors. Strength alone is not an indication of physical health. Fitness involves the simultaneous development of several factors, of which strength is only one. Ac-cording to researchers Karpovich and Sinning, "Strength tests do not permit us to draw satisfactory conclusions regarding the efficiency of the entire body."[19]

Certain aspects of training are confusing to many teachers and students. Recently, terms such as *isometrics, isotonic training,* and *weight training* have received considerable attention. These procedures are not new. During the early years of this century, Swoboda employed the same principles and called the system "conscious evolution." A little later, Charles Atlas called it "dynamic tension." The physiological principle involved in all these systems of developing strength is *overload.* Advocates of muscle-building have taken this established principle and have manufactured new titles for it in an effort to promote their programs and to sell mechanical equipment and contrivances.

The Principle of Overload

The principle of overload is simple. All individuals have definite patterns of physical activity: we walk, climb, run, dance, sit, and participate in other routines for a certain amount of the time in our usual schedule of work or play. When there is an increase in the usual exercise pattern, necessitating more work and muscle effort, the increment in activity is known as overload. There are many ways of overloading a muscle in order to develop strength. Some of these are acceptable as sound physical education procedures and others are of questionable value. In order to discriminate among them, the teacher should be familiar with the three types of overload.

Natural Overload. Any time that a muscle is required to perform or contract with greater effort than before, the overload principle is in use. A person who has been walking a mile daily will be overloading various muscle groups if he runs the mile instead of walks; thus sprinters practice overloading more than distance runners. Natural overloading involves movement and is physiologically sound. The standard sports instruction program that constitutes the bulk of the physical education curriculum provides sufficient overload for normal growth and development.

Special Overload for Sports Training. Certain types of overloading are effective and physiologically acceptable for developing the strength of a specific group of muscles to improve performance in a particular skill. An illustration of this is the training of basketball players. Medicine balls should be used for developing the shoulder and arm muscles, a heavy basketball for strengthening the fingers, and a standard ball for practicing the skills. These procedures may be applied to other sports skills, such as swinging a heavy bat for developing hitting strength in baseball, or jumping with weights on the shoulders for improving jumping ability. It is important to overload the muscles involved in the skill rather than simply to lift weights indiscriminately with the assumption that this

will develop better performance in all sports. Weight lifting is a good overload activity for training in lifting weights.

Nonfunctional Overload. Nonfunctional overload involves many systems that have been practiced under various names but that still involve the physiological principles of overload. *Isometric training* includes all methods in which a muscle is stimulated but either is not allowed to contract or is contracted very little and then held. Isometric training does not allow or develop flexibility; it excludes natural movements and is therefore physiologically unsound as a physical education activity. Even as a training program for sports, it is of questionable value. *Isotonic training* overloads the muscle but allows complete contraction. Isotonic contraction is more functional but also is of questionable value as a physical education activity. Both types will improve muscular strength and numerous studies have been made to determine the superiority of one type over the other.

Figure 7-6. Vigorous activities such as soccer make a greater contribution to physical fitness than gymnastics and calisthenics. (Courtesy Hamilton High School, Los Angeles City Schools.)

These reveal that one group is about as effective as the other in developing strength.[20]

Physical Education and Overload

Physical education teachers are faced with the decision of whether to include the overload program of isometrics involving weights and mechanical equipment in the curriculum. Considerable evidence reveals the inadvisability of incorporating these activities in the regular program. Training athletes may need some type of overload; however, there is great disparity between the level of strength needed by most students and that needed by training athletes. Physical educators are concerned with developing strength on the level necessary for normal growth and development and not at the level for competitive athletics.

Considerable research has been conducted in isometric and isotonic regimens and their value for physical education. The basic conclusions are:

1. Physical fitness is more than muscular strength and muscular endurance; a third essential component is circulatory-respiratory endurance. Thus, both isometric and isotonic regimens of exercise are deficient as an adequate approach to physical fitness.
2. Motivation is generally superior with isotonic than with isometric exercises.
3. Isometrics can be performed anywhere, while isotonics require limited space and may require special equipment.
4. Both isometric and isotonic forms of exercise improve muscular strength. Most studies do not favor one method over another; however, several investigators have reported greater strength gains for the isotonic form.
5. No study reviewed verified the strength gain of 5 percent per week from a single daily 6-second contraction against resistance equal to two-thirds of the muscle's strength as reported by Hettinger and Muller in Germany. A more realistic figure seems to be 1–2 percent.
6. Isometric training at one point in the range of motion of a joint develops strength significantly at that point but not at other positions throughout this range.
7. Isometric exercise of a gross nature, such as pressing the body upward against a bar, does not permit precise application of contractions to specific muscle groups.
8. Recovery from muscle fatigue is faster after isotonic than after isometric exercise.
9. Muscular endurance is more effectively developed through isotonic than through isometric exercise.
10. Improvement in muscular power occurs from isotonic but not from isometric exercise.
11. In strong isometric exercise, the circulation to the contracting muscles is occluded, thereby interfering with the oxygen supply to the exercising muscles.
12. In isometric as contrasted with isotonic exercise, oxygen debt is greater, oxygen income is less, and the debt-income ratio is much larger.
13. Diastolic blood pressure increases during isometric but not during isotonic exercise.
14. In contrasting isometric and isotonic (with circulatory involvement) training regimens, isotonic training decreases blood coagulation time, increases hemoglobin concentration, and elevates the red corpuscle count in the blood.
15. Isometric exercise as contrasted with bicycle riding is more prone to produce irregular heart beats, premature ventricular contractions, and abnormally fast heart beats in heart disease patients. (Evidence of such heart reactions does not exist with noncardiac disease subjects.)[21]

Law of Reciprocal Innervation

The law of reciprocal innervation as defined by Sherrington has served as a guideline in teaching for many years.[22] It is involved in all movement, because when the brain sends an impulse to a muscle to contract, a corresponding impulse is sent to the antagonistic muscle to relax. In flexion of the arm, for example, the stimulus to the biceps is sent simultaneously with an impulse to the triceps to relax. This physiological phenomenon is nature's way of achieving smooth coordination and is fundamental to attaining proficiency in all skills and movements. Many resistance movements labeled isometric that violate this principle are nevertheless included in some physical education programs. Because they contradict established principles of movement, they should be excluded from the curriculum.

Furthermore, isometric exercises are inadvisable, as they impede the normal range of joint movements and do not incorporate the natural body movements necessary for normal growth and development. Overload can be involved in all physical education activities without excluding the natural movements. Wrestling, for example, not only provides an acceptable overload for developing strength but also includes the speed, skill, and endurance factors. Different types of running provide overload and develop physiological endurance, which is not promoted by isometric exercises. Medical opinion disapproves of isometrics, particularly for those with circulatory problems. Schultz states: "Isometrics, for example, are now considered inadvisable; such exercises tend to raise both blood pressure and pulse rate to an unsafe degree. Most authorities feel that rhythmical exercise is best."[23] This observation is substantiated by Clark, who examined the results of studies made of isometric and isotonic exercises and their effect on the circulatory system. The studies reveal that isometric exercises are more likely than isotonic exercises to produce irregular heartbeats, premature ventricular contractions, abnormally fast heart beat in heart disease patients, and a rise in blood pressure.[24]

THE HEALTH OBJECTIVE

Students of physical education may be confused as to their role in relating physical fitness to physical education. They may ask, "How much fitness is necessary?" "To what extent should I pursue the various testing programs?" "What should be my objectives relative to fitness?" Obviously, teachers and administrators should be concerned with the health needs of individual students and should guide the programs toward the health and fitness objectives of physical education. If the physical education program does not contribute to good health, it would be failing to meet its most basic objective, and therefore make justification for its inclusion in the curriculum quite difficult.

Physical fitness may be viewed sci-

entifically because it involves more than just exercise. Fitness requires proper nutrition, good eating habits, sufficient sleep and relaxation, periodic health examinations, and instruction. Evidently, the exercise approach to fitness is not enough; supporting services and instruction are also critical. To initiate a vigorous exercise program for people without sound medical histories may do more harm than good in some instances. Karpovich and Sinning observe:

... Beyond a certain indispensable minimum of physical fitness, an additional improvement in physical fitness has no effect upon health, no matter how one defines the word. Excessive physical activities, on the other hand, may be definitely detrimental to persons with some diseases.[25]

UNDESIRABLE ACTIVITIES

Teachers should understand the ways in which various types of activities become part of the physical education program. The bulk of physical education consists of instruction in team and individual sports. This involves natural movements that are popular because the sports are a part of the American way of life. On the other hand many activities involve unnatural movements that have been handed down over the years without scientific investigation.

To comprehend the nature of these exercises (calisthenics) that are common in the United States, teachers should study their origin. These movements are part of a comprehensive program of gymnastics which originated in Europe. Generally, four areas are identified: *calisthenics, apparatus, tumbling,* and *marching.* The gymnastic movement originally had preparation for military service as its primary objective. There were many systems of gymnastics, but those practiced by the Germans, Swedish, and Danish survived and have influenced physical education in this country since they were brought here during the latter part of the 19th century. For many years such programs dominated physical education in the United States.

Although these systems served a purpose in the lands of their origin, they could not satisfy the needs of a culture based on democratic principles. At the end of World War I, physical education pioneers such as Hetherington, Williams, and Nash began to eliminate the formal pattern of gymnastics. They and others introduced the natural program of physical education based on fundamental movements — using sports, games, dancing, and swimming as the media for expression. Calisthenics survived this transformation and Williams explains why:

... school people set up a number of conditions that reflected the ideas they had concerning the function of education. In effect, the schoolmen proposed that any physical training that was to be taken into the school must require very little time, must be inexpensive and not demand specifically trained teachers, must conduct its activities in the classroom (activity carried on outside the school building could not be educative), and must not require apparatus.

Unfortunately, the experts in physical training of the time came forward and said in effect: We have just what you want. We propose systematic exercises that can be taught by the regular teacher in the classroom. No apparatus will be required, and the expense is very moderate. These exercises will correct the schoolroom stoop, provide relief for the mind, and bring health and vigor to the body. The antiseptic request of the schoolmen was accorded a sterilized program, vestiges of which remain today as "10 minutes a day of calisthenics."[26]

When related to teaching a sport, conditioning exercises are important for their warm-up value and should be given a place in the curriculum. But they do not result in fitness, and the individuals who promote calisthenics need to study what constitutes fitness. Even in the early part of the century, when calisthenics were at their peak of popularity, many leaders disapproved of them. Hetherington emphasized the need for natural movements rather than calisthenics:

The natural physical-training activities arise out of children's play tendencies. They are satisfying because they meet growth needs. These needs are not met by any other kind of activity. The natural activities are an essential part of the child life. On the other hand, gymnastic drills or calisthenic movements are pure adult inventions. They are artificial or invented movements derived from the army idea of "training" and were incorporated into the school program in Germany and Sweden when formal discipline was in vogue.[27]

Siedentop, in a more recent discussion of calisthenics, states:

For many years, however, physical fitness has been functionally defined in physical education as the ability to do push-ups, sit-ups, and other such exercises. There is no evidence that practice for such activities causes a meaningful increase in either health fitness or in the ability to perform in specific sports activities.[28]

These opinions show rather conclusively that many of the unnatural calisthenic movements are in the physical education curriculum without any scientific reason. Instead, they have been handed down from year to year and teachers have accepted them without question. Not only do they not do what they are supposed to do, but they may seriously injure the individual. Some exercises in this category are the deep-knee bend, leg lift, sit-up, toe-touch, dip (unless correctly executed), and back arch. Although some of the movements have been derived from experiments that have been used for corrective purposes, they are not desirable for the majority of students.

Natural movements are beneficial for normal growth and development; unnatural calisthenics may cause serious damage to the alignment of the body if used improperly. Many teachers do not know which muscles are actually used in calisthenic exercises, and therefore more harm than good frequently results. Warm-up exercises should incorporate as nearly as possible the actual movement that will be involved in the major activity that follows. For example, a batter swings one or two bats before batting; a pitcher warms up by pitching with moderate speed.

QUESTIONS FOR DISCUSSION

1. What is the principle of overflow? How can it be used in the class?
2. Identify the principles of class organization and briefly explain each.
3. Discuss the advantages and disadvantages of allowing students to perform exercises and activities based on their physiological limits.
4. How should the intensity of an exercise program be determined?
5. Explain the importance of classifying students for participation in physical education.
6. Why should students be grouped for instruction in physical education?
7. Discuss the advantages of ability grouping.
8. Distinguish between grouping for instruction and grouping for competition.
9. Discuss the pros and cons of the warm-up as part of the physical education program.
10. What is meant by *tort*? Cite some examples of tort that may occur in physical education.
11. Indicate the precautions that the teacher can observe to help deter accidents.

REFERENCES

1. Clark Hetherington, *School Program in Physical Education* (New York: World Book Company, 1972), pp. 74–76.
2. "Half the Physical Education Grade is Based on Outside Activity," *Physical Education Newsletter* (Old Saybrook, Conn., January 15, 1976).
3. Laurence E. Morehouse and Augustus J. Miller, *Physiology of Exercise,* 7th ed. (St. Louis: The C. V. Mosby Company, 1976), p. 157.
4. "Classification of Students for Physical Education," A Committee Report, *JOHPER* (February, 1967), p. 16.
5. "Sudden, Vigorous Exercise May Harm Even Healthy Hearts, Scientists Warn," American Medical Association, Health Education Service (December, 1972).
6. Tom Neuberger, "What the Research Quarterly Says About Warm-Up," *JOHPER* (October, 1969), p. 77.
7. The Readers' Digest Great Encyclopedic Dictionary, *The Readers' Digest Association* (New York, 1975), p. 1414.
8. Herb Appenzeller, *From the Gym to the Jury* (Charlottesville: The Michie Company, 1970), pp. 46–51c.
9. *Ibid.,* pp. 63–65.
10. Helen M. Zimmerman, "Accident Experience With Trampolines," *Research Quarterly of AAHPER* (December, 1956), p. 452.
11. Appenzeller, *op. cit.,* p. 74.
12. *Ibid.,* p. 77.
13. *Ibid.,* p. 81.
14. Joseph B. Tremonti, "Legal Liability for Accidents in Physical Education," *Physical Education Newsletter* (Old Saybrook, Conn.: Physical Education Publications, November, 1969).
15. Appenzeller, *op. cit.,* p. 83.
16. *Ibid.,* p. 102.
17. *Ibid.,* p. 109.
18. Tremonti, *op. cit.*
19. Peter V. Karpovich and Wayne E. Sinning, *Physiology of Muscular Activity,* 7th ed. (Philadelphia, W. B. Saunders Company, 1971), p. 282.
20. H. Harrison Clark, "Basic Understanding of Physical Fitness," *Physical Fitness Research Digest,* President's Council on Physical Fitness and Sports (July, 1971), p. 10.
21. *Ibid.*
22. Charles Sherrington, *The Integrative Action of the Nervous System* (New Haven: Yale University Press, 1961).
23. Dodi Schultz, "Family Doctors Health Guide," *Ladies Home Journal* (August, 1971), p. 38.
24. H. Harrison Clark, *op. cit.,* p. 11.
25. Karpovich and Sinning, *op. cit.,* p. 270.
26. Jesse Feiring Williams, *Principles of Physical Education,* 8th ed. (Philadelphia: W. B. Saunders Company, 1964).
27. Clark Hetherington, *School Program in Physical Education* (New York: World Book Company, 1927), p. 54.
28. Daryl Siedentop, *Physical Education, Introductory Analysis* (Dubuque, Iowa: William C. Brown Company, 1972), p. 81.

SELECTED READINGS

Annarino, Anthony A., *Developmental Conditioning for Men and Women* (Saint Louis: Mosby, Times Mirror, 1976).

Appenzeller, Herb, *From the Gym to the Jury* (Charlottesville, Virginia: The Michie Company, 1970).

Strasser, Marland K., Aaron, James E., and Ralph C. Bohn, *Fundamentals of Safety Education* (Riverside, New Jersey: MacMillan Publishing Company, 1973).

Van Der Smisson, Betty, *Legal Liability of Cities and Schools for Injuries in Recreation and Parks* (Cincinnati: The W. H. Anderson Company, 1968).

Chapter 8

Courtesy Los Angeles Unified School District

INTERNAL ORGANIZATIONAL PROCEDURES
  DISCIPLINE
  RECORDING ATTENDANCE
  STUDENT RECORDS
    INDIVIDUAL RECORD CARDS
    SQUAD CARDS
    DAILY CHECK SHEETS
    PERMANENT RECORD CARDS
  EXCUSES FROM PARTICIPATION
    TEMPORARY EXCUSES
    PERMANENT EXCUSES
  TOWEL PROGRAM
  UNIFORMS AND SHOES
  LOCKERS
    LOCKER ASSIGNMENTS
  SHOWERS
  STORAGE
  PARENT-TEACHER RELATIONS
    HANDBOOK
    LETTERS
    REPORTS
  STUDENT INVOLVEMENT
    STUDENT INSTRUCTORS
    SQUAD LEADERS
    STUDENT CLASS MANAGERS
    ASSISTANT STUDENT INSTRUCTORS
  ORGANIZING TEACHING STATIONS
  PROVIDING SUPPLIES AND EQUIPMENT
    THE INVENTORY
    BUDGETING
    REQUISITIONS
      INSTRUCTIONAL CONTENT AS A
        DETERMINANT
  IMPROVISING
  SAFETY PRECAUTIONS
  TEAM TEACHING
  SELECTIVES IN PHYSICAL EDUCATION
EXTERNAL ORGANIZATIONAL PROCEDURES
  THE PHYSICAL EDUCATION REQUIREMENT

CREDIT FOR PHYSICAL EDUCATION
TEACHING LOAD AND CLASS SIZE
SCHEDULING FOR PHYSICAL EDUCATION
  TRADITIONAL SCHEDULING
  FLEXIBLE SCHEDULING
    EXAMPLE OF FLEXIBLE SCHEDULING
    A CRITICAL LOOK AT FLEXIBLE
      SCHEDULING
  CLIENT-CENTERED APPROACH
  INDIVIDUALIZED SCHEDULING
PLANNING FACILITIES
  PRINCIPLES OF PLANNING
  CONSIDERATIONS IN PLANNING
    SIZE OF SCHOOL
    GENERAL RECOMMENDATIONS
    REVIEW OF THE GENERAL PLAN
    SPECIFIC RECOMMENDATIONS
INDOOR FACILITIES
TEACHING STATIONS
  THE AUXILIARY GYMNASIUM
  IMPROVISED TEACHING STATIONS
  THE MAIN GYMNASIUM
  THE SWIMMING POOL
    TYPE OF POOL
    LOCATION OF POOL
    SIZE OF POOL
    CHECK LIST FOR PLANNING THE
      POOL
OUTDOOR FACILITIES
  SURFACES
    SYNTHETIC SURFACES
    SURFACES FOR MULTI-USE AREAS
    SURFACES NEAR FIXED EQUIPMENT
  OTHER AREAS
NUMBER OF TEACHING STATIONS
GUIDELINES FOR EXTERNAL ORGANIZATION
QUESTIONS FOR DISCUSSION
REFERENCES
SELECTED READINGS

ESSENTIALS IN CLASS ORGANIZATION

Effective instruction is the purpose of education. Although many factors are involved, the most influential is the actual teaching situation.

It is during the instructional period that physical education must serve the needs of the students. Nevertheless, in too many instances the class period is poorly organized and ineffective, and either serves as a training ground for the interscholastic program or is a free-play program in which the teacher throws out the ball and watches the students play. This is not teaching.

The purpose of this chapter is to discuss the various techniques and strategies essential to organization for effective instruction. These are grouped into two general categories: (1) internal organizational procedures and (2) external organizational procedures.

INTERNAL ORGANIZATIONAL PROCEDURES

The teacher is solely responsible for the various organizational procedures that exist within the physical education class. External factors also affect the operation of the class, but it is with the internal procedures that instructors must be concerned first.

Discipline

For ten consecutive years, the Gallup Poll has revealed that discipline in public schools is a major national concern. The 1977 poll lists the distress over discipline ahead of all other problems facing schools.[1]

For some teachers, developing student-teacher rapport is one of the most difficult tasks in the organization of the class. Physical education classes include students of various temperaments, abilities, and life-styles. These students approach the physical education class anticipating the release of inhibitions. Unless instructors are able to control this situation positively, the teaching process may be adversely affected.

Physical education teachers should

not be confronted with the same disciplinary problems that exist in classrooms of academic instruction. Biehler believes that the causes of misbehavior are (1) boredom, (2) release of frustration and tension, and (3) desire for attention, recognition, and status.[2] Because physical education is a program based on the natural urge for movement, a well-planned class should satisfy these feelings before they manifest themselves in misconduct.

When classes meet for the first time, a teacher-student rapport is established that lasts for a long time. New teachers should never minimize the importance of developing a positive relationship with students during the first few days of instruction. Invariably, teachers who seek popularity and place themselves on the level of their students lose control and jeopardize their future as successful teachers. Instructors must always maintain their status with dignity. At the same time, they must be friendly and firm, informal and forceful.

There are two strong deterrents to class disorder: *careful organization* and *quality instruction*. If classes are planned properly and the program provides instruction for student achievement, teachers prevent confusion in the gymnasium.

However, despite all the efforts made by teachers in class control, there are always some students who develop attitudes that are disruptive and demand direct action by the teacher. For years, many teachers have resorted to the use of aversive controls such as physical punishment, sarcasm, and ridicule for disciplinary purposes. Generally, psychologists and educators feel that this approach to handling deviant behavior should be avoided. Instead, they suggest a positive approach that attempts to develop better communication and understanding between the student and the teacher. Neal, on the other hand, shows in a study of aversive control that this approach is receiving new attention and support. He presents evidence that challenges those who find such procedures objectionable, revealing that in some instances aversive methods may be effective and that undesirable side effects need not occur.[3]

Many disruptive students possess great leadership ability, and society could benefit enormously from their seemingly innate capacity to influence and guide others. One challenge for teachers is to provide them with an environment that will develop their abilities along socially acceptable channels. Among adolescents, at least average physical ability is essential for group acceptance. It seems that if children are markedly deficient in skill development, an improvement of these skills would provide a better chance for the child to adjust to peer expectations and win at least a minimal achievement status.

The problem students in the physical education class have the potential to be good squad leaders and to handle constructive responsibility. Their feeling of importance and the opportunity for them to assume leadership roles not only will provide a valuable education for them but will also develop a more positive climate in class.

Physical education teachers can learn from an experiment in Woodbourne Junior High School in Baltimore, Maryland. Troublemakers were placed on the Student Security Patrol and given positions comparable to those of lawmen. Vandalism decreased 99 per cent, gang wars were prevented, and drugs almost disappeared.[4] This positive approach to handling discipline problems is advocated by many educational leaders who feel that self-discipline is the answer. They stress the need for teachers and administrators to have faith in the students.

Many behavioral problems arise from the lack of parental control during the early years and the child's resultant mistaken interpretation of freedom. When young children are not given proper instruction in responsibility, their relationship to society, and their obligations to the rights of others, their concept of freedom in later years may include doing exactly as they please. Certain restraints must be taught with freedom, and educators have a responsibility to see that this relationship is developed. Sometimes rewards are necessary to support the restrictions, as all people need reinforcement for a job well done. Positive support is needed to show students that doing the right thing does mean approval.

At the National Conference on America's Secondary Schools in Denver, Colorado, in April 1976, considerable emphasis was placed on the rights and responsibilities of students. Although these rights have been affirmed by court decisions, parents, teachers, and students are confused as to what rights are guaranteed. The participants of the conference were concerned that student responsibilities are not comparable to student rights. As a result of the conference, a model policy on student rights and responsibilities was developed:

Student Rights:

1. All constitutional rights
2. The right to learn
3. The right to pursue an education without interference
4. The right to be respected and accepted as a human being
5. The right to be appropriately involved in their own education on an equal basis

Student Responsibilities:

1. The responsibility to respect the constitutional rights of others
2. The responsibility to learn
3. The responsibility to be involved in setting up and observing the necessary constraints to freedom
4. The responsibility to participate in their own governance[5]

These have significant implications for class management because, when confronted with disruptive behavior, teachers must consider students' legal rights before reacting. The administrator of the school should establish definite procedural policies for handling disruptions in the physical education class. These should be explained to students and should be strongly enforced as problems arise.

From the foregoing discussion, the reader should develop a philosophy concerning student discipline. Specific guidelines may also prove helpful to teachers in maintaining normal class control. Biehler offers these suggestions:

1. Consider establishing some class rules.
2. Be friendly but firm. Act confidently, especially the first day.
3. Have a variety of influence techniques planned in advance. They include watching the troublemaker more closely, use of humor, use of restraint, etc.
4. Whenever you have to deal harshly with a student, make an effort to establish rapport.
5. Try to avoid threats.
6. Be prompt, consistent, reasonable.
7. Consider using behavior modification techniques.
8. When you have control, ease up some.[6]

Recording Attendance

Recording attendance is important because it has administrative implications. In most places, students are required by law to attend school, and teachers are legally responsible for the students enrolled in their classes.

Checking attendance is one of the most difficult and time-consuming elements in the organization of a physical education class. Probably the most practical method is to have numbers painted on the walls, about waist height, or on the floor around the gymnasium. The numbers, in numerical order, should be of sufficient range to accommodate the largest class. Each student is assigned a number, and at the beginning of each class should promptly stand on or in front of that number. Students assigned to all exposed numbers are marked absent; these numbers are recorded on a slip of paper and placed on the student's individual record card or in the roll book. Arrangements must be made to change the status of students who come in late from *absent* to *tardy*.

Many school systems receive state financial aid based on daily average attendance, and the failure to check rolls and report absentees may adversely affect this support. There have been instances where rolls have not been checked and students have failed to report to classes for months. A procedure for recording attendance is shown in Chapter 9, and other methods are discussed in the *Resource Manual*.

Student Records

To a large extent, successful instruction depends on how the daily routine of recording absences, tardinesses, excuses, and evaluations is handled. Practical tools for assisting teachers with this type of bookkeeping should be available. Usually this information is recorded on individual cards, squad cards, and permanent record cards. These teaching tools are not as widely used as they were at one time. However, some teachers find them helpful. A few examples of these techniques are discussed.

Individual Record Cards. Individual record cards should be filled out the first day the class meets and will thereafter serve as the class roll. They may be used for recording other items in the program such as test scores, locker numbers, and matters involved in instruction. An example of such a card is shown in Figure 8–1.

Squad Cards. Many teachers prefer to use squad cards. These may be used alone or in conjunction with the individual record cards. They are meaningful only if the squad plan is predominantly used for class organization. Usually the cards include the name of

CINCINNATI PUBLIC SCHOOLS
DEPARTMENT OF PHYSICAL EDUCATION

PERIODS
M. T. W. TH. F.

NAME ______ HOME ROOM ______

SQUAD ______ NO. ______ LOCKER ______ LOCK ______ GRADE LEVEL ______

	SEPTEMBER					OCTOBER					NOVEMBER					DECEMBER					JANUARY					SEMESTER
TOWEL FEE:	M.	T.	W.	Th.	F.	M.	T.	W.	Th.	F.	M.	T.	W.	Th.	F.	M.	T.	W.	Th.	F.	M.	T.	W.	Th.	F.	I
ATTENDANCE KEY:																										
	FEBRUARY					MARCH					APRIL					MAY					JUNE					II

											AVERAGE
ATTITUDE											
APPEARANCE											
SHOWERS											
PREPARATORY EXERCISES											
GAMES PROGRAM											
APPARATUS AND TUMBLING											
TRACK AND FIELD											
SWIMMING AND DIVING											

P.E. - 13 BOYS' CLASS CARD–SECONDARY SCHOOLS

Figure 8–1. An individual record card. (Courtesy Cincinnati Public Schools.)

SQUAD	SHW. NO.	PHYSICAL EDUCATION ATTENDANCE CARD											SIT-UPS	BROAD JUMP	BENT-ARM HANG	SHUTTLE RUN	SOFTBALL THROW	50 YD. DASH	600 YD. WALK-RUN
DAYS PER.		1	2	3	4	5	6	7	8	9	10							
1 LEADER																		
2																		
3																		
4																		
5																		
6																		
7																		
8																		
9																		
10																		
11																		
12																		
13																		
14																		

FORM D-64

Figure 8–2. A squad card is desirable when the classes are organized by squads. (Courtesy Davenport, Indiana, Public Schools.)

the squad member, attendance record, homeroom or grade, test results, and other important information that will assist the teacher in record-keeping. A sample squad card is shown in Figure 8–2.

Daily Check Sheets. A check sheet is practical for keeping daily records of such items as attendance, dress, and showers. A form that may serve this purpose is shown in Figure 8–3.

Permanent Record Cards. In a well-planned physical education program, a system is provided for permanent records that are available for future reference. Grades, teachers' comments, intramural points earned, and results of special activities are some of the many aspects of the program that should be recorded for permanent files.

Excuses from Participation

Excusing students from physical education, which appears at first to be a minor issue, can become a major problem for the teacher whose administrators have not established a firm policy on the matter.

Temporary Excuses. Students should be required to have a physician's letter specifying disability in order to be excused permanently from physical education. Temporary excuses from home should first be submitted to the school nurse for examination and then brought to the teacher. Two or three of these excuses should necessitate a physician's examination and recommendation concerning the student's condition as it pertains to his or her participation in the physical education program.

PERIOD ____________

CHEYENNE PUBLIC SCHOOLS

DAILY CHECK LIST

WEEK OF ____________

1. EXCELLENT
2. GOOD
3. SATISFACTORY
4. UNSATISFACTORY

V–OKAY
T–TARDY
A–ABSENT
E–EXCUSED

	MONDAY					TUESDAY					WEDNESDAY					THURSDAY					FRIDAY					
NAME	ATTENDANCE	DRESS/SHOWER	EXERCISE	CONDUCT	SKILLS	ATTENDANCE	DRESS/SHOWER	EXERCISE	CONDUCT	SKILLS	ATTENDANCE	DRESS/SHOWER	EXERCISE	CONDUCT	SKILLS	ATTENDANCE	DRESS/SHOWER	EXERCISE	CONDUCT	SKILLS	ATTENDANCE	DRESS/SHOWER	EXERCISE	CONDUCT	SKILLS	COMMENTS

Figure 8–3. A daily check sheet is essential for accurate accounting. (Courtesy Cheyenne Public Schools, Cheyenne, Wyoming.)

Permanent Excuses. It is inadvisable to excuse students permanently from physical education class so they can participate in extracurricular activities such as cheerleading, band practice, drill teams, or athletics. If physical education is important for growth and development — as it has been shown to be — then students should not be excused from it for other activities. Physical education teachers too often permit students to take part in extracurricular activities during the class period. This practice eventually undermines physical education instruction; moreover, it is difficult to curtail, once a precedent has been established.

Students should not be excused from physical education for athletic competition. Although there are some arguments in favor of such a practice, the following reasons show why they are not sound:

1. Students participating in sports often miss the important instruction offered in the physical education class. In addition to the conditioning they would get in the class, they would also be learning skills that could be used in later life, long after school participation is over.
2. Where physical education is required for credit, teachers cannot justify giving a grade if the student does not attend class. A student would never be excused from academic subjects and still expect a grade. If this policy does not apply to all other subjects, it should not apply to physical education.

Frequently, students are permanently excused because of some disability that prevents them from participating in the regular program. Decisions regarding these cases should be made only

SCOTIA-GLENVILLE HIGH SCHOOL
Scotia, New York

Date _____

To Dr. _____

_____, a pupil at Scotia-Glenville High School, has requested to be excused from some physical education activities. It is the policy of the school and the Regulations of the Commissioner of Education that all pupils be enrolled in physical education classes and that activities be adapted in individual cases where needed and as recommended by either the school or family physician.

In order to place the student in the most appropriate physical education program, we would appreciate it if you would consider the enclosed possibilities and recommend the type of activity that should be pursued.

Respectfully,

Craig B. Hitchcock
Director of Health and Physical Education

_____ (Pupil's name)   Date _____

(   ) is able to participate in all physical education and athletic activities

(   ) should participate only in limited physical education with activities restricted to those indicated below.

    (   ) 1. Individual, carry-over activities (indicate)
        (   ) Archery   (   ) Golf   (   ) Badminton
        (   ) Paddleball   (   ) Bowling   (   ) Tennis

    (   ) 2. Mild team activities
        (   ) Softball   (   ) Volleyball

    (   ) 3. Physical fitness activities (indicate)
        (   ) Concepts of physical fitness (a study of physical fitness and cardiovascular health)
        (   ) Weight training (activities may be prescribed in 4 below)
        (   ) Aerobic activities (running-jogging)
        (   ) Gymnastics

    (   ) 4. Adapted activities specifically suggested by the physician _____

        _____

    (   ) 5. Assisting with record keeping and scoring for research projects.
    (   ) 6. Assisting in the physical education class as a scorer or a nonparticipating assistant.

This recommendation is to be effective   Signed _____M.D.

From _____ 19____   Address _____

To _____ 19____   _____

                                Telephone _____

Please briefly indicate the nature of the handicap _____

Figure 8–4. Physician's recommendation for modified physical education. (Courtesy Scotia-Glenville High School, Scotia, New York.)

through the recommendation of a physician, and in some cases, students may be placed on a modified program that the physician recommends. Special cards or letters should be provided in these instances. However, it is inadvisable to excuse students permanently unless a serious heart condition is present. A well-planned physical education class will provide for the needs of *all* students. Figure 8–4 shows the type of card to be used for this purpose.

Towel Program

A towel room with a check-out window should be installed at the exit end of the showers. It should be large enough to store towels and to provide space for one person to issue towels. Used towels can be placed in carts or bins to be picked up for laundering.

An important aspect of overall organization is cleanliness. One of the essentials is the provision of a towel for each student. There are several ways to arrange the daily showering program. Some schools launder the towels on the premises. This presents a number of problems: a washing machine operator must be employed, and the costs of equipment, water, detergents, and the other items make this system quite expensive. Probably the most practical way to handle the problem is to have all students pay a small towel fee each year. This money can be kept in a central fund and used to cover the cost of laundering the towels outside. Indigent students must, of course, be provided for by school funds or other sources. Local laundries may bid for the towel contract; they usually make daily deliveries. However, many school districts prohibit the charging of fees. In such cases, the district usually provides all instructional materials. These, of course, should include towels.

Some cities use the large paper towel which is discarded by the student after use. This plan eliminates all problems of laundering, loss, and other details involved in the use of regular towels. The cost of these towels is about the same

as the expense of laundering the usual type.

Another important aspect of the towel program is checking the inventory. Wherever local laundries service towels, a strict inventory procedure must be developed.

Uniforms and Shoes

Requiring standard dress for physical education has been common practice for many years. However, recent trends have somewhat eroded this rule. Many students feel that regulation uniforms are unnecessary and too expensive. They wish to dress as individuals and wear the types of uniforms that they feel are appropriate.

Teachers who advocate standard uniforms claim that conformity leads to better discipline, a more aesthetic and sanitary environment, better class appearances, and improved public relations. Others contend that if the outfit is comfortable and adequate for safe participation, it does not need to be a standard uniform. These teachers also argue that as there are no dress codes in other classes, students in physical education should not be forced to comply with a dress code. A local policy should be established concerning appropriate physical education attire for the students. As a rule, student morale, performance, and discipline are improved when students dress uniformly.

If a policy requiring a standard uniform is established, it is desirable that girls wear one-piece suits and boys wear trunks and shirts. In some places, students of both sexes wear trunks and shirts. These may be provided through local retail stores. Some schools order uniforms from the manufacturer and sell them in the school bookstore or in the physical education classes. There may be objections to this plan by local dealers, and many school authorities disapprove of the use of class time to sell materials of any kind. An alternative program practiced in some schools provides all students with uniforms, and the school board underwrites the total cost, including laundry. This plan is extremely expensive and many schools have abandoned it.

There should be no debate over requiring proper shoes for physical education participation as they are necessary to insure safety in the various activities. Tennis and basketball shoes are most suitable for athletic activity.

Lockers

Several types of lockers may be used, both for storage of clothes while the student is in the physical education class and for storage of uniforms. Teachers have to decide which is the best arrangement for the program. Experience has shown that the basket system is not as satisfactory as the box-locker arrangement. The baskets are easily damaged and the contents are often stolen. Probably the best type is the box locker-storage unit (a 5 foot × 1 foot × 1 foot dressing locker with 1 foot × 1 foot storage lockers attached) as illustrated in Figure 8–5.

Each unit should have both padlock attachments and combination locks. After enrollment has been determined, enough lockers should be made available to accommodate the highest number of students that might dress at the same time. For instance, if two classes of 40 students each are the day's peak load, there should be a minimum of 80 dressing locker units. This would provide 480 storage lockers for students to use for shoes and uniforms during a six-period day.

Another arrangement is to have all the storage units in a separate room. Students enter the box-locker storage room, take their uniforms and locks from their box lockers, and enter the

Figure 8–5. The box-locker storage unit is a functional and practical type of locker for physical education.

		School			
	Period			Teacher	

Number	Student's Name	Serial Number	Combination	Paid	Returned

Figure 8–6. A master form for keeping locker assignments is both practical and efficient.

dressing room. There must be enough dressing lockers to accommodate the largest class. This plan is recommended for situations in which outside groups use the dressing facilities. These areas should be locked to prevent outside groups from entering.

Locker Assignments. All locker assignments should be made during the first week of classes. Locker numbers and combinations should be recorded on the individual record cards or on a master sheet filed in the office. In addition, regulations concerning locks must be explained. Another form that may be used for recording locker informa-

tion is shown in Figure 8–6. This may be used when two or more people share a locker.

Showers

Construction of showers should be considered when planning new buildings. Walk-around showers are both practical and economical. Shower heads are placed five feet high on two sides of a corridor and the water is controlled by a master valve in the physical education office. Students walk through the corridor as water sprays on them from both sides. A group of 100 students can pass through the showers in three minutes. This type of shower plan has several advantages:

1. *Costs less.* The initial cost is considerably less because of the small amount of space as compared with the space required for individual showers.
2. *Saves time.* An entire class can shower in three or four minutes. There is no loitering.
3. *Prevents discipline problems.* Because time is limited, there is no opportunity for loitering and misbehavior in the showers.
4. *Lowers water cost.* The entire system is controlled by a master valve in the physical education office. There is no chance of students leaving the showers on and wasting water.

Showers for girls present a different situation. In many places, religion, modesty, and other considerations make it advisable to have individual showers and booths, in addition to the walk-around shower, for girls who wish privacy.

An administrative policy should be developed regarding showering for students. If regulations require showering, they should be strictly enforced. Before classes begin, an educational program should be initiated to show students why they should take showers. Many schools put showering on an optional basis. However, unless strong educational measures are taken, few students will choose to shower.

Storage

It is essential to provide adequate storage space for physical education equipment and supplies. Many new buildings do not allow sufficient storage room, and this can present a serious problem for the teachers. A large area should be available for assembling mats, table tennis tables, and other heavy equipment. In addition, a smaller area is needed for items such as balls, bats, and golf clubs. Three factors that should be considered in planning storage facilities for small equipment are security, accessibility, and portability. (Refer to the *Resource Manual* for an illustration.)

Parent-Teacher Relations

Teachers should communicate with parents at every opportunity and should interpret the physical education program in a way that gives parents at least an overview of what goes on in class. Several channels of communication have been proved effective.

Handbook. The handbook is a practical and effective tool for explaining the program to parents. If used properly, it can help to secure parental assistance and to aid the teacher in implementing a successful program. Figure 8–7 illustrates an outline of a type of handbook that is both practical and informative. It discusses the important areas involved in the organization and administration of the program. These handbooks are usually taken to the parents by the students only once during the years the students attend the school.

Letters. Letters may be written to parents describing the program, although their limitations make them less satisfactory than handbooks. A letter usually consists of one page, whereas the handbook consists of several pages. However, if the teacher wishes to acquaint the parent with a specific area of instruction, the letter may be an effective medium. Figure 8–8 shows one example of how letters may be used.

Reports. Many teachers devise some type of report to give parents an indication of their child's status in the physical education class. Although the usual report card carries a mark in physical education, something more comprehensive is important if parents are to have a clear understanding of their child's progress. These cards accompany the periodic report card devised by the school and are delivered to the parents by the students. A special physical education report is illustrated in Figure 8–9.

Text continued on page 155.

TABLE OF CONTENTS

THE MEANING OF PHYSICAL EDUCATION 3
THE PROGRAM 3-4
    Primary Grades 3
    Recess 3
    Upper Elementary, Junior and Senior High 3-4
THE DEPARTMENT 4
THE COURSE OF STUDY 4
IN-SERVICE TRAINING 4-5
    The Physical Education Library 4
    Visiting Days 4
    Supervisory Help 5
    Physical Education Committees 5
    In-Service Training Classes 5
PROFESSIONAL ORGANIZATIONS 5
RULES AND REGULATIONS 6-11
    Class Plans 6
    Grading 6
    Dressing 7
        Pupils 7
        Teachers 7
    Showering 7
    Outdoor Activities 7
    Excuses 7-8
    Inspection of Pupils 8
    Accidents 8
    Equipment 8
    Requisition Forms 9
    Public Relations 9
    Testing 9
        Physical Fitness Tests 9
        Skill Achievement Tests 9
        Tests of Knowledge 9
    Class Organization 10
    Supervision and Liability 10
    Planning Work 10
    Free Play 10
    Roll Call 10
    Conditioning Activities 11
JUNIOR HIGH SCHOOL PLAY DAY 11
ATHLETIC ASSOCIATION 11

Figure 8–7. The physical education handbook can be an important instrument in teacher-parent relations. (Courtesy South Bend School Community Corporation, South Bend, Indiana.)

Dear Parent:

This letter contains the regulations of the physical education department. We feel that to provide you with this information will enhance the splendid relations already existing between the home and school. It is the feeling of the teachers that with the number of students involved, in order to establish decorum in the department, the following regulations are necessary.

The student must have:

1. White socks
2. Gym suit
      Blue and white suit for girls
      Blue shorts and white T-shirt for boys
3. Tennis shoes
4. Combination lock

The student must:

1. Dress for each physical education period. If suit is misplaced, inform the teacher and use an emergency suit.
2. Present note from physician to be temporarily excused from participation.
3. Be on the proper number for roll call three minutes after tardy bell rings.
4. Take suit home to be laundered at the end of physical education week.
5. Deposit all jewelry, combs, pencils, etc. in secure place before entering the gymnasium.
6. Shower at the end of each period. If unable to do so, inform the teacher on duty in locker room.
7. Be on time for dressing, roll call, and health class. If students are tardy more than once each nine weeks, they will remain 15 minutes after school.
8. Not chew gum in class. This rule is for safety reasons. Violators will stay 20 minutes after school.
9. Be responsible for all work missed during absence.

You may be interested in the physical education curriculum, which includes instruction in lifetime sports, team sports, rhythms, and physical proficiency tests. The lifetime sports instruction is provided in tennis, golf, bowling, table tennis, and rhythms. Instruction in team sports includes volleyball, touch football, field hockey, basketball, and softball. Instruction is also given in wrestling, track and field, and tumbling.

_____
          Teacher's name

Figure 8-8. Letters to parents help to interpret the physical education program. (Courtesy Rosemont Junior High School, Norfolk, Virginia.)

CEDAR RAPIDS COMMUNITY SCHOOLS

Physical Welfare Department
PUPIL PHYSICAL FITNESS REPORT

NAME_____ SCHOOL_____ DATE_____ TEACHER(Fall)_____

PRINCIPAL_____TEACHER(Spring)_____

TO THE PARENTS: A series of physical fitness tests has recently been given to all pupils in grades 4–12. They are being given twice each school year. This is a report on the performance of your child. In each test you may compare your child's score with the performance score of other children throughout the state. The state scores are given in terms of percentile rank. For example, a percentile rank of 75 means that a child's performance surpasses that of 75 per cent of the children of the same grade tested through the state. The state norms were constructed on data obtained by testing boys and girls in 104 schools in Iowa during the 1960–61 school year. Thus, the percentile scores cannot necessarily be interpreted as the ultimate in achievement. They can be assumed to represent the achievements for the 1960–61 school year of those schools where attention was given to motor fitness.

If your child has a low performance score, it might be because of a particular height, weight or other physical characteristic. The important thing is for each child to show continued improvement in his own performance.

This department is making strenuous efforts to assist our young people to attain and maintain health and physical fitness. The physically underdeveloped youngsters are being identified and programs geared to individual needs. We are giving increased emphasis to the more vigorous type activities. It is recommended that parents encourage their children to participate regularly in physical activity.

TEST	WHAT IT TESTS	YOUR CHILD'S SCORE		PERCENTILE RANK		HOW TO INTERPRET THE RESULTS
		Fall	Spring	Fall	Spring	
SIT-UPS	Strength/endurance of abdominal muscles					The object was to do as many as possible in 1 min. (2 min. boys, Gr. 10–12)
STANDING BROAD JUMP	Power in the legs and coordination	in.	in.			The greater distance jumped, the better the performance.
SHUTTLE RUN	Agility					The greater number of trips in a 15 second interval, the better the score.
FORWARD BEND	Flexibility	in.	in.			The higher score (plus) measured in the nearest $\frac{1}{2}$", the better the performance.
GRASSHOPPER	Endurance					The object was to do as many as possible in 30 sec. (1 min. boys, Gr. 7 & up.)
DASH	Speed	sec.	sec.			The faster time the better the performance; 40 yd., Gr. 4–6; 50 yds., Gr. 7–12.
PULL-UPS (Boys) BENT ARM HANG (Girls)	Arm, shoulder and upper back strength					Boys—one point each time chin goes above the bar. Girls—the longer the time (in sec.) with arms fully bent, chin above bar, the better the performance.

ARNOLD SALISBURY
Superintendent of Schools

EMIL A. KLUMPAR
Physical Welfare Consultant

Figure 8–9. Parents appreciate information showing how their children perform in physical education. (Courtesy Cedar Rapids Community School District, Cedar Rapids, Iowa.)

Student Involvement

Part of the organizational details of the first week of classes should be a plan for student involvement in certain phases of the program. A group of student leaders that assists with many of the instructional procedures and routine details can be a tremendous help to the teacher. It also provides the students with leadership experience. The group can be responsible for checking attendance, issuing towels and equipment, recording results, and other details important to the smooth and effective functioning of the class. The student leaders from each class should meet periodically. Under the teacher's direction, they can be trained to assist in the various mechanics of the program. The Student Leader Association may be organized in a simple yet functional plan, as shown in Figure 8–10.

Student Instructors. In each class, the teacher should have a group of older, experienced students that assists with the instruction. These are usually students who have become proficient in certain activities by participating on the varsity team, in intramurals, or in a community program. For example, it is important in tumbling that one group of students check the movement of the students performing the skills, in order to prevent accidents. Student instructors should be trained to assist in this procedure.

Squad Leaders. Many teachers feel that a good organizational procedure is to divide all classes into squads, each having a leader. These units may be formed by having an entire class nominate a number of students for the leadership positions. Those nominated would then select the students who would constitute their squads. The chief function of the squad leaders is to expedite such procedures as taking attendance, urging members to report on time, checking uniforms, and managing the squad.

Student Class Managers. Students should be selected to serve as class managers. These managers would have as their chief responsibility the issuing of equipment to the squad leaders. They would also work directly with the squad leaders in the duties outlined for them.

Assistant Student Instructors. Each class would have several *assistant* student instructors whose chief duty is to work with the class manager and assist the teacher with the overall administration of the class.

Many schools throughout the country utilize student leaders to a great advantage. These leaders may assume many

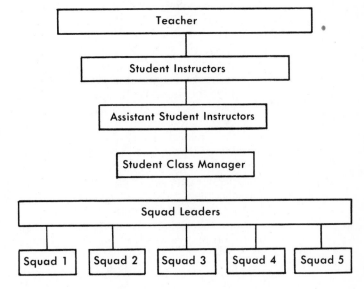

Figure 8–10. Organization of the student leader association.

of the burdensome administrative details and thus enable the teachers to devote most of their time to teaching.

Organizing Teaching Stations

Organizing teaching stations can be time-consuming and should be done well in advance. For example, when wrestling or tumbling is scheduled, mats must be unrolled and placed properly. This requires tremendous manpower because mats are heavy and cumbersome. Volleyball instruction involves the proper installation of nets, which must be strung tightly for efficient ball handling. Lines must be placed on play fields for softball, hockey, and soccer. All these details necessitate a cooperative effort by teachers and students. The Student Leader Association may assume the responsibility for many of the details that are involved in organizing teaching stations.

Providing Supplies and Equipment

Physical education leaders are usually responsible for submitting requisitions when equipment and supplies are needed. Teachers should be familiar with the types of equipment that are scientifically adequate for the program, and in addition should know how to prepare the inventory, budget wisely, and care for all supplies.

Any materials being employed for a class should be set up at the beginning of each period. In order to conserve valuable instruction time, this procedure may be the responsibility of the Student Leader Association. Equipment must also be securely stored at the end of each class period. Many accidents occur on the play field and in the gymnasium because equipment is left out, and students who are reporting early or are not scheduled for a class take advantage of the teacher's absence. They often injure themselves by using the equipment unsupervised.

The Inventory. A detailed inventory should be made at the end of each year. This inventory is of inestimable value in assisting teachers with selecting equipment and determining the budget. Teachers are expected to know how much equipment is on hand and are responsible for maintaining accurate records of where the equipment is stored. Damaged and unused materials should be included in the inventory. Local schools and districts usually develop standard check lists for this purpose.

Budgeting. An annual budget should be prepared, showing the allocation of funds for each activity. A stipulated amount of money is usually set aside for the health and physical education budget. Teachers must work within this budget in planning each aspect of the program.

In many school systems, the budget for physical education is dependent upon gate receipts from athletic contests. This is not a recommended procedure. Physical education instruction is of vital importance for the health and fitness of all students and should not be dependent upon a fluctuating income. Regular allocations should be provided by the same instructional resource that supports other subjects in the curriculum.

Requisitions. Materials should not be ordered without justification of their need. The type and amount of supplies needed for the program are determined by (1) the instructional content of the program and (2) the teaching procedures used.

INSTRUCTIONAL CONTENT AS A DETERMINANT. Before selecting activities for any instructional program, the teacher must determine the availability of the needed materials. For example, bowling cannot be taught unless pins, balls, and alleys can be procured. The teacher should make every effort to make arrangements so that the activity can be included in the curriculum. Local bowling establishments are usually willing to furnish used balls and pins at little or no cost. This approach should be used in making supplies and equipment available for any activity that is a desirable addition to the curriculum.

TEACHING PROCEDURES AS A DETERMINANT. The teaching approach will always determine the quantity of supplies and equipment for the program. If the teacher is content with an informal play program in basketball, for instance, two or three balls will suffice. However, if the teacher is eager to provide effective instruction, the class should be divided into eight or ten units, each with one ball. This will require more supplies, but only by working in small groups can students learn and practice skills.

After determining the necessary materials, the teacher should be careful in the selection of items. He should try to find the most reliable sources of materials and place all orders on bid. Specifications should be written out concerning quality, design, and safety factors. Standard school forms, designed locally, are helpful in requisitioning the equipment and supplies needed for the program.

Improvising

A considerable amount of equipment is necessary for teaching effectively, and providing it may be very costly. However, many items used in the instructional program can be constructed or secured locally for a portion of the usual price. Some examples of these items are starting blocks; hurdles; jumping and volleyball standards; table-tennis tables, nets, and paddles; bowling alley and basketball backstops; archery racks; batons; and rope-jumping equipment.

Safety Precautions

The importance of planning for safety has been discussed in Chapter 7. It should be emphasized again that instruction in sports safety, equipment safety, locker room safety, and class behavior should receive high priority in the physical education program. It is recommended that Chapter 7 be reviewed at this time.

Team Teaching

When more than one teacher is employed for the physical education program, team teaching may be used. In team teaching, two or more teachers work cooperatively to devise better ways of teaching student groups. When giving individual sports instruction, for example, one teacher might instruct a small group in golf while another teacher instructs larger groups in volleyball or basketball skills.

Some physical education leaders strongly endorse team teaching. They claim that this innovation provides the best teacher for the particular activity, students find the program more interesting, and instruction is improved. However, there is disagreement as to the effectiveness of team teaching. Some feel that less planning is done, team teaching is difficult to administer, the large groups are not scheduled by ability, and small group instruction does not produce the desired results because of teacher shortage. However, a modified program of team teaching in which several teachers combine their efforts to arrange small and large groups *within a period* can be successfully implemented. The Secondary Physical Education Department of the Norfolk, Virginia Public Schools has used a combination plan of selectives and team teaching for over 25 years.

Selectives in Physical Education

A widely accepted trend in secondary physical education is to offer students a choice of activities within a stipulated framework. Physical education is still required, but students may periodically select the activities in which they wish to receive instruction. The term for this is *selectives*. (It is different from an *elective* program, which allows students the option of not participating if they so desire.)

When selective scheduling is implemented, students are no longer forced to participate in those sports and games that are uninteresting to them and to which they are neither anatomically nor psychologically suited. However, before students are allowed to select activities, they should participate in a comprehensive exploratory program that provides them with experience in a variety of activities. Junior and senior students attending Terra Linda High School in San Rafael, California, are allowed to select activities from the curriculum every nine weeks. These students take exploratory mini-courses in their freshman and sophomore years. The courses introduce them to various activities, providing the students with the exposure that enables them to choose their curriculum more wisely in the junior and senior years.[7]

A well-organized physical education class is appreciated by students, teachers, administrators, and parents alike because it is the best medium for effective instruction. Orderly classes also lessen disruptive behavior, provide students with the satisfaction of having improved their performance, and assure teachers that their efforts have been successful. The well-organized class has a number of characteristics that are a visible testimony to the teacher's success:

1. The program shows evidence of planning to motivate and maintain interest.
2. The students are enthusiastic and inspired.
3. The students assemble quickly for roll call and instruction.
4. All students are dressed for participation.
5. There are no discipline problems, and morale is high.
6. The instruction is superior; has direction, and shows planning.
7. The activities are meaningful and scientifically selected.

8. The teacher demonstrates, leads, and allows student discussion.
9. Emphasis is on teaching, with the teacher providing individual instruction whenever possible.
10. Students are grouped by ability.
11. Emphasis is on teaching of skills, and all students are active and interested.

EXTERNAL ORGANIZATIONAL PROCEDURES

External procedures that affect the management of the class require the cooperative effort of the teacher and the administrator of the school. This rapport largely determines whether or not the program will be conducive to good teaching; many have failed because the proper administrative framework was never fully established. *Teachers have a responsibility to assist administrators with the formulation of policies that will provide a strong foundation for the program.* They should have access to authoritative opinion on the various procedures necessary for program development. These procedures are discussed on the following pages.

The Physical Education Requirement

Chapter 12 shows that one of the crucial issues in physical education is a daily requirement for all grades. Establishing this requirement is the first and most important step in planning and organizing a program.

The President's Council on Physical Fitness and Sports summarizes the recommendations of many national organizations, including the National Medical Jury, in the suggestion that daily physical education classes be required in grades seven through twelve.[8] The Council also reveals that 91 per cent of the 3875 men and women interviewed support physical education in the secondary schools.[9] These findings support the proposition of a physical education requirement, and teachers must continually strive for the implementation of adequate daily programs. Through interpretation and presentation of the need for daily requirements, administrators can be convinced of the importance of making the physical education program mandatory for all grades.

The authors feel that a physical education requirement for students in kindergarten through grade twelve is not an end in itself. It is misleading to say that physical education should begin or end at any specific time because exercise in varying degrees starts with birth and stops only at death. It is the responsibility of physical educators to guide children through an effective program during the school years and thus motivate them to remain physically active throughout life.

Credit for Physical Education

An essential corollary to the daily requirement is the awarding of credit for physical education, which is also discussed in Chapter 12. If physical education is to attain the status it deserves in education, it must carry the same credit value as other subjects in the curriculum. Teachers and physical education leaders have long been apathetic about this matter and must therefore assume the blame for the status of the program in this respect. It must be emphasized again that the strongest source of improvement lies within the profession itself; the program must be interpreted and the objectives explained in a continuing effort to convince administrators that, in education, the physical is as important as the mental.

Teaching Load and Class Size

Another important policy to be established for overall organization concerns class size. Although the ideal size for any subject has not yet been determined, the limitations for effective classroom instruction that have been empirically established apply to physical education as well as to academic subjects. Class size is even more consequential for physical education than for other subjects. Teachers of physical education are concerned not only with excellence of instruction but also with the safety of each student in the class. There is a high correlation between large classes and accidents; large numbers of students cannot be taught safely or effectively.

Scheduling for Physical Education

Students should be scheduled by grade to maintain the proper sequence of learning. Each class should be composed of students from only one grade level whenever possible. Although there may be some topical overlap, repetition will be avoided through the spiral of learning — an educational principle long accepted as fundamental to good teaching. The spiral of learning, when applied to teaching of skills, involves the progression from a simple movement to the complex game situation. Throughout the learning process, a continuous thread of multi-patterned fabric is noticed, which represents the spiral-of-learning concept (Figure 8–11). Each succeeding grade should require a little more content, a different approach, and higher goals.

Grade levels have often determined the way in which students are arranged for instruction. This involves two generally recognized procedures: (1) traditional scheduling and (2) flexible or modular scheduling. Although scheduling is the responsibility of the administration, teachers should be familiar with the process. In some instances, they may assist the administration with the details of assigning students.

Traditional Scheduling. In this plan, students are assigned to blocks of time; the school day may be divided into five, six, or seven periods. Students have the same teacher every day for the number of days allocated to physical education. Each subject is allotted

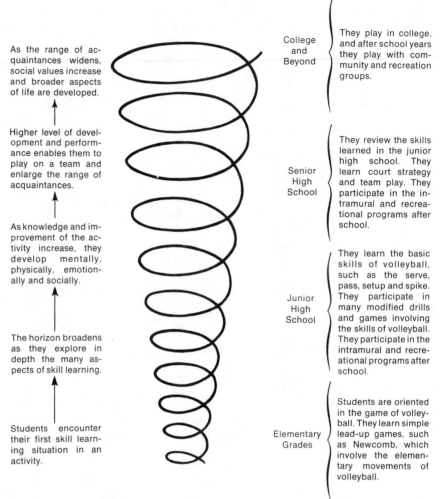

As the range of ac-
quaintances widens,
social values increase
and broader aspects
of life are developed.

Higher level of devel-
opment and perform-
ance enables them to
play on a team and
enlarge the range of
acquaintances.

As knowledge and im-
provement of the ac-
tivity increase, they
develop mentally,
physically, emotion-
ally and socially.

The horizon broadens
as they explore in
depth the many as-
pects of skill learning.

Students encounter
their first skill learn-
ing situation in an
activity.

College
and
Beyond

They play in college,
and after school years
they play with com-
munity and recreation
groups.

Senior
High
School

They review the skills
learned in the junior
high school. They
learn court strategy
and team play. They
participate in the in-
tramural and recrea-
tional programs after
school.

Junior
High
School

They learn the basic
skills of volleyball,
such as the serve,
pass, setup and spike.
They participate in
many modified drills
and games involving
the skills of volleyball.
They participate in the
intramural and recre-
ational programs after
school.

Elementary
Grades

Students are oriented
in the game of volley-
ball. They learn simple
lead-up games, such
as Newcomb, which
involve the elemen-
tary movements of
volleyball.

Figure 8–11. The spiral of learning. (Adapted from Daughtrey, Anne S.: *Methods of Basic Business and Economic Education*. Cincinnati: South-Western Publishing Company, 1974, p. 156.)

the same amount of time, and the teacher-student ratio is determined by the administrator. The recommended ratio for physical education is 30 to 40 students per teacher each period.

Flexible Scheduling. Probably the most popular innovation in education today is flexible scheduling. This plan was developed to provide more free-dom in the daily schedule and to give teachers more time for individual in-struction. The plan elminates the tradi-tional allocation of one daily period, usually 50 or 60 minutes, to each sub-ject, substituting a number of modules

which are not necessarily allocated each day. Some subjects will be given more modules than others. These mod-ules are usually 20 minutes long, but they may vary, depending on school policy. In developing flexible scheduli-ng, three types of learning are usually involved: (1) large group instruction, (2) small group instruction, and (3) inde-pendent study.

Large group instruction involves in-struction to groups of students ranging from 75 to 300 in number. Classes are given once or twice each week by a team of teachers. Various instructional media are used, including films, filmstrips, and overhead projectors. Students are not given the opportunity to ask questions but are required to take notes and study the materials provided by the teaching team.

In *small group instruction,* students are organized into groups of 5 to 20. The teacher instructs, answers questions, encourages discussions, and evaluates student progress. These groups usually meet two or three times per week.

Independent study involves unscheduled time during which the student is allowed to pursue his own interests. He may do research, visit the laboratory, study independently, or work with another student. In the case of physical education, he would report to the gymnasium, playground, or pool.

Physical educators should carefully evaluate flexible scheduling. Who determines the number of modules allotted to each subject? How many modules will be assigned to physical education? Will successful programs have to lose their hard-earned gains for some experiment that has not, as yet, proved to be successful? These questions and others should be resolved if physical education is to maintain its respectability in the curriculum. Figure 8–12 illustrates assignments in secondary schools using a flexible program arrangement.

EXAMPLE OF FLEXIBLE SCHEDULING. Students and teachers should study the following example of flexible scheduling and evaluate it, remembering that change is not always progress.

Washington High School, located in Germantown, Wisconsin, adopted the modular scheduling plan in 1968. The plan includes all three phases of modular scheduling: large group instruction, small group instruction, and independent

TIME	M	T	W	Th	F
8:00	English	Indep. Study	English	Social Studies	English
8:30				Indep. Study	
9:00	Indep. Study	Math	Guidance	Math	Social Studies
9:30			Social Studies		
10:00	Math	English	Math	English	
10:30	Indust. Arts	Typing	Indust. Arts	Typing	Math
11:00	Boys' Chorus		Boys' Chorus	Physical Education	
11:30	Indep. Study		English		
12:00	L	U	N	C	H
12:30	Social Studies	Social Studies	Indep. Study	Indep. Study	Guidance
1:00		Studies	Study	Study	
1:30	Physical Education	Indust. Arts		Indust. Arts	Physical Education
2:00			Physical Education		
2:30		Arts	Education	Arts	English
3:00					Boys' Chorus

Figure 8–12. A modular schedule for students in the secondary school. (Courtesy "Organizational Patterns for Instruction in Physical Education," *AAHPER,* 1971, p. 13.)

study. The purposes for adopting the modular scheduling plan were:

1. To provide students greater opportunity for individualized instruction.
2. To foster more student responsibility.
3. To provide opportunity for student self-discipline.
4. To provide opportunity for student self-direction.

Instead of a traditional seven-period day, five-day week schedule, the system operates within a six-day cycle, each day consisting of twenty-one 20-minute modules. Each of the six days is given a letter: Monday is "A"; Tuesday is "B," Wednesday, "C"; Thursday, "D", Friday, "E"; and the following Monday "F"; Tuesday, "A", and so on. Students are required to attend physical education class four days out of the six-day cycle for three modules each time. Three classes involve instruction and the fourth is a laboratory class. Instruction in a laboratory situation depends on the type and length of the unit, the number of students, and the number of skills to be learned.

Twelve laboratories exist within the six-day cycle. Students are assigned to these laboratories at the beginning of the school year. Freshman-sophomore and junior-senior classes are combined for laboratory work. All teachers are required to instruct within each laboratory. This procedure provides for a smaller teacher-student ratio, more individualized instruction, and better personal contact with students.[10]

A CRITICAL LOOK AT FLEXIBLE SCHEDULING. Flexible scheduling has been in existence long enough to allow some practical observations to be made concerning its relative value. Students enjoy modular scheduling, and to bright students it offers several advantages. However, there appears to be no significant difference between the mean achievement scores of students in schools using flexible modules and those in traditional schools.[11] The independent phase of flexible scheduling has been somewhat abused by certain students who, when allowed free time, invariably choose activities of an antisocial nature. For them, independent study is not synonymous with individualization of instruction.[12]

An important two-year study commissioned by the California Bureau of Health Education, Physical Education, Athletics, and Recreation revealed the advantages of daily scheduling over modular scheduling in physical education. The study involved 2400 students in 12 high schools, six of which were on flexible scheduling and six on daily scheduling. H. Harrison Clark, chairman of the project, stated that "the results . . . supported the value of the daily physical education requirement." The director of the project, Stan LeProtti, made the following analysis of the study:

. . . the advantage alluded to by exponents of flexible scheduling . . . is not attainable under the conditions which presently exist. Students do not respond according to theory; staff does not function effectively to the extent claimed; and existing facilities do not accommodate the scheduling practice.

In those flexible schedules which provide elongated time periods, i.e., 90 or 120 minutes for physical education on an irregular basis, the process of program administration instruction is simply slowed down. That is, students take longer to dress, teachers take longer to take the roll, and students spend more time standing or sitting during the instructional phase of the program.[13]

The major problem in flexible programming, according to the committee, is the use of unscheduled time. A large number of students, instead of reporting to independent study, resource centers, and conferences, were found visiting friends, sitting around, and actually leaving the campuses. Unscheduled time also contributed to increased locker room theft, which necessitated more supervision of parking lots, hallways, dining areas, and other places where students meet. The report showed that in one school, teachers were scheduled for 36 modules of instruction and 43 modules of general supervision per week. These situations not only are expensive but also are a gross misuse of professional time.

Adjusting physical education to flexible scheduling presents a variety of problems, as substantiated in the following:

1. Some teachers are neither educated in, nor

experienced with, this concept, and others have been uncomfortable in the situation or unwilling to participate.

2. Some state laws and local regulations require a daily period of physical education.

3. Locker rooms and gymnasiums that have been designed and outfitted for a traditional peak student load may require revisions before the program can be completely operative.

4. If the student's schedule calls for longer, less frequent meetings, absences cause more detriment to the learning process.

5. Staffing requirements may be more than those traditionally allotted to physical education.

6. A period of acclimation, organization, and public relations must be undertaken before the program can be implemented successfully. This period should extend for at least two years before the program is inaugurated. Teachers, students, and parents must be fully ready for transition.

7. Identification of various learning groups and the establishment of a differentiated learning process can take more time and effort than grouping students traditionally by year in school.

8. Not all students feel secure in, or can profit from, unscheduled class time. Special counseling and supervision of these students is needed.[14]

Gard, in a timely analysis of flexible scheduling, discusses the problems that arise when administrators attempt to handle all the variables involved in regular daily scheduling. He shows that only through the use of a computer-produced schedule can the more complex flexible plan become a reality. Although there are advantages to such a system, Gard points to the problems of time, space, and personnel, all of which involve huge expenditures.

In addition to the requirements of scheduled subjects, space and personnel are necessary for *unscheduled* time. Whether the students are in large groups, small groups, or independent study, the ratio of students to seats does not change and the need for more personnel to supervise these groups is evident.

Gard also discusses the human element involved. In the flexible scheduling plan, there is the opportunity for team teaching, supervising independent work, and meeting with small groups. Working with these groups may demand 25 to 40 per cent more teacher time. On the other hand, this problem may be offset by the use of aides, and the result may be a greater service for a lower cost than the traditional schedule. However, Gard is concerned with the 40 per cent of unassigned time during which students are released from supervision. This phase of flexible scheduling too often results in vandalism, off-campus problems, petty theft, loitering on the premises of homeowners and businesses, absenteeism, and the increased incidence of smoking of cigarettes and marijuana.

Gard feels that the following arrangements should be made in those schools that decide to initiate the flexible scheduling approach:

1. Planning of the "master schedule" should be truly adequate to minimize the number of impossible student schedules.

2. Students should not be scheduled for larger loads than the school can support.

3. Faculty members should expect to work harder and to put in longer hours with students.

4. Administrators, board members, students, and community should recognize the price of reduced control — in absenteeism, failure, and even possible violence to person and property. (The community must be prepared for the cost and unpopularity of firm grounds-control measures should this eventually prove necessary.)

5. Ample space should be available for study and research — adequate even for the necessary inefficiency of voluntary usage — and to accommodate the one in four who probably will need full-time supervision.

6. Faculty support measures (aides, supervisors, materials, services) should be adequate to leave teachers free to teach and to plan.[15]

Flexible scheduling has been successful in some schools and has failed dismally in others. The major concern of physical education in considering this plan is the status of the physical education program. As was pointed out earlier in the chapter, approximately 60 minutes of physical activity is necessary every day, and many school systems have incorporated this into the curriculum. Will flexible scheduling affect this daily allotment of time? If it interferes with fulfilling this requirement, teachers must urge the administration to allot the minimum recommended time each day for physical education.

The schedule based on selectives is practical, functional, relatively easy to administer, and may be easily adapted within the class period. It is the authors' opinion that a wise choice of activities within the daily requirement is the most satisfactory arrangement for physical education. Schools that have experimented with this approach find that it meets the needs of students without creating the problems that arise when physical education programs deviate from the daily requirement. Many students terminate their education at the end of high school. If the program of physical education is to have meaning, it should offer students a program that encourages their participation in activities beyond the school years.

New patterns of organizing physical education programs have emerged throughout the country. All have been tried in the field of general education, and some offer a welcome change in the traditional curriculum. These patterns may affect an entire system or merely a single school. Regardless of how they are used or to what extent they are applied, they should pass the experimental stage before being applied to physical education. Sometimes physical educators, in their efforts to improve their programs, are likely to adopt experiments made by general educators. Although physical education has some goals in common with general education, it is a different discipline. Physical education is basically a *movement* program. As such, it is planned differently, is organized differently, and makes unique contributions to the education of children.

Client-Centered Approach. The need for a realistic plan that accommodates those students whose needs are not met by flexible scheduling is obvious. Such a plan is described by Thomson as the client-centered plan. In the client-centered plan, a diagnostic unit is established to determine interests, skills, attitudes, and needs of students. Using

the information gathered, student types are determined. Instructional modes are developed from these studies to provide a degree of individualization. The instructional system operating in the client-centered school is shown in Figure 8–13.

The instructional mode is essential to the success of the client-centered school. Its effectiveness depends on its adaptability to the individual student; to the bright and dull and to different attitudes, values, psychological patterns, and lifestyles. An instructional mode is shown in Figure 8–14.

Although no research is available to guide the way toward solving the inadequacies of flexible scheduling, Thomson feels that:

what does appear to be true from the present vantage point, however, is that unscheduled time and independent study at present do not benefit a significant number of students. Alternative arrangements must be found. The search will continue for new approaches. The client-centered school seems to be a promising direction to pursue.[16]

Individualized Scheduling. Each student needs and is entitled to a good physical education program. Because each child develops at his or her own pace physically, mentally, and emotionally, instruction must be personally geared. This concept has strengthened the individualized instructional approach to the teaching-learning process for all students — normal, gifted, handicapped, poorly coordinated, and slow. There are many forms of individualized instruction; effective teachers always use it to some extent for each student. Individual instruction is intended to give the student personal attention, allow the student selection, and give the student the chance for involvement.

Leaders in physical education have

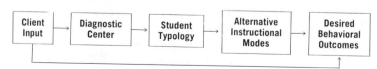

Figure 8–13 The instructional system operating in the client-centered school. (Courtesy of Scott Thomson, *Phi Delta Kappan*, April 1971, p. 484.)

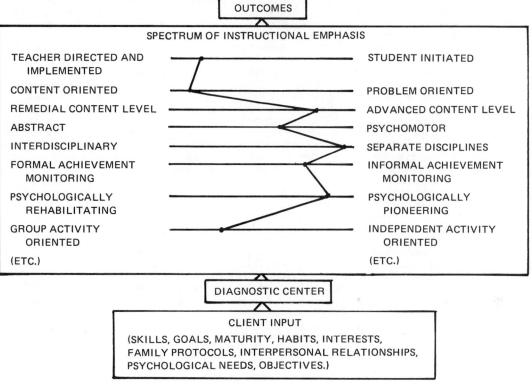

Figure 8–14. Profile of an instructional mode. (Courtesy of Scott Thomson, *Phi Delta Kappan*, April 1971, p. 484.)

been seeking new ways to resolve the dilemma of teaching large numbers of students with limited equipment and facilities and at the same time meeting the particular needs of the individual student. Teachers in the secondary schools have been applying various methods to individual instruction. In 1976, the American Alliance for Health, Physical Education and Recreation introduced a new publication jointly sponsored by the Secondary School and College Commissions of the National Association for Sport and Physical Education. The publication, *Personalized Learning in Physical Education,* contains material applicable to the secondary school.

Individualizing means different things to different people. Larry Locke, Hal Lawson, Anthony Annarino, Muska Mosston, and others have attempted to solve the problem of terminology. The definition of

terms used in the AAHPER publication is useful. Four types of individual instruction are explained: cohort instruction, individualized instruction, personalized instruction, and humanistic instruction.

Cohort Instruction. Cohort instruction makes subject matter and the characteristics of groups of students the two paramount factors in determining teacher behavior. Cohort instruction includes any pedagogical strategy which leads the teacher to teach the same thing to all students at the same time, by the same method, and requires all the students to practice in the same way, at the same pace, for the same length of time, and to be subject to the same kinds of standards and the same criteria for evaluating achievement.

Selection of objectives, method, and content is determined by the internal logic of the subject matter and an appraisal of the group. The assumption is made that it is not possible to deal with students whose needs and interests deviate significantly from the type selected as the target for instruction (often the average of the group, though sometimes a higher ability segment) without an unreasonable loss in educational efficiency. It further is assumed that any disadvantage which accrues to students who are not well matched to the instruction is unfortunate, but inevitable and therefore tolerable.

Individualized Instruction. Individualized instruction makes the learning characteristics of individual students the paramount factor in determining teacher behavior. Individualized instruction includes any pedagogical strategy which leads the teacher to adjust objectives (ends) or content, instruction and practice (means), or all those elements, to produce the most appropriate match with the characteristics of individual students. The process of matching educational ends and means to student needs and interests may be controlled by the teacher or the student, or shared by both. In short, this process adjusts learning to the student.

The assumption is made that it is possible for the teacher to deal with most students as individuals (irrespective of the diversity of their unique needs and interests) and to maintain or improve educational efficiency. It further is assumed that individualizing is necessary because some of the consequences of cohort instruction are intolerable.

Personalized Instruction. Personalized instruction has been used as a generic term intended to encompass all methods of instruction in which students, or students in concert with teachers, undertake to adjust what is to be learned to the needs and characteristics of the learner. When the term is employed in this way, it ordinarily implies particular emphasis on personalizing learning products. Thus, contract learning systems are an appropriate illustration of this kind of method.

A second and quite different meaning has been assigned to personalized instruction. Here the term is used to designate any version of individualized instruction in which there is use of, or emphasis upon, the learner's involvement with others in the learning environment. This either may involve the learner in a tutor-student relationship with the teacher or may involve the learner in transactions with peers.

Personalized instruction is distinguished from independent study, or those group settings for individualized instruction which may be non-interactive, such as learning stations or circuit training.

Humanistic Instruction. Humanistic instruction includes any version of individualized instruction which, in addition to being a strong component of personalization through social transactions, stresses primacy of the individual's feelings (and a variety of related affective goals); the value of long-range outcomes such as self-actualization and personal awareness; and involvement in such processes as continual self-examination and open communication with others in the learning environment.

Great stress is placed on active participation and immediate personal experience, rather than passive learning processes employing verbal abstraction. Humanistic instruction often involves substantial student participation in the selection of learning content as well as learning method.

There are reservations about the ability of the secondary student to be self-directive. Concerns also center on evaluation and discipline. The humanistic approach to teaching has numerous alternatives. Some teachers may find it a challenge, while others may view it as a threat to the teacher's role. At any rate, the beginning teacher of physical education needs to be aware of the opportunity for individualizing the instruction in the secondary schools.[17]

Planning Facilities

Just as adequate facilities are needed for effective instruction and goal fulfillment in other subjects, so are they needed for successful teaching in physical education. Lack of sufficient teaching stations and play areas is one of the reasons that poor programs in physical education still exist throughout the country. This does not imply that good programs cannot be carried on in older and apparently inadequate facilities; it does imply that at least enough space should be available in which to teach a class effectively. Some of the finest programs exist in old facilities, and some of the worst programs exist in beautiful modern stations.

Much has been written about physical education facilities and equipment. Teachers are expected to be well informed about all phases of their special field and are often asked to make recommendations on facilities and equipment. It is the purpose of this chapter to give an overview of the facilities needed for physical education and to suggest references for more extensive study in these two areas.

Teachers should insist that they be allowed to participate in the planning of facilities. This is of extreme importance, because once final plans are drawn and approved, the school program must adjust to the facility regardless of whether the final construction is functional.

Principles of Planning. These are important if the construction is to provide functional areas for teaching. Principles that may be used by administrators and architects in developing plans for the physical education plant are:

1. Every community needs space and facilities for physical education, athletic, and recreational programs.
2. Every community requires a master plan based on a study of its needs.
3. The type, location, and size of essential areas and facilities must be related to the total community pattern.
4. Facilities should be planned in relation to the social and economic characteristics of the community.
5. Areas and facilities should be planned with due regard for the full potential use of existing and available physical resources.
6. Programs should serve the interests and needs of all the people.
7. Plans must conform to state and local regulations and, as far as possible, to accepted standards and practice.
8. Close cooperation among all public and private agencies concerned with the location is essential. Acquisition, development, and operation of areas and facilities designed for athletics, physical education, and recreation are of the utmost importance.
9. All interested organizations, individuals, and groups should have an opportunity to share in the planning of areas and facilities intended for public use.
10. Individuals qualified to give expert advice and assistance in planning should be consulted as often as possible.
11. Every available source of property or funds should be explored, evaluated, and utilized whenever appropriate.
12. Widespread publicity, sound interpretation, and public discussion facilitate the implementation of area and facility plans.

Considerations in Planning.   There is now a trend to bring teachers into the planning process and to use their suggestions for formulating more functional designs for physical education. Several important factors are involved in planning facilities for the physical education pro-

gram, and the teacher should be familiar enough with them to plan them sequentially.

SIZE OF SCHOOL.   For a new school, an enrollment estimate is necessary to determine the number of teaching stations needed. This is crucial because one gymnasium may be adequate for 200 pupils (40 pupils per period, five periods daily), but for a larger student body, the architect and the administration must begin to think in terms of additional stations.

GENERAL RECOMMENDATIONS.   Teachers should make general recommendations as to the needs of the program. The required number of teaching stations and a general plan for location of stations, showers, and other items should be outlined for the architect. A rough sketch presented with the recommendations is always helpful.

REVIEW OF THE GENERAL PLAN.   The architect should study the recommendations of the teacher and use them in planning the building. After he has drawn a rough sketch of the entire facility, he should ask the teacher to review the plans.

SPECIFIC RECOMMENDATIONS.   At this point the teacher should be ready to make specific recommendations regarding the size of the teaching stations, showers, storage rooms, towel room, lockers, and other needed components for a functional facility. It costs no more to design a building for functional use than to design it so that teachers and pupils are handicapped in the day-by-day operations.

An authoritative check list is tremendously helpful to the teacher in reviewing specific details involved in the construction of physical education facilities. A check list developed by the Athletic Institute and AAHPER is shown in Figure 8–5.

Indoor Facilities

Planning indoor facilities for functional operation is extremely important. Often the entire responsibility for this is left to the architect, who may not have had experience with physical education structures. As a result, the architect usually resorts to the traditional gymnasium plan designed for the varsity
Text continued on page 170.

CHECK LIST for FACILITY PLANNERS

As an aid to those responsible for planning facilities for athletics, physical education, and recreation, a check list has been prepared. The application of this check list may prevent unfortunate and costly errors.

Place the appropriate letter in the space indicated in the right-hand margin after each statement.

A—The plans meet the requirements **completely.**

B—The plans meet the requirements **only partially.**

C—The plans **fail** to meet the requirements.

Soundly conceived plans for areas and facilities are **not** achieved by chance or accident, but by initiative and action of knowledgeable people acting individually, in groups, and as agencies.

GENERAL

1. A clear-cut statement has been prepared on the nature and scope of the program, and the special requirements for space, equipment, fixtures, and facilities have been dictated by the activities to be conducted. _____
2. The facility has been planned to meet the total requirements of the program as well as the special needs of those who are to be served. _____
3. The plans and specifications have been checked by all governmental agencies (city, county, and state) whose approval is required by law. _____
4. Plans for areas and facilities conform to state and local regulations and to accepted standards and practices. _____
5. The areas and facilities planned make possible the programs that serve the interests and needs of all the people. _____
6. Every available source of property or funds has been explored, evaluated, and utilized whenever appropriate. _____
7. All interested persons and organizations concerned with the facility have had an opportunity to share in its planning (professional educators, users, consultants, administrators, engineers, architects, program specialists, building managers, and builder—a team approach). _____
8. The facility and its appurtenances will fulfill the maximum demands of the program. The program has not been curtailed to fit the facility.
9. The facility has been functionally planned to meet the present and anticipated needs of specific programs, situations, and publics. _____
10. Future additions are included in present plans to permit economy of construction. _____
11. Lecture classrooms are isolated from distracting noises. _____
12. Storage areas for indoor and outdoor equipment are of adequate size. They are located adjacent to the gymnasiums. _____
13. Shelves in storage rooms are slanted toward the wall. _____
14. All passageways are free of obstructions; fixtures are recessed. _____
15. Facilities for health services and the first-aid and emergency-isolation rooms are suitably interrelated. _____
16. Buildings, specific areas, and facilities are clearly identified. _____
17. Locker areas are arranged for ease of supervision. _____
18. Offices, teaching stations, and service facilities are properly interrelated. _____
19. Special needs of the physically handicapped are met, including a ramp into the building at a major entrance. _____
20. All "dead space" is used. _____
21. The building is compatible in design and comparable in quality and accommodation to other campus structures. _____
22. Storage rooms are accessible to the play area. _____
23. Workrooms, conference rooms, and staff and administrative offices are interrelated. _____
24. Shower and dressing facilities are provided for professional staff members and are conveniently located. _____
25. Thought and attention have been given to making facilities and equipment as durable and vandalproof as possible. _____
26. Low-cost maintenance features have been adequately considered. _____
27. This facility is a part of a well-integrated master plan. _____

28. All areas, courts, facilities, equipment, climate control, security, etc., conform rigidly to detailed standards and specifications. _____
29. Shelves are recessed and mirrors are supplied in appropriate places in rest rooms and dressing rooms. _____
30. Dressing space between locker rows is adjusted to the size and age of students. _____
31. Drinking fountains are conveniently placed in locker-room areas or immediately adjacent thereto. _____
32. Special attention is given to provision for locking service windows and counters, supply bins, carts, shelves, and racks. _____
33. Provision is made for the repair, maintenance, replacement, and off-season storage of equipment and uniforms. _____
34. A well-defined program for laundering and cleaning towels, uniforms, and equipment is included in the plan. _____
35. Noncorrosive metal is used in dressing, drying, and shower areas except for enameled lockers. _____
36. Antipanic hardware is used where required by fire regulations. _____
37. Properly placed hose bibbs and drains are sufficient in size and quantity to permit flushing the entire area with a water hose. _____
38. A water-resistant, coved base is used under the locker base and floor mat, and where floor and wall join. _____
39. Chalkboards and/or tackboards with map tracks are located in appropriate places in dressing rooms, hallways, and classrooms. _____
40. Book shelves are provided in toilet areas. _____
41. Space and equipment are planned in accordance with the types and number of enrollees. _____
42. Basement rooms, being undesirable for dressing, drying, and showering, are not planned for those purposes. _____
43. Spectator seating (permanent) in areas that are basically instructional is kept at a minimum. Roll-away bleachers are used primarily. Balcony seating is considered as a possibility. _____
44. Well-lighted and effectively displayed trophy cases enhance the interest and beauty of the lobby. _____
45. The space under the stairs is used for storage. _____
46. Department heads' offices are located near the central administrative office, which includes a well-planned conference room. _____
47. Workrooms are located near the central office and serve as a repository for departmental materials and records. _____
48. Conference area includes a cloak room, lavatory, and toilet. _____
49. In addition to regular secretarial offices established in the central and department-chairmen's offices, a special room to house a secretarial pool for staff members is provided. _____
50. Staff dressing facilities are provided. These facilities may also serve game officials. _____
51. The community and/or neighborhood has a "round table" for planning. _____
52. All those (persons and agencies) who should be a party to planning and development are invited and actively engaged in the planning process. _____
53. Space and area relationships are important. They have been carefully considered. _____
54. Both long-range and immediate plans have been made. _____

Figure 8–15. A check list for planning facilities in physical education. (Courtesy *AAHPER*, "Planning Facilities for Athletics, Physical Education and Recreation," 1974, p. 7.)

(Continued on opposite page)

55. The body comfort of the child, a major factor in securing maximum learning, has been considered in the plans. _____
56. Plans for quiet areas have been made. _____
57. In the planning, consideration has been given to the need for adequate recreational areas and facilities, both near and distant from the homes of people. _____
58. Plans recognize the primary function of recreation as being enrichment of learning through creative self-expression, self-enhancement, and the achievement of self-potential. _____
59. Every effort has been exercised to eliminate hazards. _____
60. The installation of low-hanging door closers, light fixtures, signs, and other objects in traffic areas has been avoided. _____
61. Warning signals—both visible and audible—are included in the plans. _____
62. Ramps have a slope equal to or greater than a one-foot rise in 12-feet. _____
63. Minimum landings for ramps are 5 by 5 feet, they extend at least one foot beyond the swinging arc of a door, have at least a six-foot clearance at the bottom, and have level platforms at 30-foot intervals on every turn. _____
64. Adequate locker and dressing spaces are provided. _____
65. The design of dressing, drying, and shower areas reduces foot traffic to a minimum and establishes clean, dry aisles for bare feet. _____
66. Teaching stations are properly related to service facilities. _____
67. Toilet facilities are adequate in number. They are located to serve all groups for which provisions are made. _____
68. Mail services, outgoing and incoming, are included in the plans. _____
69. Hallways, ramps, doorways, and elevators are designed to permit equipment to be moved easily and quickly. _____
70. A keying design suited to administrative and instructional needs is planned. _____
71. Toilets used by large groups have circulating (in and out) entrances and exits. _____

CLIMATE CONTROL

1. Provision is made throughout the building for climate control—heating, ventilating, and refrigerated cooling. _____
2. Special ventilation is provided for locker, dressing, shower, drying, and toilet rooms. _____
3. Heating plans permit both area and individual-room control. _____
4. Research areas where small animals are kept and where chemicals are used have been provided with special ventilating equipment. _____
5. The heating and ventilating of the wrestling gymnasium have been given special attention. _____

ELECTRICAL

1. Shielded, vapor-proof lights are used in moisture-prevalent areas. _____
2. Lights in strategic areas are key-controlled. _____
3. Lighting intensity conforms to approved standards. _____
4. An adequate number of electrical outlets are strategically placed. _____
5. Gymnasium and auditorium lights are controlled by dimmer units. _____
6. Locker-room lights are mounted above the space between lockers. _____
7. Natural light is controlled properly for purposes of visual aids and avoidance of glare. _____
8. Electrical outlet plates are installed three feet above the floor unless special use dictates other locations. _____
9. Controls for light switches and projection equipment are suitably located and interrelated. _____
10. All lights are shielded. Special protection is provided in gymnasiums, court areas, and shower rooms. _____
11. Lights are placed to shine between rows of lockers. _____

WALLS

1. Movable and folding partitions are power-operated and controlled by keyed switches. _____
2. Wall plates are located where needed and are firmly attached. _____
3. Hooks and rings for nets are placed (and recessed in walls) according to court locations and net heights. _____
4. Materials that clean easily and are impervious to moisture are used where moisture is prevalent. _____
5. Shower heads are placed at different heights—four feet (elementary) to seven feet (university)—for each school level. _____
6. Protective matting is placed permanently on the walls in the wrestling room, at the ends of basketball courts, and in other areas where such protection is needed. _____

7. An adequate number of drinking fountains are provided. They are properly placed (recessed in wall). _____
8. One wall (at least) of the dance studio has full-length mirrors. _____
9. All corners in locker rooms are rounded. _____

CEILINGS

1. Overhead-supported apparatus is secured to beams engineered to withstand stress. _____
2. The ceiling height is adequate for the activities to be housed. _____
3. Acoustical materials impervious to moisture are used in moisture-prevalent areas. _____
4. Skylights, being impractical, are seldom used because of problems in waterproofing roofs and the controlling of sun rays (gyms). _____
5. All ceilings except those in storage areas are acoustically treated with sound-absorbent materials. _____

FLOORS

1. Floor plates are placed where needed and are flush-mounted. _____
2. Floor design and materials conform to recommended standards and specifications. _____
3. Lines and markings are painted on floors before sealing is completed (when synthetic tape is not used). _____
4. A coved base (around lockers and where wall and floor meet) of the same water-resistant material used on floors is found in all dressing and shower rooms. _____
5. Abrasive, nonskid, slip-resistant flooring that is impervious to moisture is provided on all areas where water is used —laundry, swimming pools, shower, dressing, and drying rooms. _____
6. Floor drains are properly located, and the slope of the floor is adequate for rapid drainage. _____

GYMNASIUMS AND SPECIAL ROOMS

1. Gymnasiums are planned so as to provide for safety zones (between courts, end lines, and walls) and for best utilization of space. _____
2. One gymnasium wall is free of obstructions and is finished with a smooth, hard surface for ball-rebounding activities. _____
3. The elementary school gymnasium has one wall free of obstructions, a minimum ceiling height of 18 feet, a minimum of 4,000 square feet of teaching area, and a recessed area for housing a piano. _____
4. Secondary school gymnasiums have a minimum ceiling height of 22 feet; a scoreboard; electrical outlets placed to fit with bleacher installation; wall attachments for apparatus and nets; and a power-operated, sound-insulated, and movable partition with a small pass-through door at one end. _____
5. A small spectator alcove adjoins the wrestling room and contains a drinking fountain (recessed in the wall). _____
6. Cabinets, storage closets, supply windows, and service areas have locks. _____
7. Provisions have been made for the cleaning, storing, and issuing of physical education and athletic uniforms. _____
8. Shower heads are placed at varying heights in the shower rooms on each school level. _____
9. Equipment is provided for the use of the physically handicapped. _____
10. Special provision has been made for audio and visual aids, including intercommunication systems, radio, and television. _____
11. Team dressing rooms have provisions for the following:
    a. hosing down room _____
    b. floors pitched to drain easily _____
    c. hot- and cold-water hose bibbs _____
    d. windows located above locker heights _____
    e. chalk, tack, and bulletin boards, and movie projection _____
    f. lockers for each team member _____
    g. drying facility for uniforms. _____
12. The indoor rifle range includes the following:
    a. targets located 54 inches apart and 50 feet from the firing line _____
    b. three to eight feet of space behind targets _____
    c. 12 feet of space behind firing line _____
    d. ceilings eight feet high _____
    e. width adjusted to number of firing lines needed (one line for each three students) _____
    f. a pulley device for target placement and return _____
    g. storage and repair space. _____
13. Dance facilities include the following:
    a. 100 square feet per student _____
    b. a minimum length of 60 linear feet for modern dance _____

Figure 8–15. *Continued.*

(Continued on following page)

c. full-height viewing mirrors on one wall (at least) of 30 feet; also a 20 foot mirror on an additional wall if possible ____

d. acoustical drapery to cover mirrors when not used and for protection if other activities are permitted ____

e. dispersed microphone jacks and speaker installation for music and instruction ____

f. built-in cabinets for record players, microphones, and amplifiers, with space for equipment carts ____

g. electrical outlets and microphone connections around perimeter of room ____

h. an exercise bar (34 to 42 inches above floor) on one wall ____

i. drapes, surface colors, floors (maple preferred), and other room appointments to enhance the room's attractiveness ____

j. location near dressing rooms and outside entrances. ____

14. Training rooms include the following:

a. rooms large enough to administer adequately proper health services ____

b. sanitary storage cabinets for medical supplies ____

c. installation of drains for whirlpool, tubs, etc. ____

d. installation of electrical outlets with proper capacities and voltage ____

e. high stools for use of equipment such as whirlpool, ice tubs, etc. ____

f. water closet, hand lavatory, and shower ____

g. extra hand lavatory in the trainers' room ____

h. adjoining dressing rooms ____

i. installation and use of hydrotherapy and diathermy equipment in separate areas ____

j. space for the trainer, the physician, and for the various services they provide ____

k. corrective-exercise laboratories located conveniently and adapted to the needs of the handicapped. ____

15. Coaches' rooms provide the following:

a. a sufficient number of dressing lockers for coaching staff and officials ____

b. a security closet or cabinet for athletic equipment such as timing devices ____

c. a sufficient number of showers and toilet facilities ____

d. drains and faucets for hosing down the rooms where this method of cleaning is desirable and possible ____

e. a small chalkboard and tackboard ____

f. a small movie screen and projection table for use of coaches to review films. ____

Figure 8–15. *Continued.*

basketball team. This is nonfunctional and usually results in insufficient space for effective teaching. The design for indoor facilities is so critical because it determines which activities can be taught. A group of 40 or 50 students may have had adequate space outdoors, but problems arise when the group comes inside for instruction.

At this point the term *adequate* should be discussed. A teacher will often say facilities are inadequate, when in reality they are adequate — and it is simply a matter of changing the activity. As an illustration, consider a class of 40 students that has been outside for touch football instruction. Space is usually ample because almost every school in the country has a football field. If the class is divided into several groups, the area will be large enough for all students to learn the skills of touch football. Now this same group comes inside to a standard gymnasium. At this point, many teachers will say that the space is inadequate because all 40 students cannot *play* basketball at the same time. In such a situation, the alert and creative teacher teaches the *skills* of basketball. Instantly, the situation changes. The class is divided into several groups: four with ten students, five with eight students, eight with five, or any division of students compatible with the

number of balls available. Not only is the space now entirely adequate, but the objectives of physical education are more nearly attained. Remember that the teaching of skills is a basic objective of physical education.

Another situation might arise wherein an additional group of students is assigned to physical education. Teachers sometimes say that it is impossible to teach 80 or 100 students in one gymnasium. This is not true, because a folding door can be used to divide the gymnasium into two teaching stations. Again, the answer to the problem is the teaching of skills, not play, during the instructional period. The divided-gymnasium plan affords the possibility of including many activities in the program. Effective instruction can be given in volleyball, rhythm, basketball, tumbling, wrestling, table tennis, or bowling — in either or both stations.

A third illustration of maximizing the facilities is a situation in which the administrators of the school attempt to schedule still another group (40 to 50 students) in the same standard gymnasium. The facility becomes inadequate and the teaching program is jeopardized. The teacher and administrators must find a third station. If not alleviated, this overcrowding will contribute to the eventual breakdown of the program. A recommended solution to the problem of the third teaching station is the auxiliary gymnasium.

Teaching Stations

Throughout the text, the term *teaching stations* has been used. Teaching stations are comparable in importance to classrooms for academic subjects if physical education instruction is to be successful. Teaching stations have been described as any space or area used for physical education and health instruction; they do not have to be traditional gymnasia. Teachers usually think of the standard gymnasium with the high ceiling as the only area for physical education instruction, when actually the only sport that requires a high ceiling is basketball. All other activities can be taught successfully in stations with 12 to 14-foot ceilings.

The Auxiliary Gymnasium. In schools with large enrollments, auxiliary teaching stations are recommended. These stations should be about 25 to 40 feet wide and 50 to 70 feet long, with ceilings 12 to 14 feet high. These auxiliary stations may be used for wrestling, tumbling, rhythms, bowling, archery, table tennis, and other activities that do not require a high ceiling.

Improvised Teaching Stations. The teacher in need of extra space should study the building and attempt to find some old room, corridor, or oversized dressing room that can be converted into a teaching station. Obviously the result will not be ideal, but using such improvised stations is better than blaming inadequate facilities for poor teaching.

The Main Gymnasium. Usually when buildings are planned, the gymnasium is designed for varsity competition and is to be used in conjunction with the physical education department. The gymnasium should be of regulation size for varsity competition and should have a folding partition to provide two separate stations for the regular physical education program. Some of the items that architects should include in their plans are:

1. Backboards for basketball goals

2. Heating and ventilation facilities
3. Mountings for bars, ropes, etc.
4. Drinking fountains
5. Safety mats behind goals
6. Bleachers
7. Recessed lights
8. Floor or wall electrical outlets
9. Bulletin boards
10. Floor markings
11. Wall numbers for roll checks
12. Public address outlets and horns

One aspect of planning indoor teaching stations that requires particular attention is the material to be used for constructing floors. For many years, the standard material was wood and, in some instances, tile. Recent experimentation with synthetic surfacing gives teachers, administrators, and architects new options for gymnasium floors. (Dimensions for indoor areas are shown in Figure 8–16.)

The Swimming Pool. Planning a swimming pool requires the help of specialists. Certain decisions involved in the construction of a pool can make it both nonfunctional and extremely costly.

TYPE OF POOL. Teachers and administrators must determine the purpose for which the pool will be used. Usually in the secondary schools it is used jointly for physical education instruction and athletic competition. Several types may be used: (1) an all-purpose pool with the instructional and diving areas in the same unit; (2) a pool with the instructional area located in a separate unit; (3) a pool with the diving area in a separate unit; and (4) a pool with the diving, swimming, and instructional areas all planned separately. The most practical pool for the secondary school is one that combines instructional, swimming, and diving areas in one unit.

LOCATION OF POOL. Location is one of the most important factors in planning the pool if the overall cost is to be kept at a minimum. The pool should be planned in conjunction with the physical education dressing rooms and showers to facilitate usage and to lower cost. If the pool is treated as a separate unit, new showers, locker rooms, and dressing areas must be constructed; this may increase the cost by one third.

Activity	Play Area in Feet	Safety Space in Feet*	Total Area in Feet
Badminton	20 x 44	6s, 8e	32 x 60
Basketball			
Jr. High instructional	42 x 74	6s, 8e	
Jr. High interscholastic	50 x 84	6s, 8e	
Sr. High interscholastic	50 x 84	6s, 8e	62 x 100
Sr. High instructional	45 x 74	6s, 8e	57 x 90
Neighborhood El. Sch.	42 x 74	6s, 8e	54 x 90
Community Junior H. S.	50 x 84	6s, 8e	62 x 100
Community Senior H. S.	50 x 84	6s, 8e	62 x 100
Competitive—DGWS	50 x 94	6s, 8e	62 x 110
Boccie	18 x 62	3s, 9e	24 x 80
Fencing, competitive	6 x 40	3s, 6e	12 x 52
instructional	3 x 30	2s, 6e	9 x 42
Rifle (one pt.)	5 x 50	6 to 20e	5 x 70 min.
Shuffleboard	6 x 52	6s, 2e	18 x 56
Tennis			
Deck (doubles)	18 x 40	4s, 5e	26 x 50
Hand	16 x 40	4½s, 10e	25 x 60
Lawn (singles)	27 x 78	12s, 21e	51 x 120
(doubles)	36 x 78	12s, 21e	60 x 120
Paddle (singles)	16 x 44	6s, 8e	28 x 60
(doubles)	20 x 44	6s, 8e	32 x 60
Table (playing area)			9 x 31
Volleyball			
Competitive and adult	30 x 60	6s, 6e	42 x 72
Junior High	30 x 50	6s, 6e	42 x 62
Wrestling (competitive)	24 x 24	5s, 5e	36 x 36

*Safety space at the side of an area is indicated by a number followed by "e" for end and "s" for side.

Figure 8–16. Space for selected indoor activities in secondary schools. (Courtesy The Athletic Institute and *AAHPER*, "Planning Facilities for Athletics, Physical Education and Recreation," 1974, p. 12.)

SIZE OF POOL. Pools designed for instruction and interscholastic competition may vary in size. The width should always be planned to allow for several lanes 7 feet wide, with buffer space on each side. The length may vary from 60 to 75 feet or more. A pool 30 feet wide should provide four 7-foot lanes with a buffer of 1 foot on each side. A practical and adequate pool should be 75 feet 1 inch by 42 feet, providing six lanes.

CHECK LIST FOR PLANNING THE POOL. Authoritative information should be secured on the items shown in Figure 8–17.

Outdoor Facilities

Teachers frequently feel that if there is not a large amount of space available for outdoor activity, they will be unable to have an effective program in physical education. Such reasoning is illogical. Surveys of available outdoor space usually reveal that there is ample room to conduct a program that meets all the objectives of physical education. Effective use depends on the activities; many can be taught successfully in limited areas. For instance, volleyball skills may

SWIMMING POOLS

1. Has a clear-cut statement been prepared on the nature and scope of the design program and the special requirements for space, equipment, and facilities dictated by the activities to be conducted? _____

2. Has the swimming pool been planned to meet the total requirements of the program to be conducted as well as any special needs of the clientele to be served? _____

3. Have all plans and specifications been checked and approved by the local Board of Health? _____

4. Is the pool the proper depth to accommodate the various age groups and types of activities it is intended to serve? _____

5. Does the design of the pool incorporate the most current knowledge and best experience available regarding swimming pools? _____

6. If a local architect or engineer who is inexperienced in pool construction is employed, has an experienced pool consultant, architect, or engineer been called in to advise on design and equipment? _____

7. Is there adequate deep water for diving (minimum of 9' for one-meter boards, 12' for 3-meter boards, and 15' for 10-meter towers)? _____

8. Have the requirements for competitive swimming been met (7-foot lanes; 12-inch black or brown lines on the bottom; pool 1 inch longer than official measurement; depth and distance markings)? _____

9. Is there adequate deck space around the pool? Has more space been provided than that indicated by the minimum recommended deck/pool ratio? _____

10. Does the swimming instructor's office face the pool? And is there a window through which the instructor may view all the pool area? Is there a toilet-shower-dressing area next to the office for instructors? _____

11. Are recessed steps or removable ladders located on the walls so as not to interfere with competitive swimming turns? _____

12. Does a properly-constructed overflow gutter extend around the pool perimeter? _____

13. Where skimmers are used, have they been properly located so that they are not on walls where competitive swimming is to be conducted? _____

14. Have separate storage spaces been allocated for maintenance and instructional equipment? _____

15. Has the area for spectators been properly separated from the pool area? _____

16. Have all diving standards and lifeguard chairs been properly anchored? _____

17. Does the pool layout provide the most efficient control of swimmers from showers and locker rooms to the pool? Are toilet facilities provided for wet swimmers separate from the dry area? _____

18. Is the recirculation pump located below the water level? _____

19. Is there easy vertical access to the filter room for both people and material (stairway if required)? _____

20. Has the proper pitch to drains been allowed in the pool, on the pool deck, in the overflow gutter, and on the floor of shower and dressing rooms? _____

21. Has adequate space been allowed between diving boards and between the diving boards and sidewalls? _____

22. Is there adequate provision for lifesaving equipment? Pool-cleaning equipment? _____

23. Are inlets and outlets adequate in number and located so as to insure effective circulation of water in the pool? _____

24. Has consideration been given to underwater lights, underwater observation windows, and underwater speakers? _____

25. Is there a coping around the edge of the pool? _____

26. Has a pool heater been considered in northern climates in order to raise the temperature of the water? _____

27. Have underwater lights in end racing walls been located deep enough and directly below surface lane anchors, and are they on a separate circuit? _____

28. Has the plan been considered from the standpoint of handicapped persons (e.g., is there a gate adjacent to the turnstiles)? _____

29. Is seating for swimmers provided on the deck? _____

30. Has the recirculation-filtration system been designed to meet the anticipated future bathing load? _____

31. Has the gas chlorinator (if used) been placed in a separate room accessible from and vented to the outside? _____

32. Has the gutter waste water been valved to return to the filters, and also for direct waste? _____

INDOOR POOLS

1. Is there proper mechanical ventilation? _____

2. Is there adequate acoustical treatment of walls and ceilings? _____

3. Is there adequate overhead clearance for diving (15' above low springboards, 15' for 3-meter boards, and 10' for 10-meter platforms)? _____

4. Is there adequate lighting (50 footcandles minimum)? _____

5. Has reflection of light from the outside been kept to the minimum by proper location of windows or skylights (windows on sidewalls are not desirable)? _____

6. Are all wall bases coved to facilitate cleaning? _____

7. Is there provision for proper temperature control in the pool room for both water and air? _____

8. Can the humidity of the pool room be controlled? _____

9. Is the wall and ceiling insulation adequate to prevent "sweating"? _____

10. Are all metal fittings of noncorrosive material? _____

11. Is there a tunnel around the outside of the pool, or a trench on the deck which permits ready access to pipes? _____

OUTDOOR POOLS

1. Is the site for the pool in the best possible location (away from railroad tracks, heavy industry, trees, and open fields which are dusty)? _____

2. Have sand and grass been kept the proper distance away from the pool to prevent them from being transmitted to the pool? _____

3. Has a fence been placed around the pool to assure safety when not in use? _____

4. Has proper subsurface drainage been provided? _____

5. Is there adequate deck space for sunbathing? _____

6. Are the outdoor lights placed far enough from the pool to prevent insects from dropping into the pool? _____

7. Is the deck of nonslip material? _____

8. Is there an area set aside for eating, separated from the pool deck? _____

9. Is the bathhouse properly located, with the entrance to the pool leading to the shallow end? _____

10. If the pool shell contains a concrete finish, has the length of the pool been increased by 3 inches over the "official" size in order to permit eventual tiling of the basin without making the pool "too short"? _____

11. Are there other recreational facilities nearby for the convenience and enjoyment of swimmers? _____

12. Do diving boards or platforms face north or east? _____

13. Are lifeguard stands provided and properly located? _____

14. Has adequate parking space been provided and properly located? _____

15. Is the pool oriented correctly in relation to the sun? _____

16. Have windshields been provided in situations where heavy winds prevail?[2] _____

Figure 8–17.   A check list for swimming pools. (Courtesy The Athletic Institute and *AAHPER*, "Planning Facilities for Athletics, Physical Education and Recreation," 1974, p. 193.)

be taught in an area of 90 by 60 feet. But when teachers think of outside activities, they usually think of football, track, or softball. These sports are desirable, but they are not essential to physical education. If volleyball and softball are compared, it will be found that the values derived from volleyball far exceed those from softball. Surely a teacher would not say that a school without a golf course could not have a valuable physical education program.

Earlier in the chapter, it was pointed out that when teachers begin to place emphasis on the teaching of skills, the entire situation changes; they often find that a good program can be conducted in small areas. The following information will assist teachers in planning activities for an outdoor program.

Surfaces. The surface used for outdoor areas is important, and teachers should have a general knowledge of the different types needed for the program. The most common are turf, asphalt, and concrete, but synthetic surfaces offer a promising alternative.

Turf is the most widely used surface for all field games, such as softball, touch football, hockey, soccer, speedball, and lacrosse. Considerable attention is needed for upkeep and maintenance. In many climates, a good amount of water must be applied to prevent grass from dying and to promote its growth. *Asphalt* surfaces are popular for multi-use areas and small play spaces and are relatively inexpensive. However, asphalt must be treated to prevent grass from growing in it. *Concrete* surfaces are used for general play areas and small play spaces. Many physical education leaders and administrators prefer this surface because it requires little maintenance, is usable in all types of weather and is relatively inexpensive.

SYNTHETIC SURFACES. Synthetic surfaces are becoming more popular each year for all outdoor areas. Astroturf, Polyturf, Uniturf, Synthoturf, Robbinsturf, Dynaturf, Proturf, and Axonturf are all trade names of synthetic surfacing. This type may eventually replace the surfaces discussed above. A further discussion of synthetic surfaces will be found in the *Resource Manual.*

SURFACES FOR MULTI-USE AREAS. Probably the most practical outside space is the multi-use area that accommodates several activities on one hard surface. These areas are usually covered with concrete or asphalt and are usable all year. The well-planned multi-use area may be used for teaching the skills of basketball, tennis, and volleyball.

SURFACES NEAR FIXED EQUIPMENT. The surfacing around fixed equipment, such as chinning bars, ropes, and apparatus, should be of soft materials. Considerable experimentation is in progress with rubber, cork, sponge, and air cell materials to determine which has the greatest safety features.

Other Areas. Adequate space for touch football, track, softball, and tennis is desirable in a well-rounded physical education program. The amount of space needed for these playing areas and the lay-out diagrams are shown in the *Resource Manual.*

Number of Teaching Stations

We have already noted that the first and most important step in planning facilities is to determine the number of teaching stations needed. A formula that takes into account school enrollment, class sizes, and the number of periods per day determines the number of teaching stations needed:

$$\text{Minimum Number of Teaching Stations} = \frac{\text{Number of students}}{\text{Average number of students per instructor}} \times \frac{\text{Number of physical education periods per week per class}}{\text{Total number of physical education class periods in school week}}$$

If a school with a projected enrollment of 700 students has six class periods a day with an average class size of 30 students, and physical education is required on a daily basis, the formula application is as follows:

$$\text{Minimum Number of Teaching Stations} = \frac{700 \text{ students}}{30 \text{ per class}} \times \frac{5 \text{ periods per week}}{30 \text{ periods per week}}$$

$$3500$$

$$= \frac{3500}{900} \qquad = \qquad 3.9 \text{ or 4 Teaching Stations}[18]$$

When new buildings are planned, teachers must provide the best available information to assist the architect. Sometimes, for the sake of economy, teachers and administrators make compromises and approve construction that is nonfunctional and impractical. An example is the trend in some parts of the country to combine the gymnasium with the lunchroom or the auditorium. None of these set-ups has ever been satisfactory; in fact, the conflicts resulting from the joint use of these facilities frequently demoralize students, teachers, administrators, lunchroom employees, and outside groups who use the auditorium. Effective use of

---

Guidelines for Secondary School Physical Education

A position paper published in 1970 by the American Association of Health, Physical Education and Recreation provides a rationale for developing sound programs in physical education. The stands taken on scheduling, time allotment and class size are included in the following recommendations.

Scheduling, time allotment, and class size have a direct bearing on the health, safety, and extent of participation by students, on the type of activities that can be offered, and on the student outcomes which can be expected.

A daily instructional period of directed physical education should be provided for all secondary school students equivalent in length to that found in the regular school pattern.

Schools organized on other than the traditional schedule should provide physical education experiences for each pupil comparable in time to that allocated to other major courses.

The instructional program should be scheduled to allow for maximum participation and adequate time for each pupil to have an opportunity to gain the satisfaction that comes from achievement.

All students should be enrolled in physical education classes. Time should be scheduled in the physical education program for pupils handicapped by functional or structural disorders and those who find it difficult to adjust to the regular program.

Assignment to physical education classes should take into consideration sex, skill, maturation, grade level, and health status.

The pupil/teacher ratio should be the same for physical education classes as for other subject areas with variations possible depending upon the activity.

There should be no substitute for the instructional program.

The teacher's schedule should allow time for preparation.

Figure 8–18. Guidelines for secondary school physical education. (*AAHPER*, 1970.)

the combined facilities by any group becomes impossible.

Research shows that another common mistake in planning has been the multi-purpose room. Classes that meet intermittently may use these rooms advantageously, but classes in subjects that are offered daily, such as physical education, usually suffer, and the entire program can be undermined. If the physical education program is to fulfill its objectives, there must be a sufficient number of stations to meet the needs of the program without interference from or conflict with other subjects in the curriculum.

Guidelines for External Organization

The American Alliance for Health, Physical Education and Recreation has summarized the external organizational procedures necessary for effective instructional programs in physical education (Figure 8–18).

QUESTIONS FOR DISCUSSION

1. Discuss ways in which the teacher may contribute to disciplinary problems.
2. Differentiate among the policies involved in excusing students from participation in physical education.
3. Suggest some alternate activities for students who are temporarily or permanently excused from the regular physical education class.
4. Discuss the pros and cons of requiring a uniform for physical education. Indicate your preference.
5. Cite some methods for encouraging student involvement in organizing the class.
6. Indicate how instructional content and teaching methods will affect equipment usage. Give several examples.
7. Discuss how team teaching and selectives may influence the overall effectiveness of the instructional program.
8. Indicate how the three phases of learning can be incorporated into a traditional class in basketball. In gymnastics.
9. Do you favor the flexible scheduling procedure? Why or why not?

REFERENCES

1. George H. Gallup, "The Ninth Annual Gallup Poll of the Public's Attitude Toward the Public Schools," *Phi Delta Kappan* (September, 1978), p. 34.
2. Robert Biehler, *Psychology Applied to Teaching,* 2nd ed. (Boston: Houghton-Mifflin Company, 1974), p. 700.
3. Daniel C. Neal, "Aversive Control of Behavior," *Phi Delta Kappan* (February, 1969), pp. 335–337.
4. George Karner, "All Kids Want to Be the Good Guy," *Parade* (April 18, 1971), p. 18.
5. Shirley Boes Neill, "Two R's for Students," *New Dimensions for Educating Youth* (United States Department of Health, Education and Welfare and the National Association of Secondary Principals, 1976), p. 26.
6. Biehler, *op. cit.,* p. 702.
7. "Required Electives for Juniors and Seniors," *Physical Education Newsletter* (Physical Education Publications, Old Saybrook, Connecticut, January, 1973).
8. "What Physicians Say About Physical Education," *Newsletter* (President's Council on Physical Fitness and Sports, 1972).
9. "National Adult Physical Fitness Survey," *Newsletter* (President's Council on Physical Fitness and Sports, May, 1973), p. 6.
10. "Flexible Modular Scheduling in High School Physical Education," *Physical Education Newsletter* (Physical Education Publications, Old Saybrook, Connecticut, May 1, 1971).
11. Scott D. Thomson, "Beyond Modular Scheduling," *Phi Delta Kappan* (April, 1971) p. 484.
12. *Ibid.* p. 485.
13. "California Study Supports Value of Daily Program," *Newsletter* (President's Council on Physical Fitness and Sports, December, 1971).

14. "Organizational Patterns for Instruction in Physical Education," *AAHPER* (1971), p. 15.
15. Robert S. Gard, "A Realistic Look at Flexible Scheduling," *The Clearing House* (Teaneck, New Jersey: Fairleigh Dickenson University, March, 1970), p. 429.
16. Thompson, *op. cit.,* p. 487.
17. Lawrence F. Locke, "Personalized Learning in Physical Education," *Journal of Physical Education and Recreation* (Vol. 47, June, 1976), pp. 32–35.
18. "Planning Facilities for Athletics, Physical Education and Recreation," The Athletic Institute and *AAHPER* (1974), p. 14.

SELECTED READINGS

Heitman, Helen M., Chairperson, *Organizational Patterns for Instruction in Physical Education* (AAHPER, 1971).
Lessinger, Leon, Jr., *Every Kid a Winner* (New York: Simon and Schuster, 1970).
Long, Nicholas, et al., *Conflict in the Classroom,* 2nd ed. (Belmont, California: Wardsworth Publishing Company, 1971).
"Planning Facilities for Athletics, Physical Education and Recreation." (The Athletic Institute and *AAHPER,* 1974).
Willgoose, Carl E., *The Curriculum in Physical Education* (Englewood Cliffs: Prentice-Hall, 1974).
Yost, Charles Peter, ed., *Sports Safety (AAHPER).*

Chapter 9

Courtesy Cedar Shoals High School, Athens, Georgia

METHODS OF INSTRUCTION
    INDIVIDUAL INSTRUCTION
    COEDUCATIONAL INSTRUCTION
PLANNING RESOURCE UNITS
BASIC OUTLINE FOR DAILY PLANNING
    PREPARATION
        DRESSING
        ROLL CALL
        ANNOUNCEMENTS
        CLASS FORMATION
    DEVELOPMENT
    TEACHING OF SKILLS
        ORIENTATION
        DEMONSTRATION OF THE SKILL
        ORGANIZATION FOR INSTRUCTION
        INVENTORY OF PERFORMANCE ABILITY
        INSTRUCTION AND ABILITY GROUPING
    SKILLS LABORATORY
    CLOSING
INTENSITY CURVE

SKILL EVALUATION
COMPETENCY-BASED INSTRUCTION
    DEVELOPING SUB-COMPETENCIES
        PSYCHOMOTOR DOMAIN
        COGNITIVE DOMAIN
        AFFECTIVE DOMAIN
    PRETESTING
    CRITERION-REFERENCED PLANNING
TEACHING THE SPECIAL STUDENT
TEACHING THE SKILLS OF INDIVIDUAL AND
GROUP ACTIVITIES
INDIVIDUAL ACTIVITIES
GROUP ACTIVITIES
QUESTIONS FOR DISCUSSION
REFERENCES
SELECTED READINGS

TEACHING STRATEGIES FOR SELECTED ACTIVITIES

METHODS OF INSTRUCTION

Several teaching strategies are acceptable for the physical education class. Instructors should always remember that teaching physical education is quite different from teaching academic subjects; it is based on movement, whereas learning in academic areas is sedentary. For example, lectures play an important role in academic instruction but in most cases are irrelevant to physical education because they negate its very purpose — activity. Instruction in movement is crucial to the total physical fitness program. (Chapter 5 should be reviewed at this time.)

Individual Instruction

Effective teaching strategies allow the teacher to spend considerable time helping students to develop their potential. Group instruction may be used in some instances, but individual instruction provides the interaction between student and teacher that prepares students for healthful living.

Grouping students by ability assures them the opportunity to make decisions and improve their performance. The teacher, after having grouped the students, can spend the majority of the class time with those who need individual instruction. After reaching the skill level of one group with the assistance of the teacher, students can advance to the next group. The authors favor ability grouping because it fosters personal attention from the teacher where it is needed (see Fig. 9–1).

Coeducational Instruction

Title IX legislation has produced important administrative changes in physical education that affect both males and females throughout the country. It has challenged teachers and administrators to treat women equally in areas such as scheduling, facilities, finances, and equipment. Although the techniques of

Figure 9–1. Grouping students by ability is essential for effective instruction. This figure shows 16 students learning table tennis skills in four ability groups. Courtesy Rosemont Junior High School, Norfolk Public Schools, Norfolk, Virginia.

teaching coeducational classes will remain the same, the attitudes of many teachers must change. Ability grouping alleviates most of the problems of performance differences, but teachers who formerly taught boys or girls exclusively must learn to work with and understand students of the opposite sex.

A survey of teachers in the Norfolk, Virginia, public schools revealed some interesting reactions to Title IX:

1. Title IX has a very definite place of importance in the physical education program. As with any new idea there is much that needs to be understood and improved. With time this program will have a positive effect on the educational programs.
2. The class size should be lowered when both sexes are included. Social, academic, or psychomotor problems occur that need the attention of the teacher; large classes would preclude this.
3. Closer study needs to be given to contact sports (basketball, football, and wrestling). Research on differences in development of girls and boys, especially in the seventh and eighth grades, needs further investigation.
4. Better guidelines for evaluation of students in psychomotor skills are needed. Grading is difficult. There is a need for consistency among department members

in using standards for performance and methods of evaluation.
5. More male instructors need to become aware of the physical capabilities of the female student.
6. Regardless of the subject, all educational experiences should be coeducational. A more diversified, elective program will meet the needs of both boys and girls.
7. The coeducational program is long overdue. Student adjustment has been very smooth. Successful experiences for both students and teacher should increase.[1]

Figure 9–2 shows a successful coeducational unit in volleyball.

PLANNING RESOURCE UNITS

One of the most important aspects of good teaching is careful planning. (A review of Chapters 7 and 8 may help the reader.) Plans should not only outline daily procedures but should also include weekly and monthly goals. Each moment must be used constructively if instruction is to be accomplished, motivation generated, and student interest maintained.

Long-range planning involves the resource unit, which includes all the ma-

Figure 9–2. Coeducational volleyball instruction. Courtesy Wood Junior High School, Davenport Community School District, Davenport, Iowa.

terial to be covered within a block of time. The complete unit consists of several parts: (1) history of the activity; (2) value of the activity; (3) rules, regulations, and scoring; (4) safety precautions; (5) equipment needed; and (6) basic skills involved. After sufficient time has been spent on the cognitive parts of the unit, the psychomotor teaching process begins. This involves the use of daily lesson plans, which will be described in the remainder of the chapter.

BASIC OUTLINE FOR DAILY PLANNING

An outline in which each procedure is given a definite time allotment should be prepared for each class period. Poor instructional habits can be eliminated by following a basic time pattern. Every teacher should know how to implement a daily lesson plan for a 60-minute period. A well-organized class should consist of five distinct phases:

1. Preparation (10 minutes)
2. Development (10 minutes)
3. Teaching of skills (20 minutes)
   a. Orientation
   b. Demonstration

c. Organization
d. Inventory
e. Ability grouping
4. Skill laboratory (10 minutes)
5. Closing (5 to 10 minutes)

Preparation

The success of the class depends on the teacher's thoroughness in planning the preparation phase. Preparation should take only 10 minutes. If certain procedures are not well organized, they become time-consuming and troublesome.

Dressing. Students should be given a definite time limit for dressing and reporting to the gymnasium. Students who fail to dress on time should be penalized, because too much teaching time is wasted. Motivation diminishes when students are kept waiting.

Roll Call. This should take no more than one or two minutes. Several plans are designed to expedite the checking of attendance. Probably the best is one in which numbers are placed on either the floor or the wall. Students are assigned numbers; when they report, they stand on their number or in front of it. The numbers showing at the end of a specified time represent students who

Figure 9–3. A simple but functional roll check expedites the teaching process. Courtesy Rosemont Junior High School, Norfolk, Virginia.

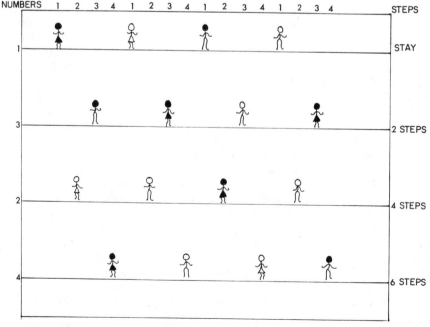

Figure 9–4.   A practical organizational plan for developmental exercises.

are absent. An example of this plan is shown in Figure 9–3. Other plans are discussed in the *Resource Manual.* However, this one is practical and involves a minimum of time.

Announcements. These should be brief, concise explanations of what will take place during the period.

Class Formation. A highly recommended formation plan is to have students count off by fours, beginning from the left end of the line. At a given command, students take a number of steps forward, as shown in Figure 9–4. From this position, developmental exercises can be performed properly.

Another commonly used method is that in which the class is divided into squads, each with an assigned place to assemble on the floor. Other plans are shown in the *Resource Manual.*

Development

Ten minutes are set aside for developmental exercises that are designed to prepare the students for more vigorous movements. However, these exercises must be carefully selected; some exercises may actually injure the student. For example, the deep-knee bend, which was commonly used for many years, is undesirable. Exercises should be scientifically selected for each period so that they "warm up" the muscles used in the activity being taught that day. The warm-up is discussed in Chapter 7.

The teacher should announce the exercise and give the commands clearly and forcefully. Commands always consist of three parts: (1) explanation, (2) pause, and (3) execution. In addition, exercises should be given rhythmically, accompanied by music. Rope jumping to music is popular for this part of the lesson. It is not only interesting but also has tremendous developmental value. Figure 9–5 illustrates this activity. After the students have had sufficient developmental movements, they are ready to receive skill instruction.

Teaching of Skills

The teaching of skills is the nucleus of the entire course. Good programs depend on the manner in which the teacher organizes and imparts to his or her students the scientific procedures involved in basic skills.

Chapter 4 describes the scientific approach to the selection of activities and should be reviewed at this time. The

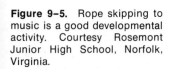

Figure 9–5. Rope skipping to music is a good developmental activity. Courtesy Rosemont Junior High School, Norfolk, Virginia.

following outline should be used in the sequence shown for teaching the skills of each activity in the curriculum. Skill instruction should take about 20 minutes of each class.

Orientation. In introducing a new activity to students, teachers should:
1. Acquaint the class with the history and importance of the activity and emphasize the need for learning the skills thoroughly.
2. Use visual aids. A textbook can be helpful.
3. Allow students to participate briefly with a superior player.
4. Initiate a discussion about the activity.
5. Determine the extent of previous experience in the sport or activity.
6. Ask the student to read about the activity in newspapers and magazines and to bring clippings to class.
7. Outline the rules and discuss them with the class.
8. Help the students to learn how to keep score.

Demonstration of the Skill. In order to increase student comprehension of the activity or sport, teachers should:
1. Have the skill demonstrated by students who are able to perform it well.
2. Analyze the skill and discuss it with the class.
3. Determine which of the methods discussed earlier should be used in teaching.
4. Use members of the varsity team, professionals, or other outstanding performers to demonstrate the skills.
5. Use films, filmstrips, and slides to demonstrate the skills.
6. Use bulletin boards, wall charts, and pictures shown through an opaque projector or transparencies to show students correct techniques.

Organization for Instruction. After the informational groundwork has been laid, teachers should:
1. Organize the class into teaching formations, keeping in mind how to make the best use of the available time.
2. Divide the class into as many groups as space, facilities, and equipment permit.

3. Allow students to perform the skill as many times as possible.
4. Motivate the students to practice beyond the school hours.

Inventory of Performance Ability. When students are organized and ready to begin practicing, teachers should:
1. Allow each member of the class to try the skill.
2. Have students practice skills in groups so that no student remains idle.
3. Walk around the groups, point out faulty techniques, and comment on good and improved techniques.

Instruction and Ability Grouping. This pertains to all the lesson plans in the chapter. Teachers should:
1. Group students according to ability into as many sections as space, facilities, and safety permit, based on the inventory described above.
2. Allow students to practice the skill and advance from the less proficient to the most proficient groups or from one component of an activity to another, as in a tumbling sequence.
3. Allow students who perform skills well to assist others or to serve as spotters in activities such as tumbling.
4. Evaluate the students subjectively through continuous observation.
5. Use individual instruction throughout this phase of the period. Particular attention should be given to the exceptional child.

The *Resource Manual* includes several types of formations.

Skills Laboratory

Skills should be practiced competitively for 10 minutes at the end of the period. Relays, games, or any activity requiring little organization that places the skill in a contest situation is suitable. Teachers should be creative and devise several activities in which large groups can participate. One illustration is the basketball dribble-and-shoot relay race. Figure 9–6 illustrates how a skill may be made competitive.

Figure 9–6. The basketball dribble and shoot relay race illustrates how a skill may be placed in competition. Courtesy Rosemont Junior High School, Norfolk Public Schools, Norfolk, Virginia.

Closing

For 5 to 10 minutes, students should assemble for announcements, a brief discussion of the next day's lesson, and dismissal to the locker room. During this phase, activity comes to a close and movement is inhibited, allowing students to proceed to other classes refreshed and relaxed.

INTENSITY CURVE

Classes should follow a definite physiological exercise pattern, beginning with an absolutely quiet formation and gradually increasing in vigor and intensity until a peak is reached. After a period of sustained movement at this level, the exercise program should diminish in intensity until effort is as inhibited as it was at the beginning of the period. The daily lesson guide described in the preceding paragraphs is based on this intensity curve. The *Resource Manual* includes more material on this concept.

SKILL EVALUATION

Periodically, students should be evaluated on the skills that were taught in a series of lessons. It is important for students to recognize their progress and to identify their weaknesses. Teachers should refer to Chapter 13 for suggested evaluative procedures.

COMPETENCY-BASED INSTRUCTION

Competency-based instruction was developed because of widespread dissatisfaction with past educational accomplishments. Students were not performing well in the basic academic subjects and were underachieving in physical education as well. The public demand for accountability necessitated more comprehensive methods for evaluating student progress.

In competency-based programs, performance objectives are used to chart the instructional program. These set forth precisely what is expected of the participant under specified conditions. Objectives are usually written separately for each of the three domains, psychomotor, cognitive, and affective. In physical education, several teaching methods that measure the extent of students' skills are acceptable. However, the basis of each is the requirement that students be able to perform at a standard competency level. The following is an example of a competency-based lesson plan.

Psychomotor

Component 1. Identify in a statement the aspect of the performance that is measurable.

Example: The student will successfully serve a tennis ball.

Component 2. State the conditions under which the task is performed.

Example: The student *standing behind the service line* will successfully serve a tennis ball into the service area.

Component 3. Define the criteria or standards of performance to be used for measuring the task.

Example: The student standing behind the service line will successfully serve a tennis ball into the service area *8 out of 10 times.*

Cognitive

Component 1. The student will describe the advantages of each type of serve.

Component 2. The student will describe the advantages of each type of serve *by answering questions on a written test.*

Component 3. The student will describe the advantages of each type of serve by answering questions on a written test with *60 per cent accuracy.*

Note: This is the complete objective.

Affective

Component 1. The student will show inhibition and control in serving.

Component 2. The student will show inhibition and control in serving *when he or she misses the ball.*

Component 3. The student *consistently* will show inhibition and control in serving when he or she misses the ball.

Note: This is the complete objective.

Developing Sub-Competencies

All skills involve sub-skills or sub-competencies. Because proficiency in one usually depends on another, sub-competencies should be taught in the proper sequence.

Psychomotor Domain. The tennis serve, for example, is composed of the following sub-competencies:

Grip
Body angle
Position of feet
Height of ball toss
Extension of serving arm
Position of racquet
Transfer of weight to left foot (right-hand server)
Use of wrist
Follow-through

After these have been determined, the sequential arrangement of teaching the tennis serve may be:

1. The student, standing behind the service line, will successfully serve a tennis ball into the service area 8 out of 10 times.
2. The student, standing behind the service line, will correctly demonstrate the sub-competencies in the proper order.

Cognitive Domain. The intellectual process of the learner is developed as follows:

1. The student will describe the advantages of each type of serve by answering questions on a written test with 60 per cent accuracy.

2. The student will describe the advantages of each type of serve by:
   a. Tracing the origin of each type.
   b. Listing players who use each type.
   c. Listing opinions of well-known players.
   d. Stating when each type should be used.
   e. Discussing research in this area.

Affective Domain. Good behavior is essential to sportsmanship. In this case it can be promoted if:

1. The student will consistently show inhibition and control in serving when he or she misses the ball.
2. The student will consistently show inhibition and control by:
   a. Respecting advice from the teacher.
   b. Ignoring ridicule from peers.
   c. Making a greater effort to concentrate.
   d. Requesting suggestions from other players.
   e. Refusing to quit practicing the skill.

Pretesting

Earlier in the chapter, it was suggested that an inventory of performance should be made before grouping students by ability. This inventory depends on pretesting, an important process that measures competencies and subcompetencies before the student attempts to attain a specific performance standard. Pretesting can also serve as a prerequisite for individual instruction, prescribing how each student may work at his or her own rate. When students reach the established goals, they may proceed to more difficult challenges.

After performance objectives have been identified, they should be made available to students, administrators, parents, and other interested individuals. Class instruction is no longer an indefinite procedure involving huge outlays of money, with no assurance that objectives will be developed or

achieved. When the public is apprised of the instructional goals, educators are held accountable for achieving them.

It is vital that objectives be written in a functional style that makes them applicable to class instruction. Further discussions of competency-based programs and performance objectives are in the *Resource Manual.*

Criterion-Referenced Planning

Performance measures should be developed for each ability group. In the foregoing example, the criterion of 8 out of 10 correct tennis serves becomes the goal for the best group. This objective should be adjusted downward for the other groups within the class. A criterion-referenced plan might be arranged as follows:

Fair Group	*Good Group*
2 out of 10	4 out of 10

Better Group	*Best Group*
6 out of 10	8 out of 10

Performance standards in each group may be quantitative or qualitative. If the performance is quantitative, absolute proficiency in the task is specified. In the tennis serve, for example, the best group would demand 10 out of 10. A qualitative performance standard would be more like 8 out of 10.

Continued assessments are made for each group as the instruction progresses. Students with poor coordination need guidance and individual attention from the teacher. If the grade is based on this type of performance standard, the program is criterion-referenced.

TEACHING THE SPECIAL STUDENT

Including special or handicapped students in regular physical education classes presents problems because, as

Puthoff states, "Even students of normal intellectual and physical range do not learn cognitive or psychomotor skills at the same rate."[2] But when both normal and handicapped students are placed in groups on the basis of ability, need, knowledge, and interest, everyone can progress at his or her own rate. Physical education programs that consist of varied activities and involve ability grouping and pretesting provide adequate opportunity for *all* students to participate.

TEACHING THE SKILLS OF INDIVIDUAL AND GROUP ACTIVITIES

The lesson plans included in this section illustrate the sequential procedures for teaching the skills of selected individual and group activities. Although the plans are designed for groups of 40 students, they may be adapted to varying class loads. To insure that progress is evaluated fairly, the *objectives are written in terms of performance*. Teachers should use these examples as guides in writing other performance objectives that relate to the specific situation. (Sub-competencies are not shown, but students may refer to the preceding pages for this information.) Refer to Chapter 3 for a review of performance objectives.

Five plans are developed progressively for each activity and may be used for varying time periods. In some instances, the five plans might occupy one or two weeks or even a month, depending on the physical education background of the students. Plans provide teachers with procedures and approaches for teaching large groups of students effectively and safely.

Students and teachers should review the overflow principle described in Chapter 7, as this approach is used throughout this section. Volleyball is selected for the overflow activity because it safely accommodates large numbers with a minimum of supervision. When planning the overflow activity, the teachers should not be concerned with having a fixed number of participants on each side. Overflow activity may be informal or highly organized, according to the discretion of the teacher, *and some activities may be taught without using the overflow plan.*

Emphasis is placed on grouping by ability or performance, regardless of the activity. The number of groups depends on the size of the class, the previous experience of each student, the size of the teaching station, and the equipment available. After analyzing these factors in relation to the specific activity, teachers must determine which instructional method will be most effective.

INDIVIDUAL ACTIVITIES

Individual activities are those in which achievement is based entirely on one person's independent performance. Bowling is an illustration; even though the participant may be a member of a team, the student's score is not dependent upon the activity of others.

Team sports have excellent immediate value but very little carry-over potential. This opinion has been held by physical education leaders for many years; nevertheless, probably because of the impact of interscholastic competition in team sports, it has been suppressed. As a result, individual sports such as golf, bowling, tennis, swimming, table tennis, tumbling, and handball — which have greater participative value for the future — have been neglected.

The lack of instruction in individual sports is obvious. Plans for new buildings invariably include facilities for basketball and football; one rarely finds provisions made for tennis, bowling, or golf, for example. The difficulty of offering a varied program when only a football field (which is frequently restricted to football playing) and a basketball court are available is a major impediment to including individual activities in the program.

Instruction in individual sport skills using limited facilities requires a great deal of organization. The purpose of this section is to develop the teacher's ability to adapt instruction to the situation while maintaining the value and integrity of the program. Remember that the intensity curve should be applied to the plan for all teaching periods.

Teaching Tennis Skills

GENERAL OBJECTIVES:

    A. **Psychomotor.** The students will demonstrate the correct form in executing the intricate skills of tennis.

    B. **Cognitive.** The students will demonstrate their knowledge of tennis by checking the correct answers among a list of choices on a test.

    C. **Affective.** The students will demonstrate their ability to:

        Control emotions under stress.
        Show good sportsmanship.
        Exhibit team loyalty.
        Accept responsibility.
        Assume leadership.
        Respect decisions of officials.

I. *HISTORY OF TENNIS*

(See references at end of chapter.)

II. VALUES OF TENNIS

Leisure time carry-over
Social potenial
Development of physiological fitness

III. RULES, SCORING, AND STRATEGY

IV. *SAFETY PRECAUTIONS*

Warm up to prevent muscle injury.
Hold ball until instruction begins.
Be careful in using racquets.
Stay in assigned area.

V. EQUIPMENT NEEDED

Racquets
Balls
Areas or courts
Nets or ropes

VI. *BASIC SKILLS*

Grips —	Eastern	Backhand
	Western	Serve
	Continental	Volley
Strokes —	Forehand	Lob

LESSON ONE

PERFORMANCE OBJECTIVES:

Psychomotor. The student will demonstrate the correct form in bouncing the ball with the racquet for a distance of 30 feet and back without losing possession of the ball.

Cognitive. The student will list advantages of each of the three grips by answering questions on a written test with 60 per cent accuracy.

Affective. The student will exhibit inhibition and control each time the ball is lost while being bounced between two lines.

LESSON ONE

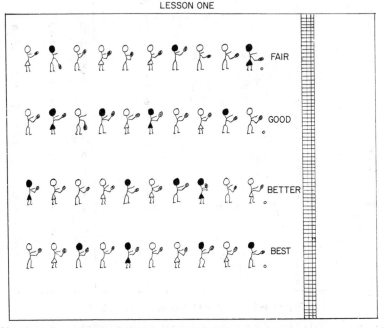

Figure 9–7. Grip and hitting ball formation.

The class is arranged as shown. The first student in each line is given a ball and a racquet. After the correct grip is demonstrated, students bounce the ball with the racquet up to the line and back. The balls are then transferred to the next student, and this continues until everyone has practiced once. Students are then asked to bounce the ball while running to the line. For variation, repeat the procedure with students bouncing the ball in the air. The same plan can be used in competitive relay races for motivation.

LESSON TWO

PERFORMANCE OBJECTIVES:

Psychomotor. The student will stand in the center of the court and demonstrate the correct position of the feet and arms in executing the forehand and backhand return, returning the ball 3 out of 5 times.

Cognitive. The student will describe the footwork in the forehand and backhand return in one paragraph as a written test.

Affective. The student will display patience each time the ball is missed in the forehand and backhand return from the back court.

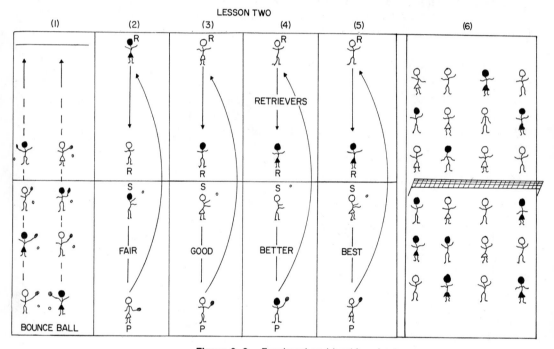

Figure 9-8. Forehand and backhand return.

The class is divided into six groups: (1) those who did not show improvement in bouncing the ball; (2) fair; (3) good; (4) better; (5) best, in the backhand and forehand; and (6) volleyball overflow. Each of the four players (P) is given a racquet. The set-up (S) students have six balls each, which they throw with one bounce to the players, who practice making a forehand or backhand return in their lane. The retrievers (R) throw the balls to the set-up pupils. After the players (P) have practiced sufficiently, they rotate as shown in the figure. This continues, with students advancing from group 2 toward group 5 as they improve. Students in group 1 continue practicing and are advanced to group 2 as they improve. As group 5 becomes crowded, group 1 will have advanced, leaving section 1 open for another advanced group (5). The tennis groups periodically change with the volleyball groups.

LESSON THREE

PERFORMANCE OBJECTIVES:
Psychomotor. The student will stand behind the service line and correctly serve the ball into the left and then the right service area 7 out of 10 times.
Cognitive. The student will discuss in three minutes why the power serve is essential for championship tennis.
Affective. The student will display self-control each time the serve is incorrectly made.

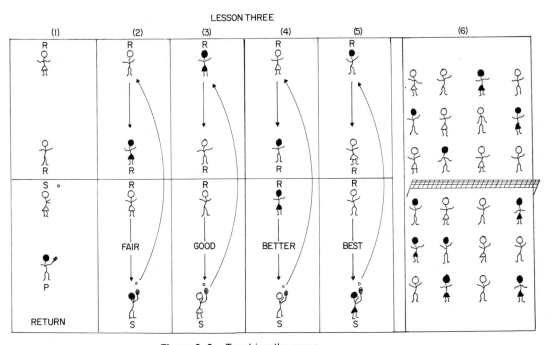

Figure 9–9. Teaching the serve.

The class is divided into six groups: (1) those who need more practice in returning the ball; (2) fair; (3) good; (4) better; (5) best, who are ready for practice in serving; and (6) the volleyball overflow group. Each of the four servers (S) is given a racquet and two balls. They practice placing the serve over the net in their lane. The retrievers (R) throw the balls to the server. After practicing the serve sufficiently, the servers rotate, as shown in diagram. This continues, with students advancing from group 2 toward group 5 as they improve. As group 5 becomes crowded, group 1 will have advanced to group 2, leaving section 1 open for another advanced group (5). All students in groups 1 through 5 change with the volleyball overflow group after practicing tennis skills sufficiently.

LESSON FOUR

PERFORMANCE OBJECTIVES:

Psychomotor. From a position close to the net, the student will successfully volley the ball 3 out 5 times.

Cognitive. The student will list three advantages of the volley in tennis with 80 per cent accuracy on a written test.

Affective. The student will display temper control if hit by the ball while attempting to volley it.

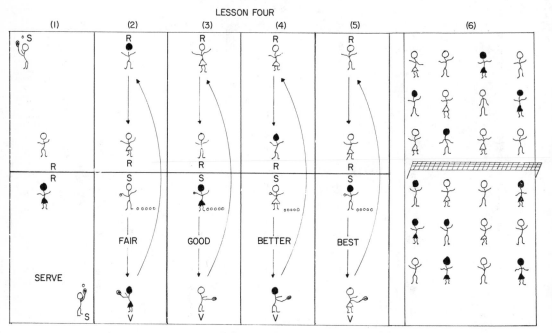

Figure 9–10. Teaching the volley.

The class is divided into six groups: (1) those who did not progress well with the serve; (2) fair; (3) good; (4) better; (5) best; and (6) volleyball overflow. Each of the four volleyers (V) is given a racquet. The four set-up (S) students are given about six balls each. They toss the balls so that the volleyers are able to return the ball in their lane. Retrievers (R) gather the balls for their lane and throw them to the set-up students. The volleying groups rotate within their lanes. This continues with students advancing from group 2 toward group 5 as they improve. Students in group 1 advance to group 2 as they improve. As group 5 becomes crowded, group 1 will have advanced to group 2, leaving this space open for another advanced group. All students in groups 1 through 5 change places with volleyball overflow group 6 after they have practiced tennis skills sufficiently.

LESSON FIVE
PERFORMANCE OBJECTIVES:
Psychomotor. The student will successfully lob the ball over the opponent's head 3 out of 5 times from mid-court.
Cognitive. On a written test, with 90 per cent accuracy, the student will list tennis champions who used the lob to their advantage.
Affective. The student will exhibit kindness to the opponent who fails to return the lob.

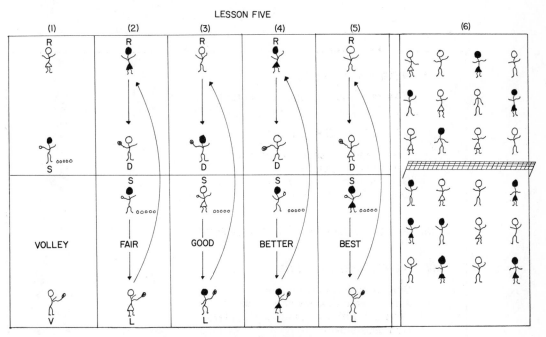

Figure 9–10. Teaching the lob.

The class is divided into six groups: (1) students from the last lesson who continue to practice the volley; (2) fair; (3) good; (4) better; (5) best (students who progressed enough to practice the lob); and (6) the volleyball overflow. Each of the four students (L) is given a racquet to practice the lob. Each of of the four defense (D) students nearest the net is given a racquet. The set-up (S) students are given several balls and make a one bounce toss to the lobbers. The lobbers (L) attempt to return the ball over the heads of the defense students (D). After the lobbers have practiced sufficiently, they rotate as shown in the figure. This continues, with students advancing from group 2 toward group 5 as they improve. Students in group 1 advance to group 2 as they improve. As group 5 becomes crowded, group 1 will have advanced to group 2, leaving that space open for another advanced group (5). After sufficient practice, all students in groups 1 through 5 change with volleyball group (6).

Teaching Bowling Skills

GENERAL OBJECTIVES:
   A. *Psychomotor.* The students will correctly perform the basic movements of bowling as described in class.
   B. *Cognitive.* The students will demonstrate knowledge of bowling by matching correct statements in a written test.
   C. *Affective.* The students will demonstrate their ability to:
      Control emotions under stress.
      Show good sportsmanship.
      Exhibit team loyalty.
      Assume leadership.
      Respect decisions of officials.

I. *HISTORY OF BOWLING*

(See references at end of chapter.)

II. *VALUES OF BOWLING*

Social and recreational potential
Family participation
Development of coordination
Leisure time carry-over

III. *RULES, SCORING, AND COURTESIES*

IV. *SAFETY PRECAUTIONS*

Stay away from flying pins.
Always watch balls when returned.
Stop ball with foot (improvised alleys).
Roll balls slowly.
Remove balls from rack properly, keeping fingers away from on-coming balls.
Release ball only when pin setter is away (improvised alley).
Control ball at all times.

V. *EQUIPMENT NEEDED*

Six alleys (improvised — see Figure 9–14)
60 pins — 18 balls
Six pieces of indoor-outdoor carpeting, 40 to 60 feet long
Score sheets

VI. *BASIC SKILLS*

Grip   Release
Stance   Delivery
Approach   Follow-through

LESSON ONE

PERFORMANCE OBJECTIVES:

Psychomotor. The student will demonstrate correct delivery form from the starting position by hitting the headpin 3 out of 5 times.

Cognitive. The student will list five values of bowling as a written test with a time limit of five minutes.

Affective. The student will display emotional control if a foul is made.

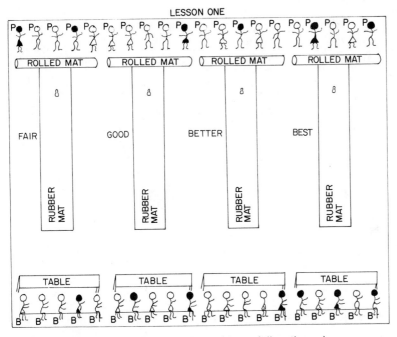

Figure 9–12. Grip—stance—release—follow-through.

Students are arranged in ability groups of four as shown. The B's are bowlers; they are seated on benches behind the tables. The P's are pin-setters, who roll the balls slowly on the rubber runners back to the bowlers. One pin per mat is used. Each bowler walks to the foul line, places his left foot on it, and releases the ball, aiming it at the pin and following through. Each bowler repeats this several times. Bowlers then change places with pin-setters. Students are grouped by ability into one of the four groups. Bowlers advance from one group to another as they improve.

LESSON TWO
PERFORMANCE OBJECTIVES:

Psychomotor. Using the four-step approach from behind the foul line, the student will hit the headpin 3 out of 7 times.

Cognitive. The student will give a one-minute oral report to the class on the four-step approach.

Affective. The student will display emotional control if a foul is made when releasing the ball.

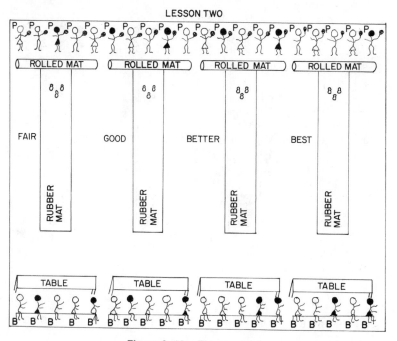

Figure 9–13. The approach.

Follow the same organizational procedure outlined in lesson one, but use three pins per mat instead of one. Students practice the four step approach instead of releasing the ball from the stationary position. Bowlers advance from the fair group to the best group as they improve.

LESSON THREE
PERFORMANCE OBJECTIVES:

Psychomotor. The student will demonstrate the correct form in the hook delivery by hitting the 1-3 pocket 4 out of 10 times.

Cognitive. The student will write a description of the straight delivery, showing its advantages.

Affective. The student will display courtesy to an opponent whose ball has rolled into his or her alley.

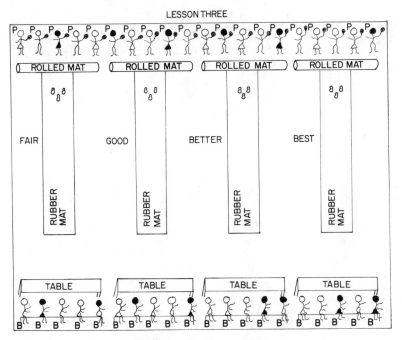

Figure 9–14. The delivery.

Students are organized as shown in lesson one. Three pins per mat are used. Emphasis is on the hook and straight deliveries. Students advance from one group to another as they improve.

LESSON FOUR
PERFORMANCE OBJECTIVES:

Psychomotor.   After selecting a spot 15 to 20 feet from the fou line, the student will hit the 1-3 pocket 3 out of 7 times.

Cognitive.   The student will prepare a one-page paper on the advantages and disadvantages of the two types of aims.

Affective.   The student is patient when he or she fails to hit the proper pin in spot aiming.

LESSON FOUR

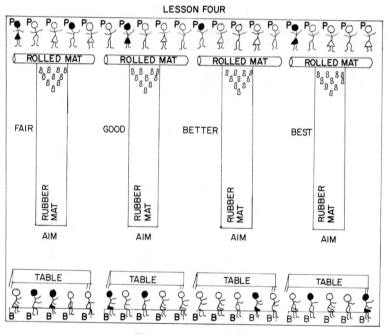

Figure 9-15.   The aim.

The organizational plan for the preceding lessons is used. All ten pins are set up on each mat. Students practice both head pin and spot aiming. They advance as they improve.

LESSON FIVE

PERFORMANCE OBJECTIVES:

Psychomotor. The student will use the four steps of bowling — grip, approach, delivery, and aim — to hit the 1-3 pocket 6 out of 10 times.

Cognitive. The student will identify the correct form of the four stages from a series of pictures that shows both correct and incorrect form.

Affective. The student will show good sportsmanship when consistently missing strikes.

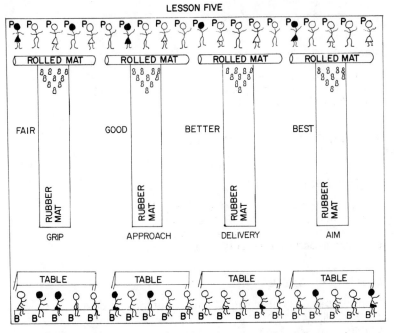

Figure 9–16. Teaching all skills; grip—approach—delivery—aim.

Based on the inventory, students are placed as shown above. They should practice those skills in which they are weakest. All ten pins are used on each mat.

Teaching Golf Skills

GENERAL OBJECTIVES:
  A. **Psychomotor.** The students will exhibit correct form in the complex movements of golf as described by the teacher and demonstrated by a professional.
  B. **Cognitive.** The students will demonstrate their knowledge of golf by checking correct answers on a true-false test.
  C. **Affective.** The students will demonstrate their ability to:
       Control emotions under stress.
       Show good sportsmanship.
       Exhibit team loyalty.
       Accept responsibility.
       Assume leadership.
       Respect decisions of officials.

  I. HISTORY OF GOLF

  (See references at end of chapter.)

  II. VALUES OF GOLF

  Leisure time carry-over
  Social and recreational potential
  Development of coordination

  III. RULES, SCORING, AND COURTESIES

  IV. SAFETY PRECAUTIONS

  Always be aware of danger of swinging clubs.
  Stay in individual squares while swinging.
  Stay away from other pupils who are practicing.
  Intensive supervision is required at all times.

  V. EQUIPMENT NEEDED

  Eight rubber mats or pieces of indoor-outdoor carpeting
  Plastic balls
  Clubs

  VI. BASIC SKILLS

  Grip   Pivot
  Stance   Follow-through
  Swing   Putt

LESSON ONE
PERFORMANCE OBJECTIVES:

Psychomotor. Following instruction in class, the student will execute a correct golf swing 3 out of 7 times.

Cognitive. In one minute, the student will draw a diagram showing a player position that insures safe practice.

Affective. The student will show tolerance for classmates when they violate rules of safety.

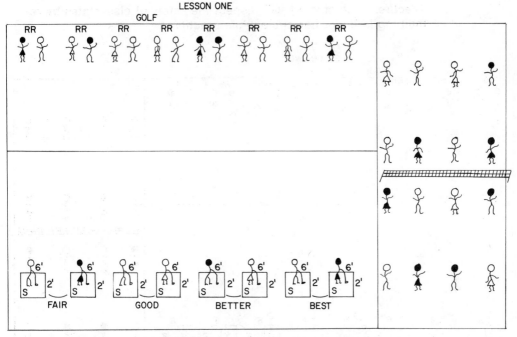

Figure 9–17. Grip—stance—swing—follow-through (indoors).

Students are arranged as shown. The golf group has 24 students—eight swingers (S) and 16 retrievers (R). The volleyball overflow group has eight on each side. Students in the golf swing group practice the stance and swing at the plastic balls placed in the center of each square. It is imperative that they stay in the square. A swinging golf club is a lethal weapon, and the organization must be such as to insure safety at all times. The retrievers (R) approach the restraining line and throw the plastic balls back to the swingers (S). The swingers periodically change places with the retrievers. Students progress from the fair to the best groups based on ability. Overflow groups change with the golf groups at set intervals.

LESSON TWO

PERFORMANCE OBJECTIVES:

Psychomotor. The student will use an iron and hit a plastic golf ball into a target circle 3 out of 5 times.

Cognitive. In a two-minute quiz, the student will identify the functions of the irons by matching the correct iron with the yardage shown on a chart.

Affective. The student will respect the safety of classmates by remaining in his or her circle while practicing.

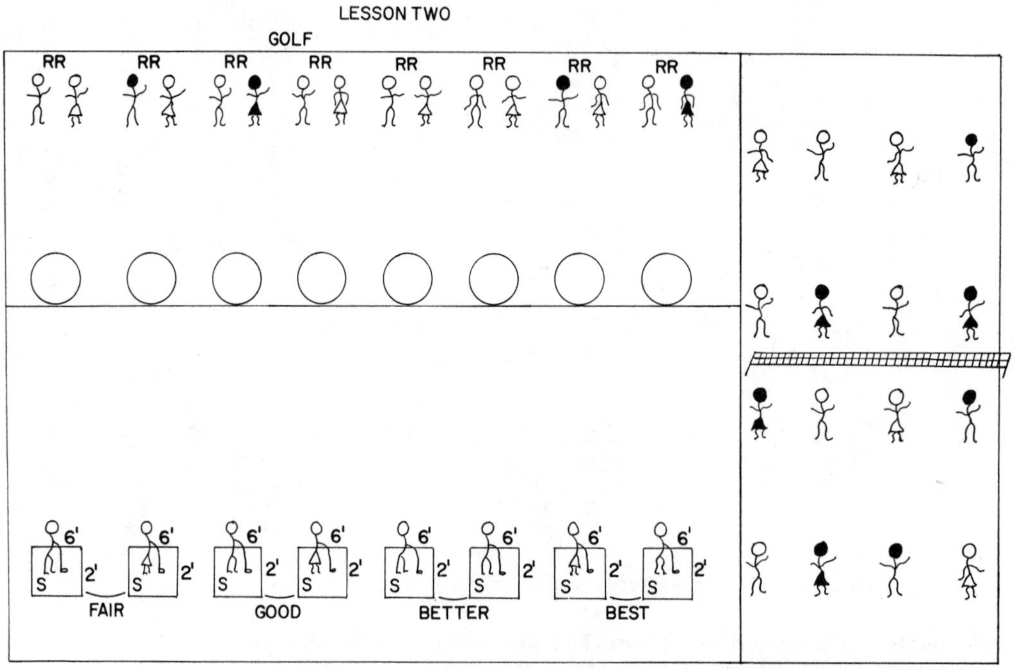

Figure 9–18. Accuracy (outdoors).

The plan shown in lesson one is used again. Students attempt to place the ball in the circle corresponding to their squares. Plastic balls are used. Students advance from the fair groups to the best groups as they improve.

LESSON THREE

PERFORMANCE OBJECTIVES:

Psychomotor. The student, using a regular golf ball and selected iron, will hit the ball in the target circle 3 out of 5 times.

Cognitive. In two minutes, the student will describe the reason for using an iron rather than a wood during early instruction.

Affective. Using the terms taught in class, the student will show proper courtesy before hitting the ball.

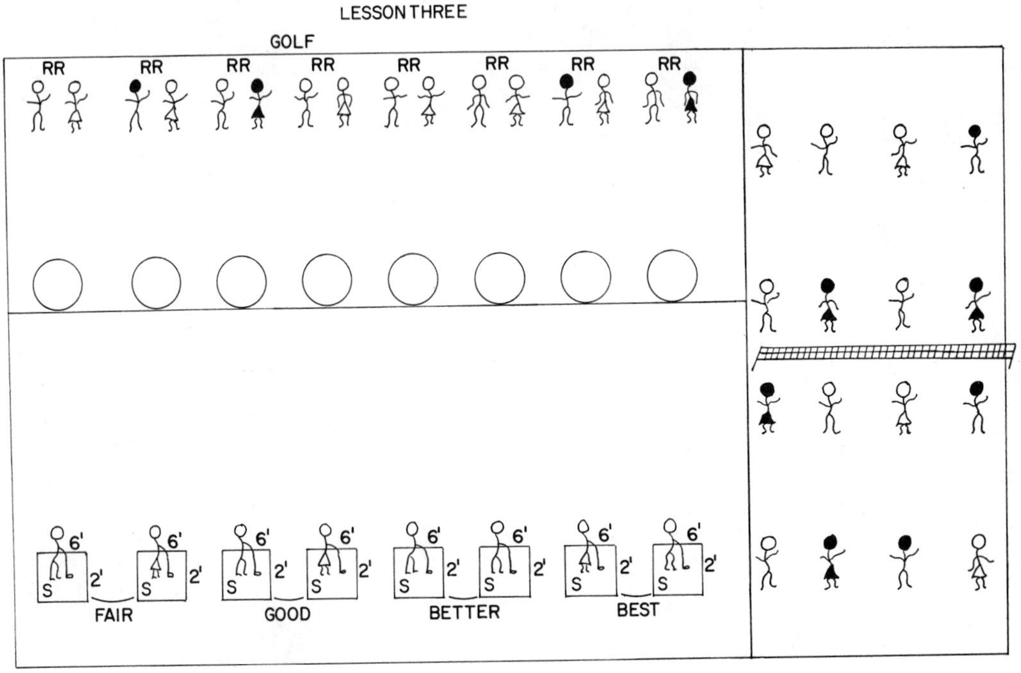

Figure 9–19. Using regular balls (outdoors).

The students are organized as shown in lesson two. Standard golf balls are now used, thus limiting this exercise to outdoor practice. Because the previous two lesson plans call for the use of plastic balls, they can be implemented either indoors or outdoors.

When the regular golf ball is used, the circles are drawn farther away from the practice squares. Students advance as they improve.

LESSON FOUR
PERFORMANCE OBJECTIVES:
  Psychomotor. The student will putt the ball into the metal cup (or hole) 3 out of 7 times.
  Cognitive. As a written test, the student will write two 50-word paragraphs describing the stance used in putting and explain how it differs from the other stances.
  Affective. The student will show courtesy for classmates by awaiting his or her turn for putting.

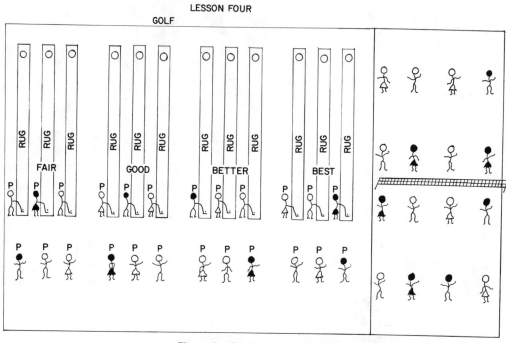

Figure 9–20. Putting indoors or outdoors.

The students are divided into two groups as shown. The golf group consists of 24 putters (P), and the volleyball overflow group consists of 16 students with eight on each side. Students practice putting on rugs that have metal cups at the end. The students advance from the fair group to the best group based on their ability. Periodically, the volleyball overflow groups change with the golf groups. Regular balls are used.

LESSON FIVE

PERFORMANCE OBJECTIVES:

Psychomotor. The student will score par on the pitch and putt course 3 out of 5 times.

Cognitive. The student will orally explain his selection of clubs and demonstrate his knowledge by answering questions on a written test with 70 per cent accuracy or better.

Affective. The student will show tolerance for the poorly coordinated classmate who makes a mistake.

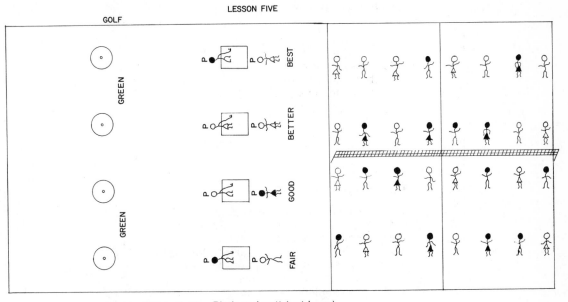

Figure 9-21. Pitch and putt (outdoors).

Students are arranged in two groups as shown. The golf group (P) has eight students, and the volleyball overflow group has 32 players on two courts. The golfers pitch and putt, and are grouped from fair to best based on ability. The volleyball groups and the golfers change places periodically. Regular balls are used. Golfers advance from fair to best as they improve.

Teaching Tumbling Skills

GENERAL OBJECTIVES:

A. Psychomotor. The students will correctly demonstrate the various skills of tumbling as described by the teacher and practiced in class.

B. Cognitive. The students will demonstrate their knowledge of tumbling by checking the correct answers on a true-false test.

C. Affective. The students will demonstrate their ability to:

Control emotions under stress.
Show good sportsmanship.
Exhibit team loyalty.
Accept responsibility.
Assume leadership.
Respect decisions of officials.

I. HISTORY OF TUMBLING

(See references at end of chapter.)

II. VALUES OF TUMBLING

Safety rules transfer to other sports
Contributes to emotional stability
Contributes to physiological fitness
Leisure time carry-over

III. RULES, SCORING, AND COURTESIES

IV. SAFETY PRECAUTIONS

Never leave group unsupervised.
Follow recommended sequence in teaching.
Always use spotters in all skills.
Do not allow students to overextend their efforts.
Do not urge students to progress too fast.
Check mats for unseen objects.
Always have students warm up.
Always have students complete a movement; do not allow them to hesitate.
Have student stay off mat until tumbler in front has left mat.

V. EQUIPMENT NEEDED

Two 20-foot mats   Teaching aids
Two safety belts   Test

VI. BASIC SKILLS

Forward roll   Front handspring
Backward roll   Back handspring
Kip-up   Front somersault
Headstand

LESSON ONE

PERFORMANCE OBJECTIVES:

Psychomotor. After the demonstration in class, the student will properly perform a forward roll 3 out of 5 times.

Cognitive. The student will take a written test and answer questions with 80 per cent accuracy on the proper sequence of steps in performing the forward roll.

Affective. The student will follow instructions given by the teacher to insure the safety of classmates.

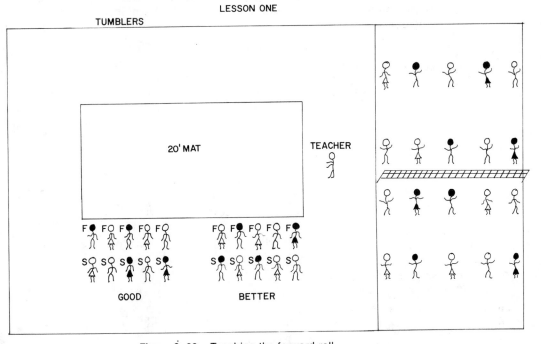

Figure 9-22. Teaching the forward roll.

The class is divided into two groups as shown. The tumbling group consists of ten tumblers, who will practice the forward roll (F), and ten spotters (S). The volleyball overflow group consists of two teams with ten on each team. The forward roll has been demonstrated in the second part of the teaching procedure and the pupils are ready to begin, with the spotters beside them ready to assist. As the tumblers improve, the "better" group becomes larger and the "good" group is absorbed. If students improve in the simple forward roll, they may add a dive. The tumbling group changes with the volleyball overflow either several at a time or as a group, at the discretion of the teacher.

LESSON TWO
PERFORMANCE OBJECTIVES:
  Psychomotor. The student will perform a correct backward roll, as demonstrated in the filmstrip shown in class, 7 out of 10 times.
  Cognitive. The student will prove his knowledge of the backward roll, which was gained by reading the recommended text, with 50 per cent accuracy on a written test.
  Affective. The student will demonstrate tolerance for the poor performance of other students and assist them in learning the correct form.

LESSON TWO

TUMBLERS

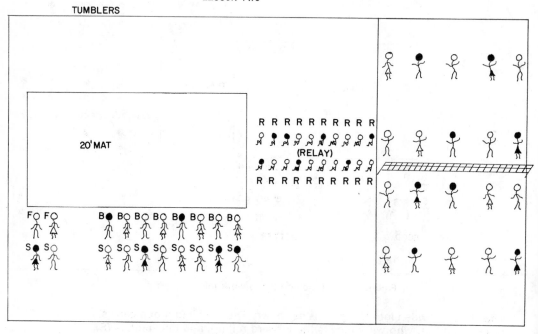

Figure 9–23.   Teaching the backward roll.

Students are grouped as shown. Students (F) who failed to execute the forward roll continue to practice. Those who learned the forward roll practice the backward roll (B) with spotters (S). The tumbling group changes with the volleyball group, either several at a time or as a group, at the discretion of the teacher. Spotters change with learners also at the discretion of the teacher. A forward roll relay race may be used as shown.

LESSON THREE

PERFORMANCE OBJECTIVES:

Psychomotor. The student will demonstrate correct form for the headstand and maintain it for 25 seconds.

Cognitive. The student will exhibit an understanding of the headstand by assisting a classmate in performing it correctly.

Affective. The student will show appreciation for the teacher by following instructions without disruption.

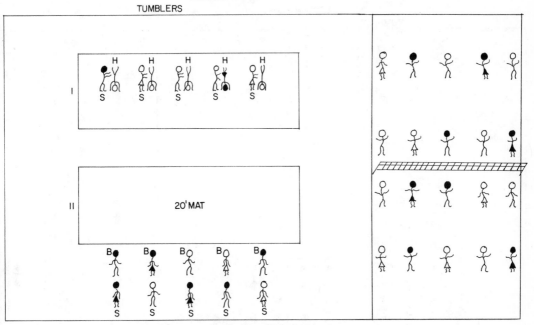

Figure 9–24. Teaching the headstand.

Students are arranged in two sections as shown. The mat is placed against the wall. Students learning the headstand (H), assisted by their spotters (S), place their head and hands on the mat and their feet against the wall. A mat is not necessary for this activity but is desirable if available. At the teacher's discretion, the spotters change places with those learning the headstand. Students who failed to execute the backroll in the previous lesson practice on mat II with their spotters. Tumbling sections change with volleyball sections either in pairs or as a group.

LESSON FOUR

PERFORMANCE OBJECTIVES:

   Psychomotor. The student will perform the kip-up correctly on a standard mat 3 out of 5 times.

   Cognitive. The student will demonstrate an understanding of the kip-up by observing a classmate and pointing out any incorrect movements.

   Affective. The student will demonstrate good sportsmanship by overlooking remarks made by a classmate when poor movements are made.

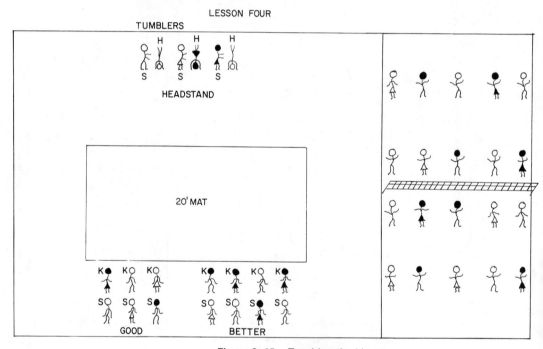

Figure 9–25.   Teaching the kip-up.

Students are grouped as shown, with those who failed to execute the headstand (H) still practicing, and those who are ready to practice the kip-up (K) starting with the spotters (S) helping them. Students progress as they improve, from headstand to good and from good to better. A constant interchange, either in pairs or by entire groups, goes on between the tumbling groups and the volleyball overflow. Spotters change with learners at the discretion of the teacher.

LESSON FIVE

PERFORMANCE OBJECTIVES:

Psychomotor. The student will execute the handspring 3 out of 5 times on a 5 foot × 10 foot mat in proper sequence and without hesitating.

Cognitive. From a series of pictures made by students, the student will identify the one showing correct form with 75 per cent accuracy.

Affective. The student will show kindness toward poorly coordinated classmates and assist them in performing the handspring.

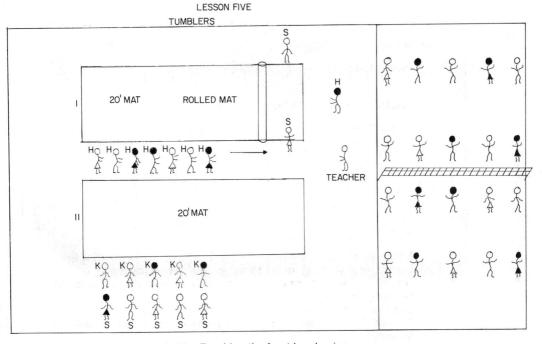

Figure 9–26. Teaching the front handspring.

Students are grouped into two sections: 20 tumblers and 20 volleyball overflow pupils. The eight students learning the handspring (H), assisted by the two spotters (S), begin to execute the handspring over a rolled mat. These students have executed the kip and are ready to advance. Students who did not perform the kip correctly continue to practice on mat II as shown. When students learn the kip, they proceed to the handspring. As the handspring group learns the skill satisfactorily, they change with one of the volleyball overflow groups. Spotters change places with learners at the discretion of the teacher.

Teaching Swimming Skills

GENERAL OBJECTIVES:

A. Psychomotor. The students will exhibit the correct form in the complex movements of swimming as described and demonstrated by the visiting professional.

B. Cognitive. The students will demonstrate their knowledge by giving the correct answers on a true-false test.

C. Affective. The students will demonstrate their ability to:
Control emotions under stress.
Show good sportsmanship.
Exhibit team loyalty.
Accept responsibility.
Assume leadership.
Respect decisions of officials.

I.   HISTORY OF SWIMMING

(See references at end of chapter.)

II.   VALUES OF SWIMMING

Safety values
Physiological development
Recreational values

III.   RULES

IV.   SAFETY PRECAUTIONS

Never go into pool alone.
Wear swim suit at all times to be ready to aid students.
Do not permit dangerous behavior such as pushing, ducking, and climbing in water.
Use the "buddy system."
Do not allow students to dive in water unless depth of water is known.
Do not allow students to run around the pool.
Always have life preservers available.

V.   EQUIPMENT NEEDED

Pool or tank	Films and filmstrips
Swim suits	Texts

VI.   BASIC SKILLS

Learning to swim:		Strokes:	
	Breath control		Crawl
	Submerging		Back crawl
	Face floating		Breast
	Flutter kick		Side
	Arm stroke		

LESSON ONE
PERFORMANCE OBJECTIVES:

Psychomotor. The student will bob correctly in the shallow end of the pool by holding his breath, remaining under water for three seconds, coming up for air, and repeating the process 10 times.

Cognitive. After instruction by the teacher, the student will describe the importance of bobbing in one 50-word paragraph.

Affective. The student will show understanding of his or her "buddy's" fear of water and help him or her to bob properly.

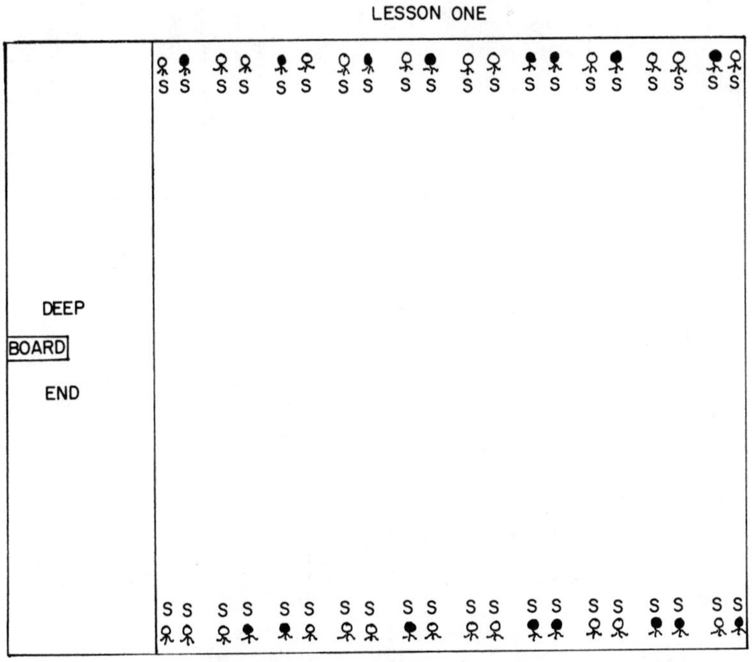

LESSON ONE

Figure 9–27. Dispelling fear of water.

The entire class of 40 students is grouped in pairs ("buddy system"). Students enter the shallow water and practice "bobbing", or submerging to dispel the fear of water. This is done in a leisurely, unpressured manner, since fear of the water is one of the biggest impediments to teaching swimming. Once students have become accustomed to the water, they should begin to practice rhythmical breathing.

LESSON TWO

PERFORMANCE OBJECTIVES:

Psychomotor. The student will demonstrate the float by pushing from the side of the pool and floating for at least 30 seconds.

Cognitive. The student will show his knowledge of floating in a true-false test by scoring 8 correct answers out of 10.

Affective. The student will show respect for the teacher by following instructions and floating the requested distance without complaining.

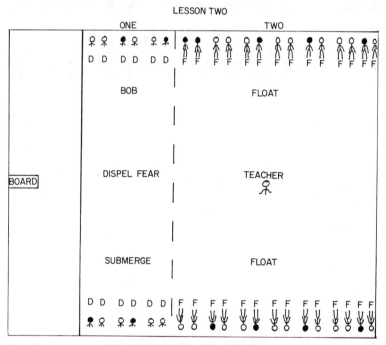

Figure 9–28. Teaching the float.

Students are organized in two groups as shown. Students who have not learned to bob and breathe rhythmically will continue to practice in group one. Students in group two are ready to practice the dead man's float, by holding their breath and pushing off from the side of the pool with arms outstretched. Breathing may be practiced in conjunction with the floating procedure. Students in group one practice floating as they improve in the bobbing and submerging. Because of improper buoyancy, all students may not be able to float without slight arm and leg movements. However, practicing floating is important in learning to swim.

LESSON THREE

PERFORMANCE OBJECTIVES:

Psychomotor. The student will demonstrate the flutter kick by holding his or her breath, grasping the edge of the pool, and executing the flutter kick with straight knees for 15 seconds.

Cognitive. The student will demonstrate his knowledge of the flutter kick by answering 8 out of 10 questions correctly on a true-false test.

Affective. The student will overcome fear of water by performing the flutter kick without hesitation for the width of the pool.

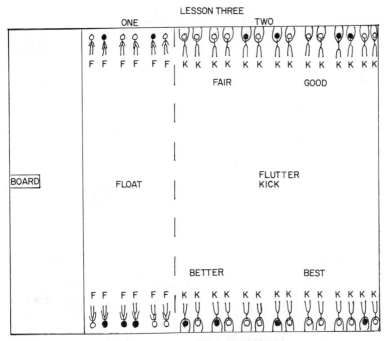

Figure 9-29. Teaching the flutter kick.

Students are grouped in two sections as shown. Students in group one continue practicing the float (FF), and as they improve they advance to group two. Students in group two are ready to learn the flutter kick (KK), and are divided into four ability groups. Students grasp the edge of the pool and practice the flutter kick first with the head out of water and then with it under water. They advance as they improve.

LESSON FOUR

PERFORMANCE OBJECTIVES:

Psychomotor. The student will demonstrate the push-off from the side of the pool and will propel himself the width of the pool by using the flutter kick.

Cognitive. The student will display his knowledge of the push-off by observing his classmates and pointing out incorrect procedures.

Affective. The student will show respect for those who lack confidence by offering assistance in the push-off demonstration.

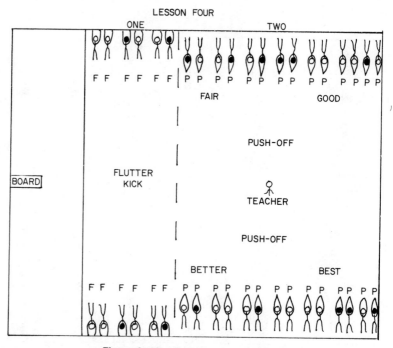

Figure 9-30. Teaching the push-off.

Students are placed in two groups as shown. Students in group one (FF) continue to practice the flutter kick, and as they improve they advance to group two. Students in group two are ready to learn the push-off (PP), and are divided into four ability groups. One student from each of the pairs (PP) takes a deep breath and pushes off with outstretched arms and his head under water. The flutter kick is executed vigorously as the pupils try to travel the width of the pool. Finally, they push off, flutter, and use two or three strokes with their arms. They advance as they improve.

LESSON FIVE

PERFORMANCE OBJECTIVES:

Psychomotor. The student will correctly perform the crawl stroke by coordinating the arms and legs and swimming 10 yards.

Cognitive. The student will demonstrate his knowledge of the crawl stroke by comparing the form of classmates with that shown in the films seen in class.

Affective. The student will show sympathy for a classmate who has trouble mastering the crawl stroke by offering assistance.

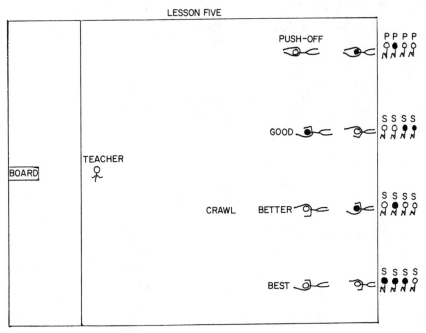

Figure 9-31. Teaching the crawl stroke.

The class is organized in two groups as shown. The students who failed to execute the push-off in the preceding lesson continue to practice. Those who learned the push-off are ready to practice the crawl, with the first student in each group swimming to the teacher, to the side of the pool, and out. This goes on with the push-off group advancing to the crawl group as they improve. Students advance from the good group to the best group as they improve.

Teaching Rhythms

GENERAL OBJECTIVES:
  A. **Psychomotor.** After studying a film on rhythms, students will demonstrate correct form in these movements.
  B. **Cognitive.** The students will demonstrate their knowledge of rhythms by writing two-page essays on these activities.
  C. **Affective.** The students will demonstrate their ability to:
    Control emotions under stress.
    Show good sportsmanship.
    Exhibit team loyalty in demonstrations.
    Accept responsibility.

I. HISTORY OF RHYTHMS

(See references at end of chapter.)

II. VALUES OF RHYTHMS

Social potential
Development of poise, grace, and confidence
Development of physiological fitness
Provides emotional release of tension

III. SAFETY PRECAUTIONS

Intricate movements should be taught progressively.
All pupils should warm up before beginning movements.

IV. EQUIPMENT NEEDED

Record player with microphone	Drums
Records	Piano
Tomtoms	

V. TYPES OF RHYTHMS

Basic movements:

Running	Sliding
Walking	Galloping
Leaping	Folk dancing
Jumping	Square dancing
Hopping	Modern dancing
Skipping	Social dancing

LESSON ONE

PERFORMANCE OBJECTIVES:

Psychomotor.   After viewing a film on basic dance steps, the student will demonstrate the proper form in leaping 3 out of 5 times.

Cognitive.   The student will exhibit his or her knowledge of basic dance movements by sketching them on the chalkboard with 80 per cent accuracy.

Affective.   The student will exhibit inhibition by controlling his or her temper when the teacher strongly criticizes a poor performance.

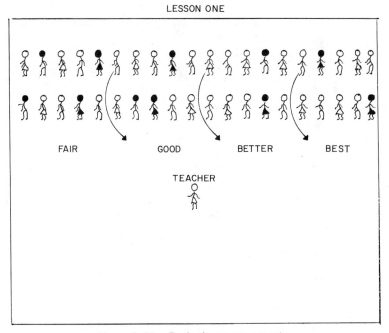

Figure 9–32. Basic dance movements.

Teaching dance movements to large groups does not present a procedural problem. Methods for instructing rhythmic groups are generally known, and dance is an activity that is easily adapted to sizable numbers. The class is organized as shown. Students form two lines and execute various movements around the gymnasium. They may or may not hold hands. Students should be classified according to ability, and advanced as they improve.

LESSON TWO

PERFORMANCE OBJECTIVES:

Psychomotor. After listening to a musical number, the student will demonstrate the allemande movement correctly 2 out of 3 times.

Cognitive. The student will demonstrate his or her knowledge of square dancing by writing a one-paragraph paper.

Affective. The student will demonstrate his or her positive character traits by assisting an awkward partner in performing intricate movements.

LESSON TWO

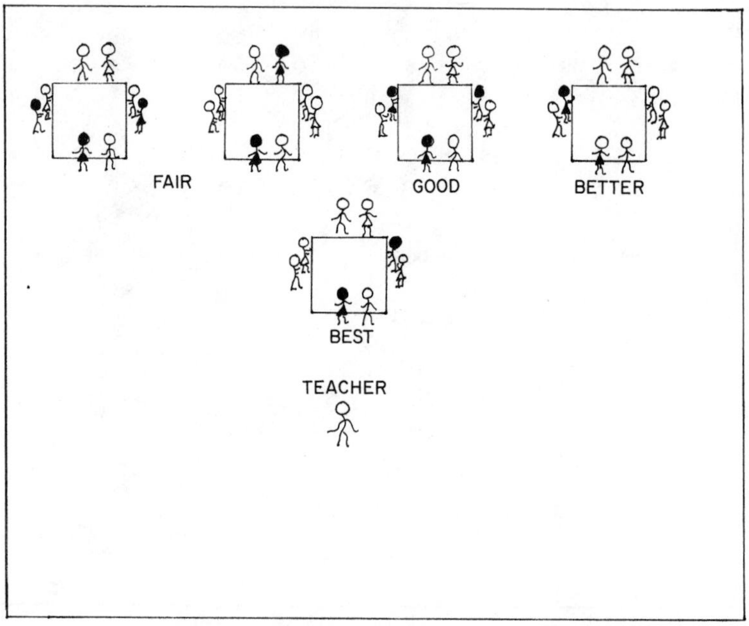

Figure 9-33. Square dance formations.

Teaching square dancing does not present problems. There are several possible group formations. When the quadrille is used, students may be placed as shown. They should advance from the fair group to the best group as they improve.

LESSON THREE

PERFORMANCE OBJECTIVES:

Psychomotor. The student will demonstrate correct form in the mazurka, which was taught in the class, 3 out of 7 times.

Cognitive. The student will exhibit his or her knowledge of folk dancing by answering questions with 75 per cent accuracy.

Affective. The student will show respect for the teacher when corrected for a poor performance.

LESSON THREE

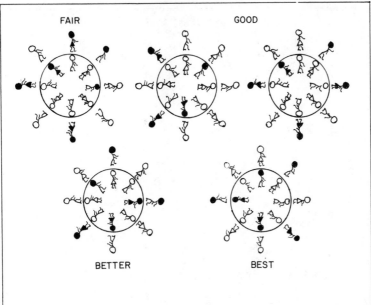

Figure 9-34. Folk dance formations.

There are many variations in the formations for teaching folk dancing. The procedures shown here can be used for all dances involving double circles. Students should be placed in ability groups as shown, and should advance as they improve.

LESSON FOUR

PERFORMANCE OBJECTIVES:

Psychomotor. The student, after studying a film, will demonstrate the waltz correctly 4 out of 8 times.

Cognitive. The student will exhibit his or her knowledge of the waltz by writing a one-paragraph paper describing the dance.

Affective. The student will assume leadership in performing the waltz with a partner without showing embarrassment.

LESSON FOUR

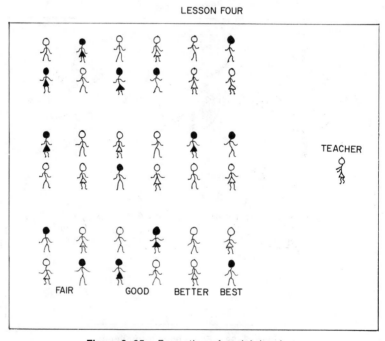

Figure 9–35. Formation of social dancing.

In teaching social dancing, students may be grouped in pairs as shown. They progress from the fair group to the best group as they improve. Teaching social dancing does not present a procedural problem.

LESSON FIVE
PERFORMANCE OBJECTIVES:

Psychomotor. After viewing a professional demonstration, the student will exhibit correct form in flexion 3 out of 6 times.

Cognitive. The student will display knowledge of modern dance by describing it to the class.

Affective. The student will overcome a feeling of embarrassment in performing the steps of modern dance by seeking assistance from a classmate.

LESSON FIVE

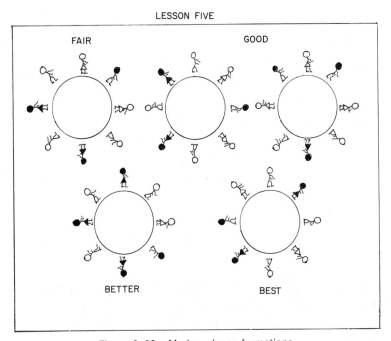

Figure 9–36. Modern dance formations.

Teaching fundamental forms of modern dance may be approached in two ways: (1) group the entire class as shown in lession one and teach the same movement to all, or (2) break the class into several groups and allow each person to interpret the music as he or she feels it. The figure above shows a class divided into five groups with eight in each group. Students will interpret the same musical composition individually, and advance from the fair group to the best group as they improve.

Teaching Wrestling Skills

GENERAL OBJECTIVES:

A. Psychomotor. Students will correctly execute the intricate techniques of wrestling, which were studied in class, several times.

B. Cognitive. Students will exhibit knowledge of wrestling by identifying the various holds when they are flashed on the screen.

C. Affective. The students will demonstrate their ability to:

Control emotions under stress.
Show good sportsmanship.
Exhibit team loyalty.
Accept responsibility.
Assume leadership.
Respect decisions of officials.

I. HISTORY OF WRESTLING

(See references at end of chapter.)

II. VALUES OF WRESTLING

Development of fitness
Development of strength, speed, skill, and endurance
Immediate carry-over
Development of confidence
Tremendous self-defense practice

III. RULES AND SCORING

IV. SAFETY PRECAUTIONS

Students should be matched by weight and ability.
In physical education classes, wrestling should be limited to maneuvers from the referee's position.
Mats should be adequately padded and frequently cleaned.

V. EQUIPMENT NEEDED

Mats	Covers

VI. BASIC SKILLS

Referee's position	Pin holds
Breakdowns	Escapes
Advantage	Counters
Disadvantage	

LESSON ONE

PERFORMANCE OBJECTIVES:

Psychomotor. After a demonstration, the student will correctly execute the spinning movement by circling his partner for 30 seconds without stopping.

Cognitive. The student will describe the spinning maneuver and use the chalk board to illustrate it in a two-minute talk.

Affective. The student will protest to the teacher whenever violations of the safety rules occur.

LESSON ONE

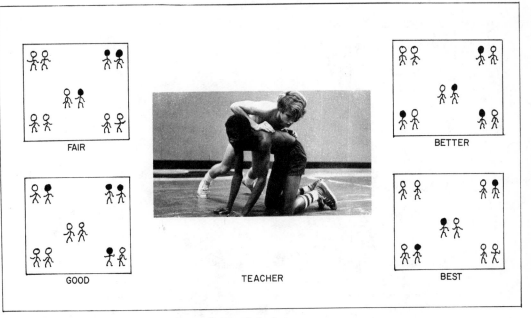

Figure 9–37. Spinning.

Teaching wrestling skills does not present a procedural problem. An average class can be accommodated on the standard mat. Students should be matched according to ability and weight, as shown in the figure, and should advance as they improve.

LESSON TWO

PERFORMANCE OBJECTIVES:

Psychomotor. After observing the referee's position, the student will demonstrate it properly with a classmate 2 out of 3 times.

Cognitive. The student will draw a diagram of an official wrestling mat and list the correct dimensions of it.

Affective. Following instruction, the student will display a positive attitude toward the teacher..

LESSON TWO

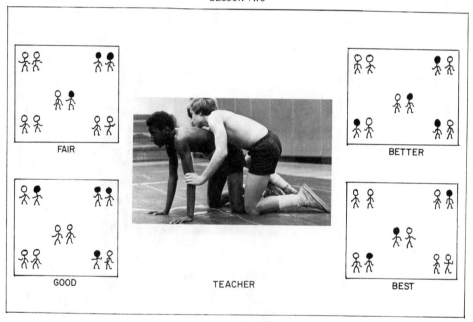

Figure 9–38. Referee's position.

Wrestling maneuvers from the referee's position are recommended for physical education classes because they are safer and require less space. In the plan above, students are arranged around the mat in pairs according to ability. They advance from the fair group to the best group as they improve.

LESSON THREE

PERFORMANCE OBJECTIVES:

Psychomotor. After observing a demonstration, the student will perform the near-wrist breakdown correctly 3 out of 5 times.

Cognitive. The student will explain the steps in executing the near-wrist breakdown in sequential order.

Affective. The student, under close supervision, will not lose his temper when he is pinned.

LESSON THREE

Figure 9-39. Maneuver from position of advantage.

From the referee's position, there are many breakdowns that may be used. The one shown above is the near-wrist breakdown. Students should practice this hold and, at the discretion of the teacher, change from the position of advantage to the position of disadvantage. They progress from the fair group to the best group at the discretion of the teacher.

LESSON FOUR
PERFORMANCE OBJECTIVES:
Psychomotor. After observing a film, the student will correctly demonstrate the side switch maneuver 3 out of 5 times.
Cognitive. The student will write one paragraph describing the correct form for the set-out and switch maneuver.
Affective. The student will never exhibit rowdiness in class while learning the set-out and switch maneuver.

LESSON FOUR

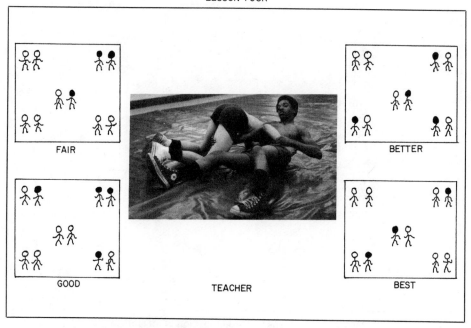

Figure 9-40. Maneuver from position of disadvantage.

There are several good maneuvers from the position of disadvantage. The side switch movement shown above is one illustration. Students are grouped by ability in pairs and advance from the fair group to the best group as they improve.

LESSON FIVE

PERFORMANCE OBJECTIVES:

Psychomotor. The student will execute the half-nelson and crotch combination correctly 3 out of 5 times.

Cognitive. After instruction, the student will describe to the class the ordered steps involved in the half-nelson with 90 per cent accuracy.

Affective. The student will display respect for the teacher and the classmates by reporting to class on time.

LESSON FIVE

Figure 9–41.   Pin holds (half-Nelson and crotch combination).

There comes a moment in a match when the opponent can be pinned. Many holds may be used to do this, one of which is shown above. Students are grouped as shown and progress from the fair group to the best group as they improve.

GROUP ACTIVITIES

Group activities are those in which the successful performance of the individual depends upon close teamwork. For instance, an end in football cannot receive a pass unless the passer forwards the ball properly. Although individual sports are of great importance for their carry-over value, they do not, as a rule, provide the rugged physiological development that team sports offer. The strength, speed, skill, and endurance developed through participation in hockey, touch football, soccer, or basketball are not acquired in many of the individual activities.

Team activities have long dominated the physical education curriculum, and their importance cannot be questioned. For immediate carry-over and for physiological development they are unexcelled. Moreover, team competition develops traits of cooperation and leadership and provides both emotional release and social acceptance — all essential factors for health and personality development.

It is impossible to measure the deterrent effect that a well-planned intramural program of team activities has on deliquency, but associating with other students and experiencing intelligent adult supervision while participating as a member of a team is of inestimable value in developing character. The tendencies toward gregariousness and play are two of nature's most basic drives. It is the responsibility of physical education teachers to organize and guide these instincts along socially accepted channels.

Teaching Basketball Skills

GENERAL OBJECTIVES:
  A. **Psychomotor.** Students will demonstrate the correct form in the various basketball skills studied in class, several times.
  B. **Cognitive.** Students will demonstrate knowledge of basketball by identifying the various shots when demonstrated by other students.
  C. **Affective.** The students will demonstrate their ability to:
    Control emotions under stress.
    Show good sportsmanship.
    Exhibit team loyalty.
    Accept responsibility.
    Assume leadership.
    Respect decisions of officials.

I. HISTORY OF BASKETBALL

(See references at end of chapter.)

II. VALUES OF BASKETBALL

Physiological development
Develops skill, speed, and endurance
Immediate carry-over
Develops teamwork
Contributes to emotional stability

III. RULES, SCORING, AND STRATEGY

(See references at end of chapter.)

IV. SAFETY PRECAUTIONS

Conduct warm-up drills before activity to prevent pulled muscles.
Hold balls when whistle blows.
Roll balls on the floor when asked for by instructor or student instructor.
Report all injuries, blisters, floor burns, and bruises to the instructor.
Have properly fitted shoes.
Note any obstructions on the floor.
Be conscientious about training rules; take care of your body.

V. EQUIPMENT NEEDED

Ten balls
Six baskets
Court 'inside or outside'
Films and filmstrips
Texts

VI. BASIC SKILLS

Dribbling	Guarding
Passing	Pivoting
Shooting	Strategy

LESSON ONE
PERFORMANCE OBJECTIVES:

Psychomotor. The student will dribble the ball down the length of the court without losing possession of it.

Cognitive. The student will draw a diagram of a basketball court and list the dimensions and height of the goal.

Affective. The student will await his or her turn in the relay race without creating a disturbance.

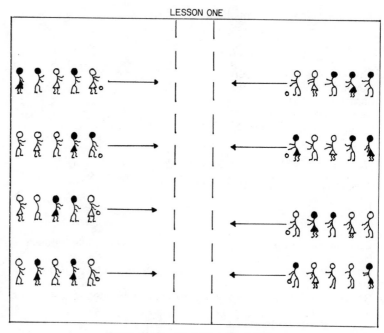

Figure 9-42. Teaching the dribble.

Students are arranged in eight lines of five each as shown; one ball per line is distributed. The first student in each line dribbles to the line and back, passes the ball to the next dribbler, and returns to the end of the line.

LESSON TWO
Performance Objectives:
  Psychomotor. Students will form a circle and demonstrate the bounce pass correctly 4 out of 5 times.
  Cognitive. The student will write a 50-word description of the bounce pass.
  Affective. The student will refrain from interfering with class procedure while waiting for his or her turn to pass the ball.

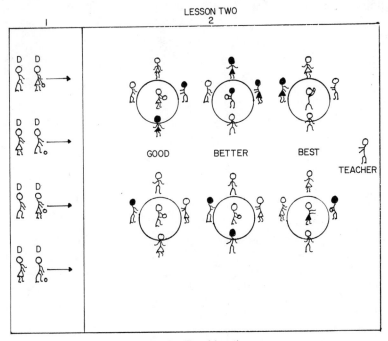

Figure 9–43. Teaching the pass.

The class is divided into two sections as shown. In section one, the students who failed to learn the dribble (D) continue to practice dribbling to the line and back. The students who are ready to learn the passes are grouped in circles of five. Various passes are used, with the inside student passing to the outside students, who pass back; this should be done in standing formation. Then the outside students should walk around the circle, and finally run, as the passing routine continues. Students should progress from the dribble to the pass, then from good to better and best as they improve.

LESSON THREE

PERFORMANCE OBJECTIVES:

Psychomotor. The student will stand behind the foul throw line and use the correct form to shoot a basketball through the goal 7 out of 10 times.

Cognitive. The student will show his knowledge of the foul shot by answering questions on a written test with 90 per cent accuracy.

Affective. After failing to score the required number of foul shots, the student will demonstrate tenacity of purpose by practicing after school.

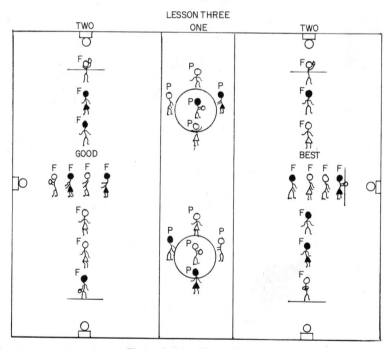

Figure 9–44. The foul shot.

Students are organized in two categories as shown. Section one consists of the students who failed to learn the pass (P). They continue to practice. Students in section two are ready to learn the foul shot (F). They may be grouped by ability as shown and advance as they improve. The passers advance to the foul shot lines as they improve.

LESSON FOUR

PERFORMANCE OBJECTIVES:

Psychomotor. The student will stand 20 feet from the goal and use the set shot to shoot the basketball through the goal 7 out of 10 times.

Cognitive. In a 75-word written report, the student will describe the situations in which the set shot should be used.

Affective. The student will display willingness to assist other students in mastering the form for the set shot.

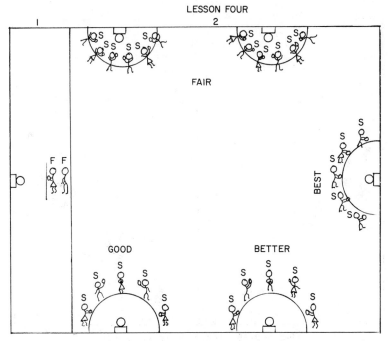

Figure 9–45. The set shot.

Students are placed in two sections as shown. In section one, students who did not learn the foul shot (F) continue to practice. In section two, students who have mastered the foul shot practice the set shot, and progress from the fair to the best group as they improve. The students in the foul shot advance to the set shot group as they improve.

LESSON FIVE

PERFORMANCE OBJECTIVES:

Psychomotor. The student will execute the correct placement of the ball on the backboard 4 out of 5 times.

Cognitive. The student will describe in sequence the steps involved in the lay-up shot with 95 per cent accuracy.

Affective. The student will recognize the need for following safety precautions in executing the lay-up shot.

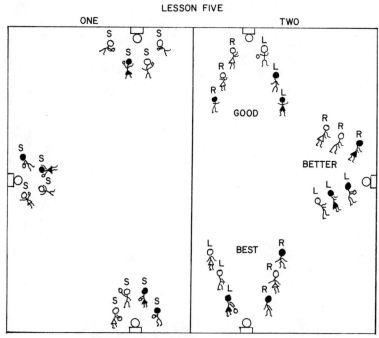

Figure 9–46. Teaching the lay-up shot.

Students are grouped in two sections as shown. Those who failed to perform the set shot are placed in section one (S) and continue to practice. Students ready to learn the lay-up shot are placed in section two, with L's executing the lay-up shot and R's retrieving and passing to L's. Both L's and R's run to the end of the opposite lines. In the next step, the ball is shot from the left side of the basket using the same procedure. Students advance from the good to the best group as they improve.

Teaching Field Hockey Skills

GENERAL OBJECTIVES:
   A. *Psychomotor.* The students will demonstrate the complex motor skills involved in field hockey by executing the movements that incorporate them.
   B. *Cognitive.* The students will demonstrate knowledge of the game by identifying and describing the various skills involved.
   C. *Affective.* The students will demonstrate their ability to:
   Control emotions under stress.
   Show good sportsmanship.
   Exhibit team loyalty.
   Accept responsibility.
   Assume leadership.
   Respect decisions of officials.

I. *HISTORY OF FIELD HOCKEY*

   (See references at end of chapter.)

II. *VALUES OF FIELD HOCKEY*

   Contributes to emotional stability
   Physiological development
   Carry-over
   Develops teamwork and cooperation

III. *RULES, SCORING, AND STRATEGY*

   (See references at end of chapter.)

IV. *SAFETY PRECAUTIONS*

   Warm up adequately before participating.
   Learn to handle the stick correctly.
   Never hit a moving ball.
   Never strike in the direction of another player.
   Use shin and ankle guards, and glasses if necessary.

V. *EQUIPMENT NEEDED*

40 sticks	Films and filmstrips
20 balls	Ankle guards
Pinnies	Shoes
Goal-keeper equipment	Texts
Shin guards	

VI. *BASIC SKILLS*

Dribbling	Dodging
Driving	Right
Straight	Left
Left	Triangular Pass
Right	Scoop
Fielding	Bully
Push Pass	Corner
Flicking	Long corner
Tackling	Short corner
Left-hand lunge	Free Hit
Front or straight	Roll-in
Circular	Strategy

LESSON ONE
PERFORMANCE OBJECTIVES:

Psychomotor. The student will correctly execute the dribble and evade his or her opponent 3 out of 5 times.

Cognitive. The student will orally describe the dribble to the class, pointing out the importance of mastering this skill.

Affective. The student will display self-control if struck on the shin with the hockey stick.

LESSON ONE

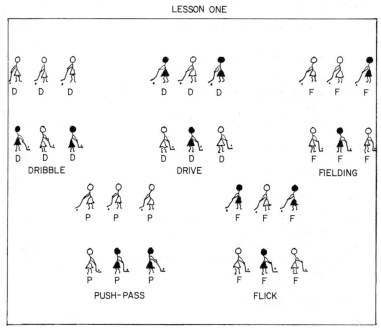

Figure 9-47. Teaching the strokes.

Students are divided into groups as shown. A stick is given to each student, and as many balls as possible are provided per group. The dribblers dribble back and forth and the drivers practice their drives, using as many balls as they can. The fielding, push pass, and flick groups all work back and forth as they execute their specific skills. Students rotate among the groups until everyone has adequately learned each skill. An alternate to this procedure is to teach each stroke separately, proceeding only after each stroke is mastered.

LESSON TWO

PERFORMANCE OBJECTIVES:

Psychomotor. The student will gain control of the ball from the advancing dribbler 2 out of 3 times.

Cognitive. The student will draw the stages involved in the tackle on the chalk board.

Affective. The student will show cooperation with the teacher by offering assistance with the instruction.

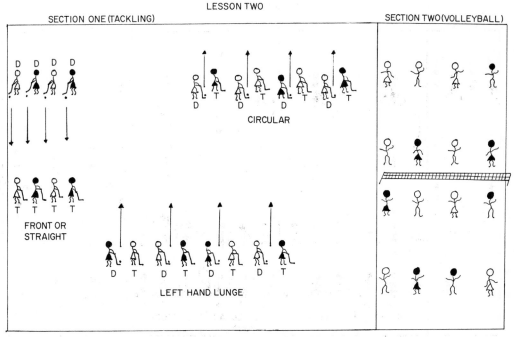

LESSON TWO

SECTION ONE (TACKLING)   SECTION TWO (VOLLEYBALL)

CIRCULAR

FRONT OR STRAIGHT

LEFT HAND LUNGE

Figure 9–48. Teaching tackling.

Students are divided into two sections as shown. Section one has three groups of students learning the three types of tackling. A stick is given to each of the students, and a ball is given to each dribbler (D). The dribblers in the front group carry the ball toward the tacklers (T), who stop the ball. Then they trade places. The lunge and the circular groups work in pairs (DT), with the student in possession of the ball (D) placed on the right or left of the tackler (T). The dribbler carries the ball in the direction of the arrows, and the tackler attempts to capture the ball. Students change with the volleyball overflow pupils at the discretion of the teacher.

An alternative is to teach each skill separately, based on ability grouping.

LESSON THREE

PERFORMANCE OBJECTIVES:

Psychomotor. The student will execute the triangular pass correctly 3 out of 5 times.

Cognitive. After viewing several executions of the triangular pass, the student will spot errors and describe the correct performance.

Affective. The student will volunteer to assist a poorly coordinated classmate in learning the dodge.

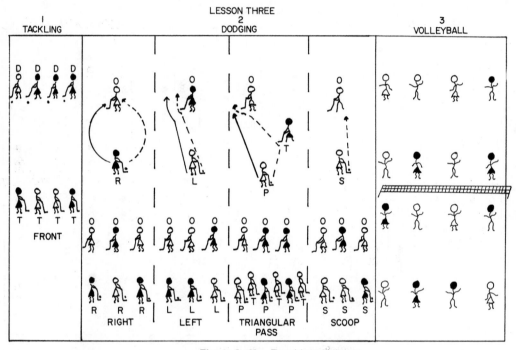

Figure 9–49. Teaching dodging.

Students are divided into three sections as shown. Students in section one continue to practice tackling. Section two is divided into four groups, with each group practicing the types of dodge shown. The students (R and L) in the right and left dodges are given sticks and balls. The diagrams at the top illustrate the path of the ball (---->), the player (→), and the opponent (O). In the triangular pass, the player (P) with the ball passes to teammate (T), who returns it to the player behind the opponent (O). In the scoop, each scooper (S) is given a ball and stick and carries the ball (---->) toward the opponent. Students change with the volleyball overflow group at the discretion of the teacher.

An alternative is to teach each skill separately using ability grouping.

LESSON FOUR

PERFORMANCE OBJECTIVES:

Psychomotor.   The student will execute the bully correctly 3 out of 6 times.

Cognitive.   The student will give an oral report to the class on the proper execution of the bully.

Affective.   The student will be patient when a classmate violates a safety precaution in the use of the hockey stick.

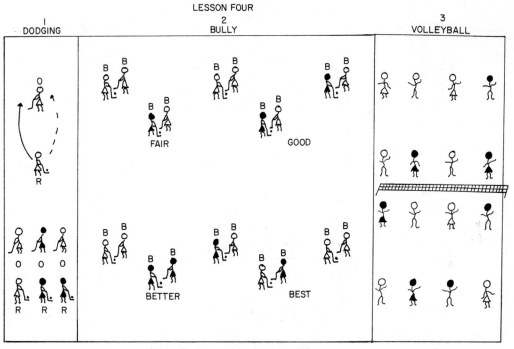

Figure 9-50.   Teaching the bully.

The class is divided into three sections as shown. The students in section one continue to practice dodging, and those in section two are divided into ten pairs, each pair practicing the bully. Students advance from the fair group to the best group as they improve. The hockey group changes with the volleyball group at the discretion of the teacher.

LESSON FIVE
PERFORMANCE OBJECTIVES:
  Psychomotor. After observing a demonstration by a varsity player, the student will execute the roll-in correctly 4 out of 7 times.
  Cognitive. The student will identify and describe the roll-in from a series of hockey techniques flashed on the screen.
  Affective. The student will assume a leadership role in settling a dispute between two classmates who collided during a roll-in.

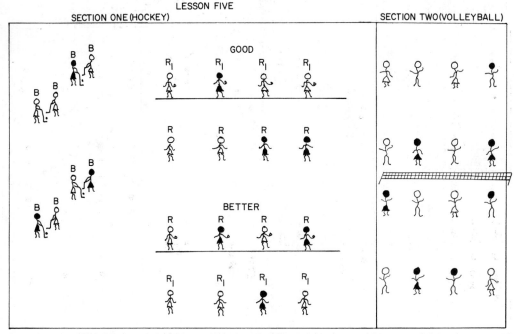

Figure 9–51. Teaching the roll-in.

Students are divided into two sections as shown. In section one, the bully group (BB) students continue practicing until they have improved enough to advance to the roll-in group (R_1). The retrievers (R) roll the ball back to the roll-in group. Students advance from the good to the better group as they improve. The roll-in group changes with the volleyball group at the discretion of the teacher.

Teaching Soccer Skills

GENERAL OBJECTIVES:
A. *Psychomotor.* The students will demonstrate the complex skills and techniques of soccer by executing the movements involved.
B. *Cognitive.* The students will demonstrate their knowledge of soccer by correctly answering questions on a true-false test.
C. *Affective.* The students will demonstrate their ability to:
Control emotions under stress.
Show good sportsmanship.
Exhibit team loyalty.
Accept responsibility.
Assume leadership.
Respect decisions of officials.

I. *HISTORY OF SOCCER*

(See references at end of chapter.)

II. *VALUES OF SOCCER*

Contributes to physical fitness
Develops teamwork
Provides immediate carry-over

III. *RULES, SCORING, AND STRATEGY*

(See references at end of chapter.)

IV. *SAFETY PRECAUTIONS*

Always warm up before practicing skills.
Be careful to protect head when opponent kicks ball.
Learn to relax.
Avoid collisions with opponents.

V. *EQUIPMENT NEEDED*

Ten soccer balls
Films and filmstrips
Texts

VI. *BASIC SKILLS*

Dribbling	Intercepting
Kicking	Heading
Passing	Chesting
Trapping	Tackling
One foot	
Both feet	

LESSON ONE
PERFORMANCE OBJECTIVES:
Psychomotor. The student will dribble a soccer ball 50 yards in a zigzag manner in 30 seconds.
Cognitive. After observing several demonstrations of the dribble, the student will select the correct one and describe it.
Affective. The student will show respect for the teacher after being reprimanded for unnecessary roughness.

LESSON ONE

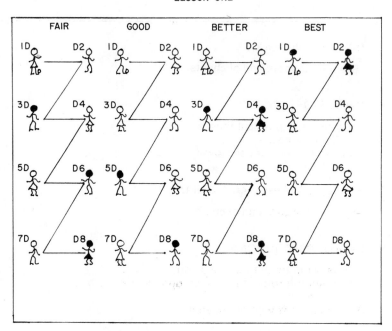

Figure 9-52.   Teaching the dribble.

The class is divided into eight groups of four each. The number 1 student in each group is given a soccer ball and dribbles, as shown in the diagram (number 1 to number 2 and takes his place; number 2 to number 3 and takes his place; finally number 8 replaces number 1). Students may be grouped according to ability as shown and advance from the fair to the best group as they improve.

LESSON TWO

PERFORMANCE OBJECTIVES:

Psychomotor. The student will kick a soccer ball to within five feet of a classmate standing 30 yards away 3 out of 5 times.

Cognitive. In two minutes, the student will draw a diagram on the chalkboard showing the correct form for kicking the ball.

Affective. When necessary, the student will protest a violation of the rules established by the teacher.

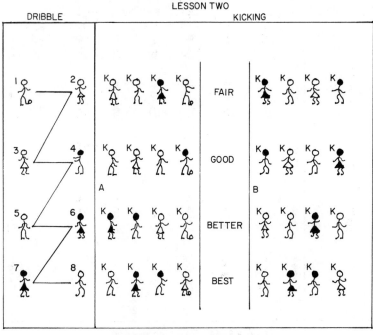

Figure 9–53. Teaching kicking.

The class is divided into two sections as shown. Those who failed to learn the dribble continue practicing, and advance to the kicking section as they improve. The first students in the A groups kick to the first students in the B groups and then run to the end of the line. The first students in the B groups kick to the second students in the A groups and run to the end of the line. Students may be grouped by ability as shown and advance from the fair to the best group as they improve.

LESSON THREE

PERFORMANCE OBJECTIVES:

Psychomotor. Using the inside of the foot, the student will successfully pass to a target point 20 feet away 3 out of 5 times.

Cognitive. The student will demonstrate his knowledge of soccer by identifying the various passes and describing the value of each.

Affective. The student will offer no alibis for performing poorly after having studied the pass in class.

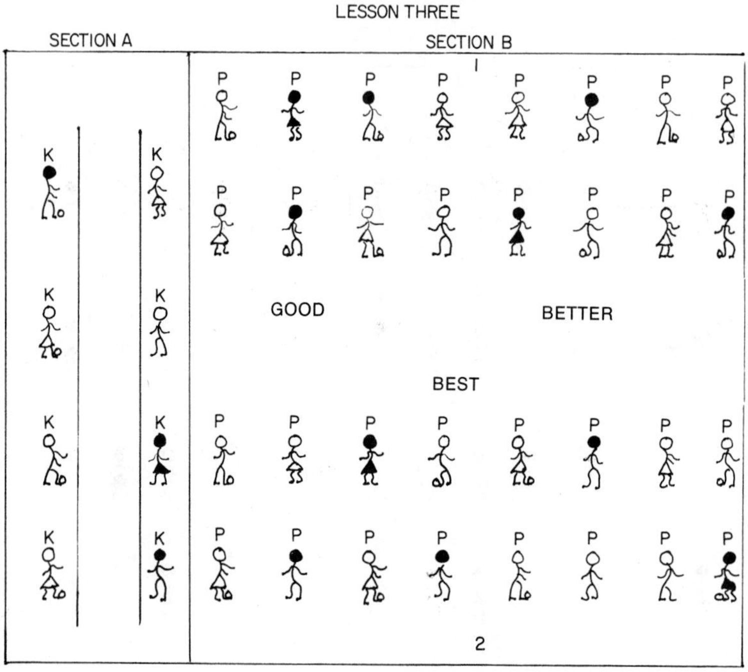

Figure 9–54. Teaching passing.

The class is divided into two sections as shown. Section A includes students who did not learn the kicking skills. Section B consists of students who learned how to kick and are ready to learn passing skills. The first pairs in group 1 of section B are given a ball. They pass to each other, advance the ball to the first pairs in group 2, and run to the end of the line. The first pairs of the opposite group 2 pass to each other, advance the ball back to group 1, and run to the end of the line. As this procedure continues, the teacher points out mistakes and assists with instruction. Students advance from the good group to the better group as they improve.

LESSON FOUR

PERFORMANCE OBJECTIVES:

Psychomotor. The student will successfully trap the ball, which was kicked by his classmate, 3 out of 5 times.

Cognitive. The student will demonstrate his knowledge of trapping by showing two students how to trap properly.

Affective. The student will cooperate with the class by assuming his or her share of responsibility for the distribution of equipment.

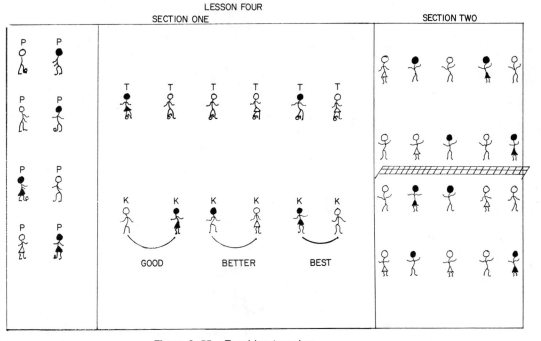

Figure 9–55. Teaching trapping.

The class is divided into two sections as shown. In section one, those who failed to learn the pass (P) continue to practice, and advance to the trappers as they improve. The kickers (K) kick the ball in an effort to cross the trapper's line. The trappers (T) attempt to trap the ball and kick it back to the kickers. This procedure continues. Students may be grouped by ability as shown and advance from the good to the best group as they improve. The volleyball overflow group changes with the soccer group at the discretion of the teacher.

LESSON FIVE

PERFORMANCE OBJECTIVES:

Psychomotor. The student will successfully intercept a soccer ball from the class formation 4 out of 5 times.

Cognitive. After viewing a film on soccer, the student will identify an interception and describe what is wrong with the execution.

Affective. While practicing in the class formation, the student will control his or her temper after being tripped.

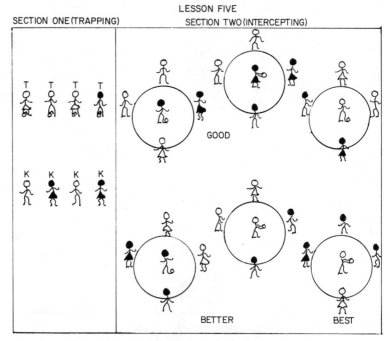

Figure 9–56. Intercepting.

The class is divided into two sections as shown. Students who did not learn how to trap continue practicing, and advance to the interception group as they improve. Students learning how to intercept are placed in six groups with five in each group. The center player in each group is given a ball, and he or she throws it so that the other players in the circle may head or chest the ball. The object of the procedure is to keep the ball in the air as long as possible. Students advance from the good to the best groups as they improve.

Teaching Softball Skills

GENERAL OBJECTIVES:
  A. **Psychomotor.** The students will demonstrate the complex motor skills involved in softball by executing the movements incorporating them.
  B. **Cognitive.** The students will demonstrate knowledge of the game by identifying and describing the various skills involved.
  C. **Affective.** The students will demonstrate their ability to:
     Control emotions under stress.
     Show good sportsmanship.
     Exhibit team loyalty.
     Accept reasonsibility.
     Assume leadership.
     Respect decisions of officials.

   I. *HISTORY OF SOFTBALL*

       (See references at end of chapter.)

   II. *VALUES OF SOFTBALL*

        Carry-over
        Develops skill

   III. *RULES, SCORING, STRATEGY*

         (See references at end of chapter.)

   IV. *SAFETY PRECAUTIONS*

        Always stay clear of the batter.
        Swing the bat in the designated area only.

   V. *EQUIPMENT NEEDED*

       Ten softballs and bats   Films and filmstrips
       Bases   Texts

   VI. *BASIC SKILLS*

        Throwing and catching   Batting
        Fielding   Base running
        Pitching

LESSON ONE
PERFORMANCE OBJECTIVES:
  Psychomotor. From a distance of 10 yards, the student will catch a ball thrown by a classmate 7 out of 10 times.
  Cognitive. The student will given an oral presentation to the class on the proper form for catching a fly ball.
  Affective. After missing a fast ground ball, the student will display determination by running for it.

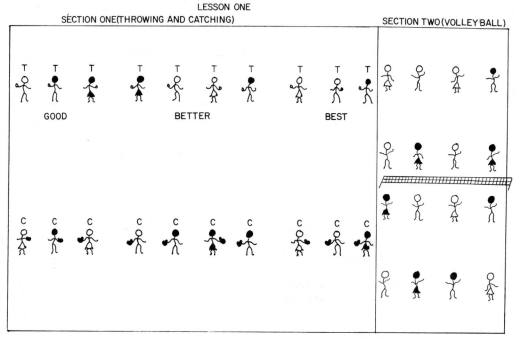

Figure 9–57. Throwing and catching.

Students are placed in two sections as shown. The throwers (T) are given balls and they practice throwing to the catchers (C). This continues with the good players advancing to the best groups as they improve. The volleyball groups change with the throwing and catching groups at the discretion of the teacher.

LESSON TWO

PERFORMANCE OBJECTIVES:

Psychomotor.   From a distance of 15 yards, the student will use the correct form in fielding the ball 4 out of 7 times.

Cognitive.   The student will illustrate the correct form in fielding by drawing stick figures on the chalkboard.

Affective.   The student will display interest in classmates by assisting them in learning how to field the ball.

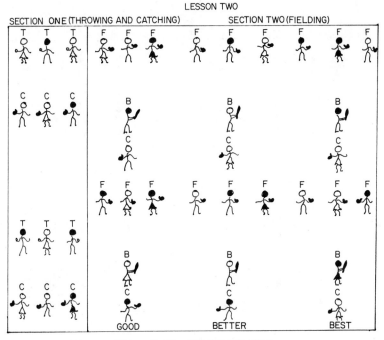

Figure 9–58.   Teaching fielding.

Students are divided into two sections as shown. Those who failed to learn how to throw and catch continue practicing, and advance to the fielding group as they improve. The batter (B) in each of the fielding groups is given a bat and ball. He hits the ball to one of the fielders, who fields the ball and throws it to the catcher (C), who gives it to the batter. This is repeated several times. The catcher and batter rotate around the fielders. Pupils are grouped by ability as shown and advance as they improve.

LESSON THREE
PERFORMANCE OBJECTIVES:

Psychomotor. The student, emphasizing the phases of pitching in proper sequence, will execute the pitch from the mound correctly 4 out of 6 times.

Cognitive. After viewing the pitches of classmates, the student will identify mistakes and describe the correct form.

Affective. The student will thank the teacher for helping him or her to pitch correctly.

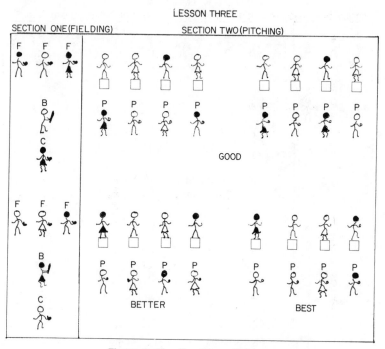

Figure 9–59. Teaching pitching.

Students are divided into two groups as shown. Those who did not learn the fielding skills continue practicing and advance to the pitching group as they improve. Each of the four groups of pitchers is given a ball, and they practice pitching the ball back and forth. Students are grouped by ability as shown and advance as they improve.

LESSON FOUR

PERFORMANCE OBJECTIVES:

Psychomotor. The student will hit a good pitch from a distance of 46 feet into fair territory 3 out of 7 times.

Cognitive. The student will demonstrate a knowledge of batting by answering questions on a written test with 70 per cent accuracy.

Affective. After striking out several times, the student will congratulate the pitcher.

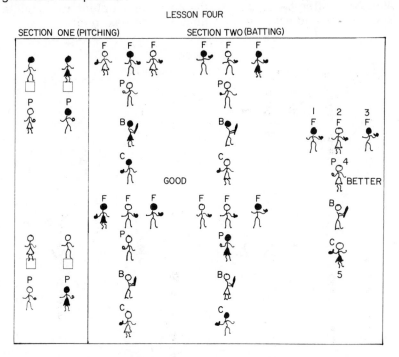

LESSON FOUR

SECTION ONE (PITCHING)   SECTION TWO (BATTING)

Figure 9–60. Teaching batting.

The class is divided into two sections as shown. Students in section one continue to practice pitching, and those in section two are placed in five groups of six each. The pitcher (P) and batter (B) in each group are given a ball and a bat. The batter hits the ball, and the fielders (F) attempt to catch the ball and throw it back to another fielder or to the catcher (C). This continues with the students rotating as shown. Number 1 goes to number 2, who goes to number 3. Number 3 goes to (P), and (P) goes to (C), who becomes the batter. (B) goes to number 1 in the outfield. Students are grouped by ability as shown and advance as they improve. Those who failed the pitching (P) continue to practice, and advance to the batting groups as they improve.

LESSON FIVE

PERFORMANCE OBJECTIVES:

Psychomotor. The student will bunt the ball into a designated zone 3 out of 5 times.

Cognitive. The student will give a two-minute oral report on the importance of bunting.

Affective. After being hit by the ball, the student will maintain self-control and assume the stance for the next pitch.

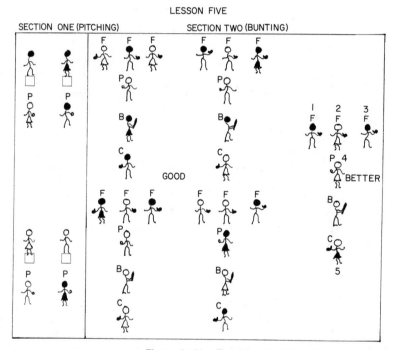

Figure 9-61. Teaching bunting.

The class is divided into two sections. The students in section one continue to practice pitching while those in section two are placed in five groups as shown. The teaching procedure is identical to that followed in Figure 9-60 (lesson four).

Teaching Volleyball Skills

GENERAL OBJECTIVES:
A. *Psychomotor.* The students will demonstrate the complex skills involved in the game of volleyball.
B. *Cognitive.* The students will demonstrate knowledge of volleyball by identifying and describing the various techniques as they are flashed on the screen.
C. *Affective.* The students will demonstrate their ability to:
  Control emotions under stress.
  Show good sportsmanship.
  Exhibit team loyalty.
  Accept responsibility.
  Assume leadership.
  Respect decisions of officials.

I. *HISTORY OF VOLLEYBALL*

  (See references at end of chapter.)

II. *VALUES OF VOLLEYBALL*

  Emotional release
  Recreational and carry-over potential
  Aid to good posture
  Developmental practice

III. *RULES, SCORING, AND STRATEGY*

  (See references at end of chapter.)

IV. *SAFETY PRECAUTIONS*

  Conduct vigorous warm-up exercises before the instruction.
  Assign pupils carefully to areas to prevent collisions.
  Organize practice around spikers, passers, and retrievers.
  Provide nonslippery playing surfaces.
  Clear area of benches, chairs, and other obstacles.
  Provide correct instruction in footwork to prevent sprained ankles.
  Require proper clothing and shoes.

V. *EQUIPMENT NEEDED*

  Three nets or rope
  Concrete area, 80 feet × 120 feet (turf area may be used)
  Inside area
  30 balls
  Films and filmstrips
  Texts

VI. *BASIC SKILLS*

  Passing   Blocking and net recovery
  Serving   Strategy
  Set-up and spike

LESSON ONE

PERFORMANCE OBJECTIVES:

Psychomotor. The student will execute passes over a line on the wall as quickly as possible for 30 seconds.

Cognitive. The student will describe the volleyball pass to the class and point out the important features involved.

Affective. The student will recognize the variance in performance of his or her classmates and volunteer to assist when needed.

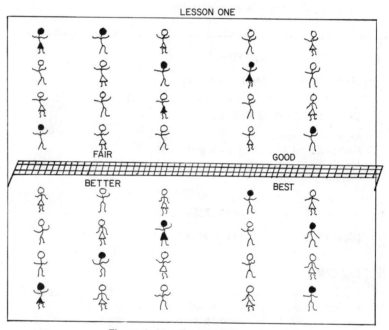

Figure 9–62. Teaching the pass.

Ten groups of four students each are arranged as shown: five groups are on each long side of the gymnasium, single file, facing the wall. The first student in each line passes the ball high on the wall and runs to the end of the line. The second student replaces the first and passes the ball, followed by the third, until all students have practiced sufficiently. Students are grouped by ability.

An alternative is to have the students face each other across the net in the same formation. The first student in each line passes the ball over the net and runs to the end of the line. The first person in each line across the net returns the ball and runs to the end of the line. This is repeated; the object is to keep the ball from falling to the floor. Another plan is to divide the class into ten circles with four students in each circle. One student of each circle stands in the center and passes the ball to the outside students, who pass it back to him. In both plans students advance as they improve.

LESSON TWO

PERFORMANCE OBJECTIVES:

Psychomotor. Using the overhand serve, the student will serve the volleyball over an 8-foot net successfully 7 out of 10 times.

Cognitive. The student will describe the merits of the overhand serve to the class in a two-minute presentation.

Affective. The student will cooperate with the teacher and classmates by reporting to class on time.

LESSON TWO

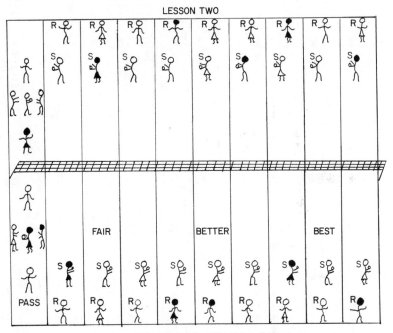

Figure 9–63. Teaching the serve.

On each side of the net or rope there are ten groups with two in each group (group one has five on each side). Two students (S) will be serving to each other; the others are retrievers (R). The servers change places with the retrievers periodically. Students who showed little progress in lesson one are placed in the first group and continue practicing the pass. If space is a problem, the number assigned to each group can be increased. Students progress from the fair to the best groups.

LESSON THREE
PERFORMANCE OBJECTIVES:
  Psychomotor. The student will correctly spike the ball into the opponent's territory 7 out of 10 times.
  Cognitive. The student will describe his knowledge of the spike to the class and show two classmates how to execute it.
  Affective. The student will volunteer to assist the teacher in teaching the spike to the class.

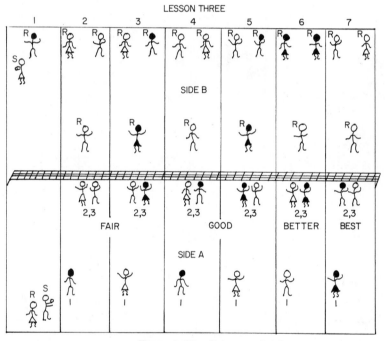

Figure 9-64. Set-up and spike.

The class is divided into seven groups as shown. Students in group one continue practicing the serve. Students in the remaining groups practice the set-up and spike. The retrievers (R) throw the balls back to the other side. Number 1 passes to number 2, who sets up for number 3, who spikes. The students on side A rotate clockwise after each spike. After sufficient practice, side A pupils become retrievers and side B pupils practice the skill. Students advance as they improve.

LESSON FOUR

PERFORMANCE OBJECTIVES:

Psychomotor.   The student will successfully block the opponent's ball 6 out of 10 times.

Cognitive.   The student will display his knowledge of blocking by answering questions on a written test with 90 per cent accuracy.

Affective.   The student will cooperate by assisting with the collection of equipment at the end of the period.

LESSON FOUR

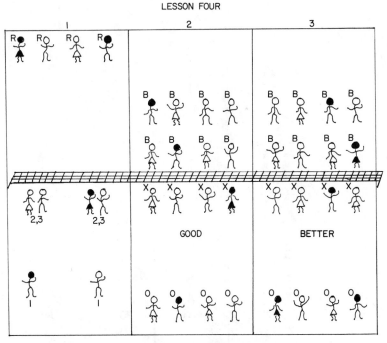

Figure 9–65.   Teaching the block.

The class is divided into three groups based on the inventory. Students in group 1 continue to practice the set-up and spike, since they showed very little progress in the previous lesson. Students in groups 2 and 3 practice the block as follows: O sets up for the spiker X, and B's are the blockers. After practicing these skills sufficiently, the students on both sides of the net change skills. The students practicing the set-up and spike gradually begin practicing the block. Students advance from the good group to the better group as they improve.

LESSON FIVE
PERFORMANCE OBJECTIVES:

Psychomotor. The student will successfully recover the ball from the net 3 out of 6 times.

Cognitive. The student demonstrates his or her knowledge by diagramming on the chalkboard the steps involved in the net recovery.

Affective. The student will assume a leadership role when someone sustains an injury while recovering the ball from the net.

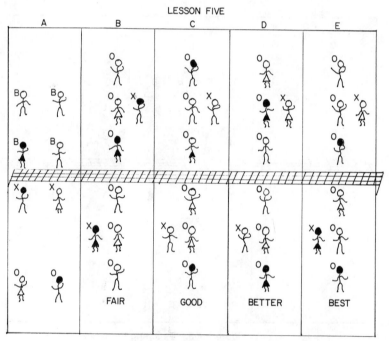

Figure 9–66. Net recovery.

The class is divided into five groups based on the inventory. Students in group A continue to practice blocking, since they showed little progress in the previous lesson. Students in B, C, D, and E practice the net recovery as follows: X throws the ball into net and the first O runs forward and recovers to X. X and O rotate clockwise. This practice continues until all pupils show improvement. The students in group A gradually begin practicing the net recovery and advance to group B. Students advance from fair to best as they improve.

Teaching Touch Football Skills

GENERAL OBJECTIVES:
  A. *Psychomotor.* The students will demonstrate the complex motor skills involved in touch football by performing movements that incorporate these skills.
  B. *Cognitive.* The students will demonstrate knowledge of touch football by describing the various skills involved in the game.
  C. *Affective.* The students will demonstrate their ability to:
> Control emotions under stress.
> Show good sportsmanship.
> Exhibit team loyalty.
> Accept responsibility.
> Assume leadership.
> Respect decisions of officials.

I. HISTORY OF TOUCH FOOTBALL

  (See references at end of chapter.)

II. VALUES OF TOUCH FOOTBALL

  Physiological fitness
  Carry-over (immediate)
  Develops teamwork
  Contributes to emotional stability

III. RULES, SCORING, AND STRATEGY

  (See references at end of chapter.)

IV. SAFETY PRECAUTIONS

  Always supervise the groups.
  Do not permit misconduct.
  Wear proper uniforms.
  Use safe playing areas.
  Use simple rules.

V. EQUIPMENT NEEDED

  Footballs   Films and filmstrips
  Kicking tees   Texts

VI. BASIC SKILLS

  Forward passing   Running with the ball
  Receiving   Blocking
  Kicking   Offensive stance
  Centering   Defense
  Ball handling

LESSON ONE

PERFORMANCE OBJECTIVES:

Psychomotor. The student will pass the ball a distance of 20 yards correctly 6 out of 10 times.

Cognitive. After observing several demonstrations of passing, the student will describe the correct form.

Affective. The student will display sportsmanship by assisting a poorly coordinated classmate.

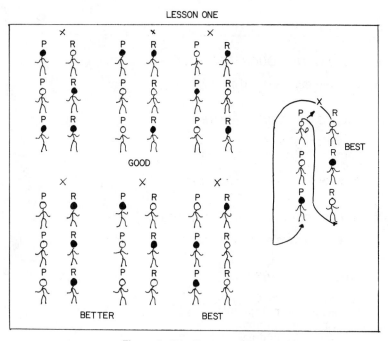

Figure 9-67. Passing and receiving.

The class is divided into seven groups of six students each. The passers (P) pass the ball to the receivers (R), and run to the end of the receivers' line. The receivers receive the ball at point X and run to the end of the passers' line. Pupils advance from good to better to best as they improve.

LESSON TWO

PERFORMANCE OBJECTIVES:

Psychomotor. The student will successfully punt the football into a marked area on the field 6 out of 10 times.

Cognitive. The student will describe the proper sequence of moves for punting the football correctly.

Affective. The student, having failed to punt the football into the proper area, will exhibit self-control by not showing dissatisfaction.

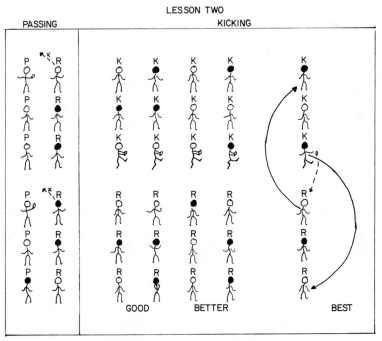

Figure 9–68. Teaching the kick.

The class is divided into two sections as shown. Those who did not learn how to pass and receive continue to practice, and advance to the kicking group as they improve. The kickers (K) punt the ball to the receivers (R), and run to the end of the receiving line. The receivers catch the ball, run it back to the head of the kicking line, and then run to the end of the line. Students advance from good to better to best as they improve.

LESSON THREE

PERFORMANCE OBJECTIVES:

Psychomotor. The student will correctly pass the ball from the center position to the receiver 8 out of 10 times.

Cognitive. After viewing several passes from the center, the student will select the correct one and describe it to the class.

Affective. The student will show admiration for the classmate who excels in this pass by congratulating him.

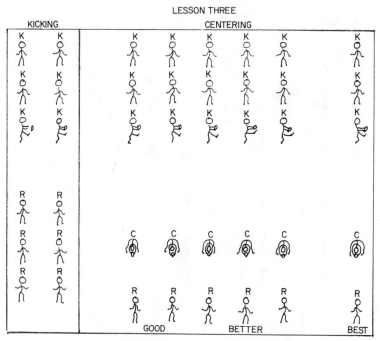

Figure 9–69. Teaching how to center.

Students are placed in two sections as shown. Those who failed to learn kicking continue to practice. The centering group practices with the centers (C) snapping the ball to the kickers (K), who kick to the receivers (R). The centers run to the receiving position, the kickers to the center position, and the receivers to the end of the kicking line. Students advance from good to better to best as they improve.

LESSON FOUR
PERFORMANCE OBJECTIVES:
Psychomotor. The student will correctly demonstrate the block from the class formation 3 out of 5 times.
Cognitive. The student will give an oral report to the class on the proper steps in blocking.
Affective. The student will exhibit self-control when hurt in blocking.

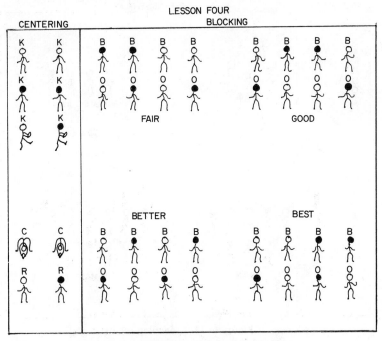

Figure 9–70. Teaching how to block.

Students are placed in two sections as shown. Those who failed to learn how to center continue to practice. Students who learned to center and punt are arranged in two groups, the blockers (B) and the opponents (O). They advance from fair to good to better to best as they improve.

LESSON FIVE

PERFORMANCE OBJECTIVES:

Psychomotor. In an offensive play, the student will demonstrate ability to handle the ball correctly 6 out of 10 times.

Cognitive. The student will present a written report on the offensive movements discussed in the class.

Affective. The student will show cooperation with classmates by passing the ball when he or she could have run with it.

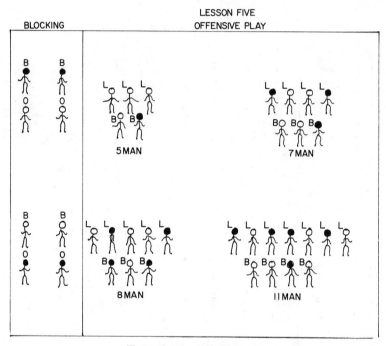

Figure 9–71. Teaching offensive play.

Students are placed in two sections as shown. Those who failed to learn blocking continue to practice, and advance to offensive play as they improve. The students in section two are placed in four groups as shown. Those groups reflect the types of teams that people organize when playing touch football away from school, under informal organization plans. It is difficult to form complete 11–man teams; they are usually organized in numbers varying from three to 11. From the formations shown above, the teacher can utilize all the offensive maneuvers that may be used when students play after school.

QUESTIONS FOR DISCUSSION

1. What is the purpose of using performance objectives in the daily lesson plan? Differentiate among the types of objectives.

2. Identify the factors involved in class grouping procedures.

3. Explain how ability grouping can be used for teaching the forehand and backhand returns in tennis.

4. How can individual instruction be administered in a class of 40 to 50 students?

5. List several intrinsic procedures and considerations for teaching individual activities that may not apply to group activities.

REFERENCES

1. Greyson Daughtrey, "Comments on Title IX by Teachers in the Norfolk Public Schools," (Norfolk, Virginia, 1977).
2. Martilu V. Puthoff, "Instructional Strategies for Mainstreaming," *Mainstreaming in Physical Education.* (National Association for Physical Education of College Women and the National College Physical Education Association for Men, 1976), p. 41.

SELECTED READINGS

Armbruster, David A., *et al., Basic Skills in Sports for Men and Women,* 6th ed. (St. Louis: The C. V. Mosby Company, 1975).

Fait, Hollis F., *et al., A Manual of Physical Education Activities* (Philadelphia: W. B. Saunders Company, 1967).

Harris, Jane, Anne Pittman, and Morlys Waller, *Dance A While,* 4th ed. (Minneapolis: Burgess Publishing Company, 1978).

Hase, Gerald J. and Irwin Rosenstein. *Modern Physical Education* (New York: Holt Rinehart and Winston, 1972).

Humphrey, Doris, *The Art of Making Dances* (New York: Grove Press, 1962).

Lockhart, Aileene and Esther Pease, *Modern Dance* (Dubuque, Iowa: William C. Brown Company, 1978).

MacIntyre, Christine and James A. Wessel, *Body Contouring and Conditioning Through Movement,* 2nd ed. (Boston: Allyn and Bacon, 1977).

Mainstreaming in Physical Education (The National Association for Physical Education of College Women and the National College Physical Education Association for Men, 1976).

McClosky, Mildred G., ed., *Teaching Strategies and Classroom Realities* (Englewood Cliffs: Prentice-Hall, 1971).

Saunders Physical Activities Series (Philadelphia: W. B. Saunders Company).

Seaton, Don C., *et al., Physical Education Handbook,* 6th ed. (Englewood Cliffs, New Jersey: Prentice Hall, Inc., 1974).

Stanley, D. K. and I. F. Waglow, *Physical Education Activities Handbook,* 3rd ed. (Boston: Allyn and Bacon, 1973).

Chapter 10

Courtesy Edmund Burke Academy, Waynes-boro, Georgia.

FUNCTION OF THE SCHOOL
    FUNCTION OF THE PHYSICAL EDUCATION
      PROGRAM
    RECENT LEGISLATION
      FEDERAL AND STATE FUNDING
AREAS OF CONCERN
    WHAT IS MAINSTREAMING?
    RECONSIDERATION OF ROLE OF THE
      PHYSICAL EDUCATION TEACHER
      COPING WITH CHANGE
    THE TEACHER AND THE PHYSICIAN
      THE PHYSICIAN'S REPORT
      ABILITY GROUPING
CLASSIFICATIONS REDEFINED
    ACTIVITIES FOR THE PHYSICALLY
      HANDICAPPED
        THE STRUCTURALLY HANDICAPPED
        THE ANEMIC
        THE ASTHMATIC
        THE DIABETIC
        THE TUBERCULAR
        THE OVERWEIGHT
        THE UNDERWEIGHT
        THE EPILEPTIC

        STUDENTS WITH CEREBRAL PALSY
        STUDENTS WITH SIGHT HANDICAPS
        STUDENTS WITH HEARING
          DIFFICULTIES
        STUDENTS WITH HEART DISORDERS
        STUDENTS WITH HERNIA
    ACTIVITIES FOR THE EMOTIONALLY
      DISTURBED
      TEACHING THE EMOTIONALLY
        DISTURBED
    ACTIVITIES FOR THE MENTALLY
      RETARDED
TEACHING THE HANDICAPPED
    INSTRUCTIONAL STRATEGIES
    PROGRAM MODIFICATIONS
    ACTIVITY MODIFICATIONS
      TEACHING/LEARNING STYLE OPTIONS
      CLASS ENVIRONMENT
PROMISE FOR THE FUTURE
    EDUCATIONAL IMPLICATIONS
    SUGGESTIONS FOR SUCCESS
QUESTIONS FOR DISCUSSION
REFERENCES
SELECTED READINGS

Chapter 10

MAINSTREAMING IN PHYSICAL EDUCATION

Secondary schools tend to have a more heterogeneous student body than any other level of American education. Their physical education programs therefore must accommodate typical, atypical, exceptionally talented, and handicapped students alike. Today there is considerable discussion concerning the use of such terms as *adapted, atypical, physically talented, low psychomotor ability, emotionally disturbed, mentally retarded, disabled, trainable, impaired,* and *handicapped.* This chapter deals with mainstreaming these types of special students into regular physical education classes. The transition must be made from treating them as abnormal students with a segregated status to regarding them as normal pupils and assigning them to integrated physical education programs.

FUNCTION OF THE SCHOOL

Education in the United States has been based on the right of all children, without exception, to an education. To insure equal educational opportunities, legal regulations now govern the integration of all students in schools, regardless of race, sex, or handicap. *Mainstreaming* refers to the inclusion of handicapped students in regular instructional programs. This process constitutes one of the greatest challenges to teachers in meeting the philosophical and methodological program objectives of the 1980's. Secondary school physical education has always had difficulty with scheduling activity classes and receiving adequate funding for equipment and supplies. More problems are anticipated as the secondary school complies with recent legislation concerning the handicapped.

Function of the Physical Education Program

Physical education programs should encourage all students to develop skills and attitudes that lead to patterns of lifetime physical activity. The student with physical, emotional, or mental problems needs this instruction as much as any other student. Ability grouping in physical education includes *all* students and makes allowances for the tremendous differences in individual growth and development. Innovative programs that incorporate this method continue to improve the quality of the learning experience for everyone involved. Mainstreaming the handicapped into regular classes provides yet another challenge to the creative ability of the secondary school teacher.

Recent Legislation

Public Law 94–142, (the Education for All Handicapped Children Act), was enacted November 29, 1975, without an expiration date. It was designed to give every person between three and twenty-one years of age, including the most severely handicapped, the educational opportunities needed to become a self-sufficient and productive citizen. Handicapped children are defined as: (1) children who are mentally retarded, hard of hearing, deaf, speech impaired, visually disabled, emotionally disturbed, or structurally impaired, or (2) children with any specific learning disabilities who require special education and related services.[1]

Public law 94–142 was designed to (1) assure that all handicapped persons will have publicly funded special education and related services made available to them no later than 1980; (2) protect the rights of handicapped children and their parents and guardians; (3) relieve state and local governments from the financial burden of providing special education services; and (4) assess the effectiveness of efforts to educate the handicapped.

Under this law, states are eligible to participate in the ongoing federal aid program that pays part of the additional cost of educating the handicapped. A brief summary of the 83-page Education for all Handicapped Children Act of 1975 includes these points of specific interest to secondary school personnel:

1. Highest priority must be given, first, to handicapped children who are not now receiving an education, and, second, to the most severely handicapped children whose education is inadequate.
2. Strong safeguards of the due process rights of parents and children must be guaranteed by states and localities. These safeguards protect parents' rights in all procedures related to identification, evaluation, and placement of their children. They also provide the opportunity to protest educational decisions made by school officials.
3. The public law emphasizes educating children in the least restrictive environment. It requires that children be placed in special or separate classes only when it is impossible to work out satisfactory placement in a regular class, using supplementary aids and services.
4. All methods for testing and evaluation must be racially and culturally nondiscriminatory and must be in the primary language of the child. No one test or procedure may be the sole means of making a decision about an educational program.
5. Individualized education plans are to be prepared for each child, with parents participating on the team that draws up the plan. All individual plans must be reviewed at least annually and revised according to the child's changing needs.
6. When children are placed in private schools by state or local educational systems in order to receive an appropriate education, this must be done at no cost to parents. These schools must meet standards set by law and must safeguard the rights of parents and children.
7. Each state must set up an advisory board consisting of handicapped individuals, teachers, and parents to advise the state on unmet needs, to comment publicly on rules and regulations, and to assist in evaluating programs.[2]

Federal and State Funding. There is a need for integrated curricular models for mainstreaming in secondary education. The Handicapped Physical Education and Recreation Training Program is working toward this goal by sponsoring projects that prepare educators to teach special students. Federal funding in 1975 and 1976 included aid to California, Connecticut, District of Columbia, Florida, Georgia, Hawaii, Indiana, Kansas, Mississippi, Missouri, New York, North Carolina, Ohio, Pennsylvania, Tennessee, Texas, Utah, Virginia, Washington, and Wisconsin.[3] Figure

---

Selected Federally Sponsored Research Projects in Physical Education and Recreation Play States*

MARCH 3, 1976

Investigator	*Project Title*
CALIFORNIA	
G. Lawrence Rarick, Professor Department of Physical Education University of California, Berkeley Berkeley, California 94720	Effects of Individualized Physical Education Instruction on Selected Perceptual, Motor, Cognitive, and Affective Functions.
DISTRICT OF COLUMBIA	
Julian U. Stein American Alliance on Health, Physical Education and Recreation 1201 16th Street, N.W. Washington, D.C. 20036	Physical Education and Recreation for the Handicapped: Information and Research Utilization Center.
MARYLAND	
Karen Littman Therapeutic Recreation Specialist Maryland National Capitol Parks Riverdale, Maryland 20840	Associative Learning Through Developmental Play: Providing Life Experiences Through Recreation and Physical Education for Handicapped Pre-school Children.
MICHIGAN	
Janet Wessell, Professor Physical Education Michigan State University East Lansing, Michigan 48823	Innovation Associated Learning Program of Mini-Curriculum Action—Learning Teaching Strategies.

Figure 10–1. Selected federally sponsored research projects. (From: *On-Going Projects*, Washington, D.C., Bureau of Education for the Handicapped, Division of Innovation and Development, 1976.)

10–1 lists some of the demonstration projects funded in 1976 that apply directly or indirectly to mainstreaming.[4]

AREAS OF CONCERN

In 1976, the Council for Exceptional Children estimated that there were about seven million handicapped preschool-age and school-age children in the United States. Since the end of World War II, more and more handicapped children have been receiving educational benefits and attending public, special, or private schools. Several factors have brought about these changes in educational opportunity, namely parent power, federal and state legislative action, research investigations, and the recent emphasis on the individual. Public law 94–142 specifies

that individual educational programs that include a statement explaining the extent to which each student is able to participate in regular classroom activities must be written annually for all handicapped students.

What Is Mainstreaming?

In essence, mainstreaming is not new. For the past 10 years, states such as California and Texas have had major programs under way that allow handicapped children to attend regular school. Other states, owing to court decisions, have made forward moves in this direction. Mainstreaming does not mean transferring handicapped children from special schools into the regular classroom. It involves identifying the physical and academic needs of individual handicapped students, assessing their readiness for integration, preparing the school for the student's entry, and providing all the back-up services required, including resources, teachers, and facilities.[5]

The current mainstreaming trend requires a review of the term *adapted physical education.* Generally, this term has applied to a varied program of developmental activities, games, sports, and rhythms suited to the interests and limitations of students with disabilities. Adapted programs were necessary for those who could not safely or successfully engage in unrestricted participation in the regular physical education program. This type of planning, more than 25 years old, reflects the practice of isolating handicapped students from their peers, rather than creating a flexible learning environment with many stations and alternate activities in which all students could participate together.

The philosophy of mainstreaming — creating learning options within the integrated setting — eliminates labels such as handicapped, disabled, impaired, crippled, blind, and awkward. It also negates the practice of distinguishing among corrective, adapted, developmental, remedial, and special physical education, because the mainstream plan includes qualities of each. Good mainstream physical education programs are flexible in order to adapt to the needs of all their participants.

Reconsideration of the Physical Education Teacher

New legislation, such as the Education for All Handicapped Children Act, that requires individual diagnosis, evaluation, and prescription necessitates the training of sophisticated special educators and adapted physical educators for work in multi-disciplinary settings with mainstream educators. Keeping individual records and files, in accordance with the growing emphasis on educational accountability, will also demand the talents of such specialists.

Educators need to identify deficiencies within the psychomotor domain and to develop and implement learning strategies that resolve these problems while preserving and building ego strength. This responsibility of educators is by no means applicable only to special students; it encompasses *all* individuals who may at one time or another experience difficulty in the psychomotor domain. *Preventive analysis* will become part of the adapted physical educator's role in the future as diagnostic screening, evaluation, and appraisal are refined.[6]

Coping with Change. The Council for Exceptional Children has recently adopted the cascade system, developed by Maynard Reynolds in 1962, as an organizational model for services offered to all handicapped students. As illustrated in Figure 10–2, accommodations range from a residential hospital for the more severely disabled to a public school classroom for the slightly handicapped. The greatest numbers are accommodated within the regular school. Realistic and flexible applications of the mainstreaming concept will allow more exceptional students to attend public schools than ever before.

Figure 10–2 also reveals that as a student is placed at a higher level within the cascade system, fewer support personnel are required. There is a tremendous difference between the staff needed to care for a person in a hospital and the staff necessary to teach a person in the normal school environment. However, even at the higher levels within the cascade system, skilled support personnel such as teachers trained for crisis situations and resource consultants are required. Unfortunately, many school districts, in their haste to integrate as many handicapped students as possible, have failed to provide the additional professionals necessary for the smooth transition from special self-contained classes to regular classes.[7]

Successful mainstreaming in physical education requires certain conditions, such as reduced class size, acquisition of additional skills by regular physical educators, provisions for support personnel, and incorporation of superior

THE CASCADE SYSTEM

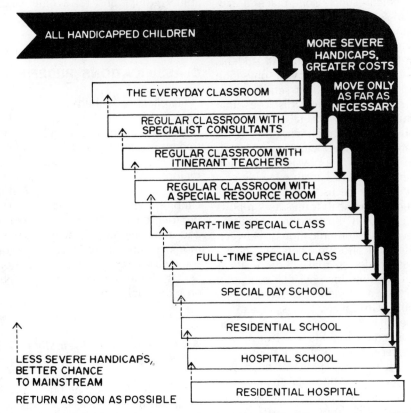

Figure 10-2. The cascade system. (Reproduced from the publication *One Out of Ten* and utilized by permission of Educational Facilities Laboratories. New York, N.Y.)

teaching methods. All physical educators must strive to insure that these conditions exist.[8]

The significance of mainstreaming for physical education is considerable. If teachers are to cope successfully with it, they must analyze the effects of integration on psychomotor learning and continue to provide an environment conducive to learning motor skills. Teachers should examine the conditions under which mainstreaming will produce desirable changes in psychomotor behavior. Methods that emphasize ability grouping and individual instruction are most effective. Pre-service and in-service programs of professional preparation are providing opportunities within the undergraduate and graduate curricula for teachers to improve their skills in working with handicapped persons. Paraprofessionals, parents, and other students can also act as support personnel to the secondary school physical educator.

The Teacher and the Physician

Teaching handicapped students is a challenge that demands great skills, courage, and dedication. The teacher must have not only a sound background in physical education and psychology but also the ability to plan and adjust the program to the individual's capability and need.

If programs are to be medically sound, there must be complete cooperation between the teacher and the physician. Individual programs designed to provide general modified activity for the slightly handicapped should be part of the regular physical education curriculum. Together, qualified teachers and medical supervisors place a student in an ability group. Continual evaluations are substantiated by regular medical supervision.

The Physician's Report. All students are usually examined by a physician several times during their school years. When the examination discloses that the student needs special attention in the physical education program, a report showing the doctor's recommendation is sent to the physical education teacher. Figure 10–3 is an example of a card that may be used in these cases.[9] (Additional medical forms and reports are included in the *Resource Manual.*) Improved communication between physical education teachers and physicians is needed to make the classification of students for physical education instruction more medically suitable.

Ability Groupings. It is logical to assume that the more efficiently the physical education class is organized, the greater the learning opportunity will be for all students. Physical education classes in which students are grouped by ability and a variety of activities is offered are the most effective. Procedures fundamental to ability grouping are:

1. According to ability, group students into as many sections as space, facilities, and safety permit.
2. Allow students to practice the skill and advance from the less proficient to the most proficient group, or from one component of an activity to another component.
3. Allow students who perform skills well to assist others.
4. Evaluate the students subjectively through continuing observation.
5. Use individual instruction throughout this phase of class. Particular attention should be given to the handicapped.

Modifications can be incorporated with a minimum amount of effort, time, and cost. Moreover, the safety element will be enhanced. Altering activities to meet the needs of all students really makes only two demands on the teacher: (1) an understanding of the activity needs and potentials of the various ability groups and (2) a little imagination.

CLASSIFICATIONS REDEFINED

Handicapped children are classified into three general categories: (1) the physically handicapped; (2) the emotionally disturbed; and (3) the mentally retarded. It has been stated that the majority of handicapped children can participate in the regular physical education program, provided that (1) the program contains a large variety of skills and activities; (2) the activity skills are modified through ability grouping or, in some cases, through modification of the activity itself; and (3) there is emphasis on individual instruction.

Activities for the Physically Handicapped

Students classified as physically handicapped usually have problems related to orthopedic disorders; anemia; asthma; diabetes; tuberculosis; weight abnormalities; epilepsy; cerebral palsy; visual, aural, or heart disorders; or hernia. The physical educator needs to have an understanding of these problems and of the desirable activities for each.

The Structurally Handicapped. These students have structural defects that prohibit them from attaining a normal level of performance. Some in this group may be so crippled that they gain very little from attending regular physical education classes. On the other hand, the majority of students in this group may benefit from participation in a diversified standard program. Wheeler and Hooley list four categories of disorders:

1. Congenital, as in scoliosis, clubfoot, spina bifida, and dislocation of shoulder or hip.
2. Osteochondrosis (as in Morquio's disease), which tends to render insufficient the functioning of the ossification centers of the body. It is seen most frequently as Perthes' hip, in which the head of the

femur undergoes dystrophy, then recalcification.

3. Injury resulting in the loss of function of all or part of the limb and pressure on a portion of the nervous system. Amputation is a frequent result of such injury cases.
4. Diseases, such as tuberculosis of the bone, osteomyelitis, and despite the availability of vaccine, poliomyelitis.[10]

Many activities in the regular physical education program may be used, in either their usual or a modified state. When only the upper extremities are disabled or affected, activities for this group can include dancing, running, soccer, and skating. In addition, golf, tennis, basketball, horseshoes, badminton, casting, bowling, and table tennis can be included when only one arm is abnormal. When the lower extremities are affected and the arms are normal, table tennis, bowling, weights, shot-put, archery, casting, billiards, bag-punching, stunts, croquet, horseshoes, swimming, and basketball shooting and dribbling are appropriate. These activities are suggested when the individuals are ambulatory and movement is facilitated by either a chair or crutches. If only one leg is afflicted, the same activities can be performed more proficiently and in some instances without modification.

The Anemic. Anemics do not have the strength and endurance of normal people. To place them in situations with stronger, healthier students can produce psychological reactions that are detrimental to development. Students suffering from anemia should participate in activities requiring skill performance. Excelling in skills will lead to the confidence and self-assurance necessary for motivation to continue the program. Some activities suitable for the anemic are dancing, archery, billiards, bowling, golf, horseshoes, table tennis, skating, softball, tumbling, volleyball, the shot-put, and the discus-throw. All these activities should be planned in moderation and frequent rest periods must be provided.

The Asthmatic. Asthmatic individuals not only suffer from physiological disturbances but also have emotional problems relating to exercise. Activities that demand increased respiration and competition with others can bring on an attack. Sports involving skill, in which one competes against a mean score rather than against another individual, are therefore desirable. Bowling is a typical activity in which the asthmatic may become involved without adverse effects. Others that might provide pleasure and promote confidence are golf, horseshoes, billiards, archery, shuffleboard, and croquet.

Recent findings seem to substantiate that the frequency and severity of asthma attacks are about the same for patients who undergo therapeutic exercise programs as for those who do not. Apparently these exercises neither prevent attacks nor cause them to occur, as was generally believed in the past. Physical educators must be aware of the exact health status of the student, including exercise tolerance, before any program can be developed. Since the health of asthmatics is subject to change, it is important that periodic physicians' reviews and written records evaluations be forwarded to the school. Once this medical cooperation is secured, a satisfactory and enriched program can be developed.[11]

The Diabetic. Diabetics can safely participate in activities that do not involve intense competition and prolonged effort. With proper supervision, plenty of rest, and the elimination of body contact, the diabetic can probably participate in most of the activities included in the standard physical education curriculum. Tennis (with frequent rest periods), golf, bowling, softball, and horseshoes are particularly suitable for the diabetic student. However, the instructor must be aware of the symptoms and treatment of insulin shock.

The Tubercular. Those with tuberculosis should never be allowed to participate in activities that require prolonged effort, endurance, and strength. If activities are properly supervised and time for sufficient rest is provided, the post-tubercular student may dance, play golf and tennis, swim, and participate in other individual sports such as

(Name of School or School District)
PHYSICIAN'S REPORT FOR SCHOOL USE

Date_____

Pupil's Name _____

Last   First   Grade   Birthdate

School_____ Address_____

PARENT'S AUTHORIZATION: I hereby give my consent to the school named above to receive from, or send to:

Dr._____ any information concerning my child.
SIGNATURE OF PARENT:_____ Address_____

REASON FOR REFERRAL: Enrollment ☐   Other ☐   (Specify): _____

HISTORY OF IMMUNIZATIONS AND TESTS (State date or age last given):
Smallpox_____Reaction_____ Report of urinalysis_____
DPT (Initial series completed)_____ Tuberculin Test (Intradermal) ___Pos.___Neg.___
Boosters for DPT or DT_____ Chest X-Ray_____Pos.___Neg.___
Polio: Salk 1_____2_____3_____4_____ Other (Specify)_____
      Sabin Type I_____Type II_____Type III_____

Medical Evaluation

Comments or Recommendations

1. Is there any *physical defect* or *condition* (orthopedic, cardiac, etc.) which limits participation in:
   (a) Classroom activities
   (b) Physical education
   (c) Competitive athletics (indicate sports)

   If yes, what do you recommend?

2. Is the child subject to any condition which may result in a classroom emergency: e.g., *epilepsy, fainting spells, diabetes, allergic reactions, (bee stings, etc.),* or a heart condition.

   If yes, what do you recommend?

3. Is there any *emotional, mental* or *physical condition* for which the child should be under periodic medical observation?

   If yes, what do you recommend?

4. Is there any *eye condition* or *defect in vision* which requires special consideration?
   Glasses required?   To be worn full time?

   If yes, what do you recommend?

5. Is there any *ear condition* or *defect in hearing* which requires special consideration?
   Are there ways in which the school could compensate by proper seating or other action?

   If yes, what do you recommend?

6. Are there any indications that this child will have difficulty in adjusting to the school experience?

   If yes, what do you recommend?

7. Other comments or recommendations:_____

8. Is this pupil under your regular care? Yes_____No_____How long?_____
   Date of last examination_____Comment:_____
   Examining physician_____Address_____

DOCTOR: PLEASE FOLD AND GIVE TO PARENT OR RETURN THIS FORM TO SCHOOL AS ADDRESSED ON BACK

Figure 10–3. Physician's report for school use. Physician's recommendation for physical education. Courtesy California State Department of Education.

Referral Form
PHYSICIAN'S RECOMMENDATION FOR PHYSICAL EDUCTION AND
OTHER PHYSICAL ACTIVITIES

Dear Physician:

All pupils enrolled in the public schools participate in physical education activities which are designed to meet their growth and developmental needs. In addition, many pupils participate in other types of activity, such as intramural programs, interschool athletics, band, and drill teams. To identify specific needs of each pupil, the physician, parents, and school personnel must work cooperatively. Will you please provide us with the information listed below so that we can provide appropriate activities for _____

(Pupil's name)

Findings and Recommendations to the School

I have examined _____ and find the following handicaps (if

(Pupil's name)

any):_____

_____

I recommend the following: (Check appropriate item or items.)

_____1. No restriction on any type of activity

_____2. Participation in all activities (intramural and other activities in addition to physical education), with the exception of inter-school athletics

_____3. No restriction on activities in physical education

4. Adaptations in physical education to fit individual needs:

_____a. Little running or jumping

_____b. No running or jumping

_____c. No activities involving body contact

_____d. Exercises designed for rehabilitation

_____e. Strenuous conditioning exercises

5. Other adaptations: (Specify)_____

_____

I recommend the adaptation for:_____two weeks,_____one month,_____three months,_____six months

Date_____ Signature_____

Address_____

Please mail this form to: (Name and address of school should be given here.)

Figure 10–3. *Continued.* Physician's report for school use. Physician's recommendation for physical education. (Courtesy California State Department of Education.)

bowling, horseshoes, and badminton. The highly contagious nature of this disease, rather than the student's ability to participate, necessitates medical approval before the student can be placed in a class. It is essential that teachers refer any suspected cases to a doctor.

The Overweight. Obesity presents one of the most difficult problems for the physical educator. Not only is the overweight student unable to achieve success in sports and physical activity, but the handicap sometimes causes emotional reactions that can seriously disturb all aspects of the person's life. In conjunction with prescribed physical activity, the overweight child must be placed on a diet by a physician. Aside from glandular conditions, overeating and lack of exercise are the common causes of obesity.

In selecting activities for the overweight student, the teacher should initially avoid those that involve prolonged running and physical contact, such as football. Emphasis should be placed on sports that progressively develop strength, endurance, speed, and skill. Eventually, with the establishment of proper eating habits and supervised programs of exercise, the student will be able to participate in the regular physical education program. Tennis, golf, bowling, horseshoes, basketball, dancing, volleyball, softball, and swimming are recommended activities for the overweight student.

The Underweight. Students who are underweight should be thoroughly examined to determine the cause of the condition. They may be suffering from disorders such as malnutrition, ulcers, tuberculosis, or glandular imbalance. Heredity may also be a cause.

Because underweight individuals usually tire easily, a medical examination is necessary before they are allowed to participate in the program. Those who are underweight usually like and excel in individual sports such as tennis, golf, bowling, swimming, and some track events. Various rhythmic activities are also recommended.

The Epileptic. Safety is the major criterion in selecting activities for the epileptic. Although there are usually warning signs before a seizure, sometimes they are detected too late to prevent a tragedy. Activities that are intensely vigorous, such as basketball, football, distance running, and contact sports, can possibly cause a seizure and therefore should be avoided. Aquatic sports and activities in which gravity and height are involved, such as tumbling and gymnastics, require close supervision at all times.

Students with Cerebral Palsy. Students who suffer from cerebral palsy need continual guidance to develop confidence in their ability to participate in moderate exercise. They can find pleasure and success in dancing, bowling, croquet, golf, horseshoes, table tennis, tennis, some tumbling, swimming, and archery. The inclusion of rest periods and light forms of competition should have high priority in the selection of activities for these students.

Students with Sight Handicaps. Too often, students who have sight difficulties are excused from physical education. This is regrettable because they are deprived of the opportunity for play and movement that specially designed programs can offer.

Students with sight problems are classified into two groups: the totally blind and the partially blind. The partially blind, when placed in situations free from hazardous equipment and unsafe activities, can participate in the standard physical education program. Teachers must be constantly aware of their limitations and provide strict supervision at all times. Suitable activities for restricted participation are basketball, bowling, horseshoes, skating, track and field events, tumbling, volleyball, and wrestling.

The totally blind students present a much greater problem, but progress has been made in providing them with physical education instruction. A program of flexible scheduling can deemphasize those activities that are difficult to alter. For example, when the regular class has swimming and the blind student happens to be an excellent swimmer, he or she attends the regular class. The student attends a special or remedial class *only* when his or her skills are so poor that they prevent the student from becoming an active member of the regular class.

Students with Hearing Difficulties. Hearing disorders range from slight difficulty in hearing to total deafness. Slight hearing problems are sometimes difficult to detect, and teachers must be alert to warning signs. Students sometimes lose interest in the program or develop hostility toward it because they are not able to hear instructions or perceive the various cues inherent in most sports. Poor balance, aversion to team activity, and lack of cooperation can be signs of a hearing defect. Teachers should frequently use visual aids and demonstrations in teaching these students. Instructions should otherwise be given in a normal manner.

If individual instruction is given, hard-of-hearing students will learn at the same pace as those who are normal. They can participate in regular curriculum activities such as basketball, volleyball, swimming, bowling, and tennis. Rhythms are recommended, because through kinesthetic sense, students with hearing defects can develop an understanding of this type of movement.

Children, young people, and adults with hearing difficulties participate at all levels of athletic competition. The International Olympic Committee granted official recognition to the Comité international des sports silencieux (CISS) in 1951. The "Deaf Olympics," as they are often called, are held every four years, the last games having been held in Bucharest, Rumania, in summer 1977.

Students with Heart Disorders. Planning programs for those with cardiac handicaps is extremely difficult. Regardless of the severity of the handicap, the student must be under constant supervision. Total exclusion from the physical education class is not recommended except in extreme cases.

Careful study of many cases reveals that students with heart abnormalities are divided into groups of recommended exercise levels:

1. No restriction of usual activity
2. Slight restriction of physical activity
3. Marked restriction of physical activity
4. Severe restriction of physical activity

The teacher should be familiar with these divisions and the types of activity suitable for each group.

Students in the class 1 are usually able to play normally with their peers in the usual activities, with the exception of highly competitive sports and those involving extreme endurance. Modification of activities, play areas, required endurance, and equipment are the criteria for the selection of activities in class 2. Highly emotional situations and strenuous contests should be avoided. Carefree games and sports that provide movement based on individual capacity are suitable, and provision for frequent rest and relaxation must be part of the planning. Golf putting, tennis doubles, croquet, limited table tennis, bowling, paddle tennis, horseshoes, skating, swimming in warm water, and boating are activities that are usually permitted.

For class 3, which requires marked restriction of activities, golf, croquet, horseshoes, moderate dancing, archery, bowling, hiking, moderate skating, and table tennis are activities that might be included. Students in this group should be under constant supervision. The program should provide time for frequent rest periods, freedom from strenuous competition, moderate movement, and a climate free of tension and pressure.

In addition to keeping up with developments in cardiac care, there are definite steps the teacher should take in planning programs for students with cardiac ailments. Wheeler and Hooley suggest:

1. Read the health history and whatever other records are available concerning the past activity and academic experience of the child.
2. Discover the interests and attitudes of the child by a conference with him.
3. Discover, by a personal interview with the physician, the classification of the child,

Figure 10–4. Mainstreaming the handicapped student into the regular program. (Courtesy Cedar Shoals High School, Athens, Georgia.)

as well as the exact activities in which he may participate and to what degree. The teacher should inquire about unusual symptoms or other aspects of the case which might help him in working with the child.

4. Get to know the child further through apparently casual interviews, by watching him in action, and from reports which parents, physicians, or teachers may submit.

5. Encourage the child to adopt and follow health practices which are particularly beneficial to him; e.g., rest, exercise, and recreation.[12]

Exercise stress testing is becoming an important diagnostic tool for the physical educator, the physician, and the applied physiologist concerned with the preventive, therapeutic, and rehabilitative aspects of coronary heart disease.

Students with Hernia. Students who have hernia problems may participate in the regular program of physical education, although common sense should, of course, prevail in deciding the extent of participation. Exhausting activities, sports that include much physical contact, and movements involving heavy lifting should be avoided. Individual sports that develop skills, such as horseshoes, tennis, bowling, golf, badminton, swimming, and dancing, and team sports such as volleyball, softball, touch football, and basketball are acceptable.

Activities for the Emotionally Disturbed

The intense pressures of living in the nuclear age, competition for academic recognition, permissiveness, and apprehension of the future are producing enormous numbers of emotionally disturbed children. Programs must be developed to help these children to understand the world in which they live and to adjust to acceptable social standards both in school and in the various phases of community life. The natural drive for play and activity can be channeled into activities that are purposeful and socially acceptable, or it may lead to antisocial behavior. It is the responsibility of parents, teachers, and educational leaders to direct the play urge positively through supervision and guidance.

Although many factors are cited as reasons for emotional disturbance, some authorities feel that organic factors are the major cause. Arnheim and his associates believe that "mental disturbances are due to faulty physiology of the nervous system."[13] Arnheim further asserts:

Disorders of the mind should be restored through procedures acting on the basic physiological mechanism that determines behavior. If this is the case, one might speculate that physical activity would be important therapy for the emotionally disturbed. It is known that volitional motor activity induces proprioceptive impulses that, in turn, effectively activate the hypothalamic cortical system, a powerful determinant of behavior.[14]

Teaching the Emotionally Disturbed. Teachers need specific guidelines to assist them in teaching emotionally disturbed students. Many students in physical education classes have emotional problems and still are able to participate as part of a group, but there are some who require special attention. Grouping such individuals by ability with other students is recommended, and Arnheim lists other guidelines for teaching the emotionally disturbed:

1. Provide overstimulation for emotionally disturbed children, with the exception of the hyperactive disturbed child.
2. Use a variety of methods of teaching and a variety of games that will accommodate children who function at different physical, social, and emotional developmental levels.
3. Remove distracting objects.
4. Manual guidance has proved to be an excellent method of teaching basic skills to younger emotionally disturbed children.
5. Limits should be required in regard to use of equipment, facilities, and conduct.
6. Motor skills and games should be within the child's ability to achieve some degree of success.
7. Know when to encourage a child to approach, explore, and try a new activity or experience.
8. Discourage stereotyped play activities that develop rigid behavioral patterns.
9. It is not essential to strive for control in all situations.
10. Inappropriate interaction among specific children in the class may result in conflicts that disrupt the whole class.
11. Provide activities capable of coping with individual abilities and levels of development.[15]

The physical education teacher is in a strategic position to observe the emotionally disturbed. Participation in physical education activities reveals deep, primitive characteristics, and through careful guidance the teacher is able to assist the disturbed student not only to understand himself better but also to adjust to life situations.

Play and movement provide normal outlets for frustrations, pent-up energy, and aggressiveness. Hostile individuals might find normal expression in swimming, batting a tennis ball, driving a golf ball, slamming a handball, hitting a baseball, and kicking a football. They can be allowed to participate until their aggressiveness is dissipated.

Some emotionally disturbed students find expression through team sports, such as volleyball, basketball, touch football, and soccer. Again, the importance of ability grouping cannot be overemphasized, as the emotionally disturbed individual must develop feelings of success and accomplishment. This is possible only when students of similar ability are grouped together.

Activities for The Mentally Retarded

The mentally retarded are classified as (1) educable, (2) trainable, and (3) totally dependent. The extent of retardation determines whether these individuals should be placed in regular or special physical education classes. Selected activities for the educable and trainable retardates provide opportunities for the students to participate in a standard movement program; totally dependent students should be assigned to special classes.

Educable and trainable mentally retarded students are often assigned to physical education together with the normal students. The educable group may even excel at various activities. Special encouragement must be given to the trainable group so they may experience a feeling of accomplishment.

Mentally retarded students who are assigned to physical education can participate in the regular program, provided all students are grouped by ability. Dancing, progressive movements involving balls, all types of relays, elementary track events, progressive swimming, and movement exploration are a few of the activities they may safely enjoy.

Studies. Research shows that the physical education program makes unique contributions to the education of the mentally retarded. Again, attention should be focused on the play urge and the importance of organized activities to adolescent development. Priority should be given to designing programs that insure the physical integration of the mentally handicapped student. These programs must be complemented by concomitant psychological integration by peers and teachers. The school environment and the attitudes of peer groups often will determine the degree of the retardate's social acceptability.

Some studies have established guidelines that underscore the importance of health and physical education to the mentally retarded. As summarized by Stein, they are:

1. For a given age and sex, the normal are superior to the mentally retarded on most measures of motor proficiency.
2. In spite of underachievement with respect to motor function, the mentally retarded are much nearer the norm physically than mentally.
3. Physical proficiency can be improved in the retarded as a result of planned and systematic programs of physical education.
4. There are real differences to be expected in working with institutionalized retardates versus those enrolled in public school classes.
5. The mentally retarded achieve better in activities characterized by simple rather than complex neuromuscular skills.
6. Achievement in the area of physical fitness development apparently does not result in corresponding differential gains with regard to sociometric status.
7. Significant IQ gains have been achieved by EMR boys participating in programs of planned and progressive physical education activities.
8. Motor proficiency and intelligence are more highly correlated in the retarded than in normal children.[16]

Local, state, and regional school systems are now integrating the mentally retarded into the regular program in physical education. This plan has a great deal of promise, as Stein reports:

... Studies have shown that the mentally retarded respond and progress as much as normal boys and girls when given specialized training or instruction in a systematic and progressive physical education program.[17]

Teaching guides are suggested by Dolores Geddes, Associate Professor of Physical Education, Indiana State University, Terre Haute, Indiana. She shows that the mentally handicapped can participate in most of the activities in which normal students participate. These suggestions refer primarily to children but are also useful in working with older students:

1. Consider mental age, environmental background, and previous activity experiences when selecting activities.
2. Progress from the known to the unknown and from the simple to the complex.
3. Be enthusiastic and participate with the students.
4. Be aware of the language understanding level of the child when giving verbal instructions.
5. Correlate physical education activities with classroom activities to provide reinforcement of academic concepts.
6. Provide success experiences and offer praise at appropriate times.
7. Provide vigorous physical activity daily.
8. Proceed with motor development from gross to fine movement and from movement of the trunk to movement of the extremities.
9. Provide greater challenges in each succeeding lesson.
10. Give short and simple instructions.
11. Encourage participation by everyone.
12. Exercise firm discipline.
13. Remove a disruptive child temporarily from the class situation and deal with him in a small group or by himself.
14. If discipline is a problem, consider the possibility that the activity is too difficult to understand, requires too much skill, has too many rules, or has too many verbal instructions.
15. Do not frustrate the child by teaching too much for extended periods of time.
16. Teach new and complex activities at the beginning of the period when the students are fresh and alert.

Recent studies show no evidence that retarded students in special classes achieve more than comparable students who are assigned to regular classes. The *Resource Manual* includes research that involves the mildly and moderately handicapped student. Most results support the concept of mainstreaming.

TEACHING THE HANDICAPPED

The success or failure of mainstreaming depends upon the capacity of the teacher to plan a meaningful and dynamic program. Since no two individuals are alike, it can be broadly stated that *all* physical education programs are special programs, and all are guidance programs as well. Through instruction, normal students progress from a lower level of skill performance to a higher level. This principle is applicable to the handicapped student also. If ability grouping is used in a program of varied activities, it becomes relatively easy to provide movement and instruction for all but a few children in each class.

Instructional Strategies

The heterogeneity of the student population in the public schools as a result of mainstreaming necessitates some differentiation among students in order to organize instruction. This should be based on individual goals and needs rather than on categorical labels. Organization of physical education programs should permit free movement of students among these groups toward normalization.

A structural model for the placement of special students is contained in the Massachusetts comprehensive special education law known as Chapter 766. Program options include: (1) regular class placement with modification, (2) regular class placement with extra instructional periods and/or use of a resource room, (3) special class placement, (4) special day-school, (5) home or hospital placement, (6) residential school placement, (7) parent-child instruction, and (8) diagnostic treatment.

In 1971, Deno recommended an organizational model of services for children with all types of disabilities that further developed class settings regularly governed by school systems. Deno added:

1. Exceptional students in regular classes, with or without supportive services
2. Regular class attendance plus supplementary instructional services
3. Part-time special class
4. Full-time special class
5. Special stations which are really special schools in the public school system.[18]

Using the foregoing models, four somewhat parallel organizational structures for physical education can be projected that provide a progressive inclusive continuum:

1. **Integrated or Combined Class** in which the handicapped student is placed in the regular class setting with the nonhandicapped. Some modification or adaptation of goals, objectives, and/or activities might need to be made, but each handicapped student in the combined class is assigned activities on the basis of condition, abilities, and limitations in the traditional block program. In an individualized instruction model each student, handicapped or non-handicapped, has a program based upon individual needs, interests, goals, and present status. Activities such as track and field and gymnastics provide an easy setting for mainstreaming exceptional students in an integrated setting since the individual's performance does not directly affect the success or failure of other students or the group.
2. **Dual Class Structure** provides for the exceptional student to be in the regular integrated class set up for certain days a week but spends supplementary instructional periods concentrating on individual special needs. In a modular scheduling system this structure is not difficult for modules are provided for large group, small group, individual, and open laboratory experiences. These supplementary instructional periods need to be looked upon not only as remedial in nature but also as individual development time. In traditional block time structure, the supplementary class assignment may be extra class time on alternative days, alternate periods, or time provided during open laboratory periods.
3. **Separate Class** may be necessary for two different populations. Some handicapped students may not be ready to be assimilated into the dual or integrated class until after intensive habilitative or rehabilitative work. Other students will need the separate class permanently. Because of the nature and severity of some handicapping conditions, it is unrealistic to believe that these students' needs can be met in integrated settings even with intensive remedial instruction. To do otherwise would run the risk of harming these students psychologically and physically along with reducing the effectiveness of instruction for the non-handicapped.

For students assigned permanently to a separate class of physical education, the least restrictive environment is attending the regular school setting interacting with non-handicapped in non-instructional environments within the school.

4. **Flexible Model Plan** provides for student assignment to an integrated class during those times when the individual can successfully and safely participate. If a unit is covered in which the student cannot participate, assignment to the special or separate class is appropriate. Another variation of this model shifts the student out of the regular integrated class in which participation is not possible (i.e. football, first period), to another class in which the student could safely and successfully participate (i.e. archery, fourth period), for the duration of the unit of instruction. In both variations of this model it should be noted that activities become the basis for participation. In other words, the program is not tailored to the student but the student is fitted into the program.[19]

The recommended class assignment options are designed to facilitate instruction by making it more feasible to meet individual needs. This does not imply that the recommended class structures are inflexible once an assignment is made. It merely suggests an organizational structure within which strategies for individual instruction might be more effective. These structures can be incorporated within both school systems using traditional block scheduling and those that have instituted flexible scheduling plans.

Program Modifications

The needs of most handicapped students can be accommodated by modifying the existing physical education program. An effective and educationally sound plan for adjusting the program, which meets not only the needs of the handicapped but also those of the normal, is ability grouping. The skill of passing in basketball can be used to illustrate the ability grouping method. After an inventory of the students in a class, the performance level was found to vary so greatly that six groups could be formed:

A majority of the students were placed in the average groups, following the normal curve of distribution. Among the students of lowest abilities were several children classified as handicapped. Those who were placed in the fair groups were students who, though not physically handicapped, had not developed the skills of basketball passing. Those who showed ease and ability in performing the skill were assigned to the excellent group. Also in this group were students who, though not physically gifted, may have been playing basketball and therefore developed skills beyond normal expectancy. It must be reiterated that except in extreme cases, handicapped individuals should be accommodated in the regular physical education class with their peers where, through ability grouping, they have equal opportunity for participation.

If students are grouped according to sequential performance objectives that increase in complexity, the learning experience will be within the ability and need of each individual.

Activity Modifications

In conjunction with grouping students by ability, specific modifications can be made to provide greater opportunity for the handicapped student without affecting the structure of the regular program. Wheeler and Hooley outline several possibilities:

1. Shorten time periods.
2. Shorten distances.
3. Change the type of signals.
4. Use guidewires, ground surfaces with different sounding textures, handrails, and similar devices.
5. Soften landing spots with mats.
6. Allow two hands instead of one where accuracy or power is involved.
7. Change the rules so that they do not contain as many limiting conditions which lessen success.
8. Lower nets, baskets.
9. Increase the size of the striking implement and the targets.

	Fair	Fair	Good	Good	Very Good	Excellent
NUMBER OF STUDENTS	6	6	6	6	6	6

10. Increase or decrease the size of the pro-jectile such as the ball, discus, or javelin.
11. Permit body positions such as sitting which increase stability in games usually played in a standing position.[20]

Elective and selective curriculum options have been offered at the secondary level. Activity selection provides variety and flexibility of movement within the capabilities of each student. The physically handicapped should choose a program according to personal interest and the physician's diagnostic prescriptions.

Teaching/Learning Style Options. Once a program is chosen, specific teaching methods can be determined. This involves options in instructional delivery systems and the amount of interaction the student will have with the teacher and other learners.

When specific objectives have been identified, the teacher develops several optional delivery systems from which the students may select. Delivery systems should be compatible with the learners, and the options developed by the teacher should be commensurate with the range of abilities of the group. Mentally retarded students need more direct teacher assistance and instruction, which can be supplemented by audio-visual aids. They might not benefit from many of the options available to the other students in the group, but the mentally retarded do gain indirectly from multiple delivery systems: because the options permit the more capable students in the class to participate in self-directed learning, the teacher is free to work more closely with mentally slow students who need more simplified delivery systems.[21]

Class Environment. Classes can be structured with multiple settings that give the student some flexibility in interacting with the teacher and other students. Adaptibility is needed, particularly when there is a broad range of student abilities, personal objectives, and appropriate delivery systems. Students who are highly motivated and capable of more self-direction should be allowed to work alone, with a partner, or in a small group of students with similar interests. In schools incor-porating flexible scheduling, it is not unusual for the physical education curriculum to include modules for large group instruction, small group instruction, practice, independent study, and open laboratory.[22]

PROMISE FOR THE FUTURE

Throughout the country, efforts are being made to provide programs for handicapped children. School, city, and state organizations joined the movement to provide equal opportunity for all children regardless of emotional, physical, and mental handicaps.

Workshops have been established to help teachers arrange testing programs and learn to screen and classify students. The workshops were designed to develop an awareness of the need of sound physical education programs for handicapped children. Properly guided participation in physical education can contribute greatly toward developing feelings of adequacy, security, and belonging in handicapped students.

Educational Implications

Teacher education programs have expanded their curriculum offerings to meet state certification requirements. Specialized training of teachers, psychometrists, school psychologists, speech therapists, and other resource personnel has become available in local and state educational school systems.

Public law 94–142 has changed the national school setting from what it was in the early 1970's. Although the implementation of the federal law has placed unforeseen pressure on educators, it also has broadened the instructional programs in the secondary schools. Competent physical educators, recreation specialists, and resource personnel are in greater demand. The need for individualized prescriptive teaching programs in turn requires certified psychometrists and school psychologists. Attitudes toward the handicapped student's place in the public school are changing. Parents and concerned parties dealing with the handicapped have long awaited this recent legislation.

Suggestions for Success

The following considerations will diminish the intensity of the problems that arise in mainstreaming students in physical education:

1. Physical education teachers should become cognizant of the regulations and legal implications of the recent federal legislation.
2. Physical education teachers should consider the part-time special instruction class plan.
3. Physical education teachers should utilize community recreational facilities and medical therapeutic facilities.
4. Physical education teachers and students should teach each other about handicaps.
5. All teachers should seize the opportunities provided for in-service education.
6. All teachers should develop alternative plans for resource support.
7. Regular classroom teachers should become aware of the characteristics of mildly handicapped individuals.
8. Secondary school principals should give leadership support by positively encouraging the faculty.

QUESTIONS FOR DISCUSSION

1. What is Public Law 94–142? Describe other recent legislation regarding the education of the handicapped.
2. What is meant by the term *adapted physical education?*
3. What are the four general categories in which handicapped children are classified? Discuss one of these categories in detail.
4. What are some of the instructional strategies that assist teachers in implementing mainstreaming in physical education?
5. In teaching the handicapped, how should programs or activities be modified?
6. What guidelines should be followed to obtain the best placement for the handicapped student?

REFERENCES

1. Ninety-Fourth Congress, Education for All Handicapped Children Act of 1975. *Public Law 94–142* (November, 1975).
2. National Information Center for the Handicapped, "The New Education Law: What Does it Mean?" *Closer Look* (Summer-Fall, 1976).
3. *Preparation of Professional Personnel in Physical Education and Recreation for Handicapped Children,* compiled by W. Hillman and M. Appell (Washington, D.C.: Bureau of Education for the Handicapped, 1976).
4. *On-Going Projects* (Washington, D.C., Bureau of Education for the Handicapped, Division of Innovation and Development, 1976).
5. Myron Brenton, "Mainstreaming the Handicapped," *Today's Education* (Vol. 63, No. 2, March-April, 1974), pp. 20–25.
6. C. Sherrill, "Arguments for a Humanistic Rationale: Mainstreaming Physical Education," *Briefings 4* (The National Association for Physical Education of College Women and The National College Physical Education Association for Men, 1976), pp. 21–22.
7. J. Dunn, "Definition, Rationale and Implications: Mainstreaming Physical Education," *Briefings 4* (The National Association for Physical Education of College Women and The National College Physical Education Association for Men, 1976), p. 3, 10.
8. *Ibid.,* p. 4.
9. California State Department of Education, *Instruction of Physically Handicapped Pupils in Remedial Physical Education* (Sacramento, California, 1973) p. 31.
10. Ruth H. Wheeler and Agnes M. Hooley, *Physical Education for the Handicapped,* 2nd ed. (Philadelphia: Lea and Febiger Publishers, 1976), pp. 326–327.
11. Martilu Puthoff, "New Dimensions in Physical Activity for Children with Asthma and Other Respiratory Conditions," JOHPER (Vol. 43, September, 1972), p. 75–77.

12. Ruth H. Wheeler and Agnes M. Hooley, *op. cit.,* pp. 273–274.
13. Daniel D. Arnheim, David Auxter, and Walter C. Crowe. *Principles and Methods of Adapted Physical Education,* 3rd ed. (St. Louis: The C. V. Mosby Company, 1977), p. 379.
14. *Ibid.,* p. 308.
15. *Ibid.,* p. 378.
16. Julian Stein, "What Research Says About Psychomotor Function of the Retarded," JOHPER (Vol. 37, April, 1966), pp. 37–38.
17. *Ibid.,* pp. 37–38.
18. M. Puthoff, "Instructional Strategies: Mainstreaming Physical Education," *Briefings 4* (The National Association for Physical Education of College Women and The National College Physical Education Association for Men, 1976), pp. 37–39.
19. *Ibid.,* pp. 37–39.
20. Wheeler and Hooley, *Op. cit.,* p. 259.
21. M. Puthoff, *Op. cit.,* p. 41.
22. M. Puthoff, *Op. cit.,* p. 42.

SELECTED READINGS

Auxter, David, "Evaluation of Perceptual Motor Training Programs," *Teaching Exceptional Children* (Winter, 1972), pp. 89–97.

Biehler, Robert F., *Psychology Applied to Teaching,* 2nd ed. (Boston: Houghton Mifflin Company, 1974).

Christensen, Dagney, "Creativity in Teaching Physical Education of the Physically Handicapped Child," JOPER (Vol. 41, March, 1970), pp. 73–74.

Godfrey, Katherine E., Louise E. Kindig, and E. Jane Windell, "Electromyographic Study of Duration of Muscle Activity in Sit-up Variations," *Archives of Physical Medical and Rehabilitation* (Vol. 58, March, 1977), pp. 132–135.

Jenkins, Joseph R. and William F. Mayhall, "Describing Resource Teachers Programs," *Exceptional Children* (Vol. 40, September, 1973), pp. 35–36.

Johnson, Richard A., James B. Kenney, and John B. Davis, "Developing School Policy for Use of Stimulant Drugs for Hyperactive Children," *School Review* (November, 1976), pp. 78–96.

Johnson, Warren R., "A Humanistic Dimension of Physical Education," JOPER, (Vol. 43, November-December, 1972), pp. 31–35.

Physical Education and Recreation for Handicapped Children, Proceedings of a Study Conference on Research and Demonstration Needs, American Association for Health, Physical Education and Recreation and National Recreation and Park Association in Cooperation with Bureau of Education for the Handicapped, U.S. Department of Health, Education and Welfare, (1969).

Spragens, Jane E., "Physical Education for the Handicapped — A Case Study Approach," *Corrective Therapy Journal* (Vol. 127, March-April, 1973), pp. 41–45.

Stoneman, Zolinda and Peggy A. Keilman, "Competition and Social Stimulation Effects on Simple Motor Performance of EMR Children," *American Journal of Mental Deficiency* (Vol. 78, No. 1, 1973), pp. 98–100.

Chapter 11

Courtesy Revere Junior High School, Los Angeles City Schools.

ACTIVITY FOR ALL STUDENTS
OBJECTIVES OF INTRAMURAL SPORTS
  A LABORATORY FOR THE INSTRUCTIONAL
    PROGRAM
  LIFETIME ACTIVITIES
  EXPRESSION OF THE PLAY URGE
  ADULT SUPERVISION
  PROVISION OF ADEQUATE FACILITIES ON
    A REGULAR BASIS
ADMINISTRATIVE PERSONNEL
  INTRAMURAL DIRECTOR
    DUTIES OF THE DIRECTOR
  STUDENT DIRECTORS
  SPORTS MANAGERS
  TEAM CAPTAINS
  OFFICIALS
TYPES OF INTRAMURAL SPORTS
  ORGANIZED INTRAMURALS
  SELF-DIRECTED PARTICIPATION
UNITS FOR ORGANIZING INTRAMURAL SPORTS
SCHEDULING INTRAMURALS
  AFTER SCHOOL
  BEFORE SCHOOL
  DURING SCHOOL
  OUTSIDE OF SCHOOL
ORGANIZATION FOR PARTICIPATION
  TOURNAMENTS
    SINGLE ELIMINATION
    CONSOLATION ELIMINATION
    DOUBLE ELIMINATION
    ROUND ROBIN
    CHALLENGE
  ORGANIZATIONAL STRATEGIES
    SECURING PARTICIPANTS

  POSTING SCHEDULES
  KEEPING RECORDS
  KEEPING SCORE SHEETS
  PROMOTING
PROGRAM OF ACTIVITIES
INTRAMURAL PARTICIPATION FORMS
POINT SYSTEMS AND AWARDS
  INDIVIDUAL POINT SYSTEMS
  GROUP POINT SYSTEMS
  AWARDS
ELIGIBILITY RULES FOR INTRAMURAL
COMPETITION
  GENERAL REGULATIONS FOR
    INTRAMURAL PARTICIPATION
INTRAMURAL SPORTS AND TITLE IX
DEMONSTRATIONS
  PLANNING FOR DEMONSTRATIONS
    PRELIMINARY PLANNING
    SELECTING PARTICIPANTS
    SECURING OFFICIALS
    CHECK LIST
    MARKING THE FIELD
    SCORING SHEETS
    AUXILIARY PERSONNEL
    PROGRAMS
PUBLIC RELATIONS
  SPONSORS
  BULLETIN BOARDS
EVALUATION OF THE PROGRAM
EXTRAMURAL PROGRAMS
QUESTIONS FOR DISCUSSION
REFERENCES
SELECTED READINGS

Chapter 11

INTRAMURAL PROGRAMS

Intramural sports are organized movement activities that occur outside of the instructional program but are supervised by the school faculty. They can be viewed as the laboratory in which students practice what they have learned in the physical education class. Intramural programs are an important phase of the curriculum because they emphasize participation by all students rather than just the gifted few.

ACTIVITY FOR ALL STUDENTS

Changes throughout the country have led to increased demands for programs that include *all* students. The President's Council for Physical Fitness and Sports and the federal government's general financial support of the educationally deprived have helped to institute programs for many children who would otherwise be ignored.

Educators and leaders in sociology and psychology have for many years advocated interschool activities, which they feel are necessary for the athletically gifted. If it is educationally sound to provide programs for the academically gifted, it seems logical that programs be developed for the physically gifted. Interschool sports serve this purpose.

However, just as academic programs are necessary for the average students, programs are needed for the physically average individuals. Intramural programs have a broader interest range than interschool athletics and offer an entirely new opportunity for participation. The emphasis is no longer on spectator sports but on participative sports. Bowling is an activity in which thousands of people can participate, and it involves very little spectatorship.

To think clearly and to function in society, individuals must be emotionally stable, physically sound, and mentally alert. Above all, they must remain healthy. As the public is granted more leisure time, the intramural program becomes more important for developing proper attitudes and providing recreational experiences that will carry over to later life, such as bowling, golf, and tennis. Experience with a sound intramural program enriches the expression of the natural play urge.

Never before in the history of this country has there been a greater need for intramural programs. It is known that during the formative years, children require periods of vigorous muscular movement. Interscholastic programs in the schools cannot provide this because the number of participants is severely limited. Regardless of the school's size, there can be only 5 students on the basketball team or 11 on the football team. The job of any varsity coach is to *cut* the squad and reduce the numbers involved as soon as possible. The job of the intramural director is to *increase* the number of participants. Interscholastic programs are not interchangeable with intramurals. Intramural sports, if organized and planned properly, can be the answer to one of the major needs of all American youth today — time for vigorous activity under adult supervision.

OBJECTIVES OF INTRAMURAL SPORTS

The general objectives of any intramural program should parallel those of the physical education instructional program. There are specific fundamental elements that should guide the planning of an effective program. Intramural sports should serve as a laboratory for the instructional program and should emphasize lifetime activities. Adult supervision and proper facilities should be provided.

A Laboratory for the Instructional Program

The authors feel that intramurals are a continuation of the instructional program and that students and teachers should be familiar with the strategies involved in developing these programs.

The required class time does not allow for the two to three hours of vigorous activity needed daily by children for normal growth and development. No matter how intense the physical education instructional program may be, several additional hours of exercise based on individual needs are still required. The intramural program provides this extension of activity and allows students to practice skills beyond the time allotted during the school day.

Lifetime Activities

Students often learn the skills of an activity during the instructional period and then find it difficult to put these skills to use in an actual game situation. When intramural sports are planned and organized properly, students are encouraged to further their exercise program and to recognize that the skills taught in class are part of an activity or sport. This reinforcement in turn leads to recreational activity beyond the school years.

Expression of the Play Urge

Intramurals are an important channel for the expression of the play urge. Everyone is born with the instinct for play and movement, but daily routine usually does not provide the opportunity for vigorous play. Students might have the desire and the time for movement, yet might have no opportunity to be with children of their own age, to be a part of a group, and to learn cooperation and teamwork in physical activity. The intramural program provides this atmosphere by organizing tournaments and informal activities and by making space, equipment, and leadership available.

Adult Supervision

Intramural sports always require supervision. An adult should be available to insure a safe environment, settle disputes, and see that the objectives of the program are met.

Adequate Facilities on a Regular Basis

It is the responsibility of the school administration to provide adequate space, equipment, supplies, and personnel for the intramural program. Schools are designed for use by all students, but too often play areas are used exclusively for the varsity athletic program. This misuse of facilities is not justifiable.

ADMINISTRATIVE PERSONNEL

A properly organized intramural program is planned as an extension of the required physical education program and financed by school board appropriations. An effective program requires competent administration. Figure 11–1 illustrates a practical administrative arrangement and the personnel involved.

Intramural Director

Responsibility for directing the intramural program varies among school systems. In some places, one or more coaches have been assigned this duty. This plan has definite limitations, as listed by Means:

1. The coach almost invariably will slight intramurals when in the midst of his varsity sport season, in some cases disregarding them almost entirely.
2. A good intramural program will include many sports not usually found on the interschool calendar, and thus a leadership vacuum would develop and have to be bridged by some staff member.
3. The plan would lack unity as each coach would seek to act independently of other staff members.
4. Individual ideas will bring in too many types of intramural organizations which might add considerable confusion to a workable program.

5. There would be great confusion on the interpretation of methods, awards, schedules, point systems, and general mechanics.
6. The great amount of detail work so essential to a good program would not be accomplished, and the program would suffer thereby.[1]

The success of the program largely depends on its direction. It would be most logical for the physical education teacher to assume the leadership role. He or she should be freed from other after-school duties; directing an intramural program is a full-time after-school job.

Duties of the Director. The intramural director must:

1. Spend a specified amount of time, outside the regular school day, organizing, supervising, and promoting the intramural program.
2. Keep accurate records of each activity on permanent record cards.
3. Accompany the intramural teams when games are scheduled away from school.
4. Keep up to date with the intramural awards system.
5. Know the mechanics of the city-wide tournaments, cooperate closely with the city chairman, and be present at all city-wide events.
6. Obtain parental permission slips from all students who are to participate in intramural programs and see that all students have insurance. Many school systems have special inexpensive arrangements with reputable insurance companies so that students pay only a small premium for this protection.
7. Keep a record of the number of participants and submit a report of all contest results to the school administration.
8. Arrange all schedules, plan meetings of those individuals responsible for conducting the program, provide officials, and prepare and administer the budget.

Student Directors

A student who has worked with the program for at least one year should be

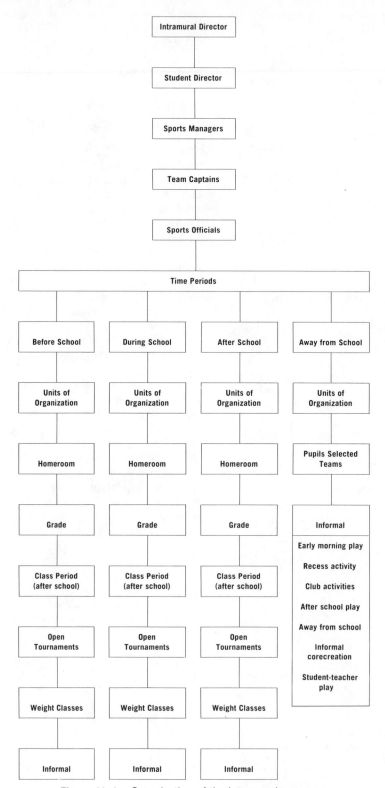

Figure 11–1.   Organization of the intramural program.

selected to assist with the overall direction of the program. He can help to record daily results, procure officials, work with the sports managers, and keep track of equipment and supplies. A good policy is to select someone from the senior class at the beginning of each year; this way, a number of students can be trained in their freshman, sophomore, and junior years, assuring the teacher of capable assistance at all times.

Sports Managers

There should be a manager for each sport in the program who is responsible for the proper functioning of that activity. He should work with the captain in procuring equipment for the particular sport and should assist with the assigning of officials.

Team Captains

Each team should have a captain to represent the unit in any situation in which the team is involved. Captains should assist the managers in approving and securing officials for each game.

Officials

Competent officials are necessary for the smooth functioning of the program. Older students and members of the varsity team can be trained to officiate; because of their youth and alertness, they frequently make good officials.

Some intramural sports leaders are planning programs without officials. Len Horyza, intramural director at Cretin High School in St. Paul, Minnesota, states, "We stopped using officials except in basketball and developed our own special rules so teams could officiate their own games."[2] This trend may solve the problem of securing officials for many of the intramural activities.

TYPES OF INTRAMURALS

A great deal of foresight is needed in planning an intramural program. Merely to organize a basketball league with eight teams playing one game per week is insufficient, because there should be enough teams to allow participation by all students every day. A well-balanced program should include several types of intramurals.

Organized Intramurals

Organized intramurals have been the basis of most programs in the past. The strategy usually used by the intramural director is to organize groups into leagues, play a round robin or elimination tournament, and present awards to the winning team. Assuming that there are eight teams in the basketball league, this means that only 40 students can participate in the tournament. This plan provides an excellent opportunity for the 40 players who are gifted in basketball, but what happens to the four or five hundred who do not want to participate on one of the teams but who enjoy practicing the skills of basketball? Obviously, another type of intramural organization is needed for this group.

Self-Directed Participation

Many students would rather participate in an informal skills program than join a team. Informal participation, in conjunction with the league plan, can enormously increase intramural participation in many situations. Self-directed participation is particularly suitable for activities that involve little teamwork, such as table tennis, basketball shooting, tennis, and track events.

Too often the pattern used for varsity programs is imposed on the intramural organization, limiting participation to a few gifted individuals. There is nothing wrong with planning activities for the athletically gifted, as long as programs are also planned for all other students, regardless of their performance capacity.

UNITS FOR ORGANIZING INTRAMURAL SPORTS

The physical education class is designed for instruction, not play, and therefore class time should not be used for intramurals. However, the physical education class can be used as an organizational unit for intramural participation. Other groups can also be used as divisions for intramural competition.

Effective group organization and planning is probably best carried out in the *homeroom,* which is already organized and is easy to reach when notices and communications are necessary.

Another unit frequently used is the *grade level.* Students from various classes may form teams and participate against other students in the same grade. This plan is most useful in small schools with few homerooms, or in schools where the number of students in a single class is insufficient to form a team.

Some intramural activities should be organized on the basis of the *weight* of the participants. Wrestling is an obvi-

ous example of a sport that should be planned in this manner.

The *one-day tournament plan* is useful when a skill or sport is being developed and performance levels are not too high. One afternoon is set aside for a particular sport, and all students interested in playing are asked to report. Teams are formed at random, a straight elimination tournament is played, and the winner is declared that day. These events may be held periodically, although ideally they should follow the conclusion of that skill lesson in the classroom. The one-day tournament can be used for any sport or activity.

Students can also form teams arbitrarily and elect a captain. The team rosters are turned in to the physical education office and organized for tournament play. Entry blanks such as the one shown in Figure 11–2 may be used. Students in various departments, such as science, mathematics, and so-

---

Intramural Entry Blank

Coeducational   Sex

Activity   Homeroom   Captain

PLAYERS   PLAYERS

Homeroom Director

Homeroom Teacher

Figure 11–2. Intramural entry blank.

cial studies, can organize their own teams for intramural competition. Vocational students can also form teams.

SCHEDULING INTRAMURALS

Providing time for intramurals frequently presents a serious problem. Students need sufficient periods of laboratory participation, and these must coincide with the general operation of the school. Because of transportation problems or conflicts with other sports or part-time jobs, different scheduling strategies can be implemented.

After School

The ideal time for intramural participation is immediately after school. However, because of the priority given to interschool athletics, facilities are usually unavailable. At some schools, time and equipment are available after the varsity teams have conducted their practice or when they are playing away from school. Neither of these arrangements is satisfactory. It is the responsibility of school administrators to provide adequate time consistently for the intramural laboratory. In Norfolk, Virginia, one hour immediately after the school day is reserved for intramural programs in all senior high schools. The varsity teams practice after this time. In the junior high schools as much time as needed is available.

Before School

Early morning programs are becoming popular. These are usually informal, and many students find this arrangement more convenient than staying after school.

During School

Intramural programs can take place during school hours; for example, they can be planned in periods normally set aside for club organization. If they are long enough, recesses might provide the opportunity for informal intramurals, although the proper timing for eating and digesting before activity must not be neglected.

Outside of School

Activities outside the school give students the chance to practice skills learned in class. An interesting program exists at the Rutland High School in Rutland, Vermont, in which half the student's grade is based on out-of-school participation. The teacher, Don Rippon, feels that if teachers can inspire students to make vigorous activity a way of life, they make an important contribution to the students' immediate development and future welfare.[3]

ORGANIZATION FOR PARTICIPATION

A number of procedures have been used to arrange competitions after the student teams have been determined. Some of the more effective ones are described here.

Tournaments

Tournaments are the most popular means for determining winners. Five

Figure 11-3. Single elimination tournament with contestants in powers of two.

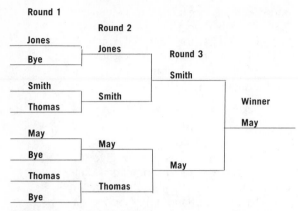

Figure 11–4. Single elimination tournament with byes. This means that Jones, May, and Thomas do not play in the first round.

types are generally used: single elimination, consolation elimination, double elimination, round robin, and challenge.

Single Elimination. When time is limited, the single elimination tournament can be used. The names of participating teams or individuals are placed in brackets, as shown in Figure 11–3. As long as the number of contestants is a power of two (2, 4, 8, 16, etc.), the first round presents no problem. However, when the number of players is not a power of two, the first round should have *byes*. The number of byes is determined by subtracting the number of players from the next

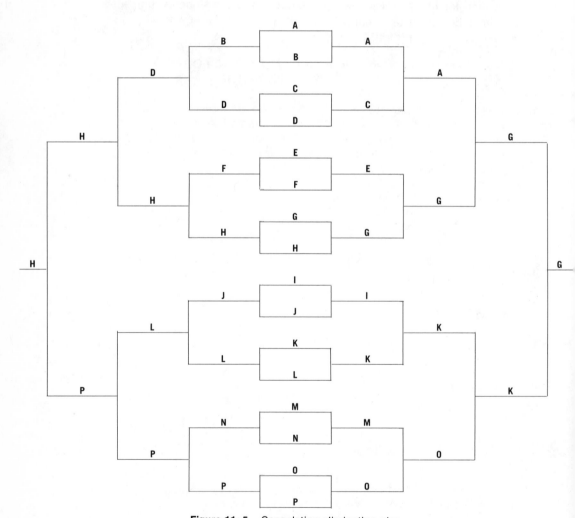

Figure 11–5. Consolation elimination plan.

power of two. For instance, if there are five players or teams, the next power of two is eight; therefore, there must be three byes in the first round, as shown in Figure 11–4.

Consolation Elimination. In the consolation elimination, the losers of the first round begin a loser's tournament the following day (Fig. 11–5). Although this type of tournament provides more playing opportunity, it is not very popular — the idea of losers playing each other does not appeal to many students.

Double Elimination. In this type of tournament, the losers in all rounds continue to play a loser's tournament. The losers from the championship brackets drop down and play the winners in the loser's bracket (Fig. 11–6).

Round Robin. The round robin is the most popular of all tournaments because of the number of times each individual or team plays. It is generally used for team play and for league competition. Round robin tournaments require a great deal of time; accordingly, leaders should first determine the number of games that will have to be played. The formula for this is simple:

$$\frac{(\text{Number of teams}) \times (\text{Number of teams} - 1)}{2} = \text{Number of games to be played}$$

$$\text{Example (8 teams): } \frac{8 \times 7}{2} = 28 \text{ games played}$$

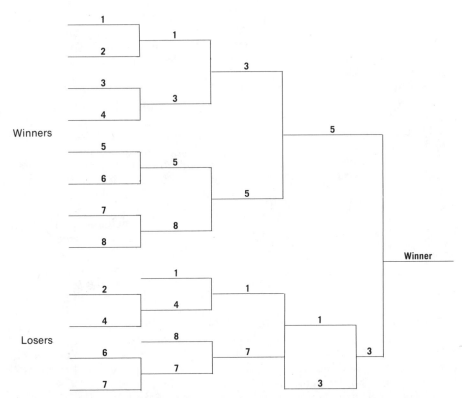

Figure 11–6. Double elimination tournament. If team 5 defeats team 3, team 5 is the tournament winner. However, if team 3 defeats team 5, these two teams must play another game since this is the first game that team 5 has lost.

The round robin schedule should not be planned for more than eight teams because of the time involved. If there are more than eight teams, a different league should be formed.

After the number of teams has been determined, the teacher has to arrange a schedule. The simplest way is to arrange all the teams in two columns:

$$1-4$$
$$2-5$$
$$3-6$$

If there is an even number of teams, number 1 remains stationary and the other teams are rotated around number 1 either clockwise or counterclockwise. The six teams shown rotated clockwise and would form the following schedule:

Round 1	Round 2	Round 3
1–4	1–2	1–3
2–5	3–4	6–2
3–6	6–5	5–4

Round 4	Round 5
1–6	1–5
5–3	4–6
4–2	3–2

When the number of teams is uneven, teams are arranged in two columns with the bye placed either at the bottom or the top and the other teams rotating clockwise. With five teams, the schedule would be as follows:

Round 1	Round 2	Round 3
1–bye	2–bye	3–bye
2–4	3–1	5–2
3–5	5–4	4–1

Round 4	Round 5
5–bye	4–bye
4–3	1–5
1–2	2–3

Challenge. Tournaments in which students challenge each other and direct their own competition are extremely popular. Several plans may be used to arrange participants for challenge tournaments, including (1) selection by lot, (2) placement upon entrance, (3) selection by ability or previous performance, and (4) placement according to ranking from previous tournaments. The following guidelines should be used when planning challenge tournaments:

1. Arrange participants by one of the foregoing selection plans.
2. Require losers to respond to a challenge before they can challenge again.
3. Set a time limit by which the players who are challenged must either play or forfeit their positions on the tournament roster.
4. Set a time limit by which players must challenge one another.
5. Allow the same participants to play each other a second time only after they have met another player in between.
6. Allow new players to enter the tournament by challenging the lowest player on the tournament sheet.

Although there are several types of challenge tournaments, only the ladder and pyramid are shown in Figures 11–7 and 11–8. Included in the illustrations are suggestions for that type of tournament. Other plans for organizing participation in the intramural sports are found in the *Resource Manual.*

Organizational Strategies

Sometimes those responsible for organizing intramural programs find it difficult to elicit student participation in the various activities. There are several methods for developing and maintaining interest.

Securing Participants. The teacher has to find the most efficient way of acquainting the students with the intramural program (dates, time of play, and activities). Probably the best medium is the physical education class — announcements can be made and entry blanks for team organization can be distributed. These blanks, to be returned to the teacher, should include the names of players and captains (see Fig. 11–2).

Posting Schedules. After the teacher has obtained the teams, schedules should be made up and posted. The

PLACES	PLAYERS	PLACES
I	DORIS	I
2	FRANK	2
3	MARY	3
4	TOM	4
5	JACK	5
6	DOT	6
7	JANE	7
8	BILL	8
9	VERNON	9
IO	MARGE	IO
II	FRED	II
I2	TED	I2

Figure 11–7. The ladder tournament.

1. Players should be seeded.
2. Participants move up if they win and down if they lose.
3. Players may challenge any of the three opponents above.
4. A deadline date should be set by which a winner is declared.
5. This type of tournament is best suited for individual sports because participants are ranked by ability when the tournament is completed.

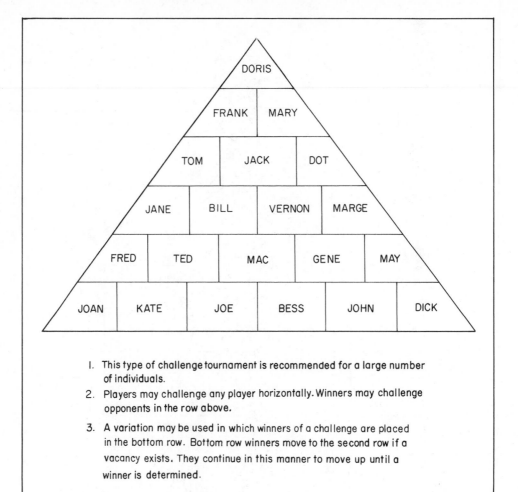

1. This type of challenge tournament is recommended for a large number of individuals.
2. Players may challenge any player horizontally. Winners may challenge opponents in the row above.
3. A variation may be used in which winners of a challenge are placed in the bottom row. Bottom row winners move to the second row if a vacancy exists. They continue in this manner to move up until a winner is determined.

Figure 11–8. The pyramid tournament.

student director should be familiar with the schedules and work with the sports managers and homeroom captains in order to keep all the participants informed.

Keeping Records. The teacher and the student director should work together to keep accurate records of all intramural results. Four by six index cards can be alphabetically arranged and placed in a filing cabinet for easy reference (Fig. 11–9).

Keeping Score Sheets. Score sheets should be available for all activities. These forms will assist officials and can also be used for record keeping and publicity purposes. Figure 11–10 illustrates how rules for the activity can be

included on the score sheet. Another type of score card is shown in the *Resource Manual.*

Promoting. Even if an intramural program is carefully planned, it will be a failure if large numbers of students do not participate. Some promotional techniques for stimulating interest are:

1. Develop a public relations program through the use of bulletin boards, television, school paper, local newspaper, and special announcements.
2. Provide coverage, in all public relations media of contest winners, future events, and outstanding performances.
3. Bring members of the faculty into

Individual Intramural Sports Record

Name _____

Homeroom _____

Intramural Awards Record

DATE	AWARDS	DATE	AWARDS
3/10/78	Certificate	10/12/78	Certificate
4/ 9/78	Cup	11/ 3/78	Monogram
5/12/78	Certificate	12/13/78	Plaque

Intramural Record

ACTIVITIES	7	8	9	10	11	12	REMARKS
Basketball							
Bowling							
Rhythmics							
Foul Shots							
Golf							
Hockey							
Managing							
Officiating							
Rapid Shooting							
Softball							
Swimming							
Table Tennis							
Tennis							
Touch Football							
Track							
Tumbling							
Volleyball							
Wrestling							
Body Mechanics							
Fitness Meet							
Total Points							

Figure 11–9. Intramural sports record.

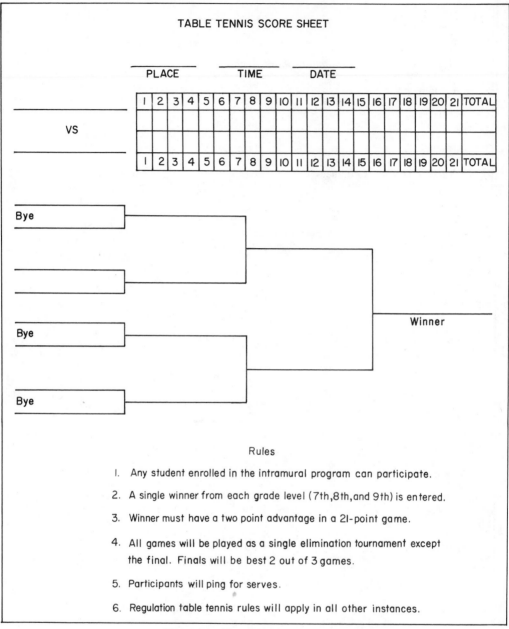

TABLE TENNIS SCORE SHEET

PLACE _____ TIME _____ DATE _____

_____
VS
_____

	1	2	3	4	5	6	7	8	9	10	11	12	13	14	15	16	17	18	19	20	21	TOTAL
	1	2	3	4	5	6	7	8	9	10	11	12	13	14	15	16	17	18	19	20	21	TOTAL

Bye

Bye

Bye

Winner

Rules

1. Any student enrolled in the intramural program can participate.

2. A single winner from each grade level (7th, 8th, and 9th) is entered.

3. Winner must have a two point advantage in a 21-point game.

4. All games will be played as a single elimination tournament except the final. Finals will be best 2 out of 3 games.

5. Participants will ping for serves.

6. Regulation table tennis rules will apply in all other instances.

Figure 11–10. Table tennis score sheet.

the program by arranging contests between students and teachers.

4. Be sure to follow the guidelines of Title IX by including coeducational activities in the program. Both team and individual sports should be offered.

5. Use all available time periods to accommodate students who cannot remain after school.

6. Include both organized and self-directed activities in the program.

7. Provide alternative tournaments, such as challenge and straight elimination, for students who cannot spare the time for round-robin play.

8. Develop an awards system that gives recognition to anyone who participates in the program.

Parental Approval Permit

I hereby give my permission for _____ to

participate in all intramural activities, _____ .
                                                    (Date)

I understand that all precautions will be taken to prevent accidents and I will not hold school authorities responsible for any injury resulting from his/her participation.

_____   _____
        (Date)   Signature of Parent or Guardian

Figure 11–11. Parental approval form.

9. Include telephonic and telegraphic tournaments, in which results from several schools are phoned into a central office.
10. Plan special programs for the handicapped.
11. Keep performance records for events such as track and swimming.

The teacher who plans carefully and uses many tools, such as record cards and official entry blanks, will be successful in organizing the program. For instance, securing and filing permission forms (Fig. 11–11) helps the director avoid problems with parents later on. Slipshod organization will result in a slipshod program. Student leaders enjoy working out many of the details involved in developing a program and should be given ample opportunities to assist.

PROGRAM OF ACTIVITIES

It is not always feasible for the intramural program to follow the instructional curriculum exactly. However, when possible, the programs should be planned to provide constant reinforcement that will enrich participation in both class activities and intramural sports. Joint planning is also more important now because of the impact of Title IX legislation on the total physical education program. Activities that have been developed for the instructional

phase meet all Title IX guidelines and can easily be incorporated into the intramural sports program.

Adjusting to Title IX has been a slow process in intramural sports. However, a few schools are conducting programs that might serve as models for future intramural competition. One such program is found in the Christianburg High School in Christianburg, Virginia. It offers 18 activities, 10 of which are conducted on a coeducational basis. With a few adjustments, this program could comply with Title IX guidelines. Figure 11–12 shows the distribution of activities.[4]

INTRAMURAL PARTICIPATION FORMS

Records should be kept of intramural participation in each activity. These records are important for publicity purposes and for program evaluation. Copies should be sent to the principal, the director of physical education, and other individuals who should be apprised of the program. Figure 11–13 shows a simple form for keeping such records.

A successful recording system has been developed by Walter Sochackl of Sandburg Junior High School in Minneapolis, Minnesota. The form is a one-page summary containing an introductory statement, an expression of appreciation to all who assisted him, an

Suggested Distribution of Activities			
Activity	*Girls*	*Boys*	*Co-Ed*
Aerial Tennis	x		x
Basketball	x	x	x
Bowling	x		x
Field Hockey	x		x
Flag Football	x		x
Soccer		x	
Softball	x		x
Tug-of-War	x	x	x
Volleyball	x	x	x
Archery	x	x	
Badminton	x		
Century Club (jog 100 miles)	x	x	
Cycle Century Club	x	x	
Miniature Golf	x	x	
One-on-One Basketball	x	x	
Ping Pong	x	x	x
Tennis	x		x
Track	x		

Figure 11–12. Distribution of activities for intramural sports. (Courtesy, Gunsten, Pamela, "Intramurals—The Christianburg Way," *JOPER*, March, 1974, p. 51.)

explanation of the program, and the percentage of participation by activities and grade. The statistics compiled from the report are made available to the administration, the parents, the taxpayers, and the members of the school board. This form makes it easy and quick to:

1. Check the summary page to see what percentage of boys and girls at each grade level participated in intramurals, extramurals, or interscholastics.
2. Study the individual sheets to determine how many boys and how many girls at each level participated in each activity and how many participated in one, two, or three activities.
3. Get a clear perspective of overall interest and participation in extracurricular physical education and see at a glance the value of the program.
4. Determine quickly which activities are popular and which ones should be eliminated or modified as the program is revised and expanded.[5]

POINT SYSTEMS AND AWARDS

The basis of any intramural awards program is a fair and practical point system. Granting points serves as an incentive for participation and provides continuity from season to season.

A comprehensive point system should be developed around both individual and group participation. Although group criteria have been used for many years, point arrangements for individual activities are becoming popular because they focus on personal performance. In addition to eliciting more participation, this recognition becomes a strong motivational factor.

Individual Point Systems

Individual point systems require considerable bookkeeping, and students can often assist with recording points. When careful and constant supervision is provided by the director, the individual point system is immensely rewarding. A study of individual scoring arrangements reveals the following advantages:

1. An increased eagerness for group participation grows out of the system, since

Monthly
Intramural Participation Record

Activities	Month	No. Teams	No. Students	Time of Day	Where Played	Type of Tournament	Comments	Total
Golf								
Tennis								
Bowling								
Wrestling								
Swimming								
Basketball								
T. Football								
Hockey								
Rhythms								
Softball								
Track								
Volleyball								
							Total	

Figure 11–13. Intramural participation record.

group play consistently adds to individual progress.

2. All individual tournaments and events will receive many more entries and will include large numbers of students who are totally unfamiliar with the particular sport but are anxious to learn and to compete.

3. Greater interest is noted in the physical education classes, since they teach the skills through which a student may become more successful in the laboratory or intramural competitive period.

4. Much more interest is created in the noncompetitive aspects of the total program, since they, too, can be recognized in the individual point scoring plan.

5. The scoring system can be used to stimulate and promote better health and safety habits.

6. The student obtains a broader knowledge of many more recreational sports, some of which can be utilized in adult leisure-time living.

7. The plan offers a splendid basis for a progressive achievement awards system, easily adapted to the local situation.

8. All individuals are recognized in measure, not just the superior athlete who more often finds himself on the championship team.

9. The plan permits the combination of all school activities in the point system, recognizing accomplishment in athletics, debate, music, declamation, and other activities.[6]

Point systems vary, depending on the type of the program, the philosophy of the school, and the status of the total intramural program. East High School in Green Bay, Wisconsin, grants an emblem to participants who earn 1000 points. Points are accumulated each year for the four-year period as shown in Table 11–1.[7]

Group Point Systems

Awarding points for group competition has been common practice in intramural programs for many years. Group point systems have great promotional value, but if they are not simply planned, record-keeping problems may develop to the extent that they become unmanageable. A functional group-scoring plan for secondary schools is shown in Figure 11–14.[8]

Rokosz suggests another simple group-scoring system involving three categories: (1) points for completing a schedule without forfeit, (2) points for each game or match victory, and (3)

TABLE 11–1. INDIVIDUAL POINT SYSTEM

Points	Distribution
League and Team Sports (Maximum of 150 points per sport)	
20	Each game played
25	Bonus, member of championship team
20	Bonus, member of second-place team
15	Bonus, member of third-place team
10	Bonus, member of fourth-place team
5	Bonus, member of fifth-place team
20	Deducted whenever team forfeits
Tournaments of Individual Nature (Maximum of 125 points per sport)	
15	Each match played or won by forfeit
20	Bonus to individual champion
15	Bonus to second-place individual
10	Bonus to third-place individual
5	Bonus to fourth-place individual
15	Deducted for each match forfeited
Meets of Individual and Team Nature (Maximum of 100 points per meet)	
20	Each event entered and completed (Number of events permissible always limited)
10	Bonus for winning each first place
5	Bonus for any record broken
8	Bonus for winning each second place
6	Bonus for winning each third place
4	Bonus for winning each fourth place
2	Bonus for winning each fifth place[7]

From Means, Louis, *Intramurals*, 2nd ed. (Englewood Cliffs; Prentice-Hall, 1973) p. 154.

Scoring Chart Junior or Senior High School				
Intergroup Games	Team Leagues and Tournaments	Individual Tournaments	Meets	Athletics
Baseball	Baseball	Foul shoot	Track	Basketball
Basketball	Basketball	Gymnastics	Skating	Tennis
Football	Football	Horseshoes	Swimming	Track
Football specialties	Football specialties	Tennis	Skiing	
Horseshoes	Horseshoes	Wrestling	Bicycling	
Pentathlon	Volleyball	Shuffleboard		
Speedball		Handball		
Softball	NOON HOUR			
Soccer				
Tennis	Baseball			
Volleyball	Basketball			
POINTS	POINTS	POINTS	POINTS	POINTS
				Entrance 25
				Squad 75
Entrance 50	Entrance 25	Entrance 25	Entrance 25	2nd–
Additional 100	Additional 100	Additional 100	Additional 100	Letter 25
150	125	125	125	Letter 75
				200

Second team intergroup sports carried in Tennis, Horseshoes, Basketball, Volleyball, and Football Goals. 25 points given for entrance in these sports, with 35 additional possible.

Figure 11–14. A group point system for secondary schools. (From Means, Louis, *Intramurals*, 2nd ed. Englewood Cliffs: Prentice-Hall, 1973, p. 137.)

bonus points for champions and runners-up.[9] The plan is shown in Table 11–2.

Awards

Award programs in schools today are highly controversial. Many people feel that the interest, the fun, and the fitness derived from intramural competition are sufficient awards. Others contend that inexpensive awards not only increase motivation but also provide tangible evidence of participation and support the American tradition of rewarding individuals for personal accomplishment.

Award systems for intramural sports should provide some sort of recognition for all the participants. The most popular kinds of awards are medals, letters,

trophies and plaques. If these are too costly, attractive certificates are recommended because they are inexpensive and can be framed and displayed in the home. Figure 11–15 illustrates one type of certificate that can be used.

Letters or monograms are universal symbols of accomplishment in intramural competition. They range in size from four to twelve inches and are made of felt or chenille. In order to lower the cost of the monograms, students in the homemaking department sometimes are willing to make them as a class project.

ELIGIBILITY RULES FOR INTRAMURAL COMPETITION

Regulations governing intramural sports should be put in writing and

TABLE 11–2. SCORING SYSTEM FOR TOURNAMENTS

	GAMES AND MATCHES			
	No-Forfeit Bonus Points	Victory Points	Championship Points	
Sport			CHAMPION	RUNNER-UP
Team Sports: One Team per Organization				
		(PER GAME)		
Touch Football	25	10	100	60
Basketball	25	10	100	60
Volleyball	25	10	100	60
Softball	25	10	100	60
Dual Sports: Two Teams per Organization				
		(PER MATCH)		
Badminton	10	5	50	30
Tennis	10	5	50	30
Golf	10	5	50	30
Table Tennis	10	5	50	30
Individual Sports: Three Men per Organization				
		(PER MATCH)		
Tennis	5	5	50	30
Badminton	5	5	50	30
Table Tennis	5	5	50	30
Wrestling	5	5 per fall 3 per decision	50	30

MEETS
Points awarded by place ranking. Three men per organization per event.

Sport	No-Forfeit Bonus Points	Places									
		1	2	3	4	5	6	7	8	9	10
Cross-country	5	50	30	25	20	15	10	8	6	4	2
Cycling	5	50	30	25	20	15	10	8	6	4	2
Foul Shooting	5	50	30	25	20	15	l0	8	6	4	2
Swimming											
50 yd. free style	5	25	15	8	6	4					
50 yd. back stroke	5	25	15	8	6	4					
50 yd. breast stroke	5	25	l5	8	6	4					
Track and Field											
100 yd. dash	5	25	15	8	6	4					
440 yd. dash	5	25	15	8	6	4					
Mile run	5	25	15	8	6	4					
Shot-put	5	25	15	8	6	4					

A team or individual must complete all schedule obligations in a tournament to earn bonus points for no-forfeits. A player or team that fails to play at least one contest in a tournament shall receive no points for any victories that may have been attained by forfeit. This guards against a situation in which a team or individual wins the first match by forfeit, then forfeits the remainder of the schedule.

Adapted from Rokosz, Francis M., *Structured Intramurals.* (Philadelphia: W. B. Saunders Company, 1975), p. 53.

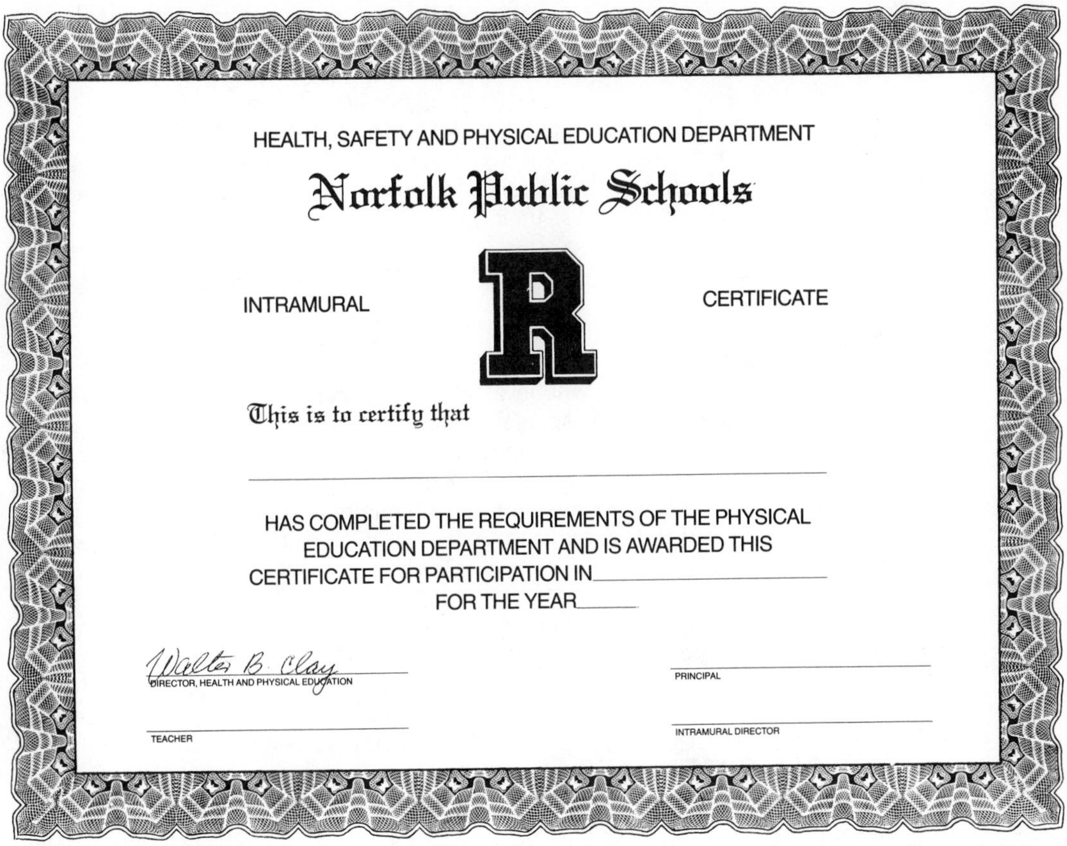

HEALTH, SAFETY AND PHYSICAL EDUCATION DEPARTMENT

Norfolk Public Schools

INTRAMURAL   CERTIFICATE

This is to certify that

_____

HAS COMPLETED THE REQUIREMENTS OF THE PHYSICAL
EDUCATION DEPARTMENT AND IS AWARDED THIS
CERTIFICATE FOR PARTICIPATION IN_____
FOR THE YEAR_____

DIRECTOR, HEALTH AND PHYSICAL EDUCATION   PRINCIPAL

TEACHER   INTRAMURAL DIRECTOR

Figure 11–15. An intramural award that is both inexpensive and attractive. (Courtesy Health and Physical Education Department, Norfolk Public Schools, Norfolk, Virginia.)

posted conspicuously. Sound and specific rules will prevent misunderstandings and embarrassment later. Common prescriptions for intramural competition are:

1. All students who are enrolled in school are automatically eligible to enjoy all intramural privileges, unless they fail to comply with the other eligibility rules.
2. No scholastic requirements are enforced unless a student is so far below the average of the class that all his spare time is needed for study.
3. Any student who is or has been a member of a varsity or junior varsity team and has participated in one or more scheduled games or practice games shall be ineligible to compete in that particular intramural sport. The same regulation applies to students who bowl on civic league bowling teams or swim on any organized teams. This rule shall be strictly enforced.
4. A player may be ruled ineligible to compete in future contests because of unsportsmanlike conduct, refusal to abide by the decision of an official, or use of improper language.
5. Players will be limited to playing on one team in any given sport.
6. Upon the decision of the intramural director, students may be ruled ineligible to compete because of infractions of any rules or any conduct that might cause embarrassment to the school.

General Regulations for Intramural Participation

There are several general policy regulations that should be printed and posted so that everyone involved in intramurals is kept informed:

1. There is no admission charge for intramurals.
2. Intramural competition is limited to groups within the school. (If intramurals were to assume the competitive aspects of interscholastics, their existence would be unnecessary. One exception to this might be extramural events.)
3. Intramurals will be scheduled outside of class periods.
4. Forfeits should be avoided whenever possible. If they do occur, special arrangements will be made and announced as quickly as possible.
5. Contests postponed because of weather conditions and administrative conflicts will be rescheduled as soon as possible.
6. A committee will be established to develop policies pertaining to protests.

INTRAMURAL SPORTS AND TITLE IX

Intramural leaders have realized for years that many activities in the physical education curriculum are suitable for joint participation by boys and girls. When they are well organized, properly supervised, and played in wholesome environments, coeducational activities make a tremendous contribution to the overall objectives of education. Psychologists and sociologists have for years advocated vigorous physical activity for the release of pent-up energy and the development of emotional stability. Furthermore, when all students play together in an acceptable manner, greater respect for the opposite sex develops.

Coeducational intramurals should be planned and administered differently from those activities segregated by sex. Placing boys and girls together in competitive situations necessitates new codes of behavior, emphasis on the scientific selection of activities, and intensive supervision. Because all aspects of school competition are governed by

Title IX, conditions that prevail for the instructional program also pertain to intramural sports. Leaders should be familiar with the guidelines established by Title IX before planning intramural programs.

DEMONSTRATIONS

At the end of a season, a program incorporating several activities that have been featured in tournaments and other competitions should be arranged. These culminating programs can take the form of school-wide demonstrations.

Planning a successful demonstration is a time-consuming and intricate task. Guidelines to assist directors with their planning are:

1. The demonstration should represent activities that are taught in the instructional program. This not only serves as a true interpretation of the physical education program but it also does not infringe on instructional time.
2. A check list should be devised showing the equipment, supplies, procedures, and all details involved in conducting the intramural program.
3. As many students as possible should be included in demonstrations.
4. Advanced planning is essential. Some of the factors that have to be arranged are (1) place to stage demonstration, (2) date, (3) use of the public address system, (4) accommodations for persons on the program, such as guest speakers, and (5) transportation.
5. All participants should be neatly dressed. If a school uniform is used, it should be cleaned and pressed.
6. Activities in the demonstration should have a time limit. If they do not, the program may drag on indefinitely and many spectators will leave. The program should move quickly and include activities that can be explained to the spectators.

7. Adequate advance publicity should be arranged through television, newspapers, and radio, and announcements to teachers and administrators.
8. A printed program is essential for giving status to the demonstration. If the financial outlay is prohibitive, a sponsor may be found to assume the cost.
9. A theme for the demonstration is desirable.
10. The content of the demonstration should reflect the local philosophy of physical education.
11. The principal, superintendent, or an important member of the school board should be given a prominent role to play in the demonstration. In this way, his or her attendance and participation are obligatory, and the intramural program benefits most when the influential people are informed and involved.

Planning for Demonstrations

Planning for demonstrations is a challenge to the teachers who are responsible for laying the groundwork. Participants must be familiarized with the surroundings, officials must be briefed, areas must be marked properly, and numerous other details must be attended to.

It is relatively easy to plan a demonstration for a small number of students, but planning for large groups presents complex problems. Regulations, participants, check lists, division groups, officials, site markings, and records are just a few of the priority items that need careful planning.

Preliminary Planning. A committee consisting of the principal, physical education teachers, and students should determine the overall policy for organizing the demonstration. Items such as time, date, events, site, and purpose should be studied by the committee.

After decisions have been made, they should be presented to the principal, who sends a letter to all teachers and other people who are involved in the demonstration. Figure 11–16 shows one example of how the decisions of the committee can be circulated.

At a later date, an announcement should be sent to all persons concerned with organizing the demonstration. It should contain more specific information relative to the preliminary planning.

Selecting Participants. Teachers should have sufficient time to select participants for the demonstration. Once students have been chosen, their names should be placed on an official entry blank. Individuals selected to participate in the demonstration should be given parental approval forms (Fig. 11–11) to be taken home, signed by the parents, and returned promptly to the teacher.

To provide fair competition and to manage large groups of students in the various events, divisions based on ability, grade, or another acceptable criteria should be made. Grouping facilitates the simultaneous participation of large numbers of students and avoids boredom by keeping the demonstration moving at all times.

Securing Officials. It is extremely important to meet with the officials who have been selected for the demonstration. If a teacher training institution exists nearby, the institution may be willing to cooperate by allowing one of the professional classes to assist with the officiating. Such an experience is invaluable to students who intend to teach when they graduate. If there is not a teacher training institution available, high school students can be trained to officiate.

There should be several meetings with the officials during which the committee explains their duties and distributes the assignments. These should be printed or mimeographed and available early in the planning period. Representatives from the planning committee work with the officials to outline their responsibilities and acquaint them with the regulations of each event.

Check List. A check list should be kept to record all the equipment need-

MARCH 10, 1978

MEMORANDUM

To: Teachers and Parents

From: The Principal

Topic: Annual Physical Education Demonstration

The annual health and physical education demonstration will be held on Tuesday, May 17, at 1:00 p.m. In the event of rain the demonstration will be held on Wednesday, May 18, at 1:00 p.m.

There is grave concern on the part of our leaders about the physical fitness of the boys and girls in this country, and this school is exceedingly anxious to provide an adequate physical education program for students in our city. The demonstration that has been planned for this year will serve as a great motivating influence and will increase student interest in exercise.

Enclosed you will find a copy of the regulations governing the demonstration. Every effort has been made to simplify the affair, and the entire program should be finished by the time school is normally dismissed. Approval has been obtained from the Superintendent to excuse all participants from classes at 12:30 p.m. Parental approval permits which will be furnished by the Health, Physical Education and Safety Department are required for all participants.

I assume that the parent-teacher organizations will assist with the transportation for the demonstration as they have done in the past, and appreciate their assistance with this phase of the program.

I sincerely hope that you will cooperate with the school on this project as you have done in the past. Any information not included in this memo will be sent to you upon request from your physical education teacher or by calling this office.

Sincerely,

The Principal

Figure 11–16

ed for holding the demonstration. Any problems or omissions should be noted in the check list file and remedied for the following year.

Marking the Field. Field marking requires careful attention because most of the students probably have never seen the site where the event is to be held. In most instances, the demonstration is unrehearsed. Field markings are needed for assembly of the students, group divisions, lanes for individual events, and the speaker's stand.

Scoring Sheets. Printed or mimeographed scoring sheets should be available for smooth operation and the keeping of official records.

Auxiliary Personnel. One person, preferably an experienced teacher, should be selected to direct the entire demonstration. This *demonstration director* should have adequate knowledge of the various sports involved and should have had previous experience with demonstrations of this kind.

The *announcer* should have experience with a public address system and should also have had experience with this type of demonstration. The demonstration director may or may not be assigned to this responsibility.

Although accidents are rare, a *nurse* or *physician* should be available at all times.

Programs. Printed programs add dignity to the event and give students and spectators a more comprehensive understanding of the demonstration.

The program should include a schedule of the events, a statement of purpose, and other details that are of interest to the public. These should be prepared far in advance of the event in order to acquaint the public with city-wide programs.

PUBLIC RELATIONS

Representatives from local newspapers and television stations should be invited to intramural programs, and all contest results should be compiled and given to reporters. Local newspapers and television stations usually acquaint the public with these programs. Members of civic clubs, parent-teacher organizations, and school administrators should also be invited. All publicity concerning demonstrations and intramurals should include the names of the principal, district superintendent, members of the board, and other persons of influence.

An intramural program is the perfect medium for presenting to the public the activities, philosophies, and objectives of physical education. Alert physical education directors can introduce a broad overview of the entire program in a single demonstration. In addition to using these media outlined in Chapter 12, there are other techniques involved in a good public relations program that merit consideration. These include the use of sponsors, bulletin boards, and public announcements.

Sponsors

It is relatively easy to find clubs and associations that are interested in sponsoring school programs. Most civic clubs have youth committees whose responsibility is to seek and support activities that contribute to the improvement of the health and welfare of children.

Although school systems frequently need the financial support of such groups, they also need the good will and manpower that they can offer. By investing small amounts of money and otherwise assisting with school events, these organizations become strong supporters of the program.

Bulletin Boards

Attractive and well-planned bulletin boards are one of the most effective publicity tools for promoting intramurals, acquainting students with contest results, and providing an overall perspective of the entire program. Students are often appointed to construct these boards. Not only will they welcome the creative challenge, but some of their ideas will enhance the promotion of the program (Fig. 11–17).

Figure 11–17. A well-planned bulletin board and display case. (Courtesy Rosement Junior High School, Norfolk Public Schools, Norfolk, Virginia.)

EVALUATION OF THE PROGRAM

The basic criterion for evaluating the intramural program is the amount of participation it elicits. Intramurals operating within limited scopes cannot meet the objectives of a good physical education program.

EXTRAMURAL PROGRAMS

Students who exhibit excellence in skills slightly below the level of the varsity players but superior to that of their classmates should receive special atten-tion. These gifted students should be encouraged to participate beyond the standard competitive challenge offered in the school. Organizing these students into one-day competitive contests is a sound educational procedure.

Criticisms of junior high school interscholastics conclude that forming leagues, keeping percentage records, and capitalizing on the extreme emotionalism of the students to incite the competitive effort is unfair. To allow the winners of the school intramurals and tournaments to compete with one another on a one-day basis is an acceptable alternative. Information on extramural programs is found in the *Resource Manual*.

QUESTIONS FOR DISCUSSION

1. Briefly discuss the role of intramural programs in today's society.
2. Identify and explain the objectives of intramural sports.
3. Differentiate among the types of intramurals and list three suitable activities for each type.
4. Briefly explain the different units of team organization. Indicate which unit may be most suitable for a large school and why.
5. What time factors should be considered when scheduling intramurals?
6. What types of competition are possible for intramural sports? What are the advantages of each type?
7. Indicate some motivational strategies that encourage student participation in the program.
8. What is the main criterion for a meaningful intramural program?
9. List several regulations that should be employed to insure an organized and effective program.
10. What influence should Title IX have on the intramural program?
11. Distinguish between intramurals and extramurals and indicate the importance of each.
12. You are to assume the job of intramural director. Prepare a general outline that indicates the areas to be considered when planning for a successful program.

REFERENCES

1. Louis E. Means, *Intramurals,* 2nd ed. (Englewood Cliffs: Prentice-Hall, 1973), p. 28.
2. Len Horyza, "Are Officials Necessary?" *JOPER* (February, 1977), p. 33.
3. "Half the Physical Education Grade is Based on Outside Activity," *Physical Education Newsletter* (Old Saybrook, Conn.: Physical Education Publications, January 15, 1976).
4. Pamela Gunsten, "Intramurals — The Christianburg Way," *JOPER* (March, 1974), p. 51.
5. "Keeping Records of Participation to Validate the Justification for Extracurricular Physical Education," *Physical Education Newsletter* (Old Saybrook, Conn.: Physical Education Publications, February 1, 1975).
6. Means, *op. cit.,* p. 153.
7. *Ibid.,* p. 154.
8. Means, *op. cit.,* p. 137.

9. Francis M. Rokosz, *Structured Intramurals* (Philadelphia: W. B. Saunders Company, 1975), p. 53.

SELECTED READINGS

Daughtrey, Greyson and John Woods, *Physical Education and Intramural Programs, Organization and Administration* (Philadelphia: W. B. Saunders Company, 1976).

Hyatt, Ronald W., *Intramural Sports, Organization and Administration* (Saint Louis: C. V. Mosby Company, 1977).

"Intramurals," *JOHPER* (February, 1977).

Means, Louis E., *Intramurals, Their Organization and Administration* (Englewood Cliffs, New Jersey: Prentice-Hall, 1973).

Rokosz, Francis M., *Structured Intramurals* (Philadelphia: W. B. Saunders Company, 1975).

Chapter 12

Courtesy Athens Academy, Athens, Georgia

PLURAL PUBLICS
    COMMUNITY
    ADMINISTRATION
    FACULTY
    STUDENTS
    PHYSICAL EDUCATION TEACHERS
COMMUNITY POWER STRUCTURES
OBJECTIVES OF SCHOOL-COMMUNITY
RELATIONS
GENERAL GUIDELINES FOR
SCHOOL-COMMUNITY RELATIONS
SPECIFIC GUIDELINES FOR REACHING THE
PUBLICS
    UNDERTAKE RESPONSIBILITY FOR
      SCHOOL-COMMUNITY RELATIONS
    KNOW THE RELATIONSHIP OF
      PHYSICAL EDUCATION TO HEALTH
    EDUCATE THE PLURAL PUBLICS
    UNDERSTAND THE IMPORTANCE OF
      HUMAN RELATIONS
    REALIZE THE NEED FOR PLANNING
    BECOME ACQUAINTED WITH THE
      POWER STRUCTURE
COMMUNICATION WITH THE PLURAL PUBLICS
    STUDENTS
    TELEVISION AND RADIO
    NEWSPAPERS
    SPEAKERS
    ASSEMBLY PROGRAMS
    DEMONSTRATIONS
    PARENT-STUDENT PROGRAMS
    HANDBOOKS
    SPECIAL PUBLICATIONS
    TOURS

    SPONSORS
    BULLETIN BOARDS
    VISITS
INTERPRETING PHYSICAL EDUCATION
    CRUCIAL ISSUES
      QUALITY INSTRUCTION
      BALANCED CURRICULUM
      PHYSICAL EDUCATION REQUIREMENT
      CREDIT FOR PHYSICAL EDUCATION
      TEACHER PREPARATION
      ADEQUATE FACILITIES
      OBJECTIVES OF PHYSICAL EDUCATION
      NORMAL TEACHING LOADS
      DEVELOPMENT OF SCIENTIFIC
        PROGRAMS
      BALANCED INTERSCHOOL ATHLETIC
        PROGRAMS
      MOTIVATION OF THE PLAY URGE
      IMPROVEMENT OF
        SCHOOL-COMMUNITY RELATIONS
      COMMUNITY PRESSURE GROUPS
      PRESTIGE
      UNANIMITY OF PURPOSE
AGENCIES AND SCHOOL-COMMUNITY
RELATIONS
    PHYSICAL EDUCATION PUBLIC
      INFORMATION (PEPI)
    PRESIDENT'S COUNCIL FOR PHYSICAL
      FITNESS AND SPORTS
SCHOOL-COLLEGE RELATIONS
QUESTIONS FOR DISCUSSION
REFERENCES
SUGGESTED READINGS

SCHOOL-COMMUNITY RELATIONS

For ten years, Gallup Polls have attempted to identify people's attitudes regarding public schools. The 1978 survey revealed that parents' lack of interest in the schools is one of the major problems in education.[1] From a national survey, Cutlip and Center compiled evidence that also showed lack of interest in and inadequate knowledge of public schools. They found that 30 per cent of those interviewed were unaware of the number of high-school dropouts; 33 per cent did not know what proportion of high school graduates enrolled in college; and 37 per cent did not know the yearly per capita cost to educate a student.[2]

Because of higher taxes and the rising costs of education, citizens are becoming increasingly concerned with the financial structure of the public school system. A few years ago, Atkinson outlined some of the major concerns of parents when they were asked to support education. He found that they wanted to be better informed — to understand modern trends, methods and innovations, and to know what the schools were trying to accomplish and to what extent the goals were being reached. Atkinson concluded that school personnel must be receptive to public opinion and use the feedback for future action.[3] These views are still valid although the educational situation today is much more complex.

Upheavals in the American social structure throughout the past 50 years have been reflected in the educational system. Decreased teacher morale, inadequate facilities, sub-standard instruction, and, in some instances, school closings have been results of certain national trends.

Public support for education is more crucial now than ever before because of the many sensitive issues that confront this country. Public schools are directly involved with busing, integration, drug abuse, and other social and moral questions. In addition, teachers and administrators must face public and student criticism concerning the curriculum. For instance, there is grave concern regarding equal educational opportunity for minority groups, special education for the handicapped, and the inclusion of controversial subjects such as sex education, in standard school programs.

Relationships between schools and communities are mutually supportive: the schools rely on the taxpayer for monetary support and the taxpayers rely on the schools for the education of their children. Community support of the school system is vital to the survival of education, as Nagle makes clear:

> The simple fact is that an American public school district is so dependent upon its public for support, financial and otherwise, that it commits educational hara-kiri when it neglects the public, isolates itself from the community, leaves its citizenry either misinformed or completely uninformed.[4]

Leaders in physical education have probably been more derelict in seeking public endorsement than have leaders in other fields of study. It is ironic that at a time when health and fitness are recognized as being of paramount importance, many schools still relegate physical education to a secondary role. Most programs are very lenient, and some not only fail to contribute to the development of youth but adversely affect their health and fitness.

As stated in Chapter 1, considerable evidence points to both the correlation between a high level of fitness and academic achievement and the importance of physical education for normal growth and development. Chapter 1 also shows evidence that physical education programs in which students can experience success can reduce the incidence of delinquency and antisocial behavior. The future of these programs depends on the work of dedicated teachers who respect physical education and see it as a chance to develop good health and fitness habits in all people, young *and* old.

Because of tight budgets and public dissatisfaction, all phases of education are under scrutiny and the value of some traditional academic programs is being questioned. In order to remain attuned to a changing society, school administrators are continually attempting to reassess student needs and to develop new curricula around them. The application of this concept to physical education is relatively simple. The contributions that a good program makes to health and fitness should theoretically make physical education an inherent and irreplaceable part of the educational system.

Why, then, is the future of physical education uncertain? The answer lies in the failure of its leaders to interpret its purposes to the public. A strong professional relationship among teachers, administrators, college authorities and an organized presentation of the program to the community are fundamental to the success of physical education. This chapter describes ways in which various public relations media can be used to involve citizens in physical education.

PLURAL PUBLICS

It is misleading to regard *the public* as one large, all-inclusive body. An infinite number of publics exists, and varying opinions are found both among and within these different factions. Public relations, or the act of influencing public opinion, can be successful only if it reaches a wide range of these interest groups.

Many of the problems confronting physical education can be resolved if the schools design their public relations strategies so that numerous influential groups in society are contacted. Two-way communication should be established and maintained between powerful public groups and school administrators.

Community. Every community has organizations that are concerned with the operation of the schools. Civic clubs, parent-teacher organizations, youth groups, church-affiliated groups, chambers of commerce, medical associations, public health organizations, patriotic agencies, business and industry, fraternal groups, and various health, cultural, and governmental agencies frequently assume active roles in the educational network.

Administration. Principals, instructional directors, coordinators, supervisors, assistant superintendents, and superintendents compose the administration. Many administrators are academically oriented and therefore are sometimes unaware of the importance of physical education. These individuals must be apprised of the need for a well-planned physical education program and the relevance of such a program to healthy growth and development. The media used to reach this group might be entirely different from those used to reach the general public.

Faculty. Although the faculty in a particular school is not directly responsible for designing the program, it can influence the value and integrity of physical education by showing respect for the subject and the teacher. Physical educators who implement a well-organized program and who strive to improve will favorably impress other teachers and inspire them to support the program. School faculties should be kept informed about the physical education curriculum through the use of announcements, bulletins, and other materials.

Students. The student body is the most important interest group. If they understand the program and their need for it, they will cooperate more willingly and benefit more directly from the instruction.

A recent survey of New Hampshire public high school students revealed widespread ignorance as to the preparatory value of physical education for adulthood. When 852 students were asked which fields of study contribute most to a good adult life, physical education ranked fifth out of eight, as shown in Figure 12–1.[5] Why should a subject that promotes health and fitness not receive a number one rating? The answer is obvious: teachers and administrators have not interpreted the program to the community. The product is excellent, but it has not been sold.

Physical Education Teachers. Physical educators are key figures in school-community relations. It is their responsibility to acquaint parents and the public with the role that physical education plays in bodily and mental development.

School-community relations can be no more effective than the teachers. Enthusiastic, knowledgeable leaders can instill respect and understanding of the program in the students, who in turn describe the program to their parents.

	All per cent	Female per cent	Male per cent
Practical arts	43	42	43
Social studies	14	14	14
English	12	15	10
Science	8	9	8
Physical education	8	6	10
Mathematics	6	4	8
Fine arts	4	5	3
Foreign language	2	3	1
No response	3	2	3

Figure 12–1. How various fields of study contribute to the good life. (From Draves, David D., "Student Opinions: Cause for Reflection," *Phi Delta Kappan*, September, 1977, p. 68.)

Items Conducive to Quality Instruction	Yes	No
Do my students show interest and satisfaction in the program?	( )	( )
Do I have an enthusiastic approach to teaching?	( )	( )
Do I provide individual instruction?	( )	( )
Do I explain the values of each activity?	( )	( )
Do I vary program content?	( )	( )
Do I provide ways for each student to attain a degree of success?	( )	( )
Do I group students by ability?	( )	( )
Do I set examples in morality, character, and fitness that students admire?	( )	( )
Do I practice what I preach regarding sportsmanship?	( )	( )
Do I actually teach rather than "throw out the ball"?	( )	( )
Do I use all available time for instruction?	( )	( )
Do I publish periodicals showing the purposes of physical education?	( )	( )
Do I solicit civic groups to sponsor programs?	( )	( )
Do I arrange for programs to be shown before civic clubs, parent groups, and on television?	( )	( )
Do I plan tournaments and demonstrations involving many students?	( )	( )
Do I invite parents and influential citizens to make comments at demonstrations?	( )	( )
Do I spend as much time planning and improving instruction as I do coaching?	( )	( )

Figure 12–2. A checklist for appraising teaching effectiveness.

This interpretation is an extremely effective public relations tool. The impact of the program on students can be determined through the use of a checklist, an example of which is shown in Figure 12–2. If the teacher can answer these questions affirmatively, he or she can assume that the students respect and admire him or her. If students are satisfied with their teacher and the program in general, they will refer to the program in favorable terms to their parents and to others.

COMMUNITY POWER STRUCTURES

In most communities and cities, a few individuals constitute the power base. In the past, it was thought that the power resided in the general public, but recent studies show this to be misleading. Relatively few people constitute the power structure and wield final authority over public affairs. Those who devise the public relations program should understand the organization of power and try to reach those who have ultimate authority over public functions.

Teachers and administrators need to have an organized public relations strategy that can induce public opinion to support quality education. The goal, of course, is to improve education and thereby to improve society. This objective provides a foundation for school-community cooperation, based on a two-way communication system through which each group acquaints the other with its needs. It is considered a good public relations approach for the people representing the schools to have clearly established objectives toward which they can direct public opinion.

OBJECTIVES OF SCHOOL-COMMUNITY RELATIONS

Predetermined goals for school-community relations can be used to evaluate the program and to assist in determining the progress made in reaching the desired goals. The following objectives are helpful:

1. *People should be aware of the purposes of physical education in a democratic culture.* These should be interpreted with emphasis on the importance of physical education to the survival of our country. Representatives from various organizations within the community should be involved in developing the curriculum in order to become acquainted with the objectives of physical education.
2. *School-community relations should develop deeper insight into and understanding of the physical education curriculum.* This can be accomplished by actual presentation of teaching methods that show the influence of instruction on the growth and development of students. (Practical use of the media outlined in this chapter can facilitate this.)
3. *Parents should be periodically apprised of the status and performance of their children.* Parents want to know of the progress and accomplishments of their children and how these achievements compare with those of other children. (More information on reporting physical education to parents is shown in Chapter 13.)
4. *School-community relations programs should acquaint the publics with the problems facing physical education.* Crowded classes, inadequate facilities, poor equipment, and ineffective instruction should be exposed and explained.
5. *The community should be informed of the results attained in the existing teaching setting.* Through the use of appropriate media, parents can learn how much is being accomplished in spite of handicaps and obstacles.
6. *The value of physical education to our country should be re-emphasized.* The publics should be made to realize that the most powerful nation on earth attained its status through the efforts of millions of people who received their education in the nation's schools. The role of physical education in developing the health and fitness that are aspects of this country's greatness should be shown.
7. *Citizens should understand the responsibilities of physical education teachers.* This is more important today than in the past both because of the great demands made on teachers in a changing society and because of the increased cost of education.
8. *School-community relations programs should encourage citizens to assume a greater responsibility for instituting quality instruction.* This can be done by showing citizens that the solution to many problems in our society depends on public support of education. Enlisting groups to sponsor various activities is one way to achieve this objective.
9. School-community relationships should take the form of a two-way communication system. This can be accomplished by initiating a partnership between parents and teachers, promoting the cooperative efforts of schools and publics, and providing joint planning committees for parents and teachers.

GENERAL GUIDELINES FOR SCHOOL-COMMUNITY RELATIONS

Physical education programs have several different aspects, each of which can be of tremendous interest to the public if it is presented properly. The very magnitude of most programs necessitates the formulation of basic principles that will guide teachers in their attempts to interpret the program to the community.

School-community relations cannot operate in an erratic or haphazard manner. Every contact that teachers have with the students, parents, and community affects attitudes toward the teacher, the physical education program, and the school. Atkinson has compiled a list of guidelines that is helpful to the teacher in formulating a school-community relations program:

1. Decisions relating to communication should be based on an understanding of the community the school serves.
2. The communication activity should involve many individuals.
3. A knowledge of the social and behavioral sciences will help school personnel to plan effective communication.
4. Communication should be so designed that messages reach the desired audience and arouse the intended response.
5. The impact of a communication is influenced by the attention it receives, the source from which it comes, and the action it proposes.
6. The outcome of communication is measured by the tenor of the feedback obtained.[6]

SPECIFIC GUIDELINES FOR REACHING THE PUBLICS

General guidelines establish a foundation for sound school-community cooperation. However, teachers should also devise some simple but specific guidelines to assist them in promoting the program. Because physical education has such an important relationship with community health, these guidelines should be fully understood by the teachers before any public relations plan is initiated. Teachers must first educate themselves in every facet of the program before attempting to interpret it to others.

Undertake Responsibility for School-Community Relations. The key to successful school-community relations is the teacher. He or she should initiate a sound program of instruction that challenges the student, appeals to

parents, and satisfies the taxpayer. Teachers must justify the need for and the importance of the program to parents, administrators, and the public. Those who have daily contact with parents and other citizens have an opportunity to gain support for their profession. Teachers will find that the following practices help to develop rapport between the school and the community:

1. Belong to community groups and become involved in various committee projects. These groups will eventually become valuable allies of the school.
2. Seek the support of diverse groups and individuals by inviting them to speak to classes, participate in school programs, and assist in planning the program.
3. Be available to talk before various clubs on topics such as physical fitness, exercise and health, and the importance of learning leisure-time skills. (Some of the material discussed in Chapter 1 should be presented to clubs and other organizations.)
4. Become acquainted with the criticisms aimed at physical education and be prepared to counter them with scientific information showing the need for the program.
5. Be able to justify some of the demands made by physical education leaders, such as school requirements and credits and adequate money for facilities, equipment, and supplies.
6. Study public relations media and plan their usage in interpreting the program to the public.

Know the Relationship of Physical Education to Health. Programs in physical education instruction need revitalization. Facts are available from various sources that reveal widespread malnutrition, the need for more exercise, and the urgency of educating citizens in healthier use of their leisure time. Although advances in medical science have virtually eliminated many diseases and have lengthened our life span, the incidence of heart disease, emotional instability, and certain geriatric ailments is increasing. The correlation between general health conditions and physical fitness must be emphasized to community leaders. The important contribution that physical education programs make in preventing and combating such conditions must be proved to the public.

Educate the Plural Publics. Although the exchange of ideas among physical educators is desirable, it is more important to reach general educators, parents, and community because in the final analysis they control the progress of the educational curriculum.

Understand the Importance of Human Relations. Teachers must be aware of the need to establish good human relations. They must be unselfish, cooperative, understanding, and capable of working with the citizenry. Teachers should never allow personal prejudices to influence their professional efforts and sway them into decisions and actions that jeopardize their public relations program.

Realize the Need for Planning. Planning is a requisite for successful school-community relations. To insure the survival of physical education, teachers must base their instruction on skills and activities that are meaningful to the students, the administrators, and the public. Teachers need to establish goals, evaluate the existing program, determine the media to be used, select the activities that reflect the needs for physical education, and assess the existing methods for interpreting physical education before they initiate new programs in school-community relations.

Become Acquainted with the Power Structure. Although it may be difficult, teachers should know the people who make up the power structure and should apprise them of the objectives of physical education before attempting to gain community endorsement.

COMMUNICATION WITH THE PLURAL PUBLICS

Teachers who understand the program and have carefully planned their in-struction are prepared to explain physical education to one or all of the publics. Determining how citizens can be reached is a problem; any publicity must reflect the philosophy and objectives of physical education and its connection to good health. The media that teachers choose must convey the message in such a manner that the various interest groups will understand and support the efforts of teachers and administrators.

Communication channels must be established between the school and the community groups. This, of course, requires educational leadership. When there is a specific individual or committee to whom the public can address itself, lines of communication can be fairly easily established.

Students. Students are an important interest group, but they also serve as effective public relations agents. When students enjoy a well-organized and well-taught physical education class, the attitudes they exhibit at home have tremendous positive value.

For the instruction to be meaningful to students, objectives must be explained and the purpose of each phase of the program must be clarified. The value of the lesson should be measured in terms of student needs — what the lesson does to and for them. Students should realize that instruction in the skills of various activities can help them become better adjusted to the rigors of adult life.

Television and Radio. Television can be of tremendous value in presenting physical education programs to the public. In 1977, a *Phi Delta Kappan* survey revealed that 45 per cent of the respondents obtained most of their information from television. (Other sources, listed in order of priority, were newspapers, schools, families, radios, magazines, and friends.)[7]

Planning and airing original television shows is an effective way to reach the people who rely on this medium for local news. For example, considerable interest can be created by a program depicting students participating in sports and activities learned in physical education class. Television and radio are also the most efficient media for reaching large numbers of people. Although not as popular as it was before the advent of television, radio is unequaled for the presentation of information in spot announcements.

Newspapers. The newspaper is another efficient means for communicating with the various interest groups simultaneously. Newspapers can be used for reporting results of various events, such as tournaments, intramural meets, or specific activities involving more than one school. Because news articles reach such a large, diversified audience, the value of this medium should never be underestimated. It can provide a written record of physical education events and has special appeal to both students and parents, who enjoy seeing their names in print.

Although parents have indicated a preference for reading about various aspects of instruction, adequate space is usually not devoted to this in the newspapers. In 1966, Ovard proved this in a survey. He ranked 13 topics of school news according to the interest expressed by parents and compared this rating to the space allotted to them in the leading newspapers.[8] The results are shown in Figure 12–3.

Student progress and achievement ranked first in parental interest but ranked fourth in the amount of space devoted to it. Extracurricular activities ranked 13th in parental interest but received the most news coverage. Physical education teachers should learn the procedures of reporting and attempt to get adequate space in the news to satisfy the public.

School newspapers reach a smaller, more selective group than public newspapers, but good school publications are important for reaching parents, teachers, and students.

Speakers. Teachers of physical education can appear before civic clubs and parent-teacher groups to explain the purpose of physical education. Visual aids or student demonstrations are useful in reinforcing certain concepts. Speeches by physical education teach-

Topics of School News	Rank According to Patron's Interest	Space in News
Student progress and achievement	1	4
Method of instruction	2	10
Curriculum	3	6
Health of students	4	9
Value of education	5	12
Discipline and behavior of students	6	11
Teachers and school officials	7	2
Attendance	8	13
Building and building program	9	8
Business management, finance	10	7
Board of education and administration	11	5
P.T.A.	12	3
Extracurricular activities	13	1

Figure 12–3. Comparison of parent's interest and space in news. (From Ovard, Glen F., *Administration of the Changing Secondary School*, New York: Macmillan, 1966, p. 453.)

ers or directors are usually most effective when made before small groups.

Teachers can also enlist the assistance of outstanding speakers in the city, acquaint them with the objectives of physical education, and arrange for them to appear before various organizations within the city.

Assembly Programs. Assembly programs are an excellent medium for educating students and teachers. A tumbling demonstration or a simple play or skit illustrating how physical education instruction is conducted can play a vital role in public relations.

Demonstrations. Demonstrations involving many students can be effective in publicizing physical education. Not only can demonstrations provide an overview of the physical education offering, but in addition they can give parents and other groups a realistic, first-hand insight into the objectives and content of the physical education curriculum. A further discussion of demonstrations is found in Chapter 11.

Parent-Student Programs.   Some teachers have been successful in developing programs in which parents and their children meet in the school for playdays, award ceremonies, banquets, and similar occasions. The program is planned to allow parents and children to participate together.

Handbooks.   The handbook is a relatively new medium of public relations. It is inexpensive to publish and extremely effective. At the beginning of each term, teachers can send this handbook home with the students and ask parents to send their comments back to the school.

Special Publications.   Certain publications are aimed at a particular audience and are presented in a more sophisticated manner than a handbook or a newsletter. This medium should be used to reach members of the power structure and other key individuals in the community.

Tours.   One week during the year can be set aside for various groups to visit the schools and see what is being accomplished in physical education. Arrangements can be made to take groups to the different schools in the district, where they can actually witness classes in progress. The school bus or a chartered bus can transport entire groups to the schools; a sponsor might be procured to defray the cost of transportation.

Sponsors.   Bringing the community into the physical education program is a powerful public relations tactic. Not only does this allow particular groups to feel they have a role in the program, but their material assistance with the operation of the program is invaluable. Sometimes individual sponsors in the community are able to provide tremendous assistance in promoting physical

education. Don Nizza, a citizen of Paterson, New Jersey, and owner of a personnel agency in Ridgewood, developed a unique school-community public relations program. The goal was to improve the physical education program in the area. Nizza sent 380 questionnaires to physical education teachers, administrators, school board members, and sports writers asking specific questions about the public schools in New Jersey. The fundamental question was, "Does the average layman understand the objectives of good physical education?" Out of 101 responses, the breakdown was:

No	92.0 per cent
Probably not	3.0 per cent
Yes	2.5 per cent
Don't know	2.5 per cent

Nizza discussed many of the facets of the program and their shortcomings in several articles in the local newspaper. He enlightened the public about physical fitness, professional standards, analysis of the curriculum, and the difference between physical education and athletics. Nizza felt that the respondents to his questionnaire had frankly reported things they would not have told educators. Many of them also wrote in and analyzed the condition of physical education in the schools.[9] Other questions and replies found in Nizza's study are included in the *Resource Manual*.

Sponsored surveys can be very helpful to both the schools and the public. Feedback on specific items helps teachers to improve their immediate programs and to plan programs for the future.

Bulletin Boards.   Bulletin boards are an excellent medium for presenting the program to students, teachers, and parents. The bulletin board may be planned by a group of students working with the teachers. Artistic displays such as announcements of activities, results of contests, and pictures of students in action can be used to portray the program. Many phases of the program are adaptable to such visual presentation.

Visits.   Scheduling time for parents to visit the school and to watch students in classes is an easy way to acquaint them with physical education. Students in each class are asked to carry notices home to parents, inviting them to the school during the period in which the student is scheduled for physical education. This allows the parent to see his child perform without spending a lot of time at the school. Because only a small group of parents visits any one class, seating is easily arranged. Other publicity techniques should be incorporated; bulletin boards should be decorated, notices and exhibits placed at strategic spots, and educational material given to the parents to take home.

INTERPRETING PHYSICAL EDUCATION

Organized interpretation of the program has unlimited public relations value for physical education. In order for the program to appeal to the public, those presenting it must know the various principles of learning, teaching methods, and class procedures. Student motivation will automatically be incited by a good teaching program, and this interest will further extend into the home, where good public relations is needed most.

Klappholz summarized the variety of available instructional strategies that assist in exposing the program to the community:

1. Give all students an opportunity to achieve status and recognition. Set up honor rolls and halls of fame. Post the names of students who qualify for these particular honors.
2. Award patches, ribbons, crests, and certificates for outstanding performance, effort, and participation in intramurals and class activities. If possible, make these presentations at assemblies or at other times when a large number of students are present.
3. Allow students to participate in planning class and extracurricular activities. This does not mean that you surrender your role as teacher. Rather, it suggests that you should give students an opportunity to voice their opinions and contribute their ideas.
4. Provide opportunities for student choice within prescribed limits by using selectives, contracting, and independent study approaches.
5. Offer a variety of different activities each year at each level so that every boy and girl

will have an opportunity to do something he or she likes and can do successfully once or twice during the year.
6. Give many youngsters an opportunity to assume leadership roles as squad leaders, exercise leaders, station leaders and so on. Do not let just the few top students monopolize these positions. Recognize that many youngsters can benefit from leadership activities and the responsibility they involve.
7. Find a way of complimenting every student for a job well done at least once or twice during the year. However, be sure that you are sincere in your praise and that there is a valid reason for it.[10]

Crucial Issues

In addition to acquainting students and parents with the objectives of physical education, there are major issues that involve interpretation on a broader scale. Physical education teachers and leaders have been concerned about several crucial aspects of general educational planning that have had adverse effects on the physical education program. These concerns have grown out of the pressures and misunderstandings to which physical education has been subjected for many years. Because of these pressures, many programs have become weak, unscientific, and aimless. Teachers should be aware of these issues and should develop plans to explain them to the public in the interest of resolving them.

Quality Instruction. Dr. Albert Ayars, Superintendent of Norfolk Public Schools, stated frankly that quality instruction is essential to physical education:

Yours is a most important job. It must be done well. I am aware that most of you have done it well. But in times of change and social unrest such as you have gone through during the past ten years, some teachers have a tendency to let down, become frustrated, give in to discouragement, to do the job half-way — lackadaisically. We cannot afford this.[11]

Teachers should assist their peers in developing quality instructional programs and in acquainting administrators with what a quality program means. Many principals and administrators, having experienced poor programs throughout their academic lives, are unaware of what a superior program entails. This can

Figure 12-4. Quality instruction provides the best medium for school-community relations. Courtesy Venice High School, Los Angeles City Schools.

be remedied by studying quality programs and simultaneously interpreting the true objectives of physical education.

Balanced Curriculum. Periodically, curriculum changes and revisions are made in order to meet new academic objectives. The need for more class time in academic subjects or the addition of new programs sometimes results in the relegation of physical education to an insecure or obscure niche in the general curriculum. For instance, in many localities, physical education teaching stations have been reassigned to expanding academic programs. Physical education classes have been uprooted and assigned to study halls or other inadequate locations.

It is not a sound educational procedure to increase the instructional offering in one subject at the expense of another area of instruction. It is the duty of administrators to provide enough time, space, and teachers to upgrade *all* instructional fields. Teachers can assist in improving physical education by developing a communications system to inform the admin-

istrators and the community of the instructional content and of its importance to the students.

Physical Education Requirement. If a subject is to maintain a permanent place in the curriculum, it must be classified as required. Because promoting good health is a basic objective of education in general, physical education should be a required course.

As a result of the emphasis placed on physical fitness by the President's Council for Physical Fitness and Sports, many parochial and private schools have increased their physical education offerings. The public school requirement, however, has remained about the same.

Credit for Physical Education. Offering credit for physical education adds meaning and credence to the program. Very few school systems grant credit for physical education comparable to that given for academic subjects. This practice suggests that the program has an inferior status and causes students to lose respect for it.

If physical education is to assume the

importance that it logically should, credit comparable to that accorded to other subjects must be granted. This will come about only when the teaching program is of a caliber that deserves such recognition.

Teacher Preparation. Teachers who are adequately prepared for their chosen fields have little difficulty in doing an effective job. However, too frequently teachers enter the profession not only lacking knowledge of many activities but also unprepared to teach skills to large groups. This is particularly true in teaching the skills of individual sports, such as golf, tennis, tumbling, swimming, and wrestling. Teachers are usually able to instruct small groups of five or six students, but problems arise when the teachers have a class of 50 students. They almost invariably attempt to teach only a few students while the remaining students are idle. This procedure creates disciplinary problems and renders the instruction ineffective. This and other shortcomings in the teacher can be avoided through thorough professional preparation. Colleges and universities that train future teachers are attempting to improve their programs, and these efforts should be intensified.

Pease and Crase noted the importance of teacher preparation in the statement that "teacher education is the heart of the education system: nearly every criticism in education can be traced back to the preparatory process."[12]

Adequate Facilities. Although adequate facilities are necessary for effective instruction in physical education, few American schools provide teaching facilities comparable to those for the academic program. The science department in a high school with 1200 students probably has a classroom and a teacher for every 150 students. A school of this size should have at least six stations and six teachers for physical education, based on 40 students per teacher, five periods per day, with one free period. Very few schools have such an arrangement.

However, teachers should not use inadequate facilities as an excuse for poor teaching. Instead, they should learn to improvise and to use the existing facilities

as effectively as possible. It is only by using inadequate facilities to their best advantage that the teacher will be able to justify the demand for better facilities.

Objectives of Physical Education. Teachers need to have clearly defined objectives if the program is to be effective. They often launch or are launched into a program without established goals; too often, the program will follow tradition rather than attempt to satisfy current needs. Selection of activities that are outdated and possibly injurious occurs because objectives were not developed adequately.

Normal Teaching Loads. If physical educators are expected to do a satisfactory job, they must have a teaching load comparable to that of teachers of other subjects in the curriculum. Physical education teachers are frequently given 50, 70, or 100 students per period to teach. Both the practicality and the safety of teaching such large classes are questionable. Students' safety should always be of primary concern to the teacher, and it is unfair to expect a teacher to be responsible for the safety of unreasonably large classes. Again, teachers should not use overcrowding as an excuse for incompetent instruction. They should continually strive to remedy the situation; until the conditions are improved, the teachers should do their best by using newer methods of organization to meet the challenge of large classes.

Development of Scientific Programs. Because physical education has such a pronounced effect on health, teachers should strive to include in the curriculum only those activities that are best suited to the developmental needs of students.

Programs in the past often consisted of group exercises. Teachers did all the planning and gave the directions, affording students little opportunity either to express themselves or to develop their physical potential. The emphasis was on developing muscle; little if any thought was given to the close relationship of physical, mental, and emotional growth. Those programs became unpopular because students began to question the value of constantly lifting weights, chinning the bar, and performing calisthenics. However, many teachers today still feel that developing strength is the sole objective of the physical education program.

Some of these unnatural programs are detrimental to the progress that physical education in general has made in this country. Many individuals and groups, aided by manufacturers of various contrivances for use in physical education classrooms, cause irreparable damage to the integrity of physical education and prevent students from receiving the type of instruction they should have. Leaders in physical education must take a stand against such procedures because they are unscientific, unrealistic, and unnatural.

One of the most difficult problems in physical education is the implementation of the empirical approach to content selection. Decisions made without scientific background have an adverse effect on the curriculum. An example is the teacher who, during high school and college, was an outstanding basketball player. In his or her opinion, basketball should dominate the program because he or she likes it. This point of view might cause the teacher to exclude from the curriculum such carry-over activities as tennis, bowling, golf, and swimming. A program based entirely on the individual whims of an administrator, coach, or physical education teacher is completely without scientific foundation.

Balanced Interschool Athletic Programs. Interschool athletics are an important part of the school program, and teachers should develop schedules and encourage student participation. It is unfortunate, however, when the interscholastic program dominates the physical education curriculum. Too often pressure is placed on coaches to win contests. If coaches also teach physical education, they sometimes neglect the instructional program by using class time for varsity practice, or using students in various classes as practice opponents for varsity players. Teachers who coach also frequently use instructional time to plan schedules, view films of games, and plan strategies for future games. These diversions result in neglect of the students. Many physical education programs

throughout the country have suffered because of these practices.

Physical education should not be confused with interschool athletics. Athletics are for the gifted few; physical education is designed for everyone. Physical education is an instructional program; interschool athletics are extracurricular activities. There is a place and a need for both programs in the schools, and with thoughtful administration and supervision, the two programs can complement each other successfully.

Motivation of the Play Urge. The play urge should be stimulated by the physical education program. Some people feel that the urge for physical activity is diminishing; when one observes the ways in which many teenagers spend their time, it is hard to disagree. High school students seem to prefer entertainment involving sitting, riding, and viewing to activities requiring a great deal of movement. At some point in their lives, the urge for play and physical activity has been discouraged or inhibited, either because of poor, artificial physical education programs or because of the lack of any program at all. Teachers must implement organized programs of physical education based on the needs and interests of students from the first grade on through high school. The play urge is instinctive, but it must be continually motivated during the school years if students are to remain physically active throughout life.

Improvement of School-Community Relations. A well-planned public relations program is the most forceful way of explaining the purposes of physical education to the public. Athletic programs are self-perpetuating, but instructional programs in physical education are rarely exposed to the public. Public administrators, teachers, parents, and students alike should be shown why physical education is essential to any educational program and basic to personal fitness and health. These objectives should be discussed, and the manner in which the program attempts to reach these objectives should be explained. When teachers are able to prove that the quality of students' lives after school and after graduation has been improved through physical education, the programs will assume the desired level of recognition and authority in the school and the community.

A well-informed and interested public is desirable if schools are to enjoy the public support that they need in order to function. The public has never been overly concerned with physical education programs. Indeed, evidence indicates that the public is not particularly concerned with health in general. A case in point is cigarette smoking — despite the overwhelming evidence pointing to the high correlation between excessive smoking and lung cancer, smoking is still a common habit.

Even though adults are sometimes negligent in their own health habits, they are usually concerned with the health of their children. Physical education teachers need to interpret the program sufficiently to parents. Teachers should have a knowledge of up-to-date health practices that will enable them to assist students in the formation of correct health habits. These procedures will eventually reach the home and help to direct public opinion toward greater interest in health and fitness and support for physical education programs.

Community Pressure Groups.   Community groups are influential in assisting the public schools with their many problems. These groups should therefore be kept informed of the content of the physical education program. Sometimes local groups become enthusiastic about certain activities and pressure school authorities to include them in the curriculum. Teachers and administrators should be aware of this trend and attempt to show influential groups how certain activities are beneficial whereas others may be injurious to the health and fitness of students.

Physical education can affect the health of young people as seriously as a regimen prescribed by a doctor, and thus the wrong prescription of exercise or activity can have an adverse effect on health. Community groups that seek to amend the curriculum should have a working knowledge of most exercises and their application in classes.

Prestige.   The status that a program enjoys in the school curriculum tremendously affects the quality of teaching.

Physical education has not occupied the same level of prestige as the academic subjects since the days of ancient Greek civilization. This is partially because of the nature of the subject itself and the types of programs that have dominated its instruction for many years. Where physical education is organized properly and taught effectively, and where the content is in keeping with recognized objectives, the program is appreciated and respected.

It is the teacher's responsibility to elicit attitudes that will foster prestige. The teacher's grooming, speech, and personality, and his or her effectiveness in interpreting the program will determine the respect that physical education receives from the community.

Physical education teachers should explore fields of knowledge in their profession with their colleagues. Leaders might discuss such items as why the law of reciprocal innervation is violated in an isometric movement or why the principle of opposition is not followed in fencing. Discussing such topics can help the teachers understand their own fields better; moreover, it will help to dispel the fallacy that there is no depth of content in physical education. Programs of physical education have important implications that permeate other phases of education, but teachers too often fail to include these implications in their "shop talk" with teachers of other disciplines.

Another factor involved in developing prestige is the use of professional terminology. Sometimes teachers and administrators refer to the physical education program as *gym* or *fizz-ed*. These terms are not at all descriptive or complimentary. Physical education teachers should continually use the proper terminology when referring to their discipline.

Unanimity of Purpose.   Individual college instructors play an important role in determining the philosophy of physical education. However, there is no common philosophy for preparing students for teaching that exists among certain institutions of higher education. Some teacher-preparation programs are dominated by athletic activities; some emphasize recreation; others stress gymnastics with emphasis on calisthenics and the apparatus. More colleges should offer intensive instruction in how to teach the important carry-over sports such as tennis, golf, wrestling, bowling, and swimming, which are basic to the achievement of current objectives in physical education.

In certain teacher-training programs, the approach has been to present two points of view and to allow students to make their own decisions. Students must be prepared to make responsible choices; successful teaching cannot exist on indecision. If there is one phase of the educational curriculum in which unanimity of purpose is needed, it is in physical education. Teachers must know what is considered the correct method of teaching a skill. It is possible that research, at a later date, may improve on this procedure; but until this happens, there is only one correct method at a given moment.

As an example, examine the procedure for teaching the front somersault in tumbling. It is generally accepted that a performer must tuck neatly at just the right moment. There is also a precise moment for coming out of the tuck and landing in the upright position. Failure to teach the somersault *correctly* might very well result in an accident. If the teacher does not emphasize the urgency of tucking properly, the performer may land on his neck or incur another serious injury. Accident statistics reveal many tragedies resulting from improper teaching procedures.

Establishing a basic philosophy in physical education is not difficult. If research and logic show that natural activities involving fundamental body movements are essential for normal growth and development, all teachers should emphasize such activities. If certain calisthenic and gymnastic movements are unsafe and do not contribute to normal physiologic growth and development, all teachers should understand why. Criteria for selecting the healthiest and safest activities must be developed.

Boxing provides an illustration of this point of view. For many years, boxing was one of the top priority activities. It was taught in the classroom and was an important intercollegiate and interschool sport as well. Today, because of safety factors, boxing is no longer part of the curriculum. Physical educators agree that the sport is incompatible with current philosophy in physical education. This kind of general consensus should be sought for all aspects of the physical education curriculum. A high degree of consistency in professional philosophy is desirable in order to achieve the objectives set forth for physical education today.

AGENCIES AND SCHOOL-COMMUNITY RELATIONS

There are several agencies that teachers may find helpful in assisting with school-community relations programs. Two of these agencies are discussed in the following paragraphs.

Physical Education Public Information (PEPI)

In an effort to educate the public regarding the need for physical education, the American Alliance for Health, Physical Education and Recreation has established a public relations program, known as the Physical Education Public Information Project (PEPI). It was designed to reach the various interest groups: students, administrators, supervisors, boards of education, teachers and professors, parent-teacher associations, civic organizations, industrial organizations, and health foundations. The main thrust of the PEPI project will be through radio and television, and it will rely mostly on the national networks. Material has been made available to teachers, directors, and administrators to assist them in sponsoring local programs.

The PEPI developed the following concepts, which may serve as guidelines for developing school-community relations programs:

1. A physically educated person is one who has knowledge and skill concerning his body and how it works.
2. Physical education is health insurance.
3. Physical education can contribute to academic achievement.
4. A sound physical education program contributes to development of a positive self-concept.
5. A sound physical education program helps an individual attain social skills.

President's Council for Physical Fitness and Sports

The President's Council for Physical Fitness and Sports was created by President Eisenhower in 1956, as a result of the findings of the Kraus-Weber Fitness Tests. Since that time, the Council has enjoyed the support of all succeeding presidents.

The purpose of the Council has been to promote physical fitness and to endorse local programs in their efforts. A complete outline of the objectives and recommendations of the Council is included in the *Resource Manual.*

SCHOOL-COLLEGE RELATIONS

It is becoming increasingly evident that more communication between teachers and college personnel is desirable. They need each other, and the polarization of the two groups may well be a major cause of the dilemmas that physical education faces today.

Teachers should request college professors to assist them in teaching and planning in-service programs. College teachers should meet with school personnel to determine what should be taught in the college classes. Both groups should jointly develop strong school-community relations programs.

QUESTIONS FOR DISCUSSION

1. What is the purpose of developing school-community relations?
2. Identify the groups that constitute the plural publics. Which is most important? Why?
3. What type of influence does a community power structure have on the public relations program?
4. What guidelines should be presented to help the public evaluate the needs and importance of physical education?
5. Why is the teacher considered to be the key to successful school-community relations?
6. What communications media are most effective in the education of a community? Give examples of how the media can acquaint people with the physical education program.
7. What effect could community sponsors have on the physical education program?
8. List some educational issues that can affect the quality of the physical education program. Should the general public be acquainted with these educational issues? Why or why not?
9. How have national organizations contributed to school-community relations?

REFERENCES

1. George H. Gallup, "Ninth Annual Gallup Poll of the Public's Attitudes Toward the Public Schools," *Phi Delta Kappan* (September, 1978), p. 33.
2. Scott M. Cutlip and Allen H. Center, *Effective Public Relations,* 4th ed. (Englewood Cliffs: Prentice-Hall, 1971), p. 566.
3. Ian Templeton, *Communicating with the Public* (Arlington, Virginia: National School Public Relations Association, 1972), p. 6. From Keith Atkinson, Communications: Closing the Widening Gap, *Clearing House.*

4. *Ibid.,* p. 5, from John M. Nagle, "How to Tell What Your Public Really Thinks," *The American School Board Journal.*
5. David D. Draves, "Student Opinions: Cause for Reflection," *Phi Delta Kappan* (September, 1977), p. 68.
6. Templeton, *op. cit.,* p. 8.
7. Draves, *op. cit.*
8. Glen F. Ovard, *Administration of the Changing Secondary School* (New York: The Macmillan Company, 1966), p. 453.
9. "The Public's Finding Out What Physical Education Is All About," *Physical Education Newsletter* (Croft Educational Services, Inc., May 1, 1970).
10. Lowell A. Klappholz, *Physical Education Newsletter* (Physical Education Publications, Old Saybrook, Connecticut, October 15, 1975).
11. Albert A. Ayars, "A Superintendent Speaks Out for Physical Education," *Directions* (Washington, D.C., January, 1976), p. 4.
12. Dean A. Pease and Darrell Crase, "Commitment to Change," *JOHPER* (April, 1973), p. 35.

SELECTED READINGS

Cutlip, Scott M., and Allen Center, *Effective Public Relations,* 4th ed. (Englewood Cliffs: Prentice-Hall, 1971).
McCloskey, Gordon, *Education and Public Understanding,* 2nd ed. (New York: Harper and Row, Publishers, 1967).
Physical Education Public Information (PEPI), *JOPER* (March, 1977), p. 6.
Ibid., (January, 1977), p. 36.
Ibid., (June, 1977), p. 10.
Ibid., (November-December, 1977), p. 14.

Chapter 13

Courtesy Rosemont Junior High School, Norfolk, Virginia.

PURPOSES OF ASSESSMENT
    DEFINITIONS
THE SCHOOL PROGRAM
THE ADMINISTRATOR
    PERFORMANCE APPRAISAL
    SELF-EVALUATION
    CONTINUOUS REVIEW
THE TEACHER
    SELF-EVALUATION
    BEHAVIOR RATING SCALE
THE STUDENT
TESTS
    PHYSICAL EDUCATION KNOWLEDGE TESTS
        SUBJECTIVE TESTS
        OBJECTIVE TESTS
    PHYSICAL EDUCATION PERFORMANCE
      TESTS
        TESTING WITH A PURPOSE
    PHYSICAL EDUCATION AFFECTIVE TESTS
    REASONS FOR TESTING
        MOTIVATION
        GRADING
        TEACHER INFORMATION
    INSTRUCTIONAL VALUE MEASURED BY
      TESTS

CHARACTERISTICS OF A GOOD TEST
    RELIABILITY
    VALIDITY
    OBJECTIVITY
    SIMPLICITY
    UNIFORMITY
STANDARDIZED TESTS
CONDUCTING THE TESTING PROGRAM
    PRELIMINARY PLANNING
    ORGANIZING THE CLASS
        MASS TESTING
        SQUAD TESTING
        INDIVIDUAL TESTING
    CONDUCTING THE TEST
    FINAL PROCEDURES
GRADING IN PHYSICAL EDUCATION
    PROFICIENCY TESTING
    GRADING ON IMPROVEMENT
    GRADING ON EFFORT
    CONTRACT GRADING
SUGGESTED GRADING PLANS
REPORTING TO PARENTS
QUESTIONS FOR DISCUSSION
REFERENCES
SELECTED READINGS

Chapter 13

ASSESSMENT AND EVALUATION

If teachers are sincere about achieving certain goals in physical education, they will judge administrators, colleagues, students, and programs in terms of fulfillment of predetermined objectives. During the past several years, emphasis has been placed on assessment and evaluation strategies in education. Taxpayers, concerned about the increased cost of education, have held physical educators accountable for the expenditure of tax dollars in their field. Teachers must therefore be competent and accurate in their appraisal of physical education programs.

New teachers often misconceive of evaluation in physical education as being primarily concerned with grading. Although grading student progress is important, the ultimate purpose of evaluation is to provide feedback that will improve the teaching and learning processes. Assessing and evaluating programs, administrators, teachers, students, and resource personnel is an essential phase of education. Appraisal is necessary for supplying parents and others with evidence that the schools are offering the best education possible.

PURPOSES OF ASSESSMENT

The primary purposes of evaluating secondary school programs are:
1. To improve physical education programs.
2. To evaluate administrative effectiveness.
3. To aid the teacher in evaluating different instructional methods.
4. To help the teacher assess student performances.
5. To enable the teacher to measure improvement objectively.
6. To discover new motivational techniques.
7. To classify students for exemption or special placement.
8. To guide students in understanding various physical education activities.
9. To determine grades and record progress.

10. To facilitate self-appraisal.
11. To collect data for research.
12. To establish educational values.

Effective assessment methods include the use of tests for cognitive, psychomotor, and affective learnings; measurement tools, both objective and subjective; scientifically applied evaluative judgments; research; and self-appraisal.

Definitions

Educational assessment can be divided into three phases, as defined by Barrow and McGee:

Evaluation is a *process* of education which makes use of measurement techniques, which when applied to either the product or the process, result in both qualitative and quantitative data expressed in both a subjective and an objective manner and used for comparisons with preconceived criteria.

Measurement is a *technique* of evaluation which makes use of procedures which are generally precise and objective, which will generally result in quantitative data, and which characteristically can express its results in numerical form. It may be applied to qualitative procedures, however, when its techniques are objectified.

Figure 13–1. Objective testing is an integral part of a physical education program. (Courtesy Los Angeles Unified School District.)

A **test** is a *specific tool of measurement* and implies a response from the person being measured.[1]

Various methods that can be used in evaluating (1) the school program, (2) the administrator, (3) the teacher, and (4) the student are described in this chapter.

THE SCHOOL PROGRAM

Most school systems devise their own process for evaluating physical education programs. The two basic systems of program evaluation are the summative approach and the formative approach.

The traditional, or summative, approach involves the evaluation of program goals at the end of the school year or another designated period of time. Formative evaluation takes place while the program is functioning, providing continual feedback. Summative evaluation is sometimes insignificant because responses and suggestions are forgotten by the beginning of the next school year. With formative evaluation, measures are developed throughout the school year to monitor strengths and weaknesses. By planning in advance, both summative and formative evaluations can be used.

Program evaluation is an integral part of any educational process that is structured around certain criteria. For the evaluation to have meaning, teachers must be familiar with the objectives of the curriculum in general and the administration of physical education in particular.

The Los Angeles city schools developed a system to assist teachers, administrators, and students in assessing the physical education programs. The staff determines the strengths and weaknesses of the program and decides what steps are necessary for improvement. Administrators are also involved in the evaluation process so that curriculum changes can be made swiftly and efficiently.[2]

Another comprehensive plan for evaluating the school program is described in *Evaluation for Physical Education,* a project of the Ohio Association for Health, Physical Education and Recreation. The entire system is based on the concept of self-appraisal. It is founded on a rating scale of zero to four in seven areas: (1) philosophy and principles, (2) organization and administration, (3) class management, (4) staff, (5) curriculum, (6) facilities and equipment, and (7) elective program.

THE ADMINISTRATOR

Evaluation of faculty, students, and programs appears to be the overriding concern of the educational system. Administrators heretofore have not been subjected to assessment and evaluation. However, because they make decisions that affect change in the programs, it is very important to examine their effectiveness. Many administrators undoubtedly have backgrounds in teaching, but it is becoming increasingly apparent that because the job descriptions of the administrator and the teacher do differ, separate evaluative methods are needed.

Three methods of evaluating the administrator are (1) performance appraisal, (2) self-evaluation, and (3) continuous skill review.

Performance Appraisal

A sound performance appraisal plan does not infringe upon the normal pursuits of the person being evaluated. The individual should be given every opportunity to develop his or her performance and should be kept fully informed of the results through immediate and continual feedback. Administrators should be encouraged and permitted to participate in all levels of their own evaluation. This approach facilitates the comparison of the results obtained during the appraisal period in relation to the performance outcomes previously agreed upon.

Performance appraisals are formulated on the basis of certain factors. *Priority responsibilities* are determined to identify the functions expected of the administrator during the particular review period. *Performance outcomes* are highly individualized goals that are agreed upon for the review period. *Formative evaluation reports* are set up as a series of ongoing reviews to determine how much progress is being made toward achieving performance outcomes. *Summative appraisals* review the results and compare them with the predetermined responsibilities and goals.

Performance appraisals are undertaken with the idea that improvement in the individual's performance eventually will result in program improvement. Program enrichment can be achieved by:

1. Affording the opportunity for mutual agreement between administrators and their superiors as to what program emphases should be.
2. Helping each administrator focus attention and effort on those things considered basic and critical functions of the position.
3. Providing the administrator with an ongoing performance review to analyze how and why the performance outcomes were or were not met.
4. Providing continual feedback to the administrator so that adjustments can be made in the performance throughout the review period.
5. Using a system of clear, orderly procedures in which full disclosure of basic decisions and specific reasons for these decisions are made available at every stage of the process.
6. Identifying specific needs for future training so that an administrator can improve performance in the present position.[3]

Self-Evaluation

One self-evaluation tool that has been devised by the authors enables the administrator to judge himself or herself on factors related primarily to affective behavior. A list of 25 semantic-differential adjectives is used to determine effectiveness, as shown in Table 13–1.

Continuous Review

The job of the administrator demands proficiency in such diverse fields as

TABLE 13–1. ADMINISTRATOR SELF-EVALUATION FORM

	Very	Quite	Slight	Quite	Very	
Articulate						Inarticulate
Energetic						Lazy
Satisfied						Frustrated
Speaks Up						Clams Up
Flexible						Stubborn
Sincere						Insincere
Responsible						Irresponsible
Prepared						Unprepared
Open-Minded						Closed-Minded
Consistent						Inconsistent
Straightforward						Deceptive
Honest						Dishonest
Patient						Impatient
Approachable						Unapproachable
Competent						Incompetent
Organized						Disorganized
Involved						Apathetic
Fair						Unfair
Interested						Disinterested
Good with Detail						Sloppy with Detail
Respected						Not Respected
Agreeable						Disagreeable
Alert						Listless
Professional						Unprofessional
Efficient						Inefficient

This form lists 25 sets of adjectives and phrases to be used as evaluative criteria. Place an X at one of the five rating terms for each pair of adjectives.

personnel, finance, recruitment, negotiations, public relations, communications, and other skills related to the successful implementation of the program. Another means of assessing the competencies of the administrator is to perpetually measure performance against a check list of the expected skills, as shown in Figure 13–2.[4]

The *Physical Education Newsletter* has compiled a list of several administrative pitfalls that must be avoided if physical education programs are to improve:

1. Scheduling such large classes that teaching and learning often are impossible.
2. Providing too little equipment to get the job done. One or two balls for a class of 30 means that most of the children stand around and wait for a chance to shoot a basket or throw the ball.
3. Failing to schedule at least 30 minutes of physical education a day — or a weekly average of at least 30 minutes a day.
4. Allowing the physical education curricula to be structured down from the high school level rather than up from the elementary level. This failure to build on a sequential body of knowledge or skills has impeded teaching, learning, and enthusiasm for physical education and led to

Directions: Place an X at the point on each continuum that most closely approximates your point of view.

Decision Making

Unaware of past experiments, programs, and traditions of the institution	Highly cognizant of institution's history and its implications for present and future directions
No theoretical, experimental, or experiential basis for decisions	Great knowledge and evidence to support his positions
No coherent plan or objectives for decisions	A carefully conceived, publicly stated set of priorities
Arbitrary and idiosyncratic regarding programs he supports	Involves faculty, students, and others in setting program priorities

Communication

Shares little to explain his decisions, values, and purposes	Open and public in sharing rationales for his actions
Is a poor, unrepresentative spokesman of school to remainder of institution and to public	Is an accurate, positive representative of school
Operates with a clique of confidantes	Makes good use of regular channels for communication
Closed and vindictive with those who disagree	Open and receptive to all points of view
Inaccessible	Available

Faculty

Selects new faculty poorly	Chooses excellent faculty
Makes unfair merit recommendations	Is equitable
Promotes wrong people	Makes wise promotion recommendations

Professional values

Places little value on teaching	Values excellence in teaching
Has little interest in community service	Values close working relations in community projects
Unconcerned with scholarly developments and research	Vitally interested in new ideas and findings

Change

Essentially a maintenance type who will keep present system functioning	A genuine change agent who will influence basic programs and their impact

Scoring: Administer test annually. X's that move to right are +; those that shift to left are −. Continua should be analyzed item by item in each category.

Analysis: Total scores (e.g., 9−, 4+, 2, no change) can also be cumulated and analyzed in terms of median change. A simple sign test will determine significance.

Figure 13-2. Check list for evaluating administrative officers. (Courtesy Journal of Teacher Education, Summer, 1972.)

undue emphasis on team sports and competition at too young an age.

5. Choosing unqualified and physically inept teachers to handle physical education when no certified or qualified physical education instructors are available.
6. Failing to provide adequate budgets.
7. Overlooking the fact that a youngster's earliest learnings are motor-oriented as a result of running, jumping, climbing, skipping, reaching, and similar activities —and that these are vital to later intellectual accomplishments.
8. Using physical education as a dumping ground so that the student load for physical education teachers is from 50 to 100 percent greater than for teachers of other subjects.
9. Emphasizing interscholastic sports so that gymnasiums, athletic fields, and pools are monopolized by the school teams after school. This cuts down on the use of the facilities by other students who can benefit substantially by participating in intramural activities.[5]

THE TEACHER

The physical education teacher is often evaluated inadequately. Teachers should be aware of the methods used by administrators to evaluate them and should demand that criteria especially designed for physical education be used.

Just as administrators have been attacked for failing to provide the elements essential for good physical education programs, teachers have been criticized for failing to use their technical knowledge and experience to conduct quality programs. Some of the shortcomings of teachers are discussed in the *Physical Education Newsletter,* on the basis of a compilation of criticisms of physical education. Teachers should study these practices and evaluate their own professional efforts in terms of the criticism aimed at them:

1. Being concerned only with the athletes — the top 10 percent of the student body from a physical education point of view.
2. Failing to provide imaginative programs; repeating the same activities each year.
3. Not using existing natural facilities such as nearby lakes or ski areas to teach carry-over sports and activities.
4. Overlooking the principles of child development in planning physical education

programs, particularly in the primary grades.
5. Pushing children into competition before they are ready for it.
6. Being coaches and not teachers. The publications charge physical educators with failing to plan classes — and being preoccupied with their coaching assignments.
7. Teaching the same old thing in the same old way. Calisthenics, more calisthenics — and taking the roll on the same old numbers on the same old blacktop.
8. Adding exercise to normal assignments as discipline, thus cheapening it in the eyes of students by making it a punishment.
9. Being unable to relate to inner-city children and imposing middle class values on ghetto students.
10. Overlooking and ignoring the best interests of about 41 million children — including the overweight, underweight, shy, scrawny, awkward, handicapped, poorly coordinated, and just plain normal.[6]

Two other strategies for measuring teacher performance are the *self-evaluation form* and the *behavior rating scale.*

Self-Evaluation

The teacher self-evaluation form in Table 13–2, devised by the authors, allows any teacher who wishes to improve to examine his or her own effectiveness.

Behavior Rating Scale

The behavior scale is a useful tool for observing and judging physical educators as they teach. Ohio State University developed the following behavioral categories to be used in measuring the value of particular teaching styles:

1. *Input teaching acts.* Includes all teacher behaviors that provide a discriminative stimulus function directly related to learning. This includes questioning (teacher asks a question), explaining (teacher elaborates or summarizes previous material or clarifies a problem for better understanding), informing (answering a question), and providing guidance (including verbal guidance, demonstration, force-responding, and physical restriction). (Rushall and Siedentop, 1972).

TABLE 13-2. TEACHER SELF-EVALUATION FORM

	High	Average	Low
Procedures and Tools			
Written assessment of your own teaching			
Student achievement you have observed in your classes			
Your work with colleagues on the staff			
Professional reading you have done			
New Position			
Conferences with the principal			
Adjustment to the school environment			
Discussion sessions with your supervisor			
Self-assessment of your knowledge and ability			
Resource Materials and Procedures			
Self-analysis of your classroom teaching			
Selection and use of various textbooks			
Use of skill tests, testing, study sheets, etc.			
Self-analysis of your activity teaching			
Observance of other teachers			
Personality			
Evaluation of self-perception			
Your behavior: "harsh-kind" scale			
Teacher-student relationship			
Set an example for students			
Tolerant of ideas of other teachers			
Discuss crucial educational issues with colleagues			
How do you rate?			
Are you improving?			

Continuous self-evaluation will result in self-improvement. Therefore, "spot-check" yourself periodically on the above items.

2. *Managerial.* Refers to teacher behaviors that provide a discriminative stimulus function indirectly related to learning. This includes establishing and maintaining order, directing the class to change activities, and giving directions for equipment, etc. Also includes roll taking, marking down performance scores, and other forms of record keeping directly related to current behavior of students. These behaviors are primarily teacher initiated (discriminative function) and are not teacher reactions to student disturbances (consequential function).
3. *Monitoring.* Refers to watching the class as a whole, a subset of the class, or an individual student. No verbal or non-verbal interaction occurs.
4. *No activity.* Refers to all teacher behaviors in which visual contact is broken and no verbal or non-verbal interaction occurs. Includes looking out the window, being out of the room, talking to another teacher, and record keeping not directly related to immediate behavior of students.

5. *Skill attempt* — positive IF. Refers to all positive verbal and non-verbal teacher reactions to an appropriate skill attempt by a student.
6. *Skill attempt* — negative IF. Refers to all negative verbal and non-verbal teacher reactions to an appropriate skill attempt by a student, including corrective feedback. Does not necessarily imply a punishing or menacing tone.
7. *Positive reaction to on-task behavior.* Refers to all positive verbal and non-verbal teacher reactions to on-task student behaviors other than skill attempts.
8. *Negative reaction to off-task behavior.* Refers to all negative verbal and non-verbal teacher reactions to off-task student behavior.[7]

THE STUDENT

One of the most important aspects of education is the assessment of student progress. Measuring students in physical education by comparing them with others is unfair and unscientific. This kind of grading might be contributing to the dropout problem that confronts educational leaders today. A meaningful evaluation of student progress is a grade based on the student's own ability and the improvement shown over a period of time.

Although lack of interest and dropouts are serious educational ills, cheating has become one of the most appalling problems in the schools today. In a study made approximately ten years ago by Columbia University, 50 per cent of the 5000 college students in 99 United States colleges admitted to cheating. The author of the study estimated that the incidence of cheating in high schools is even higher, and it is still increasing today. Apparently it is the intense emphasis on testing and grading that causes so many students to cheat:

Actually, the present situation with its heavy emphasis on tests and its insane pressure for grades, is less an invitation to learn than an invitation to cheat. Just as heavy testing is a symptom of what is wrong with our schools, cheating is a symptom of what is wrong with testing.[8]

Probably the most scathing criticism of current evaluative systems appeared in the journal of the *American Association of Colleges for Teacher Education*. The article reprinted some of the statements made at the National Advisory Council on Education Professions Development:

Evaluation of the wrong kind, at the wrong time, and for the wrong reasons has characterized too much of the current effort to appraise educational reforms. Meaningless evaluation is ruining the cutting edge of educational innovation.

It is becoming increasingly clear that a number of policies and practices . . . are having an adverse effect on efforts to provide genuine innovation and improvement. Among such practices and policies, we cite for special note the following:
1. Premature evaluation of a project or venture before it is fully operational.
2. Preoccupation with so-called "hard data" developed by mass use of standardized tests.
3. Too much concern with final results alone

leads to lack of effort to determine why project objectives were or were not met.
4. Lack of imagination in selecting types of evaluation policies that are applicable to the special nature, purposes, or stage of development of an educational activity.
5. Requirements that all projects in a program make financial provisions for project evaluation.
6. A tendency to construe tentative findings as "proof."[9]

As a result of these conditions, students develop hostility toward traditional types of evaluation. Biehler lists the four major drawbacks of these systems:

1. Too much emphasis on tests and grades limits creativity and individuality of expression. Consequently, grades may discourage rather than encourage learning that is personally relevant to the student.
2. Grades put too much pressure on the student. Learning should be an enjoyable experience; it is too often a tension-filled, disagreeable one. Students should not be forced to compete with each other to earn high grades.
3. Information learned for a test is only a means to an arbitrary end — a grade. Much of what has been learned will be forgotten as soon as the grade is achieved.
4. Teachers are too authoritative. Students are forced to spit back exactly what the book or professor says. This is not only degrading; it involves punishment if a student doesn't learn what he has been told to learn.[10]

Although these criticisms were aimed at academic subjects, many of them apply to physical education. Too often, grades given to students in physical education are based either on an invalid testing system or on subjective evaluation without a formal testing plan. Evidence strongly indicates the need for objective testing and grading systems.

Biehler agrees that in order to evaluate students fairly and accurately, some type of formal testing is essential. He lists the advantages of using certain tests and grades:

1. Evaluation provides feedback, which often functions as reinforcement, which in turn is an essential part of learning.
2. Tests help guarantee that a student will master basic facts and skills en route to mastery of concepts and general abilities.
3. In studying for exams, students usually learn material with reasonable thoroughness, which helps assure that material will be remembered. Furthermore, distortions

and faulty generalizations may be cleared up by the wrong answers being corrected.

4. Exams require students to try out their ideas under rigorous circumstances that limit "fudging." In the absence of such control, many students might never really test their ideas (or their abilities) in a literal sense.

5. Tests may be the only way to get many students to learn many important things. Test scores function as specific goals. Most students need incentives even to approach their full potential. Sometimes a student studying for an exam discovers a new interest.

6. Specific feedback may permit a student to compete against himself.

7. Under proper circumstances, performance on tests may provide a detailed analysis of the strengths and weaknesses of students. This information can be used in a variety of ways by teachers, counselors, and students themselves. Evaluation also assists a teacher to improve his or her own performance. In the absence of feedback, it is practically impossible for a teacher to make systematic efforts to change things for the better, whereas the very process of writing and reading exams aids the organization and presentation of subject matter.[11]

Teachers have always asked the question, "How can I teach students to learn on their own?" Being able to learn on one's own requires a certain independence of thought. It implies that a student who can do so is able to develop curiosity and interest without being guided, helped, or motivated by another person. This suggests genuine self-determination — the student who is self-taught not only learns without assistance but also decides what to learn. Because teachers are facilitators in the learning process, they must develop a better understanding of the factors that motivate students to learn independently.

Even though secondary school students have greater freedom in selecting what they learn, teachers still need scientifically applied standards to evaluate student performance and progress. Formal testing and grading plans are basic to a successful program of physical education. However, these plans must be developed carefully and based on adequate test items, equitable administration of tests, validity of tests, and other factors that are necessary for an accu-

rate appraisal of student performance. The remainder of this chapter is devoted to procedures involved in initiating a fair and consistent student appraisal system.

TESTS

Great disparity exists among physical educators regarding test classification. This lack of unanimity is confusing to both teachers and students. Knowledge of classifications and of the various tests that can be used within them should be acquired by all teachers and students. Figure 13–3 shows one general classification of tests by Haskins and one classification, including specific tests within it, by Mathews.[12, 13] Teachers should be primarily concerned with knowledge, performance, and affective tests.

Physical Education Knowledge Tests

Students can be given written tests to determine their retention of the material covered in class. These tests should be given periodically to measure comprehension, to discover which topics need clarification, and to provide the teacher with guidelines for future planning. Written tests are generally classified into two types, subjective and objective.

Subjective Tests. The most common type of written subjective test asks the student to discuss a topic and to justify particular statements. Considerable time is required to evaluate this kind of test, and therefore it is impractical for large classes. However, subjective tests do reflect students' knowledge of a subject because they force students to think through a problem, justify their reactions, and express themselves concisely and clearly. Subjective tests are more effective than objective tests for certain types of learning.

Objective Tests. Written objective tests require very specific answers. The most common tests are the true-false,

Haskins
- Strength
- Endurance
- Physical Fitness
- Motor Ability
- Posture
- The Concomitants
- Sports Skills

Mathews
- STRENGTH TESTS
  - Cable-Tension Strength Tests
  - Kraus-Weber Strength Tests
- MOTOR FITNESS TESTS
  - AAHPER Youth Fitness Test
  - The Physical Performance Test for California
  - Canada Fitness Award
  - Indiana Motor Fitness Test for High School and College Men
  - Elementary School Motor Fitness Test
  - Youth Physical Fitness Test
  - JCR Test
  - Division for Girls' and Women's Sports Tests (DGWS)
  - Army Air Force Physical Fitness Test (AAF Test)
  - Navy Standard Physical Fitness Test
  - Army Physical Efficiency Test
  - Texas Physical Fitness Motor Ability Test
- GENERAL MOTOR ABILITY
  - Classification Indexes
  - Tests of Motor Ability
    - Newton Motor Ability Test
    - Scott Motor Ability Test
    - Barrow Motor Ability Test
    - Cozens' Test of General Athletic Ability
    - Larson Motor Ability Test
    - Strength Tests of Motor Ability
    - Oberlin College Test
    - Sigma Delta Psi Test
    - McCloy's General Motor Ability Tests
  - Tests of Running Endurance
  - Motor Educability
    - Iowa-Brace Test
    - Johnson Test of Motor Educability
    - Johnson-Metheny Test
    - Latchaw Motor Skills Test
  - Perceptual Motor Evaluation
- SPORTS SKILL TESTING
  - Hyde Archery Test
  - Lockhart and McPherson Badminton Test
  - Miller Wall Volley Test
  - Boys' Baseball Classification Plan
  - Achievement Level in Basketball Skills for Women
  - Johnson Basketball Ability Test
  - Knox Basketball Test
  - Lehsten Basketball Test

- Bowling Norms
- Borleske Touch Football Test
- Cornish Handball Test
- McDonald Soccer Test
- Broer-Miller Tennis Test
- Dyer Tennis Test
- Brady Volleyball Test
- Russell-Lange Volleyball Test
- French-Cooper Volleyball Test
- CARDIOVASCULAR TESTS
  - Blood Pressure Measurement
  - Balke Treadmill Test
  - Modified Treadmill Test for Children
  - Barach Index
  - Burger Test
  - Carlson Fatigue Curve Test
  - Crampton Blood Ptosis Test
  - Foster's Test
  - Gallagher and Brouha Test for High School Boys
  - Gallagher and Brouha Test for Girls
  - Johnson, Brouha, and Darling Treadmill Test
  - Harvard Step Test
  - Pack Test
  - Schneider Test
  - Sloan Test
  - Tuttle Pulse-Ratio Test
  - The Ohio State University Step Test
  - Cooper's 12-Minute Test for Men
- NUTRITIONAL MEASUREMENTS AND SOMATOTYPE
  - Measuring Nutritional Status
    - Subjective Evaluation
    - Objective Measurement
- EVALUATION OF BODY MECHANICS
  - Early Posture Tests
  - Recent Posture Tests
    - Static Anteroposterior Posture Tests
    - Screening Tests
    - Functional Body Mechanics Appraisal
    - Refined Posture Appraisal
  - Muscle Power and Holding Power Measurements
  - Evaluation of the Feet
  - Evaluation of Flexibility
- EVALUATION OF SOCIAL DEVELOPMENT
  - Measuring Attitudes
  - Rating Scales
  - Sociometric Evaluation
  - The Anecdotal Record
- SPORTS HEALTH KNOWLEDGE TESTS
  - Sample Knowledge Test (Tennis Test for Women)
  - Physical Education Knowledge Tests
    - Badminton
    - Golf
    - Field Hockey
    - Softball
    - Swimming
    - Tennis

Figure 13-3. Classification of tests.

FLOOR PLAN - GOLF and TENNIS

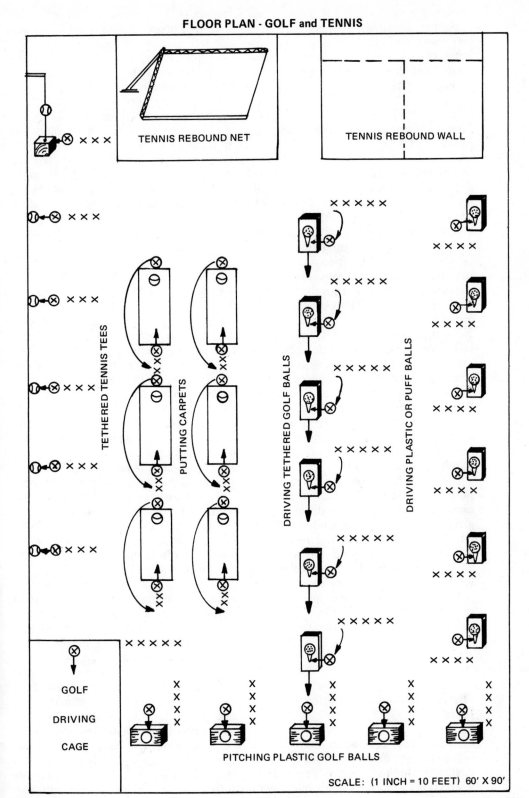

Figure 13–4. A floor plan for testing and teaching golf and tennis skills. (Courtesy New York City Public Schools.)

completion, multiple choice, and matching. These are practical and can be corrected quickly; teachers with large classes usually find them more convenient to grade and more accurate in assessing the student.

Physical Education Performance Tests

Performance tests demand entirely different procedures than do written tests. Skill measurement in physical education activities is so complex that the teacher needs to study testing thoroughly before initiating any program. Certain procedures should be followed in planning performance tests for students.

Testing With a Purpose. Teachers must decide what factors need to be tested and structure the tests accordingly. If the teacher wishes to test for physiologic fitness, students should be asked to exhibit strength, speed, skill, and endurance. If the teacher wishes to test knowledge of sports and activities, then a written objective test can be used. If the teacher wishes to measure motor ability, a more comprehensive test must be devised that will accurately reflect students' skills.

Each test should serve a definite purpose in the instructional program. Too often, tests in physical education are given to large groups of students at one time. They are graded, the results are recorded and filed, and the tests are never seen again. Time and effort are wasted. Instead, teachers should know why they are giving the test and the student should be told the purpose of the test. Whenever possible, the correct answers should later be discussed in class.

Physical Education Affective Tests

Grades that are based on affective behavior are determined by various factors, including attitude, attendance, effort, dress, and sportsmanship. Affective behavior is extremely difficult to measure. Furthermore, the cognitive and psychomotor skills are often neglected when affective skills are overemphasized. The presence of desired affective behavior in no way guarantees achievement in motor skills or understanding of movement.[14]

Educators are currently devoting unprecedented effort to the development of qualitative tools for measuring affective objectives. Teachers must take into account the values, attitudes, interests, and background of the student. Figure 13–5 illustrates commonly used affective terms measured against the continuum of general classifications of affective behavior.

Reasons for Testing

Motivating students, determining grades, and ascertaining the general performance capacity of students are among the reasons for administering tests in physical education.

Motivation. Motivation should be the real reason for testing. If a student loses all interest in an activity after he or she has completed the related test, the test contributes very little to physical education. On the other hand, if the test stimulates the student to practice an activity outside the school, its value extends into the affective domain.

Grading. Teachers might wish to use tests as indications of achievement and to assist in marking report cards. However, arbitrary grading based on performance tests is not desirable. For example, special consideration would be necessary for students with anatomic handicaps that prevent satisfactory performance. Students who are handicapped by weight and cannot chin the bar one time are not necessarily unfit; they might otherwise be in excellent health and should not be graded solely because of this poor performance.

Teacher Information. Teachers should have general knowledge of their students' performance abilities. Physical educators can study test results for assistance in developing a more effective instructional and guidance program. If

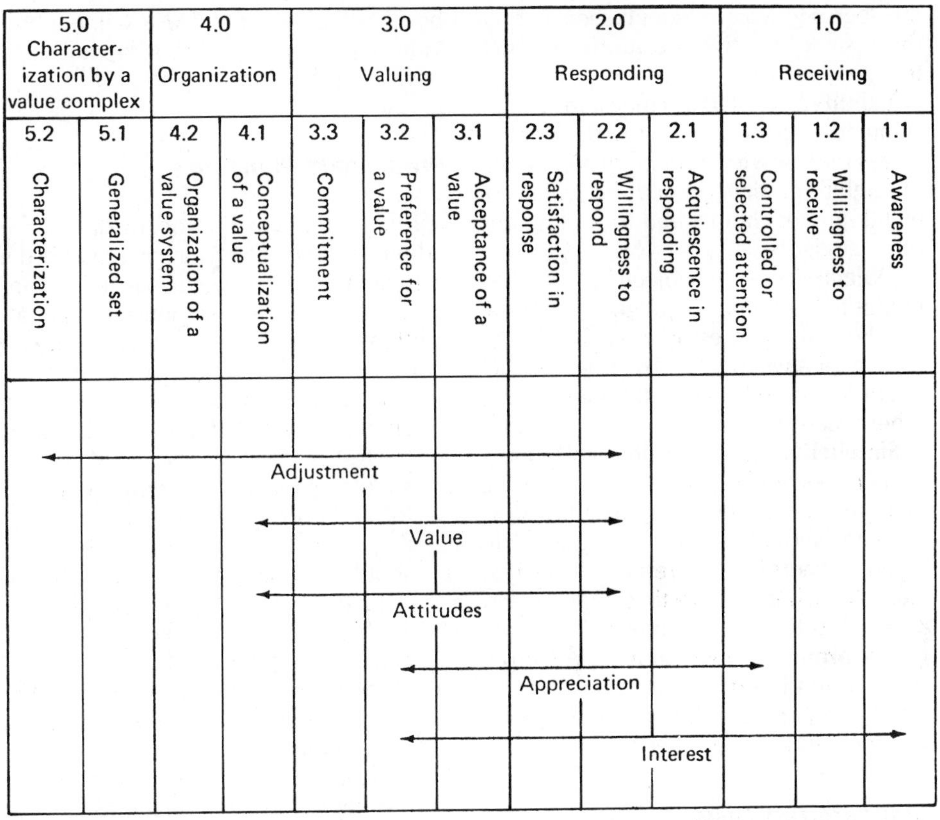

5.0 Characterization by a value complex		4.0 Organization		3.0 Valuing			2.0 Responding			1.0 Receiving		
5.2	5.1	4.2	4.1	3.3	3.2	3.1	2.3	2.2	2.1	1.3	1.2	1.1
Characterization	Generalized set	Organization of a value system	Conceptualization of a value	Commitment	Preference for a value	Acceptance of a value	Satisfaction in response	Willingness to respond	Acquiescence in responding	Controlled or selected attention	Willingness to receive	Awareness

Adjustment

Value

Attitudes

Appreciation

Interest

Figure 13–5. Evaluating affective behavior. (From David R. Krathwohl, et al., *Taxonomy of Educational Objectives: The Classification of Educational Goals: Handbook II: The Affective Domain,* New York: David McKay, 1964, p. 37. Copyright by Longman, Inc., 1977.)

many students in a class are unable to perform the 50-yard dash in less than 10 seconds, the situation merits a thorough study. The students may not be getting sufficient rest or nourishment, and there may be a need for medical attention and/or more effective instruction.

Instructional Value Measured by Tests

All tests should measure the degree to which educational objectives are being achieved. Too often, teachers identify their objectives at the beginning of the course and never refer to them afterwards. If an objective in volleyball instruction is to teach the serve, tests should measure how well the

process is improving students' serving skills. Performance objectives are as important for students as they are for teachers. Refer to the *Resource Manual* for additional examples of this kind of testing.

Characteristics of a Good Test

Although factors such as cost and ease of administration should be considered in preparing or selecting a test, the essential criteria of a good test are reliability, validity, objectivity, simplicity, and uniformity.

Reliability. A reliable test is one that the teacher can depend upon to produce consistent results. If the same test is given to a group of students at different times, the reliability of the tests is determined by the degree to which students seem to hold their same relative positions in both tests.

Validity.   A valid test measures what it is intended to measure. A test designed to assess the knowledge of body mechanics of eighth graders would be valid for eighth graders but invalid for testing any other students.

Objectivity.   An objective test precludes the influence of judgment or opinion. For example, essay tests are not objective. Essays scored by one teacher might be scored quite differently by another teacher.

Simplicity.   Because physical education classes are large and the concepts to be tested can be very complex, the testing program should be simple. Many dedicated teachers lose interest in testing their students when the testing process becomes too time-consuming.

Uniformity.   Tests should be structured around certain norms so that students can compare their test results with those of students in other areas.

Standardized Tests

Standardized tests have become common features of many aspects of secondary school curricula. School officials have used them to interpret the growth of individual students to legislators, school boards, and governors. However, the purpose and the interpretation of standardized testing are questionable. There is much disagreement about educational goals and how they are measured. Some feel that standardized testing encourages conformity at the expense of creativity.

Standardized tests are valuable if they are intended to motivate students. If the tests are used merely for passing or failing students, or for attempting to classify students as fit or unfit, the results can be extremely uninspiring. It is therefore suggested that standardized tests be used only as motivational devices in conjunction with locally prepared tests.

CONDUCTING THE TESTING PROGRAM

Careful consideration must be given to any testing program because if it has not been well planned, the tests will not provide valid measurements of the skills they have been designed to assess.

Preliminary Planning

Many problems that occur during the administration of tests can be prevented if sufficient time has been spent in planning. The following elements warrant attention before the testing program begins:

1. The purpose of the testing program should be stated. If the test is designed to test motor ability, a statement should be made explaining the reason for and purpose of the test.
2. A careful selection of the test items should be made on the basis of the objectives of the testing program.
3. The dates on which the tests will be given should be announced.
4. Students should be made aware of the purpose and importance of the testing program in general.
5. A clear and concise explanation of the test items should be made to the students.
6. A survey should be made of the needed equipment, and all necessary items should be procured.
7. A survey of the space necessary for conducting the test should be made and the space should be prepared accordingly.
8. Safety factors should be considered in planning the administration of all tests.

Organizing the Class

Organization of students for testing can prevent an unnecessary waste of time. Class arrangements for administering tests are discussed in the following paragraphs.

Mass Testing.   Some tests, such as the sit-up and the push-up, can be administered to large groups with relative facility. The class can be divided into two groups, with one taking the test while the other one scores. Figure 13–7 illustrates this.

Squad Testing.   Organization of the class into squads is a popular arrangement for administering tests. Students

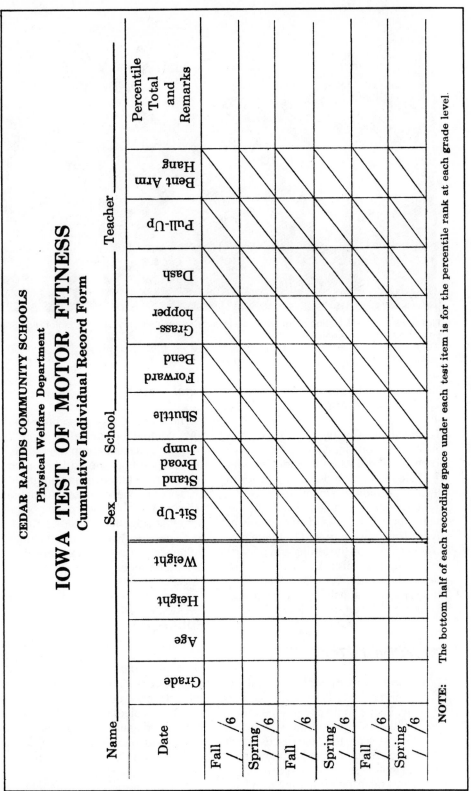

CEDAR RAPIDS COMMUNITY SCHOOLS
Physical Welfare Department

IOWA TEST OF MOTOR FITNESS
Cumulative Individual Record Form

Name _____   Sex _____ School _____   Teacher _____

Date	Grade	Age	Height	Weight	Sit-Up	Stand Broad Jump	Shuttle	Forward Bend	Grass-hopper	Dash	Pull-Up	Bent Arm Hang	Percentile Total and Remarks
Fall __/__/6													
Spring __/__/6													
Fall __/__/6													
Spring __/__/6													
Fall __/__/6													
Spring __/__/6													

NOTE: The bottom half of each recording space under each test item is for the percentile rank at each grade level.

Figure 13–6.   A practical form for recording test results.

Figure 13–7. Mass testing of an entire class in the sit-up. (Courtesy Revere Junior High School, Los Angeles City Schools.)

move from one test station to another in squad units. The results are recorded on squad cards.

Individual Testing. Some teachers prefer to test one individual at a time and to enter the results on an individual record card. Students move from one testing station to another singly instead of by squads. After completing all the test items, they participate in an overflow activity. This procedure allows the teacher to concentrate on the testing and provides activity for students after they have completed their tests. With this plan, discipline problems and the incidence of accidents are reduced. (See Figure 13–6.)

Conducting the Test

Teachers' primary concern should be to administer the tests smoothly and accurately. They should explain the importance of the test, demonstrate the proper form for taking the test, and discuss safety procedures. Students can be motivated to perform their best if teachers post average test scores near the testing area.

Final Procedures

There are several procedures that follow completion of tests. Score cards must be collected and properly filed; results of the tests should be studied and used to plan future testing programs; the tests should be analyzed to determine whether the objectives developed in the planning stage have been attained; and the degree to which the test results will influence students' grades must be carefully determined.

GRADING IN PHYSICAL EDUCATION

One of the most difficult problems in physical education is the assigning of grades to students. Unlike many other subjects in the curriculum, physical education involves numerous variables. Physical education teachers have to evaluate knowledge, performance, and affective behavior in the form of a single grade.

Probably the greatest difficulties in determining grades for physical education are oversized classes, the frequency of grading periods, and the unique nature of the knowledge and skills involved. The overwhelming complexity of evaluation in physical education leads to disagreement as to what should be tested and how tests should be given. Often, the tests that are valid and reliable are not used because they are too time-consuming. As a result, teachers compensate by using unjustifiable criteria and techniques. Instead of marking students on instruction and achievement, teachers may evaluate them on items such as attendance, dress, attitudes, sportsmanship, discipline, and other factors that have no bearing on achievement. It is difficult to justify marking students on such items, even though they do play a significant role in the teaching assignment; however, they are a reflection of overall school policy and should not be used to determine marks. Students should be evaluated on the basis of those elements that make up the learning situation. Skill tests, knowledge tests, and proficiency tests are measurable and are the best yardsticks of the learning situation.

The establishment of certain uniform guidelines for grading should be the first step in initiating a new marking system for physical education. Several fundamental principles should be included:

1. Grades given to students should be based on all of the objectives of the course, such as skills, physical fitness, attitudes, appreciation, and knowledge. These factors should be weighed according to the emphasis given in the instruction; however, a major portion of the grade should be based on skill and/or physical fitness with a minimum standard of achievement for each of the other objectives.
2. The grade for a student should be determined by the extent to which he attains the objectives with ample consideration given to attainment in terms of capacity and to improvement during the instructional period.
3. The grading procedure used for physical education should be consistent with that for other subjects in the school or school system. This includes the use of symbols (A, B, C, D, F; S or U; or Pass or Fail), distribution of grades, and the inclusion of grades in the computation for the honor roll.
4. The grade assigned to a student should be based on his performance in relation to the objectives of the course and not in comparison with other students. There can be no justification in applying the so-called curve system to assigning grades in physical education.
5. The same basic principles and plan should govern the grading procedure in all physical education classes in the school system. These principles and plan should be developed cooperatively by all teachers.
6. A variety of instruments, both subjective and objective, should be used in the evaluating process. The selection of these instruments should be in terms of the extent to which they are valid, reliable, and objective; ease with which they are understood, administered, and scored; economy in time and equipment; availability of norms and/or standards; and extent to which they serve a useful purpose; i.e., meet the purposes of tests.
7. Evaluative instruments should not be used solely or even primarily for assigning grades. Other purposes are to: provide a basis for classifying students in terms of specific objectives or competencies; motivate students to attain objectives; provide a method of instruction, i.e., in taking the test the student is drilling on the skill; provide the teacher with material for self-evaluation of teaching effectiveness; provide the teacher with additional data for reporting to parents, school administrators, and the public the achievement of students in physical education.
8. Students should be informed of the procedure to be used for assigning grades in physical education. Notification should be made in writing at the beginning of the unit, semester, or school year as appropriate.[16]

After the teacher has studied the general principles of marking, the next step is to consider proficiency testing, grading based on improvement and effort, and contract grading.

Proficiency Testing

McGee and Drews define the term *proficiency test* as a test administered to a student upon request to determine whether he or she meets a predetermined standard of performance and knowledge in a specific physical education activity. The difficulties that have arisen over such a definition have been caused by using the term *predetermined standard of performance*. High schools using a proficiency testing program must first decide what level of performance shall be required in order to declare a student proficient. Once this criterion is determined and agreed upon by the faculty, the student has a goal to which he or she can aspire. Generally, the definition of proficiency holds that the student who can perform an activity or the components of a sport reasonably well shall be considered proficient.

Proficiency tests can be used for three purposes:

1. Providing for exemption from a course that is generally required of students.
2. Placement of a student at a particular level of performance in a course of instruction.
3. Assistance in the determination of a grade or evaluation. This is usually either coupled with the presentation of the course itself or administered at a time other than in the regular course. When administered at a time other than in the course, the testing should parallel and reflect the skills and knowledges presented in the regular course of instruction testing.[17]

A proficiency testing program can allot credit to students for skills and knowledges acquired elsewhere. If grading in physical education is to be based on knowledge and physical performance, the proficiency testing program should require the same standards of achievement. Secondary school students are given the opportunity to expand their physical education experiences if this alternative program is offered.

Grading on Improvement

Most physical educators support the concept of grading based on achievement in performance. The authors believe, however, that there is a great deal of merit in evaluating students on the degree of improvement shown over a period of time. Wells and Baumgartner investigated the practicality of using the Hales method of evaluating improvement. This concept states that an individual with a good initial performance is not likely to improve his score as much as an individual who started with a poor performance. In the Hales system, however, the better the student's initial score, the more improvement credit he or she is given for progressing any fixed amount. The researchers found that this method of mea-

suring improvement does offer a practical alternative to the use of final physical performance levels.[18] Some disadvantages to this procedure do exist, but they can be overcome if the following suggestions are taken into account:

1. If students are aware that the test-retest technique is being used, they might deliberately score poorly on the initial test in order to receive a high score on the terminal test. This tendency can be avoided by giving the tests without any announcements about grading based on improvement. Students should be told that these tests are only part of the total testing program and that they should do their best.
2. Students with natural ability who score well might be penalized because the more accomplished a student is, the more difficult it is to improve. As an illustration, consider Pupils A and B. Pupil A has had considerable experience in football and Pupil B has had none. In the initial test, A punts the football 50 yards and B punts it only 20. After instruction, the terminal test is given to each. Pupil A punts 55 yards while Pupil B punts 40 yards. Pupil B shows more improvement and would receive a better grade based on improvement. This can be offset by grouping the students on the basis of ability before the initial test. Each ability group would have a different range of testing performances; this would place Pupil A in a performance division in which as much weight would be awarded to a five yard improvement as to the 20 yard improvement of Pupil B. (See Fig. 13–8.)

Grading on Effort

The effort made by a student should be considered in determining his grade. Some students, no matter how much effort they exert, never achieve above-average performance. Many students possess ability and are physically fit but are unable to score well on the tests. Body type plays a tremendous role in performance; that a student with a particular physical structure cannot attain the deter-

GROUP	INTERVAL	INITIAL TEST TALLY		TERMINAL TEST TALLY	
1	1–19	~~THL~~ ~~THL~~	10	~~THL~~ /	6
2	20–39	~~THL~~ ~~THL~~ ~~THL~~	15	~~THL~~ ~~THL~~ ~~THL~~ /	16
3	40–59	~~THL~~ ~~THL~~	10	~~THL~~ ~~THL~~ //	12
4	60–79	~~THL~~	5	~~THL~~ /	6

Figure 13-8. Grouping students by ability in testing football punt for distance. (From Greyson Daughtrey, *Effective Teaching in Secondary Physical Education*, 2nd ed., W. B. Saunders Co.)

IMPORTANT

Pupils grouped into four ability sections, based on the initial test.

Each group is evaluated on improvement as determined by the terminal test, based on scale shown below.

SCALE FOR EVALUATION

Group 1
20 yds. improvement — excellent
15 yds. improvement — very good
10 yds. improvement — good
5 yds. improvement — fair

Group 3
10 yds. improvement — excellent
5 yds. improvement — very good
3 yds. improvement — good
Below 3 yds. improvement — fair

Group 2
15 yds. improvement — excellent
10 yds. improvement — very good
5 yds. improvement — good
Below 5 yds. improvement — fair

Group 4
5 yds. improvement — excellent
3 yds. improvement — very good
2 yds. improvement — good
1 yd. improvement — fair

SCORE SHEET

PUPIL'S NAME	ABILITY GROUP	INITIAL TEST	TERMINAL TEST	YARDS IMPROVED	MARK
Frank Jones	1	10 yds.	30 yds.	20 yds.	Excellent
Joe Thomas	2	25 yds.	30 yds.	5 yds.	Good
Tom Luck	3	40 yds.	48 yds.	8 yds.	Very good
Jack Tabb	4	60 yds.	65 yds.	5 yds.	Excellent

mined standards in certain activities does not mean that the student should receive a failing grade. If students try seriously to achieve, the final grade should reflect those efforts.

A test for the 100-yard dash illustrates this point. Twelve seconds has been established as the average for the grade level or class. Assume six students, typical of the variety found in all heterogeneously grouped classes in physical education, are to run the dash. The six students complete the dash in the following times:

Student With:	Time (seconds):
Long legs	11.5
Athletically fit physique	11.7
Slight limp	11.9
Medium build	12.0
Tall, skinny build	12.3
Short, fat build	12.5

Depending on the system used by the teacher, the short, fat student might receive a failing grade. From a physiologic point of view, all the runners benefited equally. Because the short, fat student was handicapped as a sprinter, it is possible that he exerted more effort than the other students. Can a teacher justify failing a student when physiologic and health benefits were derived? This point emphasizes the value of making effort an integral factor in the grading system even if it makes evaluative criteria more difficult to establish.

Contract Grading

Student motivation is the most positive aspect of contract grading. In this system, the emphasis is on learning rather than on teaching. Contract grading is simply a written agreement between teacher and student. The teacher examines the subject matter and outlines the goals and the daily expectations of the teaching-learning experience. With this information, each student develops his or her own objectives and determines the nature of the commitment he or she wants to make to physical education. In essence, the student is responsible for fulfilling the contract. Realization of self-set goals is rewarding and fulfilling.

Contract grading is a complex and diverse grading system. On the opposite page is an example of contract grading for volleyball, as used in Beach Channel High School in Rockaway Park, New York.[19]

SUGGESTED GRADING PLANS

Some schools have made constructive efforts to devise acceptable grading plans for evaluating student achievement. The physical education program in the Norfolk, Virginia public schools includes testing as an integral part of the overall curriculum. The teachers and supervisory personnel developed a system in which the student's grade is based on ability, skill, and knowledge of games and rules. Figure 13–9 shows the grading plan and other items involved in the program.

Other schools, such as Harbor Beach Community School in Harbor Beach, Michigan, and Fife Junior and Senior High School in Tacoma, Washington, have developed testing systems to up-

grade the caliber of physical education. In the Harbor Beach School, students in grades 7 through 12 are placed in three ability groups for each activity: top, middle, and low. Each group spends proportionate time on seminar study and participation in the actual activity. Half of the student's grade in each unit is based on improvement in skills and on written tests. In addition to skills tests, students are given the AAHPER tests.[20]

At Fife Junior and Senior High School, students take fitness tests and skills and knowledge tests in football, basketball, volleyball, wrestling, badminton, and track and field. The Fife fitness test, given four times each year, includes push-ups, pull-ups, burpees, sit-ups, bar dips, vertical hang, rope climb, 600-yard run and walk, man lift and carry, extension press-ups, and overhead ladder crawl.

The skills and fitness tests are based on a 10-point scale that is translated into letter grades as follows:

10 = A	5 = C+
9 = A−	4 = C
8 = B+	3 = C−
7 = B	2 = D
6 = B−	1 = D−

The final grade for each activity unit is determined by dividing the number of points scored by the number of tests given. If a child scored 32 points in the four-item basketball test, the mark would be 8, or B+.[21]

Moriarity developed a unique plan for testing in physical education that warrants attention. She maintains that grades should be based on the successful attainment of objectives, and that the objectives of the program should decide the emphasis that measurable items should receive. Factors such as achievement and knowledge are assessed in light of their relative value. If achievement is more important than knowledge, equal weight should not be given to both factors. Moriarity suggests that letter grades be assigned numerical values of A (5), B (4), C (3), D (2), and F (1). Weighing the importance of the factors might result in the following point distribution: 3 for achievement, 2 for ability, 1 for knowledge, and 1 for attitude. In the following example, the sum of the points earned by the student is 28, which, when divided by

Volleyball Contract for Grade

The basic purposes for the use of the teaching contract are individualization and the student's acceptance of responsibility for learning.

The contract lists a variety of alternatives, giving the student a choice range which best suits his or her interests.

If students set goals for themselves, they will try harder to fulfill them. The students are responsible for fulfilling the contract.

Directions: Students are to make out an individual contract (using sheet given out in class), choosing *one* activity from Part I — team experience, and *one* activity from Part II — individualized competitive experience.

PART I — PARTICIPATION IN A TEAM EXPERIENCE
   A. *Division A:* high level competition and team play; students choosing this division should be able to perform all power volleyball techniques and strategies including overhand serve, spike, block, 4-2 defense. Rules concerning legal hits shall be enforced strictly.
   B. *Division B:* moderate level competition and team play; students choosing this division should be familiar with all power volleyball techniques; serve may be underhand and taken at a maximum of two steps in front of end line.
   C. *Division C:* modified competition and team play; students choosing this division will be able to play on a small court, with 2 tries per serve. Emphasis is on player interaction rather than highly skilled play.
PART II — PARTICIPATION IN INDIVIDUALIZED COMPETITIVE EXPERIENCE
   A. Two-person competition: 2 on 2, half-court
   B. Three-person competition: 3 on 3, half-court
   C. Volleyball-Basketball Game: 1 on 1, 2 on 2
   D. Volleyball Set to Basketball game: 1 on 1
   E. Volleyball Serve Game: placement of serves
   F. Officiating for Team or Individualized Experience: students choosing this will be responsible for calling serve violations, net and line violations, and illegal hits.
   G. Skills Performance: *Division A*
           1. Self set — 10 consecutive times
           2. Self bump — 10 consecutive times
           3. Serve — 7 out of 10 legal serves from service box
           4. Volley with partner using set and bump — 20 seconds
   H. Skills Performance: *Division B*
           1. Set to partner — 5 contacts each
           2. Bump to partner — 5 contacts each
           3. Serve — 5 out of 10 legal serves, max. 2 feet ahead of end line.
           4. Volley with partner using set and bump — 10 seconds
   I. Skills Performance: *Division C*
           1. Set to wall — 5 consecutive times
           2. Bump to wall — 5 consecutive times
           3. Serve — 5 out of 10 from anywhere behind mid-court line
           4. Volley with partner using set and bump — 3 contacts each

NORFOLK PUBLIC SCHOOLS
HEALTH, SAFETY, AND PHYSICAL EDUCATION DEPARTMENT
PUPIL RECORD CARD

Wall No. _____   Phase _____

Squad No. _____   Homeroom _____

Locker No. _____   Period _____

Grade _____

Name _____   Health Teacher _____

Address _____ Telephone _____ Age _____

ATTENDANCE

A—Absent X—Excused T—Tardy X—Excused D—Not Dressed B—Excused	Days	M	T	W	Th	F	M	T	W	Th	F	M	T	W	Th	F	M	T	W	Th	F	M	T	W	Th	F
	Dates																									

EVALUATION

PHASE	1	2	3	4
Activity Instruction				
Health Instruction				
AVERAGE				

NOTE: The final mark or grade for each nine weeks should be an average of the Health Instruction and the Activity Instruction. Each of the two areas receives the same weight.

P.E. 1-78

EVALUATION OF PROGRESS IN PHYSICAL EDUCATION
NORFOLK SCHOOL BOARD REGULATIONS ON GRADING AND REPORTING TO PARENTS:

§ 6-44 P   Each student and his parents shall be informed periodically of where the student stands in relation to the objective of his particular unit or educational plan.

Students shall not be punished academically; rather, their grades shall be based upon their achivements and progress. (Effective: 7/1/74)

§ 6-44 R   There shall be implemented a grading system or plan which is consistent throughout the school division and reflects the growth of the individual. Parents shall be advised prior to the periodic reports when their children are not meeting the academic standards in order that they might assist the student. (Adopted by School Board: 7/1/74)

SKILLS TEACHING PROGRESSION

The physical education grade should be comprised of 80% psychomotor skills assessment and 20% on knowledge of skills, rules and safety regulations. Skills should be evaluated as proficiency is acquired. Equal points should be allotted for each activity during a phase.

ACTIVITIES	GIVE AS MANY TESTS IN EACH GRADE AS TIME PERMITS					
Basketball	Passes	Dribble	Foul	Lay-Up	Set Shot	Pivot
Bowling	Grip	Stance	Approach	Delivery	Follow Thru	Aiming
Field Hockey	Grip	Dribble	Drive	Bully	Passing	Dodging
Flag Football	Punt	Pass	Block	Place Kick	Back Field Formation	Line
Golf	Grip	Stance	Swing	Follow Thru	Putting	Drive
Indv. Rhythmics	Locomotor	Exercises	Ball Rhythmics	Rope Jumping	Combinations	Dynamics
Modern Dance	Locomotor	Axial	Interpretive	Patterns	Spatial	Composition
Soccer	Dribbling	Passing	Trapping	Kicking	Blocking	Heading
Softball	Throwing	Hitting	Running	Pitching	Catching	Fielding
Table Tennis	Grip	Serve	Stroke	Drive	Chop	Doubles
Tennis	Grip	Fore Hand	Back Hand	Serve	Volley	Lob
Track	Starts	Dash	Hurdles	R. L. Jump	Shot	Relay
Tumbling	Fwd. Roll	Back Roll	Kip	Balance	Hand Stand	Hand Spring
Volleyball	Volley	Serve	Set-Ups	Spike	Block	Recover From Net
Wrestling	Take Downs	Counters	Escapes	Breakdowns	Reversals	Pins

Figure 13–9. An individual record card including a marking system based on the psychomotor and cognitive domains. (Courtesy Norfolk Public Schools, Norfolk, Virginia.)

the total of the weights (7), gives a score of 4 or a grade of B.[22]

Factors	Weight	Marks	Points
Achievement	3	B (4)	$3 \times 4 = 12$
Ability	2	A (5)	$2 \times 5 = 10$
Knowledge	1	C (3)	$1 \times 3 = 3$
Attitude	1	C (3)	$1 \times 3 = 3$

The grading system used in the Dade County Public Schools reflects overall performance by the student in the physical education class. It includes student grouping, screening tests, cardiovascular tests, fitness tests, standard tests, and sports skill tests. (See Fig. 13–10.) Different values, in the form of percentages, are assigned to performances in the cognitive, psychomotor, and affective domains.[23]

	Percentages		
Objectives	PLAN I	PLAN II	PLAN III
Psychomotor	40	50	65
Cognitive	35	30	20
Affective	25	20	15

Hanson believes that marks should be determined by the student's achievement of the basic objectives. He rules out such factors as improvement, fitness level, good citizenship, proper dress, locker room behavior, attendance, effort, and discipline. His plan reflects good motor skill performance and physical fitness as basic objectives, and he believes that knowledge and achievement in these areas should be the sole basis for grading. Hanson suggests the following formula for determining a mark in physical education:

Objectives	Weight
Motor Skills	50%
Physical Fitness	25%
Knowledge	25%
Understanding	
Sports techniques	
Rules	
Strategy	
Whys of Physical Education[24]	

Another theory of grading that is supported by some physical education teachers is based on the pass-fail concept that abolishes the traditional letter system. The teachers at Thornton Fractional High School in South Lansing, Illinois, described the advantages of pass-fail grading:

1. It eliminates many of the inequities inherent in any grading system in that one decision is better than placing students in five arbitrary categories.
2. Pass-fail is practical. It does not require intricate measurements or evaluation. Good judgment still has to be made of a student's competence.
3. Students will be encouraged to participate more willingly without the external stimulus of low grades.
4. Students should learn course content through motivation, not through the mere desire for high grades.
5. Many students become problems because they feel they cannot compete with the more skilled students.
6. Pass-fail systems of grading at college level are being accepted on a wider scale than ever before; hence our pass-fail grading would not be affected in any way by the admissions offices of colleges.
7. A pass is construed to be equivalent to at least a D grade in the regular grading system.
8. Successful completion of a course on pass or fail basis should result in a pass grade being recorded in the student's record, the credit earned being added to his credit total to fulfill his graduation requirement.
9. Unsuccessful completion in a pass-fail course should yield a fail grade, which is recorded in the student's record. At the junior-senior level, he will be held accountable for satisfactory passing of the course in physical education.[25]

The pass-fail concept has a great deal of merit for those schools that do not grant academic credit for courses in physical education. Today, however, many schools throughout the country place equal emphasis on physical education and academic subjects, requiring physical education credit for graduation. In these schools, the pass-fail concept would adversely affect the physical education program.

REPORTING TO PARENTS

After students have been tested and grades have been determined, teachers are faced with the problem of reporting to

STUDENT FITNESS TEST RECORDS

Three Screening Tests

		AGE	Flex. A or Pull-up	Stand. B. J.	Shutt. Run	Total		AGE	CARDIOVAS-CULAR TEST	RATING	STANDARD TESTS
Date							1.				Rope Skipping
Height		1st					2.				600 yard Run-Walk
Weight											
Vision W/O Glasses	R L	2nd					3.				Rope Climb
Vision with Glasses	R L										

Dates	GROUPING – LEVEL 1 2 3 4 5	FITNESS TESTS		AGE	Flex. A or Pull-up	60 sec. Sit-up	Shutt. Run	Stand. B. J.	50 yds. Dash	Softball Throw	600 Run-W.	Total %ile	Comp. Score
		1st	%ile										
			Score										
		2nd	%ile										
			Score										

Pull-ups — Arm Flexed H.

Push-ups

Bar Dips

60 Sec. Sit-up

COMMENTS:

SPORTS SKILL TESTS

(Three Basic)

1. 2. 3.

NAME: _____ LAST _____ FIRST _____ PHONE _____ SECTION

DADE COUNTY PUBLIC SCHOOLS

PHYSICAL EDUCATION STUDENT GRADE CARD

Instructor's Name

	Skills	Obs. Skills	Written T.	Soc. & Per.	Daily Av.	Subject	Effort	Conduct	Absences	Tardies

Sept. Date 4 5 6 7 8 11 12 13 14 15 18 19 20 21 22 25 26 27 28 29 **Oct.** 2 3 4 5 6 9 10 11 12 13 16 — 1ST Six Weeks

Oct. Date 17 18 19 20 23 24 25 26 27 30 31 **Nov.** 1 2 3 6 7 8 9 10 13 14 15 16 17 20 21 22 27 28 29 30 **Dec.** 1 4 — 2ND Six Weeks

Dec. Date 5 6 7 8 11 12 13 14 15 18 19 20 21 22 **Jan.** 1 2 3 4 5 8 9 10 11 12 15 16 17 18 19 22 23 24 25 26 — 3RD Six Weeks (SEM. EXAM)

Feb. Date 29 30 31 1 2 5 6 7 8 9 12 13 14 15 16 19 20 21 22 23 26 27 28 29 **Mar.** 1 4 5 6 7 8 — 4TH Six Weeks

Mar. Date 11 12 13 14 15 18 19 20 21 22 25 26 27 28 29 **Apr.** 1 2 3 4 5 8 9 10 11 12 15 16 17 18 19 22 23 24 25 26 — 5TH Six Weeks

May Date 29 30 1 2 3 6 7 8 9 10 13 14 15 16 17 20 21 22 23 24 27 28 29 30 31 **June** 3 4 5 6 7 10 — 6TH Six Weeks (Final EXAM)

Roll No.	Comp. Score	NAME					Subject	Effort	Conduct
	Level	Last First	Period	Locker No.	Combination			Final Average	
		Grade & Sec.	IBM No.	Student Classification	Fees				

Figure 13–10. Comprehensive permanent record card showing overall performance of the student in physical education. (Courtesy Dade County Public Schools, Jacksonville, Florida.)

CEDAR RAPIDS COMMUNITY SCHOOLS

Physical Welfare Department
PUPIL PHYSICAL FITNESS REPORT

NAME_____ SCHOOL_____ DATE_____ TEACHER(Fall)_____

PRINCIPAL_____ TEACHER(Spring)_____

TO THE PARENTS: A series of physical fitness tests has recently been given to all pupils in grades 4–12. They are being given twice each school year. This is a report on the performance of your child. In each test you may compare your child's score with the performance score of other children throughout the state. The state scores are given in terms of percentile rank. For example, a percentile rank of 75 means that a child's performance surpasses that of 75 per cent of the children of the same grade tested through the state. The state norms were constructed on data obtained by testing boys and girls in 104 schools in Iowa during the 1960–61 school year. Thus, the percentile scores cannot necessarily be interpreted as the ultimate in achievement. They can be assumed to represent the achievements for the 1960–61 school year of those schools where attention was given to motor fitness.

If your child has a low performance score, it might be because of a particular height, weight or other physical characteristic. The important thing is for each child to show continued improvement in his own performance.

This department is making strenuous efforts to assist our young people to attain and maintain health and physical fitness. The physically underdeveloped youngsters are being identified and programs geared to individual needs. We are giving increased emphasis to the more vigorous type activities. It is recommended that parents encourage their children to participate regularly in physical activity.

TEST	WHAT IT TESTS	YOUR CHILD'S SCORE Fall	Spring	PERCENTILE RANK Fall	Spring	HOW TO INTERPRET THE RESULTS
SIT-UPS	Strength/endurance of abdominal muscles					The object was to do as many as possible in 1 min. (2 min. boys, Gr. 10–12)
STANDING BROAD JUMP	Power in the legs and coordination	in.	in.			The greater distance jumped, the better the performance.
SHUTTLE RUN	Agility					The greater number of trips in a 15 second interval, the better the score.
FORWARD BEND	Flexibility	in.	in.			The higher score (plus) measured in the nearest 1/2", the better the performance.
GRASSHOPPER	Endurance					The object was to do as many as possible in 30 sec. (1 min. boys, Gr. 7 & up.)
DASH	Speed	sec.	sec.			The faster time the better the performance; 40 yd., Gr. 4–6; 50 yds., Gr. 7–12.
PULL-UPS (Boys) BENT ARM HANG (Girls)	Arm, shoulder and upper back strength					Boys—one point each time chin goes above the bar. Girls—the longer the time (in sec.) with arms fully bent, chin above bar, the better the performance.

ARNOLD SALISBURY
Superintendent of Schools

EMIL A. KLUMPAR
Physical Welfare Consultant

Figure 13–11. Reporting to parents. (Courtesy Cedar Rapids Community School District, Cedar Rapids, Iowa.)

parents. It is doubtful that the traditional letter grade that appears on the periodic report card can provide parents with an understanding of their child's achievement in class. Since grades are a major form of communication between the school and the parents, the report card should reflect as accurately as possible the performance of the child in physical education. (See Fig. 13–11.)

QUESTIONS FOR DISCUSSION

1. Do you consider assessment and evaluation essential at the secondary school level? Why?
2. Define the terms *evaluation, measurement, testing,* and *grading.*
3. Should administrators and teachers be evaluated on performance? Why?
4. What are the characteristics of a good test? Would you use standardized tests? State the reasons for your response.
5. What steps would you take in conducting a sound physical education testing program?

REFERENCES

1. Harold M. Barrow and Rosemary McGee, *A Practical Approach to Measurement in Physical Education,* 2nd ed. (Philadelphia: Lea and Febiger, 1971), pp. 9–11, 19.
2. Los Angeles City Schools, Instructional Planning Division, *Physical Education Departmental Self-Evaluation Checklists, Junior and Senior High Schools* (Los Angeles Unified School District, 1975).
3. Antoinette Tiburzi, "Performance Appraisal Plan for Administration," Unpublished Paper (Athens: University of Georgia, March, 1977).
4. Martin Huberman, "Evaluating Deans: A Guide to Assessment of Leadership in Schools of Education," *The Journal of Teacher Education* (Vol. XXIII, No. 2, Summer, 1972), pp. 126–128.
5. "Physical Education Teachers and Programs Attacked," *Physical Education Newsletter* (Old Saybrook: Physical Education Publications, January 1, 1971).
6. *Ibid.*
7. Daryl Siedentop, "O.S.U. Teacher Behavior Rating Scale." *JOPER* (Vol. 46, February, 1975), p. 45.
8. George B. Leonard, "Testing Versus Your Child," *Look Magazine* (March, 1966), p. 64.
9. "In-depth Study Faults Evaluation Policies," *American Association of Colleges for Teacher Education* (Washington, D.C., July–August, 1969), p. 5.
10. Robert Biehler, *Psychology Applied to Teaching,* 2nd ed. (Boston: Houghton Mifflin Company, 1974), p. 522.
11. *Ibid.,* p. 520.
12. Mary Jane Haskins, *Evaluation in Physical Education* (Dubuque, Iowa: William C. Brown Company, 1971), p. 5.
13. Donald Mathews, *Measurement in Physical Education,* 5th ed. (Philadelphia: W. B. Saunders Company, 1975), pp. VII–X.
14. Margaret J. Safrit, *Evaluation in Physical Education: Assessing Motor Behavior* (Englewood Cliffs: Prentice-Hall, Inc., 1973), p. 263.
15. David R. Krathwohl, et al., *Taxonomy of Educational Objectives: The Classification of Educational Goals: Handbook II: The Affective Domain* (New York: David McKay, 1964), p. 37. Copyright by Longman, Inc., 1977.
16. Lynn W. McGraw, "Principles and Practices for Assigning Grades in Physical Education," *JOHPER* (February, 1964), p. 24.
17. Rosemary McGee and Fred Drews, A Project of the College Physical Education Commission, AAHPER, *Proficiency Testing for Physical Education* (Washington: AAHPER Publications, 1974), p. 1.
18. W. Tom Wells and Ted A. Baumgartner, "An Investigation into the Practicality of Using the Hales' Exponential Method of Evaluating Improvement," *Research Quarterly* (Vol. 45, No. 4, December, 1974), pp. 460–464.
19. Beach Channel High School, Rockaway Park, New York (Materials sent to authors), 1977.
20. "And Here's How Schools Are Using Physical Education Tests to Upgrade Physical Education." *Physical Education Newsletter* (Old Saybrook: Physical Education Publications, October 15, 1965).
21. *Ibid.*
22. Mary J. Moriarity, "How Shall We Grade Them?" *JOHPER* (Vol. 25, January, 1954), pp. 27, 55.

23. Dade County Public Schools, Miami, Florida (Materials sent to authors), 1977.
24. Dale L. Hanson, "Grading in Physical Education," *JOHPER* (Vol. 38, May, 1967), p. 37.
25. Adolph Gentile, Chairman, Department of Physical Education, Thornton Fractional High School, South Lansing, Michigan (Materials sent to authors), 1973.

SELECTED READINGS

Barrow, Harold M. and Rosemary McGee, *A Practical Approach to Measurement in Physical Education,* 2nd ed. (Philadelphia: Lea and Febiger, 1971).

Bureau of Physical Education, Health Education, Athletics and Recreation, *The Physical Performance Test for California* (Revised), 1971.

Cohen, Karen C., "Some Workable Evaluation Strategies," *Today's Education* (Vol. 65, January–February, 1976), pp. 60–62, 95.

Greenberg, Jerrold S., "How Videotaping Improves Teaching Behavior," *JOHPER* (Vol. 44, March, 1973), pp. 36–37.

Haskins, Mary Jane, *Evaluation in Physical Education* (Dubuque: William C. Brown Company, 1971).

Johnson, Barry L. and Jack K. Nelson, *Practical Measurements for Evaluation in Physical Education,* 2nd ed. (Minneapolis: Burgess Publishing Company, 1974).

Johnson, James J., "Why Administrators Fail," *The Clearing House* (Vol. 48, No. 1, September, 1973), pp. 3–6.

Kirschenbaum, Howard, Rodney Napier, and Sidney B. Simon, *Wad–ja–get? The Grading Game in American Education* (New York: Hart Publishing Company, Inc., 1971).

Mayer, Robert F., *Measuring Instructional Intent or Got a Match?* (Belmont, California, Lear Siegler, Inc., Fearon Publishers, 1973).

McMahan, Rosemary, "Sportsmanship Questionnaire." Instrument for assessing sportsmanship attitudes (unpublished doctoral dissertation, University of Tennessee, Knoxville, August, 1978).

McWilliams, Jettie M. and Andrew C. Thomas, "The Measurement of Student's Learning: An Approach to Accountability," *The Journal of Educational Research* (Vol. 70, No. 1, September–October, 1976), pp. 50–52.

Pipho, Chris, "Minimal Competency Testing: A Look at State Standards," *Educational Leadership* (Vol. 34, No. 7, April, 1977), pp. 516–520.

Safrit, Margaret J., *Evaluation in Physical Education: Assessing Motor Behavior* (Englewood Cliffs: Prentice-Hall, Inc., 1973).

Weber, Marie, "Physical Education Teacher Role Identification Instrument," *Research Quarterly* (AAHPER, Vol. 48, No. 2, May, 1977), pp. 445–451.

INDEX

Ability grouping, 125–128, 179, *180*
  instruction and, 184
  mainstreaming and, 272
  procedures for, 276
  Title IX legislation and, 127
  use of for teaching lay-up shot, *127*
Academic achievement, 6–8
  physical growth in relation to, 7
  problems with, 6–8
Academic discipline, characteristics of, 40
  physical education and, 39–40
Accomplishment, providing students with feeling
    of, 112–113
Accountability, education and, 119
  management by objective theory and, 29
  of teachers to public, 27–32
  productivity and price of, 30
  types of, 28–29
Achievement, recognition of, 114
Activities, criteria for selection of, 74–75
  culminating, 114–115
  evaluation of, 74–75
  group, definition of, 232
  individual, definition of, 189
  modification of for handicapped students,
    286–287
  safety of, 130–131
  selection of, 76–77
    in future, 75–77
    procedures for, 76
    scientific approach to, 74–77
  teaching strategies for, 179–268
  undesirable, 136–138
Adapted physical education, 274
Administrator, common mistakes of, 340, 342
  continuous review of, 339–340, 342
  importance of education of concerning physical
    education, 321
  methods for evaluation of, 339–342, 340(t), *341*
  need for in intramural programs, 293, 295
  performance appraisal of, 339
  self-evaluation of, 339
Affective domain of behavior, 56
Aged, teaching opportunities with, 34
Agencies, school-community relations and,
    333–334
Alternative careers, 33
Alternative programs, 120
Anatomy, physical fitness and, 48
Anemia, teaching students with, 277
Announcements, in class, 183
Aritomism, physical education and, 41

Assembly programs, use of in school-community
    relations, 326
Assessment, advantages of testing as method of,
    344–345
  criticisms of current methods of, 344
  importance of in physical education, 337–362
  methods of within school systems, 338–339
  phases of, definition of, 338
  purposes of, 337–338
  scientifically applied standards for, 345–362
  self-appraisal system of, 339
  traditional or summative method of, 338–339
Assessment Center Appraisal Technique, use of in
    performance appraisal, 55
Assignments, value of beyond school, 119–120
Associated learning, 92
Associative theory of learning, 103–105
Asthma, teaching students with, 277
Attendance, problems with, 5–6
  recording of, 143–144, 181–183, *182*
Attitude, methodology in, 87–90
Audio-visual aids, as teaching device, 93, *93*
  guidelines for use of, 94–95
Awards, certificates as, *311*
  system of for intramural participation, 309

Basketball, plan for teaching skills of, 232–238,
    234–238
Behavior, affective domain of, 56
    terms used for evaluation of, *349*
    tests for, 384
  cognitive domain of, 55–56
  disruptive, 7–9
  modification of, 91
  objectives of, curriculum design and teaching
      based on, 56
    writing of, 56
  psychomotor domain of, 56
Behavioral objectives, categories of, 56
Bowling, plan for teaching skills of, 196–201,
    197–201
Budgeting, 156
Bulletin boards, 95
  use of in school-community relations, 327

Camping, *52*
Cardinal Principles of Secondary Education, 42

Cardiovascular diseases, exercise and prevention of, 10
Career alternatives, 33
Carry-over leisure sports pattern, 52–53
    camping as, *52*
    secondary school physical education and, 52–53
Cascade system, 274, *275*
Cerebral palsy, teaching students with, 280
Chalk boards, 95
Challenge, importance of providing, 113
Challenge tournament, 300
Cheating, problem of in schools, 344
Check sheets, daily, 145, *146*
Checklist Appraisal Technique, use of in performance appraisal, 54–55
Circulatory-respiratory efficiency, physical fitness and, 48
Class, closing of, 185
    effect of size on organization of, 159
    environment of, importance of flexibility in for teaching handicapped, 287
    essentials in organization of, 141–176
    large, organization of, 120–121
    organization of, five phases for, 181
    preparation for, 181–183
Classification of students, 125–128, *126*
Classroom, discipline in, 83
Cleanliness, importance of in class, 148
Client-centered plan, 164, *164*
    instructional modes in, 164, *165*
Closed-open continuum, physical education as, 90
Closing, of class, 185
Coeducation, 179–180
    curriculum revision due to, 65
    importance of, *76*
    in volleyball instruction, *181*
    Title IX legislation and, 179–180
Cognitive domain of behavior, 55–56
Cognitive-field theory of learning, 105–106
    criticisms of, 106
    introduction of into instructional program, 106
Cohort instruction, AAHPER definition of, 165
Command style of teaching, 82
Communication skills, importance of to teachers, 25–26
Community, organizations in concerned with education, 320–321
    power structures in, 322–323
    pressure groups within, 332
    school and, relationship between, 319–334
Competency-based instruction, 185–187
    affective component of, 186
    cognitive component of, 186
    example of lesson plan for, 186
    psychomotor component of, 186
Competency-based teacher education, certification criteria for, 30
    promise of, 30
Competition, against oneself, 115
    against others, 115
    in skills, 121–123
    skill instruction and, 113
    use of for practicing skills, *185*
Concomitant learning, 92
Consolation elimination plan for tournaments, *298*, 299
Consultants, use of in teaching, 90

Content, models for placement of in physical education, 71–72
Contract grading, 356, *357*
Contract teaching, 86
Creativity, development of, 6
    physical education and, 128–129
Credit for physical education, 159, 329–330
Criterion-referenced planning, 187
Culminating activities, 114–115
Curriculum, alternative models of, 66–68
    committees for planning of, 64
    definition of, 63
    design and development of, 61–79
        challenges for in future, 77
    design of based on behavioral objectives, 56
    development of components of, 69–77
    development of in secondary school, 67
    guidebook outline for development of, *71*
    importance of balance in, 329
    legislation and change in, 64–65
    need for change in, 5
    performance-based instructional model of, 65–66
    principles of construction in, 62–65
    program models for, 65–69
    purpose-process conceptual framework model of, 66
    revision of, 29–30, 65
    scope and sequence of, 72
    traditional model of, 65
    yearly calendar for, 72
Curriculum guide, 69–71
    characteristics of, 70
    committee for development of, 70
    criteria for, 70–71
    definition of, 70
Cycle plan, 71

Dance, modern, 69
Degenerative circulatory diseases, exercise and prevention of, 10
Demonstrations, 312–315
    as method of teaching, 89
    auxiliary personnel for, 314
    check list of equipment needed for, 313–314
    marking the field for, 314
    planning for, 313
    principal's announcement to teachers and parents of, *314*
    printed programs for, 314–315
    score sheets for, 314
    securing officials for, 312
    selecting participants for, 312
    steps to ensure success of, 312–313
    use of in school-community relations, 326–327
Development, challenges of for students, 110
    growth and, 109–112
Diabetes, teaching students with, 277
Discipline, 141–143
    academic characteristics of, 40
    Gallup poll on, 141
    in classroom, 83, 143
    in gymnasium, 83
    methods for teachers to deal with, 83
    problems of, 83

Discipline (*Continued*)
  teacher-student rapport and, 142
Discrimination, by sex, prohibition of in education, 65
Discussions, group, 89
Disruptive behavior, 8–9
Double elimination tournament, 299, *299*
Dressing, time alloted for, 181
Dressing area, organization of, 124
Dropouts, number of, 5
Dual class structure, handicapped and, 285

Education, accountability and, 119
  aims of, condensed, 42
  community support of, 320
  effect of social upheaval on, 319
  general objectives of, 42–44
  innovations in, 61–65
  parental concerns regarding, 319–320
  problems in, 5–9
  physical fitness as inherent part of, 320
  secondary, goals of, 62
  survival and, 4
  taxonomy of objectives of, 55–56
Education for All Handicapped Children Act. See *Public Law 94–142.*
Educators, role of in balancing physical and mental education, 14
Effect, law of, 103–104, *104*
Emotional disturbance, reasons for, 282–283
  teaching students with, 283
Emotional instability, 9
Empirical approach, physical education and, 331
Endurance, physiology in relation to, 49
Epilepsy, teaching students with, 280
Equipment. Also under *Supplies.*
  fixed, surfaces near, 174
  improvisation of, 157
  provision of, 156–157
  safety of, 130–131
Essay Appraisal Technique, use of in performance appraisal, 54
Evaluation. See *Assessment.*
Excuses from participation, 145–148
  heeding, negligence and, 132
  permanent, 146
  temporary, 145
Exercise, daily recommended hours of, 123
  developmental, 183
    commands for, 183
    organizational plan for, *182*
    rope skipping as, *183*
  growth and, 10
  heart function and, 10–11
  importance of for health and longevity, 11, 13–14
  intensity of, 123–124
  interpretation of to students, 124
  isometric, 134, 135
  isotonic, 134, 135
  law of, 103, *103*
  mental effort and, 124
  physical fitness and, 11
Existentialism, physical education and, 42
Experiments, as method of teaching, 89–90
Extramurals, 316

Facilities, check list for planning of, *168–170*
  importance of to physical education, 330
  indoor, 167, 170–172
    selection of space for, *172*
  maximum use of, 170–171
  organization of, 132
  outdoor, 172–176
    surfaces of, 174
  planning for, 166–167
  provision of for intramurals, 293
Faculty, influence of on strength of physical education program, 321
Failure, avoidance of, 115
Fencing, demonstration of as method of instruction, *88*
Field hockey, plan for teaching skills of, 239–244, *240–244*
Films, as teaching device, 93, *93*
  through television, as teaching device, 93
Flannel boards, 95
Flexible model plan, handicapped student and, 285–286
Flexible scheduling, 160–164, *161*
Football, touch, plan for teaching skills of, 263–268, *264–268*
Formations, in class, 183
Free materials, enrichment of instruction through, 95
Fundamental movement, development of, 47–48
Funding, federal and state, for mainstreaming, 272–273
  federal, research projects on mainstreaming selected for, *273*

Golf, plan for teaching skills of, 202–207, *203–207*
Grade placement, 71
Grades, reports of to parents, 359, *361, 362*
Grading, 352–359
  difficulty with for physical education, 352–353
  guidelines for, 353
  Hales method of based on improvement, 354
  suggested plans for, 356–360
  system of based on ability, 356, *358*
    based on attainment of objectives, 356, 359
    based on contracts, 356, *357*
    based on effort, 354–356
    based on improvement, 354, *355*
    based on mathematical formula, 359
    based on overall performance, 359, *360*
    based on pass-fail concept, 360
Group activities, classification of and time allotments for, 97
  definition of, 232
  specific teaching plans for, 232–268
Group discussions, as method of teaching, 89
Growth, development and, 109–112
  exercise and, 10
Gymnasium, auxiliary, 171
  discipline in, 83
  main, 171
Gymnastics, unnatural aspects of, 136–137

Hales method of grading, 354
Handbook, use of in parent-teacher communication, 151, *152*

Handbook (*Continued*)
  use of in school-community relations, 327
Handicap, structural, definition of, 276–277
Handicapped, activity modification for, 286–287
  definition of in Public Law, 94–142, 272
  dual class structure for, 285
  flexible model plan for, 285–286
  importance of adaptability in teaching of, 287
  increase in school attendance of, 273
  instruction of, promise for future, 287
  integrated classes for, 285
  medically sound programs for physical education
    of, 275–288
  performance levels among, 286
  program modifications for, 286
  reclassification of, 276–284
  separate classes for, 285
  teaching opportunities with, 33
Handspring, law of effect in teaching of, *104*
Health, longevity and, importance of exercise for,
    11, 13–14
  problems in, 9–10
  relationship of to physical education, 324–325
Health objective, 136
Hearing difficulty, teaching students with, 281
Heart disorders, exercise levels for students with,
    281
  teaching students with, 281–282
Hernia, teaching students with, 282
History, aims of physical education throughout,
    44–46
Hockey, field, plan for teaching skills of, 239–244,
    240–244
Human movement pattern, 53–54
  approach to the teaching-learning process
    through, 53
  relationship of physical education to, 53–54
Human relations, importance of to promotion of
    physical education, 325
Human values, development of through sports, 78
Humanistic instruction, AAHPER definition of, 166

Idealism, physical education and, 41
Independent study, 161
Individual activities, classification of and time
    allotments for, 97
  definition of, 189
  specific teaching plans for, 189–231
Individual testing, 352
Individualized instruction, AAHPER definition of,
    166
Individualized Prescribed Instruction, 86
Information processing, 108
Innovations in teaching, 82
Instruction, aids and strategies for, 119–137
  coeducational, 179–180
  cohort, AAHPER definition of, 165–166
  competency-based, 185–187
  grouping students for, 125–128
  humanistic, AAHPER definition of, 166
  importance of quality in, 328–329
  improvement of, 102
  individual, teaching strategies for, 179
  individualized, AAHPER definition of, 166
  in large classes, problems with, 120–121
  large groups and, 160–161

Instruction (*Continued*)
  methods of, 179–180
  negligence and, 132–133
  organization of, 184
  personalized, AAHPER definition of, 166
  programmed, 91
  quality, importance of to school-community
    relations, *329*
  small groups and, 161
  teacher-student, importance of, 22–23
Instructional objectives, 85–86
Instructional procedures, safety and soundness of,
    131
Instructors, assistant student, 155
  evidence of success of, 158
  legal liability and, 129–133
  self-evaluation of, 121, *122*
  students as, 155
  unqualified, use of, 130
Integrated class, handicapped student in, 285
Intensity curve, 185
Interschool athletics, importance of balanced
    program in, 331
Interview Appraisal Technique, use of in
    performance appraisal, 55
Intramural sports, benefits of, 6
Intramurals, 291–316
  adequate facilities for, 293
  administrative personnel involved in, 293, *294*,
    295
  adult supervision for, 292–293
  arbitrary team formation for, 296–297
  as continuation of the instructional program, 293
  assignment of coaches for, 293
  awards for participation in, 306–309
  competent officials for, 295
  definition of, 291
  director of, 293
    duties of, 293
  distribution of activities for, *306*
  effects of Title IX legislation on, 305
  eligibility rules for competition in, 309, 311–312
  encouragement of lifetime activities through, 293
  entry blank for participation in, *296*
  evaluation of, 316
  expression of play urge through, 293
  finding sponsors for, 315
  general regulations for participation in, 311–312
  group point system for, 308–309, *309*
  importance of for all students, 291
  individual point system for, 306, 308, 308(t)
  need for, 292
  objectives of programs in, 292–293
  one-day tournament plan in, 296
  organization of participation in, 297–305
  organizational strategies for, 300–305
  organizational units for, 295–297
  organized, 295
  parental approval form for, *305*
  participation forms for, 305–306
  participation record form for, *307*
  planning bulletin boards for publicity of, 316, *316*
  posting schedules for, 300, 302
  program of activities for, 305
  promotion of, 302, 304–305
  public relations for, 315–316
  records for, 302
  scheduling of, 297

Intramurals (*Continued*)
  score sheets for, 302
  securing participants for, 300
  self-directed student participation in, 295
  sports managers for, 295
  sports record for, *303*
  student directors for, 293, 295
  success of, 293
  system of awards for participation in, 309
  table tennis score sheet for, *304*
  team captains for, 295
  Title IX legislation and, 305, 312
  types of, 295
Inventory, value of, 156
Isometric exercise, 134, 135
Isotonic exercise, 134, 135

Jobs, applying for, 26–27
  interviewing for, 26–27
  letters of application for, 26

Knowledge, methodology in, 87–90

Ladder tournament, *301*
Law of effect, 103–104, *104*
  use of in teaching handspring, *104*
Law of exercise, 103, *103*
Law of readiness, 104–105
Law of reciprocal innervation, 135
Learning, associated, 92
  as two-way process, 19
  associative theory of, 103–105
  client-centered approach to, 164
  cognitive field theory of, 105–106
  concomitant, 92
  critical period approach to, 107
  guides to, 108
  in physical education, 108
  modern concepts of, 108
    instructional implications of, 108
  motivation and, 101–102
  natural approach to, 107
  primary, 92
  readiness in, 106–107
  spiral of, 159, *160*
  stimulus-response theory of, 103–105
  traditional theories of, 102–108
  transfer of, 107–108
    limitations with, 107
    principles of, 107–108
  types of, 92
Learning Activities Package (LAP), 86
Learning disabilities, organizational model of
  services for children with, 285
Learning process, 101–116
Lectures, as method of teaching, 88–89
Legal liability, instructor and, 129–133
Legislation, mainstreaming and recent changes in,
  272–273
Lesson plan, daily, 73–74
    criteria for, 73

Letters, use of in parent-teacher communication,
  151, *153*
Life, basic drives of, 46–47
Lifetime activities, 114
Listening, importance of, 25–26
Lockers, 149–150, *149*
  assignment of, 150, *150*
Longevity, health and, importance of exercise for,
  11, 13–14
Long-range planning, resource unit in, 180–181

Magnetic boards, 95
Mainstreaming, ability grouping and, 272
  areas of concern in, 273–276
  cascade system of, 274, *275*
  challenge of to teachers, 271–272
  coping with changes due to, 274–275
  definition of, 271, 273–274
  difficulties with, 271
  educational implications of, 287–288
  federal and state funding for, 272–273
  importance of flexibility in, 274
  instructional strategies for, 285–286
  philosophy of, 274
  physical education and, 271–288
  recent legislation concerning, 272–273
  requirements of for success, 274–275
  responsibility of schools in, 274
  role of adapted physical education in, 274
  role of teacher in determining success or failure
    of, 284–285
  significance of, 275
  suggestions for success of, 288
Management, devices of, 85–87
  methods and, 81–99
Management by objective theory, accountability
  and, 29
Mass testing, 350, *352*
Massachusetts comprehensive special education
  law, program options of, 285
Materials, selection of, 84–85
Maturity, relationship of to proficiency in training,
  107
Meaning in physical education, 39–59
  search for, 39–40
  teacher's search for in relation to education,
    41–42
Mentally exceptional students, teaching of,
  283–284
Method, definition of in teaching, 81
Methodology, meaning of, 82–85
Methods, teaching, implications of, 82–83
  traditional, in teaching, 82
Mind, development of, 7
Misbehavior, causes of, 142–143
  deterrents to, 142
  handling of in classroom, 142
Modern dance, 69
Modified physical education program, physician's
  recommendation for, *147*, 148
Motivation, learning and, 101–102
  strategies for development of, 112–116, *116*
  techniques of, *116*
Movement, classification of, 48
  fundamental, development of, 47–48

Multi-sensory appeal, 90–91
Multi-use area, surfaces for, 174

National Conference on America's Secondary
  Schools, 143
Natural overload, 133–134
Negligence, cases of, 131
  inadequate instruction and, 132–133
Newspapers, use of in school-community relations,
  326, *326*
Nonfunctional overload, 134–135

Obesity, teaching students suffering from, 280
Objectives, instructional, 85–86
Organization, class, five phases of, 181
  essentials in, 141–176
  external, guidelines for, 176
    procedures for, 158–176
  internal, procedures for, 141–158
Orientation of class to new activity, 184
Overflow plan, 121
  use of in teaching golf skills, *121*
  use of in teaching tennis strokes, *120*
  volleyball chosen for use in, 188
Overload, natural, 133–134
  nonfunctional, 134–135
  physical education and, 135
  principle of, 133–135
  sports training and, 134
Overmotivation, avoidance of, 115

Parent-student programs, use of in
  school-community relations, 327
Parents, reporting students' grades to, 359, *361,* 362
  teachers and relationship to, 151, *152–154*
Participation, excuses from, 145–148
PEPI. See *Physical Education Public Information.*
Performance, categories of, 54–55
Performance ability, inventory of, 184
Performance appraisal, 54–56
  achievement of program enrichment through,
    339
  basis of, 339
  of administrators, 339
  organizational management and, 54
  use of Assessment Center Appraisal Technique in,
    55
  use of Checklist Appraisal Technique in, 54–55
Performance contracting, importance of, 28
Performance objectives, as basis for teaching skills,
  188
  development of, 29
  for students, 55–56
  for teachers, 54–55
Personalized instruction, AAHPER definition of,
  166
Philosophy, as applied to physical education,
  41–42
  definition of, 40
  in physical education, 39–59
  need for in physical education, 40
  personal, need for in education, 41

Philosophy (*Continued*)
  reflection of in teaching, 41
Physical activity, lack of, 7
Physical education, AAHPER purposes of, 42
  academic discipline and, 39–40
  adapted, 274
  affective tests in, 348
  affluence and, 1–15
  assessment and evaluation in, 337–362
  basic aim of, 42–44, *43*
    historical significance of, 44–46
  contemporary designs in, 46–58
  credit for, 159
    importance of, 329–330
  crucial issues in interpretation of to public,
    328–333
  development of scientific programs in, 330–331
  education of public about, 325
  empirical approach to content selection in, 331
  federally funded research projects on
    mainstreaming in, *273*
  grading in, 352–359
  guidelines for in secondary school, *175*
  importance of establishing a philosophy in, 333
  importance of human relations in the promotion
    of, 325
  importance of requirement in, 329
  interpretation of, 328–333
  knowledge tests in, 345, 348
  learning in, 108
  mainstreaming in, 271–288
  meaning in, 39–59
  normal teaching loads in, 330
  objectives of, 330
  overload principle in, 135
  performance tests in, 348
  philosophy in, 39–59
  purposes of, 42–44
    in modern times, 46
  recommendations for, 12–13
  relationship of to health, 324–325
  requirement for, 158
  revival of objectives in, 45
  scheduling for, 159–166
  school dropout problem and, 6
  status of in American schools, 4
  status of in community, 332
  steps for promotion of to public, 324–325
  strategies for exposure of to community, 328
  strength and, 133–136
  unanimity of purpose in, 332–333
  uncertain future of, 320
  use of proper terminology in, 332
Physical education activities, classification and time
  allotments for, 96–97
Physical education program, function of, 271–272
Physical Education Public Information Project,
  333–334
Physical education vs. physical training, 42
Physical fitness, anatomical component of, 48
  circulatory-respiratory efficiency and, 48
  definition of, 49–52
  guidelines for programs of, 11
  natural patterns of, 137
  physiological component of, 49
  psychological component of, 49
  recommendations for improving, *12–13*
  vigorous activities as factors in, *134*

Physical fitness pattern, 48–49
Physical working capacity, concept of, 48
   measurement of, 48
Physician, recommendations of for physical
   education of handicapped, 276, *278–279*
   relationship of teacher and, 275–276
Physiology, physical fitness and, 49
Plan for Learning According To Needs (PLAN), 86
Planning, criterion-referenced, 187
   daily, basic outline for, 181–185
Planning of facilities, considerations in, 167
   principles of, 166–167
Play, classical theories of, *50, 51*
   importance of, 8–9
Play pattern, 46–47
Play urge, 47–48
   development of, 101–102
   intramurals and expression of, 293
   motivation of by physical education, 331
   reasons for, 50–51
Pool, check list for, *173*
Pool, indoor, location of, 171
   planning of, 171
   size of, 172
Positive health, importance of, 57
PPBS. See *Program Planning Budgeting System.*
Pragmatism, physical education and, 42
President's Council for Physical Fitness and Sports,
   334
   contributions of, 11
   purposes of, 334
   statement of about physical education
     requirements, 158
   statement of basic beliefs of, *12–13*
Prestige, effect of on quality of instruction, 332
Pretesting, 187
   as basis for performance inventory, 187
   performance objectives and, 187
Preventive analysis, of learning deficiencies as
   responsibility of physical education teacher, 274
Primary learning, 92
Private teaching, opportunities for, 33
Professionalism, 34–36, *35*
Proficiency test, definition of, 353
Proficiency testing, 353–354
   predetermined standards as basis of, 353–354
   purposes of, 354
Program, evaluation of within school systems,
   338–339
Program modification, for handicapped students,
   286
Program Planning Budgeting System, application of,
   28
Programmed instruction, 91
Programs, unnatural, disadvantages of in physical
   education, 331
Project READ, 86
Projects, as method of teaching, 89
Psychology, physical fitness and, 49
Psychomotor domain of behavior, 56
Public, attitude of towards schools, 319–320
   communication with, 325–328
   education of about physical education, 325
   guidelines for promotion of physical education
     to, 324–325
   various constituent groups in, 320–322
Publications, special, use of in school-community
   relations, 327

Public Law, 94–142, 272–273
   definition of handicapped children in, 272
   effect of on secondary school educational
     programs, 287–288
   effects of on secondary school personnel, 272
   purposes of, 272
Public relations. See also *School-community
   relations.*
   intramurals and, 315–316
Pyramid tournament, *302*

Questions and answers as method of teaching,
   87–88

Radio, use of in school-community relations,
   325–326
Readiness, law of, 104–105
Realism, physical education and, 41
Reciprocal innervation, law of, 135–136
Record cards, individual, 144, *144*
   permanent, 145
Reports, to parents concerning child's status, 151,
   154
Requirements, physical education and, 158–159
Requisitions, 156–157
   instructional content as a determinant of,
     156–157
   teaching procedures as a determinant of, 157
Resource unit, components of, 181
   planning of, 180–181
Rewards, extrinsic, 114
   intrinsic, 114
Rhythmical movement, physical education and,
   129
Rhythms, plan for teaching skills of, 220–225,
   221–225
Roll call, 181–183, *182*
Rope skipping, as developmental exercise, *183*
Round robin tournament, 299–300

Safety, 130–131
   precautions for, 157
Scheduling, daily, advantages of over modular
     scheduling, 162
   flexible, 160–164, *161*
     critical look at, 162–166
     human element and, 163
     problems in adjusting physical education to,
       162–163
     types of learning involved in, 160–161
   for physical education, 159–166
   individualized, 164–166
     cohort instruction in, 165–166
   traditional, 159–160
School, academic achievement in, 6–8
   community and, relationship between, 319–334
   development of potential in, 6
   function of concerning mainstreaming, 271–273
   parental visits to, 327–328
School attendance, problems with, 5–6
School-college relations, 334
School-community relations, 319–334

School-community relations (*Continued*)
  agencies and, 333–334
  guidelines for, 323–325
  importance of knowing power structures
    involved in, 325
  improvement of, 331–332
  need for planning in, 325
  objectives of, 323
  responsibility of teacher in, 324
  use of assembly programs in, 326
  use of bulletin boards in, 327
  use of demonstrations in, 326–327
  use of handbooks in, 327
  use of newspapers in, 326, *326*
  use of parent-student programs in, 327
  use of speakers in, 326
  use of special publications in, 327
  use of sponsors in, 327
  use of television and radio in, 325–326
  use of tours in, 327
Seasonal placement, 71–72
Secondary school, goals of, 57–58
  innovations in physical education in, 44
Selectives, 157–158
Self-appraisal, concept of in program assessment,
  339
Self-awareness, importance of, 26
Self-determination, role of in learning process, 345
Self-image, development of, 110
Self-realization, importance of, 57
Showers, 150–151
Sight handicaps, teaching students with, 280–281
Single elimination tournament, *297, 298*–299
  with byes, *298*
Skills, acquisition of, 90–91
    fixation/diversification and, 66
    ideas of movement and, 66
  basic and refined, 108–109
  competition in, 113, 121–123
  demonstration of, 184
  evaluation of, 185
  methodology in, 87–90
  physiology in relation to, 49
  practice of, use of competition in, *185*
  steps in teaching, 109
  teaching of, 183–184
    ability grouping in, 184
    for specific individual and group activities,
      188–268
    importance of demonstrations in, 184
    importance of organization in, 184
    inventory of performance ability and, 184
    on basis of performance objectives, 188
    orientation of students to, 184
    sequence for, 184
Skills laboratory, role of in physical education class,
  184
Soccer, plan for teaching skills of, 245–250,
  246–250
Socialization, importance of, 57
Softball, plan for teaching skills of, 251–256,
  252–256
Somersault, teaching of, importance of proper
  procedures in, 333
Speakers, use of in school-community relations,
  326
  use of in teaching, 90
Speed, physiology in relation to, 49

Spiral of learning, use of in physical education, 159,
  160
Sponsors, use of in school-community relations,
  327
Sportsmanship, importance of, 57
Squad cards, 144, *145*
Squad leaders, students as, 155
Squad testing, 350, 352
S-R Theory. See *Stimulus-Response Theory.*
Statewide Assessment Plans, design of, 28
Stimulus–response theory of learning, 103–105
  criticisms of, 105
  laws of learning involved in, 103–105
Storage, of equipment and supplies, 151
Strength, physical education and, 133–136
  physiology in relation to, 49
Structural handicaps, teaching students with,
  276–277
Student leader association, organization of, *155*
Students, anemic, activities for, 277
  as assistant instructors, 155–156
  as class managers, 155
  as instructors, 155
  as intramural directors, 293, 295
  as squad leaders, 155
  asthmatic, activities for, 277
  attitudes of concerning physical education, 321,
    321
  cerebrally palsied, activities for, 278
  changing, 29
  classification of by ability, 125–128
    by age and grade, 128
    by height and weight, 128
    for assignment to physical education classes,
      125, *126*
  culturally disadvantaged, 83–84
  diabetic, activities for, 277
  disadvantaged, psychological problems of, 84
  disruptive, 142
  effectiveness of as public relations agents, 325
  emotionally disturbed, ability grouping for
    teaching of, 283
    activities for, 282–283
    participation of in physical education, 283
    specific guidelines for teaching of, 283
  epileptic, activities for, 278
  evaluation of, 343–345
  expectations of for secondary education, 82
  handicapped, medically sound programs of
    physical education for, 275–288
    participation in physical education by, 276
    reclassification of, 276–284
    strategies for instruction of, 285–286
    teaching of, 284–287
  involvement of in physical education program,
    155–156
  junior high school, 110–111
    emotional and mental characteristics of, 111
    physical characteristics of, 110–111
    social characteristics of, 111
  mentally exceptional, activities for, 283–284
    guides for teaching of, 284
    importance of participation by in physical
      education, 283–284
    mainstreaming of into regular physical
      education programs, 284
  needs of, 113
  overweight, activities for, 278

Students (*Continued*)
  performance objectives for, 55
  physically handicapped, activities for, 276–282.
    Also under *Handicapped.*
  policy on number of in classes, 159
  records of, 144–145
  rights and responsibilities of, 143
  role of in planning curriculum, 77–78
  senior high school, 111–112
    emotional and mental characteristics of, 112
    physical characteristics of, 111
    social characteristics of, 111–112
  special, frequently used labels for, 271
    teaching of, 187–188
  structurally handicapped, activities for, 276–277
  tubercular, activities for, 277
  underweight, activities for, 278
  visually handicapped, activities for, 278–279
Students with hearing difficulties, activities for, 281
  with heart disorders, activities for, 281
    exercise levels of, 281
    responsibility of teacher in planning programs
      for, 281–282
  with hernia, 282
Sub-competencies, development of, 186–187
  in affective domain, 187
  in cognitive domain, 186–187
  in psychomotor domain, 186
Supervision, constant, importance of, 130
  of more than one activity at a time, 124–125
Supervisors, teachers and, 34
Supplementary teaching materials, 95
Supplies, provision of, 156–157
  requisitions for, 156–157
Surfaces, 174
  synthetic, 174
Survival, education and, 4
Swimming, plan for teaching skills of, 214–219,
  215–219
Synthetic surfaces, 174
Systems instruction, 86

Table tennis, intramural score sheet for, *304*
Teacher behavior, importance of to way students
  learn, 66
Teacher education, future of, 30
Teachers. See also *Instructors.*
  ability of to identify learning deficiencies, 274
  as students, 34
  behavior rating scale for, evaluation of, 342–343
  changing curriculum and, 29–30
  changing role of with implementation of
    mainstreaming, 274–275
  common criticisms of, 342
  duties of in the community, 24–25
    in the school, 23–24
  effective, 17–37, *20*
    personal qualifications of, 22–23
  effectiveness of, 322, *322*
  evaluation of, 342–343
  first-year, reasons for success and failure of, *8*
  goals and objectives of, 19
  human-centered duties of, 25
  importance of personal involvement by, 19
  importance of preparation of in physical
    education, 330

Teachers (*Continued*)
  influence of, 18–19
  performance objectives for, 54–55
  physical education, as key figures in
    school-community relations, 321–322
  preparation of for future, 32–34
  problems of in teaching large classes, 330
  relationship of physicians and, 275–276
  responsibility of in preventive analysis of learning
    deficiencies, 274
  responsibility of in school-community relations,
    324
  self-evaluation of, *31,* 342, 343(t)
  supervisors and, 34
  task-centered duties of, 23
Teaching, aids and strategies for, 119–137
  approaches to in physical education, 91–92
  careers in, 32–33
  challenge of with handicapped students,
    275–276
  compromise approach to, 92
  critical areas of concern in, 83–85
  definition of, 17–18
  definition of method in, 81
  developing interest in, 112–114
  effective procedures for, 113
  effective tools for in physical education, 92–95
  formal approach to, 92
  importance of methods and materials in, 81–85
  importance of to motivation, 113
  informal approach to, 92
  innovative strategies for, 129
  love of, importance of, 18
  management and methods in, 81–99
  medically sound programs of for handicapped
    students, 275–288
  modern innovations in, 82
  need for ethics in, 19
  part method of, 91
  questions and answers as method of, 87–88
  role of humor in, 18–19
  whole method of, 91
Teaching aids, free, 95
  supplementary, 95
    criteria for selection of, 95–96
Teaching guide, use of, 132
Teaching/learning styles, options in for working
  with handicapped, 287
Teaching Learning Units (TLU), 86
Teaching methods in physical education, 85–92
Teaching stations, 171–172
  improvisation of, 171
  number of, 174–175
  organization of, 156
Teaching strategies for specific activities, 179–268
Team activities, carry-over and physiological value
  of, 232
Team teaching, 86–87, 157
Television, 93
  use of in school-community relations, 325–326
Tennis, plan for teaching skills of, 189–195,
  190–195
Tension, exercise for relief of, 10
Testing, system of to upgrade caliber of physical
  education, 356
Tests, 345–350
  administration of, 352
  affective, use of in physical education, 348, *349*

Tests (*Continued*)
  classification of, 345–350, *346*
  conduction of, 350, 352
  effective, characteristics of, 349–350
  floor plan for in golf and tennis skills, *347*
  grading as reason for, 348
  importance of identifying purposes of, 348
  individual, 352
  knowledge, use of in physical education, 345, 348
  motivation as reason for, 348
  objective, *338*, 345, 348, 350
  organization of class for, 350–352
  organization of squads for, 350, 352
  performance, use of in physical education, 348
  preliminary planning for, 350
  procedures for completion of, 352
  recording results of, *351*
  reliability of, 349–350
  simplicity of, 350
  standardized, 350
  subjective, 345
  uniformity of, 350
  use of in evaluating student's physical ability, 348–349
  use of in measuring instructional value, 349
  validity of, 350
Textbooks, evaluative criteria for, 87
  use of, 87
Title IX legislation, 127–128
  coeducation and, 179–180
  effects of on intramurals, 305, *306*, 312
  implementation of in physical education, 65
  teacher reaction to, 180
Touch football, plan for teaching skills of, 263–268, *264–268*

Tournaments, 297–300. See also specific types, e.g., *Challenge tournament.*
  one-day plan for in intramurals, 296
  scoring system for, 310(t)
Tours, use of in school-community relations, 327
Towel program, 148
Tuberculosis, teaching students with, 277–278
Tumbling, plan for teaching skills of, 208–213, *209–213*

Underweight, teaching students with problems from being, 280
Uniforms, 148–149
Unit teaching, 72–73
  guidelines for development of, 73

Values, human, development of through sports, 78
  identification of, 57–58
Videotapes, as teaching device, 93, *93*
Visits, of parents to school, 327–328
Visual aids, as teaching device, 95
Volleyball, coeducational instruction in, *181*
  plan for teaching skills of, 257–262, *258–262*
Voucher system, use of in private schools, 28

Wall charts, use of as teaching device, 95
Warm-up exercises, 128
Wrestling, plan for teaching skills of, 226–231, *227–231*